Personal
Risk Management
and
Insurance

Volume I

Personal
Risk Management
and
Insurance
Volume I

CLAUDE C. LILLY, Ph.D., CPCU, CLU
*Director, Risk Management and Insurance Research
Center for the Study of Financial Institutions
University of Southern California*

GLENN L. WOOD, Ph.D., CPCU, CLU
*Professor of Finance
California State College*

JERRY S. ROSENBLOOM, Ph.D., CPCU, CLU
*Executive Director
The S.S. Huebner Foundation for Insurance Education
The Wharton School
University of Pennsylvania*

First Edition • 1978

AMERICAN INSTITUTE FOR
PROPERTY AND LIABILITY UNDERWRITERS
Providence and Sugartown Roads, Malvern, Pennsylvania 19355

Foreword

The American Institute for Property and Liability Underwriters and the Insurance Institute of America are companion, nonprofit, educational organizations supported by the property-liability insurance industry. Their purpose is to provide quality continuing education programs for insurance personnel.

The Insurance Institute of America offers programs leading to the Certificate in General Insurance, the Associate in Insurance Adjusting Diploma, the Associate in Management Studies Diploma, the Associate in Risk Management Diploma, and the Associate in Underwriting Diploma. The American Institute develops, maintains, and administers the educational program leading to the Chartered Property Casualty Underwriter (CPCU) professional designation.

Throughout the history of the CPCU program, an annual updating of parts of the course of study took place. But as changes in the insurance industry came about at an increasingly rapid pace and as the world in which insurance operates grew increasingly complex, it became clear that a thorough, fundamental revision of the CPCU curriculum was necessary.

The American Institute began this curriculum revision project by organizing a committee of academicians, industry practitioners, and Institute staff members. This committee was charged with the responsibility of determining and stating those broad goals which should be the educational aims of the CPCU program in contemporary society. With these goals formulated, the curriculum committee began writing specific educational objectives which were designed to achieve the stated goals of the program. This was a time-consuming and difficult task. But this process made certain that the revised CPCU curriculum would be based on a sound and relevant foundation.

Once objectives were at least tentatively set, it was possible to outline a new, totally revised and reorganized curriculum. These outlines were widely circulated and the reactions of more than 1,800 educators and industry leaders were solicited, weighed, and analyzed. These outlines were then revised and ultimately became the structure of the new, ten-course curriculum.

With the curriculum design in hand, it was necessary to seach for study materials which would track with the revised program's objectives and follow its design. At this stage of curriculum development, the Institute reached the conclusion that it would be necessary for the Institute to prepare and publish study materials specifically tailored to the revised program. This conclusion was not reached hastily. After all, for the Institute to publish textbooks and study materials represents a significant broadening of its traditional role as an examining organization. But the unique educational needs of CPCU candidates, combined with the lack of current, suitable material available through commercial publishers for use in some areas of study, made it necessary for the Institute to broaden its scope to include publishing.

Throughout the development of the CPCU text series, it has been—and will continue to be—necessary to draw on the knowledge and skills of Institute staff members. These individuals will receive no royalties on texts sold and their writing responsibilities are seen as an integral part of their professional duties. We have proceeded in this way to avoid any possibility of conflicts of interests.

All Institute textbooks have been—and will continue to be—subjected to an extensive review process. Reviewers are drawn from both industry and academic ranks.

We invite and will welcome any and all criticisms of our publications. It is only with such comments that we can hope to provide high quality educational texts, materials, and programs.

Edwin S. Overman, Ph.D., CPCU
President

Preface

This text builds upon the fundamental principles and concepts of risk management and insurance that were introduced and developed in CPCU Course 1. The basic purpose of this course is to apply these risk management and insurance concepts to personal loss exposures. (Courses 3 and 4 of the Chartered Property Casualty Underwriter curriculum concentrate on commercial loss exposures and their treatment.) This text is divided into two volumes. The first volume describes the nature of the various personal loss exposures and the effect that our changing society has on them. It also covers homeowners insurance contracts, automobile coverages, and life insurance. Volume 2 covers health insurance, retirement planning, investments, and business insurance and estate planning. It concludes with a detailed case analysis that provides the CPCU candidate with an opportunity to apply the concepts and ideas learned earlier.

The risk management process involves the identification and analysis of loss exposures that confront an individual or family and the evaluation and selection of the alternative methods of treating these loss exposures. Personal loss exposures considered in this text include premature death, disability, unemployment, retirement, and the various property and liability loss exposures. Following the identification and analysis of these loss exposures, various treatment techniques such as avoidance, loss control, insurance, noninsurance transfers, and retention are evaluated. Of course, since, for a family unit, insurance is one of the most widely used techniques, a substantial amount of material on all forms of personal insurance is considered, including life and health as well as property and liability insurance.

Some CPCU candidates may find that much of the information in this part is relatively new to them. Other students, who have a property and liability insurance background may be more familiar with these coverages than with life and health insurance coverages or retirement plans. Regardless of one's background, however, the material presented in this text is designed to provide an understanding of the family unit concept and the risk management techniques and insurance coverages necessary to protect this unit. Throughout this text, it must be stressed that the application of certain risk management principles is limited by an individual's or family's ability to retain exposures and negotiate insurance contracts—options that may be readily available to many commercial risks.

The authors are aware that material in this text may not agree with the approach used by every insurance company, but it is intended to be typical of the techniques and coverages of most companies.

In the preparation of this text, many individuals provided valuable assistance to the authors. The authors wish to thank the following reviewers for their thoroughness and competent advice: Everett T. Allen, Jr., LL.B., Vice President, Towers, Perrin, Forster & Crosby, Inc.; M. Forrest Briggs, Associate Director of Company Relations, Health Insurance Association of America; Jerry W. Caswell, Ph.D., CPCU, CLU, Associate Professor of Insurance, Georgia State University; Campbell K. Evans, Ph.D., CPCU, Professor of Insurance, Illinois Wesleyan University; Ralph E. King, CPCU, Professor, Canton Agricultural and Technical College; Roy C. McCormick, Editor, Policy, Form & Manual Analysis Service, The Rough Notes Company, Inc.; Robert A. Marshall, Ph.D., CLU, Professor of Insurance, Florida State University; Raymond L. Messier, CPCU, CLU, ARM, Chairman, Charles F. Andrews & Associates; J. Wesley Ooms, CPCU, CLU, Assistant Vice President, Research and Development, State Farm Fire & Casualty Company; Donald L. Strand, Ph.D., CPCU, Head, Department of Insurance, Illinois Wesleyan University; Seeman Waranch, CPCU, President, Insurance Agency of Norfolk, Inc.; and William G. Williams, Director of Group Sales Research, Provident Mutual Life Insurance Company.

A special note of thanks is due Richard L. Tewksbury, Jr., Consultant, Johnson & Higgins of Pennsylvania, for developing materials for the case analysis in Chapter 15. Special thanks are also due Curtis R. Bryant, CLU, with The Bankers Life in Santa Ana, California, for his input to the material on estate planning and to Neil D. Reznik, CPCU, CLU, Professor of Economics and Chairman, Department of Economics and Accounting, Community College of Philadelphia, for his helpful work and suggestions on the life insurance chapters.

A dept of gratitude also is owed to the many people, too numerous to mention by name, who gave us encouragement, help, knowledge, and counsel.

Claude C. Lilly
Glenn L. Wood
Jerry S. Rosenbloom

Table of Contents

CHAPTER 1

Exposures Facing Individuals and Families

INTRODUCTION

This book builds upon the basic property and liability concepts introduced in CPCU 1. Specifically, this text deals with the loss exposures confronting individuals and families. Life, health, property, and liability exposures are presented in a risk management framework in an effort to demonstrate how the financial security needs of individuals and families can be assessed and met.

APPLICATION OF THE RISK MANAGEMENT PROCESS TO INDIVIDUAL EXPOSURES

Review of the Risk Management Process

In CPCU 1, the basic risk management concepts were presented and the application of these concepts to both individuals and business firms was explained. While that material concentrated on business applications of these concepts, CPCU 2 emphasizes the use of risk management tools on an individual or family basis. After a review of the basic risk management concepts, this chapter treats the topics of exposure identification, risk analysis, and treatment techniques.

Elements of a Loss Minor financial losses occur daily, but catastrophic losses occur much less frequently. For an individual to suffer a loss, some force must act to damage an object or person so that the value of the object or person declines. Examples include the destruction of a house by fire and the disablement of an individual because of an accident.

Loss in the context of risk management means an economic loss which

> . . . is essentially a relative, rather than absolute, term. What would constitute a "severe" financial impact varies both among entities and over time for the same entity. The same dollar loss might border on the catastrophic for a recently laid-off family head but be of virtually no significance to a large firm.[1]

Thus, an entity has to consider its financial position when evaluating how to handle potential losses.

Identification   In the risk management process, an individual or family should attempt to ascertain the loss exposure possibilities since failure to do so could result in severe economic difficulties. Methods (discussed in detail later) used to identify loss exposures include (1) checklists or questionnaires, (2) flowcharts, (3) financial statements, and (4) inspections. These methods identify "pure" as opposed to "speculative" losses. Losses caused by natural disasters like fire, lightning, and so on, are examples of "pure" losses; losses from gambling or investments exemplify "speculative" losses. In the former, there is no likelihood of financial gain while that possibility does exist with the latter type.

Frequency and Severity   To select the appropriate risk management tool for handling an exposure, the frequency and severity of loss exposures must be considered. Frequency is the number of times that a particular loss will occur, while the probability of a loss is the frequency divided by the number of units exposed. Thus, if 5 out of 1,000 houses are expected to have a fire loss, the probability that any particular house will have a fire is 0.5 percent (or 5/1000).

To properly evaluate an exposure, an individual also must know the extent or severity of a loss. Although the probability of loss may be high, if the severity of a potential loss is low, the exposure may be insignificant.

Methods of Handling Loss Exposures   The methods available for handling loss exposures include avoidance, control, noninsurance transfers, insurance, and retention.

Avoidance can be utilized when an exposure does not have to be assumed or when an existing exposure can be eliminated. For example, a family can reduce automobile liability claims by not owning a car, although this alternative may not be practical or even possible.

In situations where an exposure has to be assumed, attempts should be made to *control* losses. The concept of control includes the separation, combination, prevention, and reduction of loss exposures. Combination involves the joining of a substantial number of similar exposures and therefore may be inappropriate for individuals. For example, there is a limit to the number of cars any one family needs or can afford. The physical separation of exposures is also unlikely to be a viable risk management tool for individuals and families.

Prevention and reduction are more appropriate risk management tools. For example, an individual could reduce the probability of a loss occurring by having the car's brakes checked periodically. With regard to reduction, an automobile owner who carries a fire extinguisher in his or her automobile can reduce the impact of a fire loss.

The *transfer* method for handling loss can be divided into two subcategories: (1) insurance, and (2) noninsurance. In the former case, the insurance company assumes losses up to the limits of the insurance policy in exchange for the premium. Noninsurance transfers involve shifting responsibility for a loss to a third party other than an insurer. For example, a lease may be written so that the lessor is not liable for accidents on the premises, thereby transferring the liability exposure to the lessee. Transfer is a good risk management technique only if the party to whom liability is transferred is financially strong enough to pay the losses incurred.

The *retention* method may be chosen for several reasons. First, no other risk management method may be applicable or desirable. Secondly, a person may retain an exposure because he or she is unaware of its existence or because the loss is underestimated.

The risk management techniques that have been described are not mutually exclusive but may be used quite effectively in concert. For example, with the cost of health insurance increasing rapidly, some individuals purchase protection against catastrophic loss while retaining budgetable health expenses.

The Family as a Business Unit In its traditional context, a family consists of a man, woman, and possibly, children. Like a business, a family contains individuals who earn incomes that support the family unit. A family also will possess certain assets. Any loss exposures which endanger the family unit, such as disability of a family income earner or the burning of the house, should be subject to risk management treatment. These same types of problems (income interruption and fire losses) would have a detrimental impact on a business. Therefore, the family unit can be viewed as a microcosm of the business environment.

Exposure Identification Tools

Two basic approaches may be used to assist family units in recognizing their loss exposures. One is to think through the various categories of possible losses—property, liability, and personal—faced by the family. Another, more systematic approach is to use different risk management identification techniques to develop a comprehensive list of specific loss exposures. The various risk management identification techniques should be viewed and used as complimentary tools, rather than independent alternatives. Some of the items uncovered by using one technique also may be identified by means of one of the other techniques, but overlapping is better than failing to discover an exposure. The more important types of risk management identification techniques will be discussed in the remainder of this section, while following sections will discuss separately the three major categories of possible losses.

Questionnaire A questionnaire similar to the one found in Figure 1-1 may be used to evaluate a family's exposures in detail. This questionnaire is divided so that each segment concentrates on an aspect of a family's operations. The first section deals with real property while the remaining segments cover personal property, estate, disability, health, retirement, and professional exposures.

Financial Statement Even though families typically do not prepare sets of financial statements with the same regularity and degree of precision observed by business entities, that does not lessen their effectiveness in loss exposure identification. Thus, a family's financial statement, even if somewhat brief, can be a useful means of summarizing the family's assets, liabilities (debts), and source(s) of income and therefore, its loss exposures. Like other loss exposure identification procedures, however, it is complimentary to rather than an independent alternative to other methods.

Table 1-1 contains a representative family financial statement. An unusual asset on this family's balance sheet is the life estate. The value of this asset is based on the life expectancy of the individual receiving the benefit, since all benefits cease upon the death of the recipient. A person may be given the income from a piece of property as long as he or she is alive and upon death the property reverts to some other party.

Generally, a financial statement should be used as a starting point, while a questionnaire should be used to develop more detailed information. For example, the questionnaire in Figure 1-1 forces a family to describe all personal property in detail, while the personal

Figure 1-1
Exposure Questionnaire

Real Property Data

1. Address of principal residence: _____

2. Additional Buildings (e.g., barns, greenhouses, docks, or outbuildings): ___
   _____

3. Is your property owned or rented? _____
4. Type of construction of the principal residence: _____

5. Number of rooms in principal residence: _____
6. Is the principal residence a private dwelling? _____
7. Does the principal dwelling contain any unusual glass (e.g., picture windows or expensive chandeliers)? _____

8. Type of heating system utilized in the principal dwelling: _____

9. Is there a garage? _____ If the answer is yes answer the following questions:
   a. Type of construction used in garage: _____

   b. Attached or detached to the principal dwelling: _____

   c. Living quarters in the garage: _____

10. Value of standard alterations in progress or contemplated for principal residence or garages: _____

11. Date principal residence was built: _____
12. Original (purchase) price of the principal dwelling: _____Original price of any additional building: _____Cost of any improvements that have been made: _____
13. Current appraisal value of the:
    a. principal dwelling: _____
    b. additional buildings: _____
14. Current replacement cost of the:
    a. principal dwelling: _____
    b. additional buildings: _____
15. Name and address of mortgagee, if any: _____

16. Current value of trees and shrubs: _____
17. Additional living expenses needed if principal residence cannot be occupied: _____

Continued on next page

Personal Property Data

	Principal Residence	Secondary Residence
1. Estimated Value of:		
a. Silverware and pewter:		
b. Linens (including dining and bedroom):		
c. Clothing (men's, women's, children's):		
d. Rugs (including floor covering and draperies):		
e. Books:		
f. Musical instruments (including pianos):		
g. Television sets, radios, record players and records:		
h. Paintings, etchings, pictures, and other objects of art:		
i. China and glassware (including bric-a-brac):		
j. Cameras and photographic equipment:		
k. Golf, hunting, fishing, and other sport equipment:		
l. Refrigerators, washing machines, stoves, electrical appliances, and other kitchen equipment:		
m. Bedding (including blankets, comforters, covers, pillows, mattresses, and springs):		
n. Furniture (including tables, chairs, sofas, desks, beds, chests, lamps, mirrors, clocks):		
o. All other personal property (including wines, liquors, foodstuffs, garden and lawn tools and equipment, trunks, traveling bags, children's playthings, miscellaneous articles in basement and attic) and professional equipment, if any:		
TOTAL		

2. Obtain copy of appraisal. Date of Appraisal: _____
3. Jewelry and Watches:
   a. Describe each item: _____
   b. Original cost: _____
   c. Appraised value (obtain appraisals): _____
   d. Where kept (safety deposit box, etc.): _____
4. Furs:
   a. Describe each article of fur: _____
   b. Original cost: _____
   c. Appraised value (obtain appraisal): _____
   d. Where stored (limit of liability per receipt): _____

5. Other items of unusual value:
   a. Stamp collections: _____
   b. Fine arts: _____
   c. Paintings: _____
   d. Antiques: _____
   e. Securities: _____
6. Boats or marine equipment:
   a. Length of boat: _____
   b. Power or sail (describe): _____
7. Dogs, saddle horses, or other pets (pedigreed): _____

8. Contents of barns, sheds, and other outbuildings: _____

9. Value of children's property away at school: _____

10. Airplanes, motorcycles, or motorized scooters: _____

11. Location, nature, and value of property in storage warehouses; furs (in storage); sports equipment at clubs; silver in safe deposit vault, and so on: _____

12. Cash on hand: _____
13. Automobiles:
    A. Description and year of cars (including body style and model):
       1. _____
       2. _____
       3. _____
    B. Motor and serial number:
       1. _____
       2. _____
       3. _____
    C. Name of registered owner:
       1. _____
       2. _____
       3. _____
    D. Month and year purchased (new or used):
       1. _____
       2. _____
       3. _____
    E. Purchase price, including equipment: _____

Continued on next page

F. Name of chattel mortgagee: _____
G. Where garaged: _____
_____

H. Cars used for business: _____
I. Distance driven to and from work: _____
J. Any driver under age of 25 (male or female): _____

Did they pass recognized driver training course?
_____
Get certification from: _____
K. Any trailers: _____
L. Any car trips outside continental United States and Canada: _____
_____

Estate Data

1. Principal sum in accidental death policies in event of accidental death: ____
2. Members of family:
   A. Husband: _____ Date of Birth: _____
   B. Wife: _____ Date of Birth: _____
   C. Children: _____ Date of Birth: _____
   _____ _____
   _____ _____
   _____ _____
   _____ _____

   D. Other Dependents
      Name: _____ Relation: _____
      _____ _____
      _____ _____
      _____ _____
      _____ _____

3. Income needs of family in event of a death:
   A. Cash to pay bills—medical, funeral, taxes, and so on:
   _____
   B. Cash to liquidate mortgages, chattels, and so on:
   _____
   C. Monthly income to family during school years:
   _____
   D. Funds for college or specialized training:
      $ _____
      at: _____
   E. Monthly income to widow after children are grown:
   _____

4. Income or endowment to others—in detail:
_____

5. What do you estimate your gross-estate to be?
_____

6. Is it advisable to set up a corporate trust?
_____

7. Do you have a will? _____
   Date written: _____
   Where is it? _____
8. Does your spouse have a will? _____

9. Where do you keep valuable papers (deeds, securities, etc.)? _____
10. Where do you keep your life insurance policies?
   _____
11. Where do you keep your general insurance policies?
   _____
12. Are you eligible for social security death benefits?
   _____
13. What amount of group life insurance do you have?
   _____
14. What amount of individual life insurance do you have?
   _____
15. Do you have any death benefits under retirement plans?
   _____
   If so, how much? _____
16. What types of life insurance coverage do you have?
   _____
17. Who is your beneficiary under your life insurance policies?
   _____
18. Do your insurance policies contain some provision to handle common disaster? _____
19. What types of investments do you have?
   _____
20. What is the financial size of your spouse's estate?
   _____
21. Does your estate qualify for the marital deduction?
   _____
22. Do you live in a community property state? _____

Disability Data

1. Are you eligible for social security disability payments? _____
2. If you are not eligible, when will you be eligible? _____
   _____
3. If you are eligible, what would your monthly benefit be in the event of disability? _____
4. What percentage of your salary is covered by a group short-term disability plan? _____
5. How long is coverage under the short-term disability plan provided? _____
6. What percent of your salary is covered under a long-term disability plan? __
7. How long is coverage under the long-term disability plan afforded? _____
8. Does any of your group disability coverage have a waiting period? _____
9. Do you have any individual, franchise, or association disability plan? _____
10. What percent of your salary is covered by an individual, a franchise, or an association disability plan? _____
   _____
11. Do all of your policies, both group and individual, provide coverage for accident and sickness disabilities? _____
   _____
12. What are the terms of renewability on your individual disability policies? __
   _____
13. How is the term "disabled" defined in your group and individual plans? ___
   _____
   _____

Continued on next page

14. What minimum income would be necessary if a prolonged accident or sickness occurred? _____

15. What hobbies do family members have? _____
_____

Health Data

1. What types of group health coverage do you have? (i.e., hospital, medical, surgical, comprehensive, major medical) _____

2. Are you covered under an HMO plan? _____
3. Does your group plan coordinate against other group plans? _____
4. Which family members are covered under group plans? _____
_____

5. What type of individual health coverage do you have? _____

6. If you have individual health insurance policies what are the terms of renewability? _____

7. Is anyone in your family eligible for Medicare? _____

8. Does anyone in your family have a severe health problem? _____

   If so, what? _____
_____

Retirement Data

1. When do you plan to retire? _____
2. What type of employer-provided retirement benefits do you have? _____

3. What will be the cash value in your life insurance policies when you plan to retire? _____

4. If you will qualify for social security benefits, what is the estimated benefit you should receive? _____

5. Will your spouse qualify separately for retirement benefits? _____
6. What private retirement plans (IRA, Keogh, etc.) do you have? _____
7. How much do you plan to contribute to your individual plans? _____
8. How many dependents will you have when you retire? _____
9. What savings plans do you have? _____

10. Do you have any company stock option or profit sharing plans? _____

Professional Data

Office No. 1   Office No. 2

1. Location of each professional office: _____
2. Are you in partnership? _____
3. Is your office shared with others? _____

4. If you rent your office, have
   you assumed liability under
   terms of lease? _____
5. Value of office contents: _____
6. Value of contents in office
   safe: _____
7. Value of professional
   instruments: _____
8. Number of employees in
   office? _____
   Please describe nature of
   their duties: _____
9. Value of radium owned by you
   or for which you may be
   liable: _____
10. Value of precious metals: _____
11. Do you X-ray for therapeutic
    treatment? _____
12. With what hospitals or clinics
    are you connected? In what
    capacity? _____
13. Of what professional societies
    are you a member? _____
14. If your services are under
    contract, please indicate
    to whom: _____

General Data

1. Do you act as guardian, trustee, or executor? _____
2. Occupation and other business pursuits (describe duties): _____
3. Securities held in safe deposit vault, at home, or in the hands of brokers:
   _____
4. Amount of largest personal check likely to be drawn: _____

property figure on the balance sheet is an aggregate estimate which provides little specific information.

Flowchart When examining its exposures, a business firm may utilize a flowchart containing a description of the tasks that a firm performs as well as the relationship among the tasks. The production process could be one task on the flowchart. It would be tied to raw materials and to inventory. The raw materials would go into the production process while the inventory would be a direct output of production.

A flowchart can be used by a family, but generally, the family

12—Personal Risk Management and Insurance

Table 1-1

Family Financial Statement

Assets		Liabilities	
Checking Account	$ 1,000	Charge Accounts	$ 200
Savings Account	1,500	Short-Term Notes[2]	1,700
Stocks and Bonds	10,000	Residential Mortgage	55,000
Retirement Plan	25,000	Margin on Securities	5,600
Personal Property	10,000		
Life Insurance Cash Value	3,000		
			62,500
Life Estate[1]	$ 10,000		
Residence (Market Value)	65,000	Family's Net Worth	68,000
Automobiles	5,000		
	$130,500		$130,500

1. Life interest in rental property.
2. The notes could be secured or unsecured. Generally, this type of note would apply to automobiles, home improvement, and other similar loans.

operation is so small that a flowchart is not necessary to ascertain exposures. Figure 1-2 is a flowchart of a family involved in numerous activities. These activities have been grouped into four noninclusive classes relating to exposures: (1) internal services, (2) external services, (3) activities, and (4) education. Other activity classes also could be used.

In the exhibit, all three segments of the family are providing some income (external services). However, the head of the household is providing the majority of the income, and the loss of him or her would have the greatest impact on the financial status of the family.

If the head of the household is involved in a partnership or a proprietorship, then additional problems exist. Questions on the future of the partnership or proprietorship, the location of the business, and the future of the industry all become important in the event of his or her incapacity.

The other three task groups encompass a broad spectrum of activities such as hobbies, memberships in clubs and participation in organizations. Any of these activities may create an additional liability exposure. For example, if one of the family members belongs to the board of directors of a company, his or her liability exposure would be much greater than that of an individual who is not so involved. Therefore, external activities should be evaluated carefully.

Figure 1-2
Flowchart of Family Activity

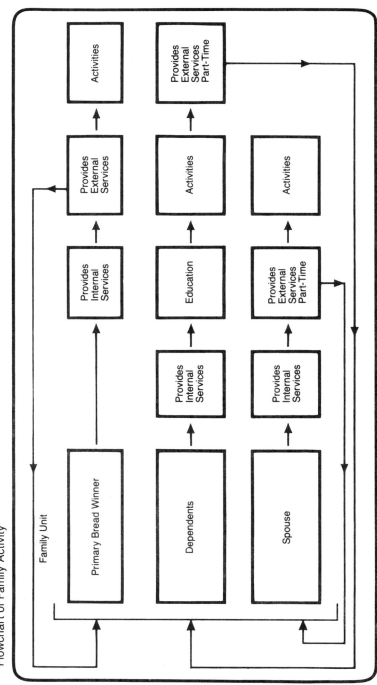

Figure 1-3

Flowchart of an Individual Family Member

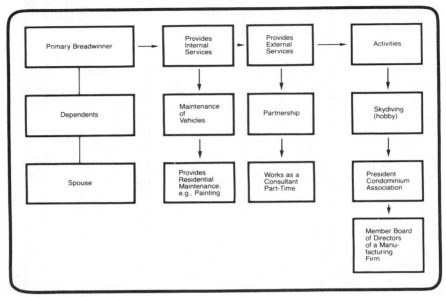

All family members provide internal services required to maintain the residence, to provide transportation, and so on. The extent to which each individual provides these services varies. Occasionally, family members may make a trade-off between providing external and internal services. For example, a woman may have a housekeeper to assist with the internal services and pursue a career outside the family.

Finally, a flowchart can show the family's education goals. One or more members of the family may be seeking to further their education.

Figure 1-3 illustrates in detail how one segment of a family flowchart can be subdivided. This flowchart outlines ten principal activities of the family's primary breadwinner.

Cash Flow   A financial flowchart can be helpful in evaluating a family's loss exposures. Assume a family analyzes its cash flow and discovers that its inflows just equal its outflows. Obviously, a worsening in its cash flow situation could result in a financial crisis. Consequently, the family should not buy insurance with high deductibles if it can afford to do otherwise.

Health coverage is typical of this type of problem. A family that does not have excess cash cannot afford to purchase catastrophe health insurance coverage which has a large deductible and a coinsurance clause. Instead, the family needs coverage that provides first dollar protection subject to a low deductible. Paradoxically, first dollar coverage is more expensive than catastrophe coverage, but the cost of the former can be budgeted accurately while the catastrophe coverage cannot.

Long-run problems also can be highlighted by using a cash flow analysis. Planning for special purchases or college education may require saving a portion of the family cash flow for an extended period of time.

PROPERTY LOSS EXPOSURES

The other major approach to loss exposure identification involves examination of the various categories of loss exposures: property, liability, and personal. This section considers property loss exposures, while the next two sections consider liability and personal loss exposures.

Almost all individuals and families are exposed to property losses. Ownership of property brings with it the chance of loss to the property itself, or *direct losses,* and the chance of indirect losses arising out of the damage to the property, called *indirect* or *consequential losses.* Direct and indirect losses to property can result from a wide variety of perils, some of which, such as fire, theft, windstorm, and automobile collision, are common, while others, such as earthquake and flood, are less common in many sections of the country.

Some of the kinds of property owned by individuals and families that may be exposed to direct loss include:

- residence;
- summer home;
- investment real estate;
- furniture, clothing, and other personal property;
- automobiles;
- watercraft (and aircraft);
- furs, jewelry, and works of art;
- securities, credit cards, and cash;
- professional equipment; and
- assets held as a trustee, executor, or guardian.

Some of the indirect losses that may arise out of a direct loss to such property include:

- loss of use of the damaged property (including additional living expenses while the residence is being rebuilt, rental of a substitute automobile while a car is being repaired, etc.);
- loss of rental income from damaged property;
- depreciation losses (or the difference between the cost to replace damaged property with new property and the depreciated value, called "actual cash value" of the damaged property);
- cost of debris removal.

Many property losses are comparatively small in size, but some are of major importance. As with disability income and medical expense loss exposures, what constitutes a small loss depends on the resources and attitudes of those involved. To understand the potential magnitude of property loss exposures and the ways they should be handled, it is necessary to review the variety of different kinds of property and property interests.

In general, property is anything an individual or family owns. Basically, there are two kinds of property—real property and personal property. Real property (or real estate) is land and everything attached to the land with the intention that it be part of the land. Personal property is all other kinds of property. Personal property can be tangible—property that has physical substance, like a car, boat, or, furniture; or, it can be intangible—property that does not have physical substance, like a stock certificate, bond, bank deposit, or life insurance policy.

Forms of Property Ownership

Property can be owned in various ways, and this can materially affect how the loss exposures should be controlled.

Outright Ownership The greatest degree of ownership is called outright ownership. The outright owner of property holds it in his or her own name and can deal with it during his or her lifetime. The individual can sell it, use it as collateral, give it away, or pass it on to his or her heirs. Examples of outright ownership are sole ownership of automobiles, furniture, boats, furs, jewelry, and so on; ownership in one's own name of stocks, bonds, bank accounts, and other accounts; and being the owner of a life insurance policy.

Joint Ownership This exists when two or more people have ownership rights in property. The more important forms of joint ownership are as follows.

Joint Tenancy (with Right of Survivorship). The main characteristic of joint tenancy with right of survivorship is that if one of the joint owners dies, his or her interest in the property automatically passes to the other joint owner(s). Thus, if Paul and Joan own their residence as joint tenants and Paul dies, Joan automatically owns the residence in her own name by right of survivorship. Joint tenancy can exist between anyone, not just husband and wife.

Tenancy by the Entirety. In some states, this form of ownership exists when property is held jointly by a husband and wife only. It is similar to a joint tenancy, but some key differences exist. First, tenancy by the entirety can exist only between husband and wife. Second, in many states, the survivorship rights cannot be terminated except with the consent of both parties. Finally, depending on the law in the particular state, the husband may have full control over the property during their joint lives and may be entitled to all the income from it.

It is incorrect to assume that all property owned by a husband or wife is jointly held property. Except in community property states, where special rules apply, only property specifically titled or received as being held by joint tenants or tenants by the entirety is so held. Other property can be owned outright by the husband alone, by the wife alone, or even by either of them jointly with others. Survivorship rights apply only to joint tenants or tenants by the entirety. Thus, a wife may not automatically get all her husband's property at his death unless specifically provided for.

The mere fact that property is held as joint tenants or tenants by the entirety does not mean such property has to stay that way. The joint owners can split their interests if they want. Sometimes splitting up joint ownership of property may be beneficial, but it depends on the individual circumstances involved. This question is discussed in greater detail later in this text (see Chapter 14).

Other Joint Interests. There are two common forms of joint ownership that have the right of survivorship somewhat similar to joint tenancy.

Joint Bank Accounts. Many individuals have joint savings or checking accounts. Generally, either party can make deposits and either party can withdraw all or part of the account. When one party dies, the survivor becomes the sole owner of the account by operation of law. This is not exactly a joint tenancy because a joint tenant can get at only his or her share of the property.

Jointly Owned Government Savings Bonds. Many individuals have purchased government savings bonds, such as Series E or H bonds, in a way that creates rights with another. Such bonds can be registered in co-ownership form and held in the name of, for example, Harry Jones or Mary Jones. This means that either Harry Jones or Mary Jones can cash in the bonds during their lifetime, and if one of them dies the other becomes sole owner.

Tenancy in Common. The main difference between tenancy in common and the other forms of joint ownership is the fact that tenants in common do not have the right of survivorship with respect to the property concerned. For example, if Ted and Joe own real estate equally as tenants in common, and Ted dies, his half of the real estate goes to his heirs as if he had owned it outright. Joe, of course, retains his half interest. Tenants in common can have different proportionate interests in property. For example, Ted and Joe could have 80 and 20 percent interests respectively in the real estate. Joint tenants and tenants by the entirety always have equal interests.

Community Property. Some states, namely, Arizona, California, Idaho, Louisiana, Neveda, New Mexico, Texas, and Washington are community property states. (The forty-two other states are called "common-law" states. In the common-law states the forms of ownership described above apply.)

In the community property states, husbands and wives can own community property and separate property. While the laws of the community property states are not uniform, separate property generally consists of property that a husband or wife owns at the time of marriage, property that each individually inherits, and property purchased with individual funds. This property remains separate property after marriage and the owner-spouse can deal with it as he or she chooses.

Community property generally consists of property that either or both spouses acquire during marriage. Each spouse has an undivided one-half interest in their community property. While the husband and wife are both living, the applicable state law would determine who has the rights of management and control over the community property. However, upon his or her death, each spouse can dispose of only his or her half of the community property.

Those living in common-law states can have community property. This can happen if the person and his or her spouse once lived in a community property state and acquired property that became community property. Such property remains community property even if the owners move to a common-law state. Conversely, property owned by a husband and/or wife in common-law states does not become community property when they move to a community property state.

Other Property Interests Other property interests are important for analyzing an individual's or family's financial situation and to determine what type of risk management and insurance planning is needed. Additional property interests may include life interests (or estates), and remainder interests, present interests and future interests, and powers of appointment.

Life Interests and Remainder Interests. A life interest in property entitles the holder to the income from or the use of the property, or a portion of the property, for the individual's lifetime. The remainder interest (or remainderman) is entitled to the property itself after a life interest has ended.

Present Interests and Future Interests. A present interest in property exists when the holder has an immediate right to use or enjoy the property. A future interest delays the use or enjoyment of the property to some future time.

Powers of Appointment. Powers of appointment commonly are used in planning a person's estate. In general, a power of appointment is a power or right given to a person that enables that person to designate, sometimes within limits, who is to get property subject to power.

The main nontax purpose of powers of appointment is to postpone the decision of who is to receive property until a later time when the circumstances about the individuals involved can be better known. This can result in better decision making about one's financial affairs. Powers also can be used to generate estate tax advantages.

Several kinds of powers of appointment exist, including (1) general powers and special powers (or limited powers), and (2) powers exercised by deed, by will, and by deed or will.

The difference between general and special powers is important especially for tax-saving reasons. A general power is a power to appoint property to the person having the power (the donee), the donee's estate, his or her creditors, or the creditors of his or her estate. In other words, a general power really means the donee can appoint the property to anyone he or she wants, including himself or herself or his or her estate. It is very close to actually owning the property. When someone who holds a general power over property dies, the property in question will be included in the decedent's estate for federal estate tax purposes.

A special power of appointment allows the donee to appoint the property only to certain persons who are *not* the donee, his or her estate, his or her creditors, or the creditors of his or her estate. The possession of a special power over property at a person's death does not result in the property's being included in his or her estate for federal estate tax purposes. This is the major tax advantage of special powers.

When the donee of either a general or special power can appoint property only at his or her death, it is referred to as a power exercisable by will (or a testamentary power). A power exercisable by deed is one where the donee can appoint the property only during his or her lifetime. The broadest power in this respect is one exercisable by deed or will.

All these forms of property ownership and property interests can apply to an almost endless variety of property. It is important to understand these property ownership and interest types in order to apply the risk management concept to individuals and families.

LIABILITY LOSS EXPOSURES

Under our system of laws, every person (and business entity) may be held financially responsible (legally liable) for any injury or damage inflicted upon the person or property of others. The events that ultimately may lead to payment for injuries or damages are as unpredictable as are the dollar amounts that can be involved. Liability loss exposures exist for all types of activities and relationships.[2] For purposes of this discussion, these exposures are classified as (1) premises, (2) general liability, (3) professional, (4) vehicular, and (5) watercraft and aircraft.

Premises Liability

Real property ownership carries with it a responsibility for losses that occur on the property. However, the degree of responsibility varies according to the status of the individual on the property. These visitors can be classified as being trespassers, licensees, or invitees. A "trespasser" may be defined as one who goes upon the private premises of another without invitation or inducement, express or implied, purely for his or her own purposes or convenience, where no mutuality of interest exists between the trespasser and the owner or occupant.[3] The primary duty owed to a trespasser by an owner or occupant is not to harass or harm him or her deliberately. Thus, a property owner may be held liable if he or she sets a trap for a trespasser who is then injured. Although a family does not have to make the premises safe for a trespasser, there are some areas where the duty owed by the property owner is unclear. If a property owner or occupier sees a trespasser and knows that the trespasser will be injured because of an existing hazard, the owner or occupier must warn the trespasser of impending danger to escape liability for the trespasser's injuries.

The duty owed to a licensee (such as a door-to-door salesperson) is greater than the duty owed a trespasser. The duty owed a licensee not only encompasses not harming the licensee but also includes warning the licensee of existing dangers.

Generally, a

> . . . "licensee" is one who stands in no contractual relationship to the owner or occupier of premises, but is permitted or tolerated thereon, expressly, implicitly or inferentially, merely for his own interest, convenience or pleasure or for that of a third person.[4]

The legal relationship between the owner and a visitor may be difficult to determine. For example, the guests to a party may be licensees or invitees. If the guests are business clients of the family, they may be invitees; however, if they are just friends, they are licensees.

Many court cases have been tried in an effort to determine if an individual was a licensee or invitee. In Crossgrove v. Atlantic Coast Line Railroad Company, the daughter of a railroad employee sued the railroad which employed her father. The girl lived with her father in a house provided by the railroad. She was injured seriously when the stairs in the house broke causing her to fall. The daughter contended that she was an invitee of the railroad but the company contended that the girl was a licensee because:

> . . . there is nothing to show an express or implied invitation upon the part of the defendant to the plaintiff to enter upon the premises; and mere permission to so do without any contractual privity of relationship between the plaintiff and defendant, or for any purpose either of mutual interest or for the benefit of the defendant, would create no more than the relation of a licensee.[5]

The court agreed with the railroad that the daughter was a licensee.

If the daughter had been an invitee the railroad would have been liable because an invitee is owed the highest degree of duty by the owner or occupier of a premises. That duty involves not only warning the invitee about danger but also taking precautions to make the premises safe.

Because of the liability exposure a family faces, it should include a premises safety program as part of its risk management planning.

General Liability

There are several areas of liability affecting individuals which do not fit into a specific category. These areas of liability are (1) absolute (or strict), (2) bailee, (3) contractual, (4) slander, and (5) libel.

Absolute Liability Absolute (or strict) liability exists when an individual is liable regardless of the reason of the loss. That is, if a person performs an act and someone or something is damaged, the person performing the act is held responsible for the loss even though he or she was not negligent.

Absolute liability is established either by statute or common law. Absolute liability evolved because of the inherent danger associated with some activities in society. Anyone who performs these acts is considered responsible for any unexpected results. For example, blasting is an activity for which an individual is held absolutely liable regardless of the degree of care used. Anyone who dams water is held absolutely liable for any damage because of accidental flooding regardless of cause. In similar fashion, anyone who owns inherently dangerous animals (e.g., lions or tigers) is generally held strictly liable for any damages caused by them.

Bailee Liability Another area of liability involves the bailor-bailee relationship. One party (the bailor) delivers goods to a second party (the bailee) but the bailor retains title to the goods and expects to have them returned at some future date. For example, a laundry is a bailee. The bailor delivers clothes to the laundry to be cleaned and then returned. Obviously the laundry (bailee) never takes title of the laundry, only possession for a temporary period of time.

The bailor-bailee relationship is important from two perspectives. First, property held by a bailee may not be covered under the bailor's insurance contracts. In addition, the bailee may deny liability for certain occurrences, such as acts of God or governmental actions. The bailor should be aware of any liability restrictions because these gaps in protection may need to be covered.

A family should be aware of the ramifications of the bailor-bailee relationship for a second reason. Occasionally, a family may be in the position of being a bailee and consequently, will be liable for items it holds as a result. For example, a family watching someone's pet and receiving compensation for so doing will be liable for any loss to the pet resulting from the negligence of a family member.

Individuals may assume liability for specific events, either knowingly or unknowingly, by entering into a contractual agreement with a second party. This contractual liability is a third area of exposure of which individuals need to be cognizant. For example, in an apartment lease, the landlord may stipulate by means of a hold harmless agreement that the tenant is responsible for all injuries, regardless of cause, that occur in the leased apartment. Obviously, this type of liability should be recognized and properly handled by the tenant.

Two final areas of liability to be considered are slander and libel. Both involve the defamation of an individual's character. Libel is:

> . . . an accusation in writing or printing . . . against the character of a person . . . which affects his reputation, in that it tends to hold him up to ridicule, contempt, shame, disgrace or obloquy, to degrade him in the estimation of the community, to induce an evil opinion of him in the minds of right thinking persons, to make him an object of

reproach, to diminish his respectability or abridge his comforts, to change his position in society for the worse, to dishonor or discredit him in the estimation of the public, or his friends and acquaintances, or to deprive him of friendly intercourse in society, or cause him to be shunned or avoided.[6]

Slander is the verbal form of libel. Any words spoken by an individual that hurt another individual's business, position, or standing can be grounds for a suit by the injured party.

Professional Liability

In the past, use of the term "professional" was generally limited to lawyers, accountants, and physicians. The term is no longer so narrowly defined, a direct result of our changing society and the desire and work of other occupations to achieve "professional" recognition and status. Many groups who call themselves professionals have no set of standards and some would certainly argue that such groups are not professionals. Regardless of which individuals should be designated as professionals, the position of a professional is a precarious one. The proliferation of suits against physicans for medical malpractice has made this fact clear. Suits against lawyers, accountants, consultants, professors, and other groups for professional malpractice are becoming increasingly commonplace.

This exposure also is important to families since one suit against a professional could totally destroy the family's financial structure. Obviously, many professionals can purchase liability insurance for protection, but in some professions, such as the medical profession, coverage has become either difficult to obtain or extremely expensive. Some physicians have responded to this situation by forming their own insurance companies or by transferring what assets they can to others and then carrying no insurance protection at all.

It cannot be emphasized too strongly that the liability exposure exists not only for physicians, lawyers, insurance agents and brokers, accountants, and consultants but also for many other professional and quasi-professional groups.

Vehicular Liability

The operation of motorized vehicles exposes families to one of their major liability problems. The exposure varies with the type of vehicle being operated and with the driver. For instance, the typical accident involving a motorcycle results in less property damage than one involving an automobile, but bodily injury is usually more severe. Moreover, elderly drivers tend to be involved in minor accidents while young drivers tend to be involved in more serious ones.

Several factors influence the liability facing an individual. For example, the driver's liability for injuries to passengers has been modified in some states so that the driver is not liable unless he or she was grossly negligent. Statutes that reduce the liability of the driver are called guest passenger statutes. However, in a majority of states a driver is liable if he or she is negligent and passengers are injured as the result of the negligent act.

The distinction between "negligence" and "gross negligence" is important. A person is negligent if he or she does not act as a reasonable individual would act given the same set of circumstances. Thus, if the driver has not acted as a reasonably prudent individual, he or she will be held liable for the accident.

Gross negligence is the:

> ... intentional failure to perform a manifest duty in reckless disregard of the consequences as affecting the life or property of another; (or) such a gross want of care and regard for the rights of others as to justify the presumption of willfulness and wantonness.[7]

The family doctrine (also known as the family automobile doctrine, the family car doctrine, and the family purpose doctrine) also may have an impact on the liability of the family. Under this doctrine, if the owner of a car permits any family member to use the car, the owner will be liable for any injuries or damage caused if the driver was negligent. The purpose of this statute is to ensure that the victim(s) will have a financially sound source to turn to for indemnification. Obviously, a parent will have more assets than a minor child.

Liability arises from the ownership of a car, not from the fact that one is the head of the household. As an example, in McNamara v. Prather, a father was held not to be liable for injuries caused by his minor son who was driving an automobile owned by the mother.[8]

No-fault insurance has affected the automobile liability area. In theory, parties to an accident are supposed to collect for their losses from their own insurers unless the accident is particularly severe (defined in terms of the size of the monetary loss or extent of bodily injury). However, since most no-fault laws have low thresholds, only minor injuries are compensated on a no-fault basis. Moreover, many states do not have no-fault statutes, and citizens involved in accidents in these states still are covered by the traditional fault system. Thus, individuals still have to be concerned about being sued. An analysis of the no-fault concept is presented in the next chapter.

Watercraft and Aircraft

Both watercraft and aircraft present a liability exposure for owners and operators regardless of their location or how they are being used. For instance, a boat being towed to a launch area poses a liability exposure just as surely as it does while it is in the water. Likewise aircraft are exposures while they are on the ground and in the air.

PERSONAL LOSS EXPOSURES

In addition to the property and liability loss exposures just described, personal loss exposures are a major consideration for all individuals and families. Such personal loss exposures occur as a result of potential financial losses that arise when an individual dies, loses income, and incurs medical expenses as a result of an accident or illness, reaches an advanced age, or becomes unemployed. All these personal loss exposures must be considered in individual and family risk management.

Premature Death

A major objective of most individuals is to protect their dependents from the financial consequences in the event of their premature death. Individuals also are concerned with the impact of their death on their business affairs. The nature of the various financial losses that may arise upon a person's death are as follows:

Loss of the Deceased's Future Earned Income   Most families live on the earned income of the husband or perhaps the husband and wife combined. The death of an income earner results in the loss to the family of the future earnings from the date of death until the income earner would have retired or otherwise left the labor force. For most families, this represents a potentially catastrophic loss because the breadwinner's earnings constitute the family's main source of future income. Several approaches can be used to value the loss of a deceased's future earning power. Three such approaches—the "human life value" approach; the "needs" approach, assuming the liquidation of capital; and the "needs" approach, assuming the preservation of capital—are discussed in detail and illustrated in Chapter 6. In most cases, this loss of future earning capacity is the most important financial loss arising out of a person's premature death.

Costs Arising at Death   Certain obligations either are created or become due at a person's death. In most cases, these obligations exist whether the deceased dies before or after retirement, so they are really losses arising at a person's death whether it is "premature" or not. Perhaps the most important obligations created by the fact of death itself are: funeral and burial expenses, cost of settlement of the deceased's estate, and any federal estate tax and/or state inheritance or estate tax that may be due.

In addition to the costs created by death itself, other obligations tend to become due at death. Most people have balances on charge accounts, credit cards, and other personal debts for which the estate would be obligated to pay in the event of death. Many people also may have larger debts outstanding that they would like to have paid off in the event of their death. For example, the balance due of any mortgage loan on a residence.

Increased Expenses for the Family   The death of certain family members, normally the wife and mother, will result in increased housekeeping expenses. This loss frequently is overlooked in personal risk management and yet can be considerable. Also, in many families, the wife is an important income earner. A wife frequently holds an outside job before she has any children, leaves her outside job to become a full-time homemaker when she becomes a mother, and then reenters the labor force when her youngest child is in school. Thus, the potential economic loss arising from the wife and mother's death may involve (1) the increased expenses incurred to hire someone to take care of the home and children and/or (2) the loss of the wife's future earning power in the outside job market, depending upon the circumstances in the particular case.

Loss of Tax Advantages   In some cases, the death of a family member can result in substantially increased taxation for the survivors. This results largely from the loss of certain tax advantages, namely, income, estate, and gift tax advantages accorded to married persons under the tax laws. The importance of the potential loss of such tax advantages depends a great deal on the individual case. Generally, the tax benefit most discussed is the potential loss of the federal estate tax marital deduction on a spouse's death. This loss may be quite important in cases where there is a large potential federal estate tax liability. These issues are dealt with later (see Chapter 14).

Business Value Losses Due to Death of Owner or Key Person   When the owner or one of the owners of a closely held business (i.e., a sole proprietor, a partner in most partnerships, or a stockholder in many smaller corporations where there are only a few stockholders who actively run the business) dies, the business also may die or experience considerable loss in value. This loss in value occurs because the business must either be liquidated at an unfavorable time or the deceased owner's interest is inherited by someone who really cannot take the deceased's place in managing the business. These potential losses in business values are directly related to the owners' personal risk management because such closely held business interests frequently constitute the major part of the owners' estates.

In addition, many businesses have employees whose services contribute greatly to the continued profitability of the business. The death of such key employees, whether owners or not, can cause considerable financial loss to the business until they can be replaced.

The above represent the types of financial losses that may arise out of the uncertainty of when death will occur. Of course, every person or family is not subject to all these potential losses; some, such as loss of tax advantages and loss of business values, arise only in certain cases. When they do exist, however, they can be of critical importance for the individuals or families involved.

Sources of Protection Against Premature Death   The various kinds of death benefits that may be available to a deceased person's family are outlined below. Each will be described in greater detail in subsequent chapters, but they are presented in outline form at this point to give an overview of the risk management devices that may be available to meet this important exposure. In most cases, a number of these sources can be used to protect against the risk of premature death.

I. Life Insurance
   A. Individual life insurance purchased on the insured's life
   B. Group life insurance on the person's life
      1. Through his or her employer or business
      2. Through an association group plan provided in cooperation with a professional association, fraternal association, etc.
   C. Credit life insurance payable to a creditor of the insured person to discharge a debt
II. Social Security Survivors' Benefits
III. Other Government Benefits
   A. Servicemen's and veteran's benefits
   B. Railroad retirement benefits
   C. Civil service benefits
IV. Death Benefits Under Private Pension Plans
   A. Life insurance under insured pension plans
   B. Return of employee contributions
   C. Vested rights in employer contributions
   D. Joint and last survivor annuity forms

E. Other survivors' benefits
V. Death Benefits Under Deferred Profit Sharing Plans
   A. Vested rights in contributions
   B. Life insurance purchased by the plan on a participant's life
VI. Death Benefits Under Nonqualified Deferred Compensation Plans
VII. Death Benefits Under Tax Deferred Annuity (TDA) Plans, Plans for the Self-Employed (HR-10 Plans), Individual Retirement Accounts (IRAs), and Personal Annuity Contracts
VIII. Noninsured Employer Death Benefits or Salary Continuation Plans
IX. All Other Assets Available to the Family After the Person's Death, Including:
   A. Jointly owned property
   B. Property inherited directly from the deceased
   C. Income or property from trusts
   D. Proceeds from the sale of business interests

Disability Income Losses

Another major objective of most individuals should be to protect themselves and their dependents from financial losses arising from their disability. Disability, particularly total and permanent disability, is a great risk faced by almost everyone, and yet, surprisingly, often is neglected in personal risk management.

Actually, the probability that an individual will suffer a reasonably long-term disability (e.g., a disability of ninety days or more) at various ages prior to age sixty-five is considerably greater than the probability of death at those ages. For example, the data in Table 1-2 shows that the probability of a long-term disability (ninety days or more) at age thirty-two is about six and one-half times the probability of death at that age.

The financial losses arising from disability tend to resemble those resulting from death. An important difference from the risk management viewpoint, however, is that there is a wide range of possible durations of total disability—from only a week or so to total and permanent disability. Thus, a person must base his or her planning decision on the assumption that he or she could be disabled for a variety of possible durations—from a few days to the rest of life. However, the individual should give greatest planning attention to protecting himself or herself and any dependents against long-term and total and permanent disability rather than being unduly concerned with disabilities that last only a few weeks or even a few months (unless there is no other way to handle the short-term disability).

Table 1-2

Comparative Probabilities of Death and Disability*

Attained Age	Probability of Disability of Ninety Days or More Per 1,000 Lives	Probability of Death Per 1,000 Lives	Probability of Disability as a Multiple of Probability of Death
22	6.64	0.89	7.46
32	7.78	1.18	6.59
42	12.57	2.95	4.26
52	22.39	8.21	2.73
62	44.27	21.12	2.10

*Adapted from O. D. Dickerson, *Health Insurance*, 3rd ed. (Homewood IL: Richard D. Irwin, 1968), p. 16.

The total and permanent disability of the family breadwinner can be a much greater financial catastrophe than premature death, because the disabled person remains a consumer, whose consumption needs may increase because of the disability. One leading insurance authority graphically labeled total and permanent disability as the "living death".

The various financial losses that may arise upon a person's disability follow. It is presumed that the disability is reasonably long-term so as to represent a severe financial loss.

1. *Loss of the disabled person's earned income for the period of disablement.* This loss parallels that of the loss of future earning power in case of death. The seriousness of the loss depends upon how long the person is disabled. From an individual's perspective, however, there is no way of knowing in advance how long a disability might last. The only sensible course, therefore, is to plan for the worst and assume the income earner could be totally and permanently disabled for life.

2. *Increased expenses for the family.* As in the case of death, the disability of a family member can result in increased expenses for the family—both medical and others. It already has been noted that the disabled breadwinner also remains a consumer. In addition, disability of the wife and mother can result in substantial expenses in hiring one or more persons to perform the economic functions she formerly performed. Moreover, the wife and mother also may be a full- or part-time outside income earner whose income is important to the financial well-being of the family.

3. *Business value losses because of the disability of an owner or key person.* While death commonly is recognized as likely to produce

business losses in the case of closely held businesses, little attention has been given to the impact of the owner's or key employee's disability on the value of the business. This contingency is complicated since the situation of a business may be considerably less clear in the event of an owner's disability than in the case of his or her death. For example, the disabled owner may recover but still be impaired in terms of his or her economic value to the firm as compared with his or her value prior to the disability. Long-term or total and permanent disability is just as important in planning for a closely held business interest as is death.

4. *Property management problems.* The disability of an income earner or property owner may give rise to particular property management problems because the disabled person might be in such a physical or mental state that he or she is unable to manage his or her affairs effectively. Advance planning is desirable to provide a means for handling this unhappy contingency.

Sources of Protection Against Disability Income Losses

As was done in the case of premature death, the various sources of protection against disability income losses are outlined below. They are described in greater detail in subsequent chapters.

I. Health Insurance
   A. Individual disability income insurance policies
      1. Purchased by the insured
      2. Purchased by his or her employer as a part of a salary continuation plan
   B. Group disability income insurance
      1. Purchased through his or her employer or business
      2. Purchased through an association group plan
   C. Credit disability income insurance payable to a creditor of the insured person to discharge a debt
II. Disability Benefits Under Life Insurance Policies
   A. Disability income riders added to some individual life insurance policies
   B. Waiver of premium benefits included with or added to individual life insurance policies
   C. Disability benefits under group life insurance
III. Social Security Disability Benefits
   A. Workers' and dependents' disability income benefits

B. Disability "freeze" on workers' retirement credits
IV. Other Government Benefits
    A. Servicemen's and veteran's benefits
    B. Railroad retirement benefits
    C. Civil service benefits
V. Workers' compensation disability benefits
VI. Disability Benefits Under Private Pension Plans
VII. Disability Benefits Under Deferred Profit Sharing Plans
VIII. Disability Benefits Under Nonqualified Deferred Compensation Plans
IX. Noninsured Employer Salary Continuation Plans
X. All Other Income, Investment or Otherwise, Available to the Family after a Person's Disability

This outline, as well as that for premature death, shows that there are often more sources of protection available than most people think. The problem is to use these sources efficiently to meet the individual's or family's needs.

Medical Care Expenses

Most people are convinced of the need to protect themselves and their family against medical care costs. Mounting medical care costs have become a national problem, and they are no less so for the individual and his or her family. For example, the average cost per patient day of a stay in a community hospital has increased from $32.23 in 1960 to $151.20 in 1975, a 469 percent increase. This daily figure ($151.20) combined with the national average length of stay (7.7 days in 1975—7.6 days in 1960) yields an average cost per (hospital) patient stay of $1,164.20 for 1975.[9]

In terms of personal planning, family medical care costs can be divided conveniently into several categories.

Normal or Budgetable Expenses These are the medical expenses that the family more or less expects to pay as a part of its regular monthly budget, such as routine visits to physicians, routine out-patient tests and X-rays, expenses of minor illnesses, small drug purchases, and the like. Just what are "normal" or budgetable expenses depends a great deal on the needs, other resources, and desires of the individual and his or her family. The federal income tax law would seem to imply that three percent of adjusted gross income is considered "normal" for tax purposes since medical expenses of less than this amount cannot be taken as itemized deductions for income tax purposes. However, the amount of medical expenses that can be assumed by an individual or family without insurance is a financial decision that should be made on the basis of each individual's or family's specific circumstances. As a general principle, however, the larger the amount of annual expenses the individual or family can afford to assume, the lower will be its overall costs. This is true because, as a group, the purchasers of insurance must pay the insurer's overhead cost of operating the insurance business, and this overhead cost is a relatively larger percentage of small claims than of large claims because most of the same insurance functions must be performed regardless of the size of the claim. Buying insurance against relatively small potential losses results in what is called "trading dollars with the insurance company," usually an uneconomical practice for an insured. Also, to the extent that an emergency fund is established to meet unexpected medical costs, the investment earnings on this fund would be available to the individual or family.

Larger Than Normal Expenses   These are medical expenses that exceed those that are expected or budgetable. If they occur, they probably cannot be met out of the individual or family's regular income. To meet such medical expenses, the individual can buy insurance, use an emergency fund, plan on using his or her sources of credit (borrowing), or some combination of these. Again, the cut-off point between "normal" and "larger than normal" expenses depends upon the individual's or family's circumstances.

Catastrophic Medical Expenses   These are expenses so large that they would cause severe financial problems for the individual or family. They are the most important for which to plan because they are potentially the most damaging. Again, the dividing line between "larger than normal losses" and "catastrophic losses" depends on individual circumstances. For example, one family may feel that uninsured medical expenses of $500 a year would constitute a severe financial strain and, therefore, are unacceptable from a risk management standpoint. Another family, however, with a larger income and an emergency fund, may feel that uninsured medical expenses of $2,000 could be tolerated, provided the annual cost savings were significant enough to justify the family's assuming this much risk. The significance of the dividing line lies in the fact that insurance generally is necessary to protect the family against truly catastrophic medical expenses, while the family may elect to assume at least some of the larger than normal expenses.[10] The traditional approach for protecting the individual or family against catastrophic medical expenses is to buy, or be covered by, so-called major medical expense insurance. This rapidly growing form of insurance has proved very popular with the public. Even major medical expense insurance, however, as it is presently written, may prove inadequate to meet some of the really large medical bills possible today. Such instances, while relatively infrequent, nevertheless point up the need for planning to meet this exposure because if it did occur, it would be truly catastrophic for the individual or family. There really is no way for an individual or family to know in advance just how large such catastrophic medical expenses might be. Since they could be very large, the individual or family should plan with that possibility in mind.

Sources of Protection Against Medical Care Expenses The following are the major sources to which individuals and families may look for coverage of medical care expenses.

I. Health Insurance
    A. Individual medical expense policies
    B. Group medical expense policies
II. Social Security Medical Benefits (Medicare)
III. Other Government Benefits
IV. Medical Payments Coverage Under Liability Insurance Policies
V. Employer Medical Expense Benefits Paid Under a Noninsured Plan
VI. Other Assets Available to the Family

Provision for Retirement Income

As noted earlier, a basic personal risk management objective is to provide a retirement income for the individual and his or her spouse. This objective is increasingly important today because of changes in our socio-economic institutions and because most people can anticipate living to retirement. As illustrated in Table 1-3, the life expectancy at all these ages exceeds the typical retirement age in the United States of sixty-five. Also, at all these ages the probability of survival to age sixty-five considerably exceeds the probability of death before age sixty-five.

This shows that for the bulk of the population the problem of preparing for retirement is far more important than preparing for premature death. It must be recognized, of course, that these probabilities are based on averages and the individual has no way of knowing for purposes of his or her planning whether he or she will be among the majority who live to retirement years. The prudent person must plan for the possibility of both contingencies. However, he or she should not give undue attention in planning to the chance of premature death at the expense of the more probable chance of outliving his or her income.

A variety of sources or instruments are available for providing retirement income. As indicated above, one of the main reasons for

Table 1-3

Life Expectancy

Age	Life Expectancy in Years[†]	Probability of Death Before Age 65	Probability of Survival to Age 65 (1 − Probability of Death)
25	46	0.29	0.71
30	41	0.28	0.72
35	37	0.27	0.73
40	32	0.26	0.74
45	28	0.25	0.75
50	24	0.22	0.78
55	20	0.18	0.82
60	16	0.12	0.88
65	13	—	—

[†]Computed from the 1958 Commissioners Standard Ordinary Mortality Table.

accumulating capital traditionally has been to provide for retirement. Before social security, and when the main obligation of the employer toward his or her retiring employees was the purchase of the "gold watch" or some other such token, the burden of providing income for retirement did rest largely with individual savings. Today, however, there are many ways a person can plan for his or her retirement—some involve government programs while others rely primarily on private insurance, and some involve tax advantages while others do not. The following is a brief outline of these sources of retirement income.

    I. Government Benefits
        A. Social Security Retirement Benefits
        B. Veteran's Benefits
        C. Civil Service Retirement Benefits
    II. Private Pensions and Annuity Plans
        A. Employer Provided Pension Plans
            1. Group type plans
            2. Individual policy pension trusts
        B. Self-Employed Persons Retirement Plans (HR-10 Plans)
        C. Individual Retirement Accounts (IRAs)
        D. Tax Deferred Annuity (TDA) Plans
        E. Individually Purchased Annuities
    III. Deferred Profit Sharing Plans
    IV. Nonqualified Deferred Compensation Plans

V. Other Employee Benefit Plans
    A. Employee Savings (or "Thrift") Plans
    B. Stock Option Plans
VI. Cash Values Under Individually Owned Life Insurance Policies
VII. Investments and Other Assets Owned by the Individual

Many of these instruments for providing retirement income offer certain tax advantages to the individual if the private retirement plan involved meets the requirements of the tax laws. Important examples of such instruments are "qualified" employer pension and profit sharing plans, HR-10 plans, IRA plans, TDA plans, and nonqualified deferred compensation plans. These tax advantages can be important to the individual or family and they have an important impact on modern retirement planning.

Because an individual today often has or will have a variety of retirement benefits available, coordination of these benefits becomes increasingly important. It does not make sense either to underprovide or overprovide retirement income. Thus, coordination becomes very important.

Unemployment

Involuntary unemployment caused by economic factors is another threat to an individual or family's financial security. The potential loss exposure can be computed in a manner similar to that for disability, i.e., total unemployment to total disability and partial unemployment to partial disability.

Sources of protection against the consequences of unemployment can be provided by several possibilities, namely, the federal-state unemployment insurance program, unemployment plans that may be available through the individual's place of employment, or through individual savings.

CAPITAL ACCUMULATION

The objective of protection against personal risks concerns the ability to make advance provision to meet the financial consequences of possible losses that generally cannot be controlled. It is essentially a "defensive" objective. The objective of capital accumulation however might be viewed as a more "positive" risk management objective.

Many people do not spend all their disposable income and thus have an investible surplus; many also have various semiautomatic plans, such as profit-sharing plans that build up capital; and some receive gifts and/or inheritances that must be invested. Thus, in one way or another one risk management objective for many people is to accumulate and invest capital.

There are a number of reasons why people want to accumulate capital. Some of the more important are for an emergency fund, for the education of their children, for retirement purposes, to guard against the consequences of unemployment, and for a general investment fund to provide them with additional income and financial security. Individuals and families also save with certain consumption goals in mind, such as the purchase of a new car or vacation trip, but these goals generally are more short term in nature. The relative importance of these reasons naturally varies with individual circumstances and attitudes. A person at age fifty-five probably will be primarily interested in preparing for retirement, while a younger person may be more concerned with educating children or perhaps the capital growth of a general investment fund.

Emergency Fund

An emergency fund is needed to meet unexpected expenses that are not planned for in the individual or family budget; to pay for the "smaller" disability losses, medical expenses, and property losses that purposely are not covered by insurance; and to provide a financial cushion against such personal situations as prolonged unemployment. This latter need for an emergency fund has been emphasized in recent years when many capable persons lost their jobs in the aerospace and defense industries. An emergency fund can help prevent the problem of temporary unemployment from becoming a crisis by giving the family time to adjust without having to change drastically its standard of living or disturbing its other investments.

The size of the emergency fund needed varies greatly and depends upon such factors as family income, number of income earners, stability of employment, assets, debts, insurance deductibles and uncovered health and property insurance exposures, and the family's general attitude toward risk management. Many people express the size of the emergency fund as so many months of family income, such as three to six months.

By its very nature, the emergency fund should be invested conservatively. There must be almost complete security of principal, marketability, and liquidity. Within these investment constraints, the emergency fund should be invested so as to secure a reasonable yield, given that the primary investment objective is safety of principal. Logical investment instruments for the emergency fund include:

1. bank savings accounts,
2. savings and loan association share accounts,
3. U.S. Saving Bonds,
4. short term U.S. treasury securities, and
5. life insurance cash values.

Education Needs

The cost of higher education has increased dramatically, particularly in private colleges and universities. For example, it has been estimated that it costs approximately $8,000 per year in tuition, fees, and room and board for a student to attend many private colleges. This can result in a tremendous financial drain for a family with college-age children, and yet it is a predictable drain.

The size of the fund obviously depends upon the number of children, their ages, the educational plans they have, and the size of the family income. However, it also depends upon the attitudes of the family toward education. Some people feel thay should provide their children with all the education they can profit from and want. Others, however, feel that children should help earn at least a part of their educational expenses themselves. What types of schools the children plan to attend also has a considerable bearing on the costs involved.

An investment fund for education often is a relatively long-term objective and, hopefully, the fund will not be needed in the meantime. Therefore, wider investment latitude is probably justified in the case of the emergency fund in order to secure a more attractive investment yield. All that is really necessary is that the principal be there by the time each child is ready for school.

Retirement Needs

A very important objective for many people is to accumulate funds for retirement. They want to make sure they can live comfortably in their old age when retired or no longer able to work. Stated another way, they want to take care of the chance that they will outlive their income.

General Investment Fund

Individuals often accumulate capital for general investment purposes. They may want a better standard of living, a second income in addition to the earnings from their employment or profession, greater financial security for the future, a capital fund to pass on to their children or grandchildren, or they simply may enjoy the investment process. In any event, people normally invest money for the purpose of maximizing after-tax returns, consistent with their financial objectives and the investment constraints under which they must operate.

The size of the investment fund depends upon how much capital the person originally has to invest, how much can be saved each year, and how successful the investor or his or her advisors are. There are, of course, wide variations in how much different people have to invest.

There are a number of ways in which people can accumulate capital and many possible investment policies that might be followed, from the very conservative to the very speculative. However, in terms of the objective of capital accumulation, the individual basically has the following factors to consider: (1) an estimate of how much capital he or she will need at various times in the future (or the financial objectives); (2) the amount of funds he or she now has to invest; (3) an estimate of how much he or she will save each year in the future; (4) the amount of time he or she has to meet objectives; (5) the general investment constraints under which he or she must operate in terms of security of principal, stability of income, tax status, and the like; and (6) the adoption of an investment program that will give him or her the best chance of achieving as much of his or her financial objectives as possible within the limitations of investment constraints.

Tables 1-4 and 1-5 give some growth rates for capital at assumed rates of return over various time periods. Table 1-4 shows how much an investment fund of $1,000 would grow at the assumed rates of return for the number of years indicated. Table 1-5 shows the amounts that would be generated from a series of annual $100 deposits made to an investment fund at various assumed rates of return and for different time periods.

The dramatic effect of compound rates of return over a number of years can be seen from Tables 1-4 and 1-5. Assume a man age thirty-five has $10,000 to invest. If he receives a *net* rate of return (after investment expenses and income taxes) of only 4 percent on his money, he can accumulate $14,800 by the time he is forty-five, $21,191 by the time he is fifty-five, and $32,430 by the time he is sixty-five. If he can increase his *net* rate of return of 6 percent on his investments, he can accumulate $17,910 by age forty-five, $32,070 by age fifty-five, and

Table 1-4

Values of a $1,000 Investment Fund Invested for Specified Periods at Various Rates of Return

Annual Net Rate of Return (Compounded)	Number of Years the $1,000 Is Invested							
	5	8	10	12	15	20	25	30
3%	$1,159	$1,267	$1,344	$1,426	$1,558	$1,806	$2,094	$2,427
4%	1,217	1,369	1,480	1,601	1,801	2,191	2,666	3,243
5%	1,276	1,478	1,629	1,796	2,079	2,653	3,386	4,322
6%	1,338	1,594	1,791	2,012	2,397	3,207	4,292	5,744
8%	1,469	1,851	2,159	2,518	3,172	4,661	6,848	10,064
10%	1,611	2,144	2,594	3,138	4,177	6,727	10,835	17,449
15%	2,011	3,059	4,046	5,350	8,137	16,367	32,919	66,212

Table 1-5

Values of a Periodic Investment of $100 Per Year at the End of Specified Numbers of Years at Various Rates of Return

Annual Net Rate of Return (Compounded)	Number of Years at $100 Per Year							
	5	8	10	12	15	20	25	30
3%	$531	$889	$1,146	$1,419	$1,860	$2,687	$3,646	$4,758
4%	542	921	1,201	1,503	2,002	2,978	4,165	5,608
5%	553	955	1,258	1,592	2,158	3,307	4,773	6,644
6%	564	990	1,318	1,687	2,328	3,679	5,486	7,906
8%	587	1,064	1,449	1,898	2,715	4,576	7,311	11,328
10%	611	1,144	1,594	2,138	3,177	5,728	9,835	16,449
15%	674	1,373	2,030	2,900	4,758	10,244	21,279	43,474

$57,440 by age sixty-five. If he can increase his *net* rate of return to 8 percent, he will have $21,590 by age forty-five, $46,610 by age fifty-five, and $100,640 by age sixty-five. Stated in a different manner, if a man age thirty-five with a $10,000 investment fund feels he needs approximately $30,000 in fifteen years for his childrens' education, he can see from Table 1-4 that he will have to earn a net rate of return of between 7 and 8 percent to accomplish his goal, assuming funds are not available from other sources ($10,000 at 8 percent per year for fifteen years— $31,720). It should be noted that it may be quite difficult for an investor to earn a *net* rate of return (after investment expenses and income taxes) of as much as 8 percent per year over an extended period of time, such as fifteen years.

In many cases, an individual also wants to know how much a certain amount saved each year will accumulate in a specified period. This can be determined from Table 1-5 which shows how much $100 per year (such as annual savings of $100 per year, for example) would grow to at the assumed rates of return for the number of years indicated. Assume that a man age thirty-five can save $1,200 per year (or about $100 per month). If he receives a *net* rate of return of 5 percent on the money he saves, he can accumulate $15,096 by the time he is forty-five ($1,258 × 12), $39,684 by the time he is fifty-five, and $79,728 by the time he reaches age sixty-five.

The results of Tables 1-4 and 1-5 also can be combined. Assume that a man age thirty-five has $10,000 to invest now and estimate he will save $1,200 per year that he can invest in the future. If he can invest these amounts at a *net* annual rate of return of 5 percent, he will accumulate $31,386 by age forty-five ($16,290 from Table 1-4 and $15,096 from Table 1-5), $66,214 by age fifty-five, and $146,168 by age sixty-five. It can be seen that substantially higher accumulations could be achieved by securing a net rate of return of even 1 or 2 percentage points higher than the 5 percent assumed above. It also can be seen that consistent saving and investment can produce rather startling results.

Investment Instruments for Capital Accumulation

A wide variety of possible investment instruments are available for an individual to use as investment outlets. These will be discussed in detail in Chapter 13, but they are outlined briefly below. The instruments are classified as "fixed dollar" and "variable dollar" (or "equity") investments. *Fixed dollar* investments mean those where the principal and/or income contractually are set in advance in terms of a specified or determinable number of dollars. *Variable dollar* (or *equity*) investments are those where neither the principal nor the income are contractually set in advance in terms of dollars. In other words, both the value and income of the investment can vary in dollar amount with changes in economic conditions.

I. Fixed Dollar Investments
  A. Bonds
    1. Corporate
    2. U.S. Government
      a. Marketable treasury
      b. U.S. Savings
    3. State and Local (Municipal)
    4. Mutual funds (bond funds)

B. Savings Accounts
  1. Bank accounts
    a. Regular accounts
    b. Savings certificates
  2. Savings and Loan Association Share Accounts
    a. Regular accounts
    b. Savings certificates
C. Preferred Stock
D. Life Insurance and Annuity Cash Values
II. Variable Dollar Investments
  A. Common Stock
  B. Mutual Funds (stock funds)
  C. Real Estate
    1. Residences
    2. Investment real estate
    3. Real estate investment trust (REIT) shares
  D. Variable Annuity Units
  E. Commodities
  F. Natural Resource Partnership Participations
  G. Business Ownership
    1. Sole proprietorships
    2. Partnership interests
    3. Close corporation stock
  H. Fine Arts and Other Miscellaneous Assets

PLANNING FOR THE ESTATE OWNER'S HEIRS

This is commonly referred to as estate planning. An estate plan is an arrangement for the distribution of one's wealth. For a great many estates, such an arrangement can be relatively simple and inexpensive to establish. However, for larger estates or estates with special problems, estate plans can become quite complex. Estate planning is a technical and specialized field where such diverse areas of knowledge as wills, trusts, tax law, insurance, investments, and accounting all are important. Thus, it frequently is desirable to bring together several professionals or specialists into an "estate planning team" to develop a well-rounded plan.

Unfortunately, there has developed over the years the impression that estate planning is only for the wealthy. However, many persons who would not regard themselves as wealthy actually do have potential estates large enough to justify use of the more advanced estate planning techniques.

Objectives of Estate Planning

In general terms, the basic goal of estate planning can be stated as planning for the arrangement and disposition of one's property to accomplish his or her wishes for the objectives of his or her heirs in the most efficient manner. This general goal, however, can be translated into the following specific estate planning objectives:

1. determining who will be the estate owner's heirs or beneficiaries and how much each will receive;
2. planning adequate financial support for the estate owner's dependents (and any others whom he or she may want to benefit);
3. providing sufficient liquid assets for the estate to enable the estate to meet its obligations (i.e., provide adequate estate liquidity);
4. reducing estate transfer costs (i.e., death taxes, expenses of administration, and the like) to a minimum, consistent with the estate owner's other objectives;
5. planning for the disposition of any closely held business interests;
6. deciding who is to settle the estate and how it is to be administered after the estate owner's death; and
7. planning how the estate owner's property is to be distributed.

Methods of Estate Transfer

For passing property to one's heirs, a variety of ways exist for an estate owner's property to be distributed at his or her death. Some involve lifetime transfers while others are transfers only at death. Most estate plans utilize several of these methods. The various methods of estate transfer may be outlined briefly as follows.

I. Lifetime (inter vivos) Methods of Estate Transfer
   A. Joint ownership of property with right of survivorship
   B. Lifetime gifts
   C. Life insurance proceeds payable to a third party beneficiary
   D. Other third party beneficiary arrangements (e.g., death benefits payable under deferred compensation agreements, pension plans, profit sharing plans, and the like)
   E. Irrevocable Living Trusts
   F. Revocable Living Trusts

II. Estate Transfer at Death
    A. Intestate distribution
    B. Outright bequests by will
    C. Testamentary trusts

Each of these methods will be covered in greater detail in a later chapter of this text.

Chapter Notes

1. George Head, C. Arthur Williams, and G. William Glendenning, *Principles of Risk Management and Insurance* (Malvern, PA: American Institute for Property and Liability Underwriters, 1978), p. 5.
2. For a detailed discussion of the tort law and negligence concepts, see Ibid., Chapter 10.
3. Keesecker v. G. M. McKelvey Co., 47 N.E. 2d 214 (1943).
4. Ibid.
5. Crossgrove v. Atlantic Coast Line Railroad Co., 118 S.E. 695 (1923).
6. Stevens v. Wright, 179 A. 215 (1935).
7. Henry Campbell Black, *Black's Law Dictionary* (St. Paul: West Publishing Co., 1968), p. 1185.
8. McNamara v. Prather, 277 KY 754, 127 S.W. 2d 160-162 (1939).
9. Source Book of Health Insurance Data, 1976-77 (New York, NY, 1977), p. 61.
10. It is recognized that in many cases this decision, in effect, is taken away from the individual consumer because his or her employer provides group medical expense insurance which the employee must either accept or in rare cases reject. Most medical expense insurance is provided on a group basis.

CHAPTER 2

Risk Management in a Changing Society

INTRODUCTION

George Bernard Shaw once said that the only intelligent man he knew was his tailor, who would take a new measure of him every time he ordered a new suit and would not assume that he always remained the same.[1]

The insurance industry has had to play the role of Shaw's tailor. It has had to constantly reevaluate its coverage and underwriting policies to meet the changing needs and circumstances of society. For example, in the 1950s, insurance companies began to market the homeowners contract, a multiline package policy providing a broad range of coverages. As segments of society began to shift from single family unit dwellings to condominiums, the insurance industry again responded by devising a package policy that meets the needs of the condominium owner. The special multiple policy for business also was approved to provide a package of coverages to meet specific needs. In the international area, some insurance companies have become involved in the insuring of overseas exports and investments.

Population changes, legal changes, and many other changes are continuously occurring in our society. These changes affect us and our institutions in varied ways. This chapter will describe some of the more important societal changes that are taking place and the implications of these changes for the insurance mechanism. Because our legal system has been one of the most fertile areas of change in recent years, and one of the most significant for insurance programs, this chapter will concentrate on this area. Because the development of the "no-fault" concept is particularly significant, it will be discussed in some detail. The remainder of the chapter describes certain insurance coverages designed to treat personal liability exposures.

SOCIETAL CHANGES AFFECTING INSURANCE

Population Changes

Demographic changes have a tremendous impact on the insurance industry. The population size, of course, effectively determines the magnitude of the insurance industry's market. Other aspects of the population, such as age distribution, income levels, marital status, and so on, also have an impact on the insurance industry and its products.

The rate of population growth is obviously one of the most important aspects of population change. Figure 2-1 provides projections of the population of the United States through the year 2050. While the underlying assumptions upon which the different projections are based vary, three of the four projections indicate that population will be growing slowly or will be declining by the year 2050. Even the growth that will occur between 1980 and 2000 will be slow. Thus, insurance markets along with others may not be expanding in future years. In addition, if the federal government expands its insurance operations, insurance companies will encounter a further reduction in market size.

The age distribution of the population also has been changing. During the 1960s, for example, the United States saw the impact of the baby boom of the 1940s. One result of this change was a drop in the median age. However, that trend now has been reversed because the rate of population growth has slowed. As children of the 1960s became adults, the population's median age began to climb, from 28.0 in 1970 to 28.8 in 1975. The median age should continue to climb because the rate of infusion of new babies into the population is declining.[2] The children of the 1960s are not having as large families as their parents and grandparents. Table 2-1 shows that the percentage of families with one or two children increased between 1970 and 1975 while those with three or more children declined over the same period.

An increasing median age affects both private and governmental insurance programs. The social security system faces additional pressures when the bulk of the population reaches retirement. The system has recognized the inevitable financial difficulty and has taken major corrective action through the 1977 Social Security Amendments.

The private insurance sector will also be made aware of the effects of an aging population. Within the next twenty years, automobile

Figure 2-1

United States Population—Projections to 2050*

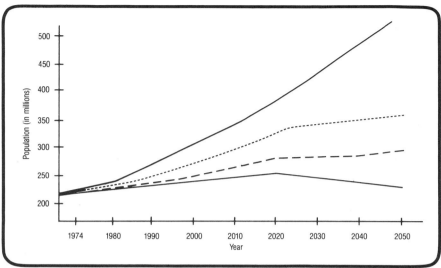

*Reprinted from United States Department of Commerce, *Statistical Abstract of the United States 1976* (Washington: Superintendent of Documents, 1976), p. 4. Each of the projections is based on different assumptions about the birth rate, immigration, and changes in mortality. A detailed analysis can be found in the *1971 Statistical Abstract.*

Table 2-1

Percent of Distribution of Families by Number of Children Under Eighteen*

	1970	1971	1972	1973	1974	1975
Percent distribution	100.0	100.0	100.0	100.0	100.0	100.0
No children	44.1	44.6	44.8	45.6	46.0	46.0
One child	18.2	18.5	18.9	19.3	19.2	19.7
Two children	17.4	17.2	17.6	17.4	17.9	18.0
Three children	10.6	10.4	10.2	9.7	9.5	9.3
Four or more children	9.8	9.4	8.6	7.9	7.4	6.9

*Reprinted from United States Department of Commerce, *Statistical Abstract of the United States 1976* (Washington: Superintendent of Documents, 1976), p. 42.

insurers, for example, will find that more of their customers will be in the "average" age bracket (twenty-five to sixty-five), but in the long run, more drivers will fall in the over sixty-five category.

Group life and health insurance companies also may find the cost of their products increasing because of an upward shift in the average age

Table 2-2

Marriage and Divorce Rate Per 1,000 Population*

	1970	1972	1973	1974	1975
Marriages— Rate per 1,000 population	10.6	11.0	10.9	10.5	10.0
Divorces— Rate per 1,000 population	3.5	4.1	4.4	4.6	4.8

*Reprinted from United States Department of Commerce, *Statistical Abstract of the United States 1976* (Washington: Superintendent of Documents, 1976), p. 69.

of workers. An older working population will also result in higher morbidity and mortality costs. Individual life insurance sales should also increase as the population matures. In the long run, however, this increase is expected to level off.

Marital status is another dimension of the population that is changing. During the past ten years the divorce rate has increased while the marriage rate has declined. As shown in Table 2-2, the marriage rate per 1,000 population was 10.6 in 1970. By 1975, the rate had dropped to 10.0. By way of contrast, the divorce rate was 3.5 per 1,000 population in 1970, but by 1975, it had risen to 4.8 per 1,000. These trends can be attributed to several factors including, but not limited to, the change in mores, elimination of discrimination against single individuals, and the mobility of society. The changing status of women is playing a major role in affecting marital patterns.

Concomitant with the decrease in marriages has been an increase in the cohabitation of couples. Cohabitation will force changes in the insurance industry just as it is causing change in the mortgage market. Until recently, a man and a woman living together would have had difficulty purchasing a dwelling together. However, as cohabitation has increased, lending institutions are being forced to make loans to unmarried couples. The effects on insurance companies may be less pronounced than on the mortgage market but are just as real. Life insurance companies will have to become accustomed to the idea that the beneficiary and/or the owner of a policy may not be related to the insured. Property and liability companies may have difficulty ascertaining who constitutes a dependent under some insurance policies.

An additional characteristic of the American population that deserves brief mention is its high mobility. By 1970, 41.8 percent of the people who had lived in a residence in 1965 lived in a different residence.

Almost 45 percent of those who moved had moved to a different county or state.

Part of the population shift in recent years has been from the rural areas to the urban centers. There have also been population shifts within the urban centers. For example, the population of the central cities comprised 32.3 percent of the total population in 1960. The corresponding figure in 1970 was 31.5 percent. During the same period, the percent of the population in the urban fringe (suburbs) climbed from 21.1 percent to 26.8 percent.[3] Thus, the urban growth has been in the suburbs not the inner city.

Population shifts can create rating problems as well as underwriting problems for property and liability insurance companies. As population changes occur, rate structures have to be reevaluated to determine if they will remain adequate. The desertion of the inner cities by middle class Americans has been instrumental in creating the need for, and the development of, the Federal Crime Insurance Program and the Fair Access to Insurance Requirements (FAIR) plans.

Inflation

Individuals and businesses alike have experienced the adverse effects of inflation, especially in recent years. While an in-depth discussion of the causes and effects of inflation is beyond the scope of this text, it is a critically important variable that affects us all.[4]

Figure 2-2 shows the annual percentage increase in the consumer price index from 1965 to 1976. Increases such as those experienced in 1974 and 1975 impact heavily on insurance companies. First, consumers have to pay more for the products they purchase. The cost of losses also has increased as the size of liability awards has grown; the cost of automobile repair parts has increased; the cost of building materials has escalated; and medical costs have risen. These increased costs have been reflected in the price of the insurance product, the premiums. This in turn has caused consumers to become concerned with insurance prices; stemming somewhat from public views that the industry is a group of profitable companies with unlimited resources. This concern may increase further since some consumers feel no choice exists as to rates charged because insurance is required or semi-required in many circumstances. For example, prospective homeowners cannot get a mortgage without property insurance and drivers in some states cannot drive a car without insurance or some other proof of financial responsibility. Likewise, physicians may be afraid to practice medicine without medical malpractice coverage, and firms that cannot afford products liability insurance may be forced out of business.

Figure 2-2

Consumer Price Index—1967 to 1976*

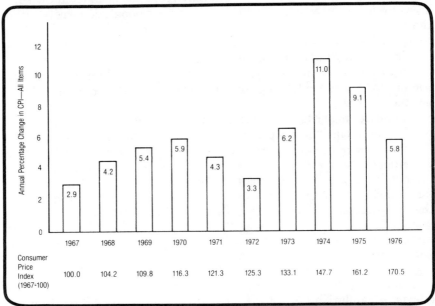

*Reprinted from United States Department of Commerce, *Statistical Abstract of the United States 1976* (Washington: Superintendent of Documents, 1976), p. 430.

Other aspects of inflation are important to insurance companies. In the area of life insurance, an agent should attempt to have a client increase his or her coverage whenever there is a change in the cost of living. The life insurance-inflation problem may be overcome to some extent, by tying the face amount of the coverage to some index or underlying investment fund, but these variable life insurance products are relatively new and have not captured a large segment of the life insurance market. It should be observed that some consumers have responded to this problem by purchasing more of the less expensive term life insurance and less of the permanent, more expensive forms of life insurance. Some consumers also are selecting higher deductibles on their property coverage, and others are simply forgoing the purchase of some forms of insurance protection altogether.

Property and liability insurers face the dilemma of how to persuade consumers to purchase adequate coverage. If an agent does not get the property owner to increase the coverage on his or her building each year, there is a chance that it will be underinsured and subject to a coinsurance penalty in the event of a loss. The inflationary problem is being overcome partially by adding inflation endorsements to property policies. Unfortunately, these endorsements increase coverage at a fixed rate, and the fixed rate does not necessarily coincide with the rate of inflation.

A Changing Work Force

The status of the American worker has undergone a dramatic evolution during the last seventy years. Children are now protected by child labor laws; women, blacks, the elderly, and other minorities are becoming a major segment of the work force; and the mandatory retirement age has just been raised from sixty-five to seventy.

The structure of the workweek also has been modified. Some companies are experimenting with the thirty-two hour workweek while other firms are trying a forty hour work schedule spread out over four days instead of five. Other organizations, including the federal government, are implementing flexible working hours.

One of the major changes in the work force is the increase in the number of women that work. Table 2-3 shows that the percentage of women in the civilian labor force has risen steadily since 1967. The increased infusion of women into the work force has led to changes in employee benefit plans. For example, there is increasing pressure to provide women and men who hold the same job and pay with the same retirement benefits. Since women, on the average, live longer than men, providing the same retirement benefits to women increases the cost of a defined benefit retirement program. However, as more women enter the work force, men can anticipate lower life insurance costs under group contracts because of the lower mortality of women.

In the health area, disability payments have been the subject of discussion. Some people argue that women should be afforded disability payments when they are absent from work because of pregnancy. Others contend that pregnancy can be prevented and, therefore, it should not be covered under a disability plan that is designed to cover only fortuitous events. Many questions concerned with employee benefits for women are not yet settled, and the debate may go on for a number of years.

Transportation

Transportation has always presented a challenge to the insurance industry. Automobile insurance, once regarded as a luxury, is now considered essential. At the same time that automobile insurance was coming to be considered a necessity, it was becoming more expensive. In

Table 2-3

Women in the Labor Force *

	Female Labor Force as Percent of Female Population	Female Labor Force as Percent of Civilian Labor Force
1967	39.7	36.7
1968	40.7	37.1
1969	41.6	37.8
1970	42.6	38.1
1971	42.5	38.2
1972	43.6	38.5
1973	44.1	38.9
1974	45.2	39.4
1975	45.9	39.9
1976 (January–April)	—	40.5

*Reprinted from United States Department of Commerce, *Statistical Abstract of the United States 1976* (Washington: Superintendent of Documents, 1976), pp. 355, 358.

fact, it has become so expensive that some poorer segments of society no longer are able to afford automobile insurance. The problem of affordability will probably become extremely critical within a few years. Some suggestions on how to control the cost of automobile insurance include price ceilings on health care costs and automobile parts and labor, revision of the tort system (no-fault), and elimination of charges for pain and suffering. The current automobile dilemma is more than just an automobile insurance problem. Air pollution and high petroleum prices also have forced the public to reevaluate its attitude toward the automobile.

Housing

The United States contains millions of acres of land, but the public has shown an unwillingness to live on some of this acreage. For example, parts of the west and southwest are not occupied because the climate is hot and adequate water supplies are not available. Other land is deemed undesirable because it is too far from major urban areas. Since all the land is not being used, increasing demand for the land that is being utilized has resulted. In California, for example, some land values have been increasing at an average annual rate in excess of 20 percent. Because of the increase in the cost of desirable land, and higher building costs, many consumers are unable or unwilling to purchase single family dwellings.

One solution to this problem has been the development of cooperatives, planned unit developments, and condominiums. When an individual purchases a condominium, he or she owns a unit in a multiple-unit building and a percentage of the land upon which the condominium is located.

Insurable interests under a condominium arrangement are divided between the condominium association and the individual unit owners.

Individual unit owners have an insurable interest in: (a) their personal property; (b) that portion of the unit in which they have sole interest; (c) additions or alterations within their units; (d) use of the unit; (e) use of limited common areas (carports, etc.); and (f) special condominium assessments caused by perils insured.

The association has an insurable interest in: (a) buildings, excluding those portions in which the unit owner has sole interest; (b) association personal property and owners' personal property in the care, custody, and control of the association; (c) pools, fences, signs, light poles and other structures on the common area; (d) retaining walls, underground utilities, sprinkler systems, driveways, walks, etc.; (e) lawns, trees, plants, and shrubs; and (f) under some declarations examined, the buildings and the units.[5]

Because of the division of insurable interest, the insurance industry has developed special coverages for condominium owners. These coverages, are discussed in detail later in this text. The move away from single family dwellings probably will continue to increase, and other types of residences will be developed. The insurance industry should have no difficulty responding to changes in housing patterns.

Crime

Table 2-4 gives the number of crimes and crime rates for selected years between 1960 and 1975 in the United States. Since 1960, both the number of crimes and crime rates have increased significantly. The impact of these increased levels of crime has not been restricted to specific income levels, races, or ages. Rather, all segments of society have been affected.

The higher crime rates have resulted in higher insurance claims, rates, and reduced insurance availability.

Commenting on crime in the *CPCU Annals*, John D. Long stated:

Table 2-4
Crimes and Crime Rate by Type—1960 to 1975*

Item and Year		Total	Violent Crime					Property Crime			
			Total	Murder	Forcible Rape	Robbery	Aggravated Assault	Total	Burglary	Larceny-Theft	Motor Vehicle Theft
Number of Offenses:											
1960	1,000	3,384	288	9.1	17.2	108	154	3,096	912	1,855	328
1965	1,000	4,739	387	10.0	23.4	139	215	4,352	1,283	2,573	497
1968	1,000	6,720	595	13.8	31.7	263	287	6,125	1,859	3,483	784
1969	1,000	7,410	662	14.8	37.2	299	311	6,749	1,982	3,889	878
1970	1,000	8,098	739	16.0	38.0	350	335	7,359	2,205	4,226	928
1971	1,000	8,588	817	17.8	42.3	388	369	7,772	2,399	4,424	948
1972	1,000	8,249	835	18.7	46.9	376	393	7,414	2,376	4,151	887
1973	1,000	8,718	876	19.6	51.4	384	421	7,842	2,566	4,348	929
1974	1,000	10,253	975	20.7	55.4	442	456	9,279	3,039	5,263	977
1975	1,000	11,257	1,026	20.5	56.1	465	485	10,230	3,252	5,978	1,001
Average annual percent increase:											
1960—1970		9	10	5.9	8.5	13	8	9	9	9	11
1970—1974		6	7	6.7	9.9	6	8	6	9	6	1
1974—1975		10	5	—1.0	1.3	5	6	10	7	14	2
Rate per 100,000 inhabitants:											
1960		1,887	161	5.1	9.6	60	86	1,726	509	1,035	183
1965		2,449	200	5.1	12.1	72	111	2,249	663	1,329	257
1968		3,370	298	6.9	15.9	132	144	3,072	932	1,747	393
1969		3,680	329	7.3	18.5	148	155	3,351	984	1,931	436
1970		3,985	364	7.9	18.7	172	165	3,621	1,085	2,079	457
1971		4,165	396	8.6	20.5	188	179	3,769	1,164	2,146	460
1972		3,961	401	9.0	22.5	181	189	3,560	1,141	1,994	426
1973		4,154	417	9.4	24.5	183	201	3,737	1,332	2,072	443
1974		4,850	461	9.8	26.2	209	216	4,389	1,438	2,490	462
1975		5,282	482	9.6	26.3	218	227	4,800	1,526	2,805	469
Average annual percent increase:											
1960—1970		8	9	4.6	7.1	12	7	8	8	7	10
1970—1974		5	6	5.6	8.8	5	7	5	8	5	0.5
1974—1975		9	4	—2.0	0.4	4	5	9	6	13	2

* Reprinted from United States Department of Commerce, *Statistical Abstract of the United States 1976* (Washington: Superintendent of Documents, 1976), p. 153.

... several dishonesty coverages will disappear from the market in certain parts of the U.S. in the decades ahead. Still other dishonesty coverages will be subject to mandatory deductibles that will have to be increased much faster than increases in price levels.

An example of a coverage that will disappear in numerous heavily populated areas is automobile theft insurance. In the automobile comprehensive coverage (D in the Family Automobile Policy) theft losses of the automobile will be specifically excluded. An example of a coverage that will be subject to larger deductibles, or unavailable in certain areas, will be fidelity insurance.

The reason for this development will be the continued disconcerting increase in criminal behavior. The crime rates that will be experienced will be incompatible with insurance that undertakes to pay for or replace the property taken and to make good the other damage done by criminals.

... fire insurance also will be seriously affected by criminal behavior. Thievery often involves arson; moreover, arson is associated with other types of anti-social behavior, such as civil disorders.[6]

Even when coverage is not eliminated because of increasing crime rates, consumers will have to pay higher costs. In one major metropolitan area, insurance experts estimate that 60 percent of all automobile claims involve fraud.

Increasing crime rates have been responsible for the development of Fair Access to Insurance Requirements (FAIR) plans. Approximately 50 percent of the states have established these joint federal-state programs to help homeowners, whose property is located in undesirable areas, secure insurance protection. In similar fashion, the federal crime insurance program is designed to ensure that property owners in high crime areas can buy insurance to protect their investments. If crime rates continue to increase, government may be forced to become more active in the insurance business.

Energy

The energy crisis will continue to impact heavily on the insurance industry. As the price of oil continues to rise, other sources of energy will become relatively more economical. Geothermal and solar energy are two sources that may be used more often in the future. An increase in the use of these two sources of energy will alter property and liability loss exposures. For example, a home that has a solar energy heating unit may cost more than an all electric home.

The demand for more oil, even at higher prices, will result in the construction of very large crude carriers (VLCC), and larger liquid natural gas carriers (LNG). The VLCC and LNG present a special challenge for the marine insurance industry. The cost of one of these vessels can run into the hundreds of millions of dollars. If the cost of the cargo is included, each of these vessels is a potential catastrophe in terms of dollar losses. And, if the pollution exposure is added, the total possible loss of one vessel could be $300 or $400 million.

In the future, the proportion of electricity generated from nuclear power is expected to increase from roughly 5 percent in 1973 to 54 percent in the year 2000. This increase in the use of nuclear power and the corresponding increase in nuclear power plants presents the insurance industry with a significant challenge.

Liability for the operation of a nuclear power plant can arise in any one of three different situations: the reactor could malfunction; disposable wastes being transported could be opened and cause radiation damage; or waste disposal areas could become radioactive because of leaks in the storage tanks. Although nuclear operational and disposal systems are designed carefully to prevent accidents, accidents may occur. The liability exposure of a nuclear power plant is difficult to evaluate. To date, no reactor has suffered a complete core melt down, and the accidents that have occurred have been minor.

Industry Responsibility

Many changes will occur in the insurance business in the future. For example, trends appear to be developing that may result in:

1. continuing simplification of policy language;
2. continuing development of computerized underwriting; and
3. changes in the role of the agent.

Whatever changes occur, they should be made only after carefully considering the social responsibility of the insurance industry. Commenting on this subject, a former editor of the *Wall Street Journal* has stated:

> I submit to you that the first task of the businessman who would contribute to the public weal is to run a successful business, and that if he fails in this, he has failed his community no matter how idealistic he is about the plight of minorities, about education, about cultural affairs or whatever.[7]

Another point of view on this subject was expressed by William G. Pritchard, who stated:

> ...I... admit to the suspicion that if the private business is not a good citizen and alert to social responsibilities that may surround it, it may quickly find that, because of the failure to react or respond, it becomes incapable of making the necessary profit.[8]

One of the changes most directly affecting society and the insurance industry has been the changing nature of the liability exposure. The next section of this chapter examines in some depth this critical element in handling personal loss exposures.

DEVELOPMENT OF THE NO-FAULT CONCEPT

Societal Attitude

Fault System   Fault can be defined as "an error; a deviation from propriety; a slight offense; a neglect of duty; a misdeed."[9] The concept of fault has been an integral part of our tort system, and it is natural for people to want to receive reparations when they are injured. The concept of fault developed from moral, as well as legal, considerations.

> In medieval England, redress for injury appears to have served the function of ameliorating the desire for revenge. The kin of an injured person were "rewarded" for abstaining from clan warfare by gaining satisfaction in damages according to the station of the victim. Concomitantly, forfeiture of the animate or inanimate instrumentality of harm was an accepted obligation in such a case.[10]

Under the current tort system, if Harrison is injured by Webb, Harrison can sue Webb. Webb will be defended by his insurance company if he has the appropriate coverage. Harrison will attempt to collect for losses, e.g., general expenses, wage loss, pain and suffering, and legal expenses. If Harrison's case is not strong (there may be contributory negligence), his claim will be reduced. The outcome of the suit will vary with the court's opinion of the amount of money necessary to compensate Harrison for the wrong done to him by Webb.

While the fault system has some intuitive appeal, numerous problems have arisen. Some of them appear in the following list taken from an automobile report by the New York Insurance Department; however, the problems cited in this list are applicable to many other areas of fault:

1. uncompensated victims,
2. delays in payment,
3. unpredictability,
4. malapportionment of benefits,
5. lack of coordination of benefits,
6. hindrance to rehabilitation,
7. inefficiency,
8. overreaching and dishonesty,

    9. instability of the insurance mechanism, and

   10. high premium rates.[11]

The relative importance of each of these problems varies widely among the different areas of tort. In general, however, it can be said that the severity of these problems has increased significantly since the late 1960s.

The fault system was devised at a time when many of the complexities of today's society did not exist. Therefore, a tort system was easier to operate. Today, for example, the highways are filled with cars; products, because of technology, have become more complex; and the practice of medicine has advanced into areas unheard of twenty years ago. These and other changes have resulted in new problems which may not be suitable for settlement under a tort system. If the present system is to remain, the courts will have to be expanded or some type of arbitration procedure established because the court dockets are filled with cases that may take years to litigate.

Some people feel that in lieu of the current system there should be a "no-fault" system. The concept is not new. No-fault programs have been discussed in the United States for over seventy years and in European countries for a much longer period. While the concept may have merit, a complete no-fault system has never been established in the United States. As a result, ascertaining the impact of a complete no-fault system in this country is impossible.

Early No-Fault Systems   Although no-fault automobile coverage has received a large amount of notoriety recently, the first no-fault legislation in the United States dealt with workers' compensation.

No-fault payments in workers' compensation were developed in response to changes in societal attitudes toward industrial accidents. First, it was accepted that occupational injuries were an inherent but unwanted part of an industrial economy. Unfortunately, workers were rarely compensated for their work-related injuries or illnesses.

Employers were armed with several possible defenses, including contributory negligence, assumption of risk, and the fellow servant rule. Even in cases where the employee had a valid case, the costly litigation process was beyond the financial reach of many employees. As a result, employees often accepted small settlements from employers rather than face extended periods of litigation and poverty. Employees who brought suit against their employers also risked losing their jobs.

Second, it was decided that the cost of industrial accidents should be borne by those who could afford to pay for them: the employer and the consumer. To provide benefits for workers who sustained job-related injury or illness, states enacted no-fault workers' compensation laws.

The first law to withstand the test of constitutionality was passed in Wisconsin in 1911.

While the workers' compensation system provides a no-fault relationship between the employer and the employee, it does not eliminate all tort remedies. For example, if an employee is injured while operating a piece of equipment, he or she can receive workers' compensation benefits. In addition, the employee can sue the manufacturer of the equipment on the grounds that the equipment was improperly manufactured and was inherently unsafe. A suit may result against the manufacturer even if the accident results from the employer's failure to modify the equipment in accordance with the manufacturer's recommended safety changes, failure to properly maintain the equipment, or improper modification of the equipment.

Current No-Fault

Proposals The no-fault concept has been suggested for many areas other than workers' compensation.

The Development of Automobile No-Fault Alternatives. In the early 1930s, the Committee to Study Compensation for Automobile Accidents at Columbia University suggested that a no-fault system be adopted in automobile insurance.

> The Columbia Plan proposed to adopt for automobile cases two basic alterations in the law. First, the plan proposed legislation that would "impose on the owners of motor vehicles a limited liability, without regard to fault, for personal injuries or death caused by the operation of their motor vehicles." Such a change from negligence to strict liability had previously been accomplished for industrial injuries by workmen's compensation. The second basic change was the proposed adoption of compulsory insurance. . . . There were other similarities to workmen's compensation. As under workmen's compensation, payments would be made periodically (rather than in lump sums) on the basis of scheduled benefits, with no compensation for pain and suffering. Disabilities would be compensated in relation to their nature, extent and permanence. Except for medical benefits, no compensation would be paid "for the first week of disability." The cost of medical care would be "paid in all cases regardless of the duration of disability. . . ."[12]

Building on this foundation, Robert E. Keeton and Jeffrey O'Connell developed a Basic Protection Insurance Plan. While this plan did not recommend the elimination of tort proceedings, Keeton and O'Connell did suggest a tort exemption for the basic coverages described in the plan. The plan precluded tort liability in the following cases:

(a) *Cases in which exemption precludes ordinary tort liability.* Every person (whether a natural person or any other legal entity) who is a basic protection insured (whether named or additional) with respect to an injury is entitled to an exemption from tort liability for the injury unless the tort damages otherwise recoverable because of the injury include either:

    (1) an amount in excess of five thousand dollars ($5,000) for pain and suffering or

    (2) an amount in excess of ten thousand dollars ($10,000) for elements of the measure of recovery other than pain and suffering.

(b) *Scope of the exemption.* Whenever one is entitled to an exemption under the terms of this section, he is nevertheless subject to liability for damage to property and, in addition, for the first hundred dollars ($100) of net loss from injury as defined in section 1.4 of this Act (which does not include damage to property) caused under circumstances such that he would be liable to pay damages in tort in the absence of this exemption; in all other respects the exemption protects him against liability in tort.[13]

Under the Keeton-O'Connell basic protection plan, each claimant was to be paid up to $10,000 for economic loss resulting from bodily injury; an optional higher limit also was proposed. All medical expenses were to be paid subject to the $10,000 limit. Loss of income was included in the economic loss and was covered up to a maximum of $750 per month. A deduction of up to 15 percent was to be made to the income benefits. This deduction was designed to offset tax savings that might accrue to an injured party since basic protection plan benefits would be received tax free. A deductible equal to the greater of $100 or 10 percent of any work loss was to be applied before economic benefits were paid. An outline summary of the basic protection plan follows.

KEETON-O'CONNELL BASIC PROTECTION PLAN

I. APPLICABILITY

    The basic protection plan is mandatory for all private passenger and commercial vehicles. They are required to purchase Basic Protection no-fault coverage and residual tort liability coverage.

II. INJURIES COVERED

    Accidental injuries arising out of the ownership, maintenance or use of an automobile, including the loading and unloading thereof.

III. TORT EXEMPTIONS

    A. The insured is exempt from tort liability for:

        1. the first $5,000 of pain and suffering,

        2. the first $10,000 of economic loss for bodily injury, and

        3. damage to vehicles.

    B. The tort exemption does not apply to:

        1. the first $100 of economic loss from bodily injury, or

        2. cases in which the injury results in death.

IV. BODILY INJURY NO-FAULT COVERAGE

A. Basic Protection pays up to $10,000 per person and up to $100,000 per accident for economic loss from bodily injury. There are no internal limits on medical expenses, but loss of income is covered only up to $750 per month.

B. A deductible of $100 or 10% of income loss, whichever is greater, applies to recovery for economic loss. In addition, a deduction, not to exceed 15% of income loss, is made in consideration of the fact that the benefits are not taxable income. Higher or lower deductibles may be offered at appropriate rates.

V. PROPERTY DAMAGE NO-FAULT COVERAGE

There are three property damage options, all applying only to damage to vehicles:

A. One option is identical to collision coverage now provided.

B. The second option pays the insured for damage to his vehicle only if he would have been able to recover in tort if there had been no tort exemption.

C. The third option, full deductible option, provides no coverage, since the deductible equals the actual cash value of the vehicle.

VI. SUBROGATION

The basic protection insurer does not have the right to subrogate against another driver insured under basic protection because of the tort exemptions. There are some very limited circumstances in which subrogation may apply, e.g., a converter.

VII. OTHER INSURANCE AND OTHER BENEFITS

If two or more basic protection policies cover a loss they share pro rata. Basic protection is excess over benefits available to the insured from health insurance, workmen's compensation, social security, salary continuance plans, and similar programs (but not life insurance).

VIII. OPTIONAL COVERAGES

All basic protection insurers must offer to each insured added protection coverage for pain and inconvenience with benefits of from $100 to $500 per month during disability.

Insurers may offer other added protection coverages and catastrophe coverage with limits of $100,000 per person and $300,000 per accident.

IX. FEES OF CLAIMANTS' ATTORNEYS

Insurer must pay 50% of fees for claimants' attorneys in all cases, and 100% of such fees if benefits are overdue.

X. ARBITRATION

No provision for arbitration.

XI. UNINSURED INJURIES

A claim which is not otherwise covered by insurance will be assigned to an insurance company or assigned claims bureau for adjustment and payment. All basic protection insurers are required to participate in the assigned claims plan.

XII. EXTRATERRITORIAL PROVISIONS

Basic protection would apply to out-of-state injuries to the named insured, members of his family and occupants of the insured vehicle, but not to others. Tort exemptions would not apply in other states.

XIII. PAIN, SUFFERING AND INCONVENIENCE
Basic protection does not cover loss from pain, suffering and inconvenience. However, insurers are required to offer optional no-fault coverage for pain and suffering with a fixed benefit ranging from $100 to $500 for each month of disability.
If the value of pain and suffering exceeds $5,000 the excess can be recovered in tort.[14]

The primary weakness of the basic protection plan is that it attempts to provide the best of both no-fault protection and the tort remedy. There is some question about retaining both systems. A basic protection plan of this type, instead of reducing the amount of litigation, might actually encourage lawyers to seek higher awards since a client would be guaranteed the basic protection coverage.

Other no-fault proposals in the automobile area were suggested. The American Insurance Association proposed a plan which almost eliminated tort remedies, had an unlimited aggregate loss of income benefit, and included property damage. The American Mutual Insurance Alliance proposed a plan that provided no-fault benefits but retained the tort system. Following are summaries of the American Insurance Association and the American Mutual Insurance Alliance Plans.

AMERICAN INSURANCE ASSOCIATION
PERSONAL AND PROPERTY PROTECTION
MOTOR VEHICLE INSURANCE PLAN

I. APPLICABILITY
The no-fault coverage and residual liability coverage would be compulsory for all motor vehicles, private passenger and commercial, registered in the state or used within the state for 30 days in any calendar year.

II. INJURIES COVERED
The no-fault benefits apply to accidental injuries arising out of the ownership, operation, maintenance or use of a motor vehicle as a motor vehicle. Injuries arising from a parked vehicle are not covered unless (1) the vehicle was parked in such a way as to cause unreasonable risk of the injury which occurred, (2) the injury resulted from contact with equipment attached to the vehicle while such equipment was being used to load or unload the vehicle, or (3) the injured person was occupying such parked vehicle, or entering into or alighting from it. Injuries resulting from certain illegal acts of the injured person are excluded.

III. TORT EXEMPTIONS
Tort liability arising from the ownership, maintenance or use of an automobile is eliminated, except for certain illegal acts.

IV. BODILY INJURY NO-FAULT COVERAGE
A. The no-fault benefits for bodily injury are:
1. medical and funeral expenses,

> 2. income loss due to disability up to the date of death, and
> 3. survivors' benefits for dependents if the injury results in death.
>
> There are no dollar limitations on medical expenses, but funeral expenses are limited to $1,000. Both disability income loss and survivors' benefits are limited to $750 per month, and will not be paid beyond the normal life expectancy of the injured person, but there is no aggregate dollar limit. Both disability and survivors' benefits include cost of substitute services as well as income loss.
>
> B. There are no mandatory deductibles, but disability income benefits will be reduced by an amount, not to exceed 15%, for income taxes which would have been paid on earned income.

V. PROPERTY DAMAGE NO-FAULT COVERAGE

No-fault benefits are provided, up to $1,000,000 per accident, for accidental damage to tangible property, except that such coverage does not apply to damage to (1) motor vehicles, or (2) property of the named insured or members of his household if a vehicle owned or operated by such person caused the damage.

VI. SUBROGATION

An insurer which pays no-fault benefits is subrogated to the right of the injured person to recover from a tortfeasor. The right to recover would be eliminated in most cases by tort exemptions.

The insurer of a private passenger car which is involved in an accident with a truck can recover from the insurer of the truck any benefits paid to occupants of the passenger car, up to a maximum of $1,000,000 per accident.

VII. OTHER INSURANCE AND OTHER BENEFITS

No-fault bodily injury benefits would not be reduced for benefits recovered from other insurance or benefit systems, except for social security.

A policy issued under the act to an individual would be primary as to injuries to the named insured and members of his household with regard to other policies issued under the act, except that:

1. a policy covering a public livery passenger vehicle would be primary with regard to injuries to passengers in the vehicle, and
2. a policy covering a car furnished to an employee by his employer is primary as to injuries to the employee and members of his household.

As to a person not insured by a policy issued to him or a member of his household, the policy of the owner of the vehicle is primary as to the policy of the operator when such person is a passenger in or is struck by the vehicle.

VIII. OPTIONAL COVERAGES

Insurers are required to offer collision insurance, subject to acceptance or rejection by the insured. Insurers also may offer:

1. coverage for expenses and loss of income in excess of the limits of mandatory coverage, and
2. benefits for dismemberment and disfigurement.

IX. FEES OF CLAIMANTS' ATTORNEYS

An insurer may be required to pay the fee of the claimant's attorney in addition to benefits, if it has unreasonably denied or unreasonably delayed payment of any part of the claim.

X. ARBITRATION
There is no provision for arbitration.

XI. UNINSURED INJURIES
There is a provision for an assigned claims plan to adjust and pay claims for persons not covered by insurance.

XII. EXTRATERRITORIAL PROVISIONS
Bodily injury no-fault benefits apply to accidents within the United States, its possessions and Canada, provided the injured person is (1) the named insured, or (2) a member of his household, or an occupant of the insured vehicle. Property damage no-fault benefits apply only to accidents occurring within the state.

XIII. PAIN, SUFFERING AND INCONVENIENCE
There is no mandatory coverage for loss due to pain, suffering or inconvenience, and no specific authorization for optional coverage for such loss. There is no specific limitation on tort recovery for pain and suffering, but the general tort exemptions would eliminate such recovery in most cases.

AMERICAN MUTUAL INSURANCE ALLIANCE
GUARANTEED PROTECTION PLAN

I. APPLICABILITY
All automobile liability insurance policies covering non-fleet private passenger automobiles would be required to include the specified minimum no-fault coverages. However, automobile liability insurance would not be compulsory.

II. INJURIES COVERED
The no-fault coverage applies to injuries sustained in an accident while occupying or being struck by an automobile. There are exclusions for drunk or drugged drivers and certain criminal activities.

III. TORT EXEMPTIONS
There would be no tort exemptions.

IV. BODILY INJURY NO-FAULT COVERAGE
  A. The no-fault benefits are:
    1. medical and hospital benefits up to $2,000 per person,
    2. income loss benefits up to 85% of the income lost or $500 per month, whichever is less, up to a maximum of 52 weeks or $6,000. Income loss benefits begin 30 days after the accident, and
    3. substitute services benefit, if the injured person was not gainfully employed, of $12 per day for 52 weeks.
  B. The income loss benefit is subject to a waiting period of 30 days. The substitute services benefit is subject to a waiting period of one week. No income benefit is paid for the first 30 days of disability. A deductible of $250 (applicable only to the named insured and his family) may be applied to the medical benefits.

V. PROPERTY DAMAGE NO-FAULT COVERAGE

The proposal does not apply to property damage.

VI. SUBROGATION

An insurer which pays no-fault benefits would be subrogated to the right of the claimant to obtain reimbursement from a tortfeasor. Subrogation claims between insurers would be subject to mandatory arbitration.

VII. OTHER INSURANCE AND OTHER BENEFITS

No-fault benefits would be excess with regard to all statutory benefit plans, including workmen's compensation. With respect to guest passengers and pedestrians, the benefits would be excess over all collateral sources of reimbursement.

VIII. OPTIONAL COVERAGES

Insurers may offer any form of optional additional coverage or broader coverage.

IX. FEES OF CLAIMANTS' ATTORNEYS

The no-fault plan does not make specific provision for legal fees. Another provision of the proposal would limit contingent fees to 25% of the amount awarded to the plaintiff.

X. ARBITRATION

Subrogation cases between insurers would be subject to mandatory arbitration if the amount of damages appears to be under $3,000.

XI. UNINSURED INJURIES

No provision is made for no-fault coverage for uninsured injuries.

XII. EXTRATERRITORIAL PROVISIONS

No-fault benefits would apply out-of-state for injuries to the named insured, members of his family, and guest passengers in the insured vehicle.

XIII. PAIN, SUFFERING AND INCONVENIENCE

There is no provision for pain and suffering in the no-fault benefits. However, another section of the proposal would limit tort recovery for pain and suffering to the sum of (a) 50% of the first $500 of medical expenses, and (b) 100% of medical expenses in excess of $500. This limitaton would not apply in cases involving death, dismemberment, disfigurement, and other serious injuries.[15]

General Liability. Workers' compensation and automobiles are not the only areas where the no-fault concept has been recommended as a method for solving the problems of rising premium costs and increased litigation. In an article in the *Insurance Law Journal* in 1973, Jeffrey O'Connell recommended the development of an elective no-fault insurance liability policy for all kinds of accidents. Emphasizing that most products liability and medical malpractice injuries were not compensated, O'Connell contended that a no-fault plan should be designed for other accident victims. Under O'Connell's proposal, businesses would be allowed the option of selecting no-fault coverage. O'Connell described his proposal as:

...a solution whereby any enterprise would be allowed to elect, if it chose, to pay from then on for the injuries that it causes on a no-fault basis, thereby foreclosing claims based on fault. The enterprise would be allowed to select all, or if it chose, just certain risks of personal injury it typically creates and agree to pay for out-of-pocket losses when injury results from those risks. To the extent—and only to the extent—a guarantee of no-fault payment exists at the time of the accident, as under no-fault auto or workmens' compensation, no claim based on fault (or a defect) would be allowed against a party electing to be covered under no-fault liability insurance.[16]

O'Connell also contended that the elective no-fault system would be very advantageous to a business firm:

The incentives to elect no-fault liability in place of traditional liability based on fault would be that, although the enterprise may have to pay more people for injury, it would pay them much less: it would not have to pay anything already covered by other insurance, nor anything for pain or suffering. This would eliminate paying *anything* in most cases of small injuries: it would also cut down substantially on what is to be paid in cases of large injury.[17]

Medical Adversity Insurance. The development of medical adversity insurance has been proposed by Clark C. Havighurst and Lawrence R. Tancredi. Under this coverage, benefits would be provided on a no-fault basis for patients inadvertently injured by the negligence of an individual or institution. The plan would function similarly to workers' compensation, with benefits being paid for three groups of specified compensable events. The first group would consist of "... medical care sequelae which can affect a nonorthopedic as well as the orthopedic patient and which arise from the overall surgical treatment and post-operative care patients." The second category of compensable events would include those "... which affect only the orthopedic patient and physician because they involve diagnosis and treatment of orthopedic conditions." The final category would include events which are consequences of conduct appropriate for specific sanctions. This group would be compiled of "... the adverse consequences of failure to obtain informed consent, abandonment of the patient, gross negligence, intentional misconduct, and illegal behavior."[18]

The no-fault concept could be applied in areas such as professional liability for accountants and lawyers and governmental liability. An additional possibility is that an individual might purchase his or her own no-fault coverage. A consumer could buy no-fault coverage under a homeowners package, for example, that would pay for injuries caused by a physician's negligence, a product's malfunction, and so on.

Current State Automobile No-Fault Laws Under Chapter 670 of the Acts of 1970, the Massachusetts legislature established the first compulsory automobile no-fault law in the United States. The law applied only to personal injury coverage and had a tort threshold (the level of economic losses required before lawsuits may be filed) of $2,000.

The legislature passed a property damage no-fault law in 1971 but later repealed it.

In concept, the Massachusetts law is similar to the Keeton-O'Connell basic protection plan. The first $2,000 of medical, funeral, wage and substitute service expense is covered. The Keeton-O'Connell plan made provision for these expenses but allowed a higher aggregate limit. Massachusetts law stipulates that only 75 percent of any wage loss or the cost of substitute services is eligible for reimbursement. The Keeton-O'Connell plan had an 85 percent limit subject to a maximum of $750 per month. The Massachusetts law also bars tort recovery for pain and suffering unless medical expenses in excess of $500 have been incurred or unless the injured party is killed, loses a body member, loses sight or hearing, is permanently disfigured, or receives a fracture. Like the Keeton-O'Connell plan, the Massachusetts plan permits tort remedies in some cases.

Massachusetts has had a problem with automobile coverage and rates for many years. This condition was a factor in the decision to enact no-fault legislation. It is uncertain whether no-fault coverage, in the long run, will be beneficial. An individual may be encouraged to defraud the system by claiming losses in excess of $2,000. The $2,000 is automatically paid; any excess over actual expenses would be profit to the victim.

In designing the personal injury legislation, the Massachusetts legislature assumed that insurance companies would realize savings as a result of the new program. The law specifically required a 15 percent reduction in rates. Since enactment of the law, rates have continued to rise in Massachusetts, and it is not known whether the personal injury protection will have a substantial long-run savings impact on rates. Cost is one of the key points upon which both proponents and critics of no-fault insurance have long disagreed. When no-fault advocates were fighting for the acceptance of the concept, they frequently claimed cost savings would accompany the implementation of a no-fault program. Opponents, on the other hand, contended that there was no evidence that substantiated this claim. No-fault plans will have to operate for a long period of time before their full effect can be determined.[19]

Residents of Massachusetts were given several options under the original 1970 legislation. Each policyholder was permitted to elect a deductible of either $250, $500, $1,000, or $2,000. Obviously the larger the deductible, the lower the premium cost. If a policyholder elects a $2,000 deductible, he or she in effect is electing to eliminate the no-fault benefits. However, the policyholder does not have the option of collecting the amount of the deductible from anyone who has been given a tort exemption under the no-fault law.

Several other states now have no-fault plans. These plans do provide some type of basic benefit but not all state plans provide tort exemptions. Table 2-5 contains a list of the no-fault benefits, limitations, or damages for pain and suffering, vehicle damage, and effective dates for each of these states.

Federal Automobile No-Fault Some insurance observers feel that the state no-fault programs will be replaced or controlled by a federal program. It is unlikely that a no-fault plan run by the federal government will be established. However, state plans may be subjected to federal guidelines. The primary piece of legislation that has been considered by Congress (S.354—A Bill to Establish A Nationwide System of Adequate and Uniform Motor Vehicle Accident Reparation Acts) would establish federal standards to be implemented by the states. Under S.354, the Secretary of Transportation would have responsibility for reviewing state no-fault laws to see if they were in compliance with federal standards. If the standards were not met, the federal government would intervene and establish a no-fault system for that state. The federal standards under S.354 stipulated minimum benefits as follows:

SEC. 204. A State establishing a no-fault plan for motor vehicle insurance in accordance with this title—

(a) may not limit basic restoration benefits for allowable expense, as defined in section 103(2) of this Act;

(b) may limit basic restoration benefits for work loss to—

    (1) a monthly amount equal to the lesser of the following—

        (A) $1,000 multiplied by a fraction whose numerator is the average per capita income in the State and whose denominator is the average per capita income in the United States, according to the latest available United States Department of Commerce figures; or

        (B) the disclosed amount, in the case of a named insured who, prior to the accident resulting in injury, voluntarily discloses his actual monthly earned income to his restoration obligor and agrees in writing with such obligor that such sum shall measure work loss; and

    (2) a total amount equal to—

        (A) $25,000 multiplied by a fraction whose numerator is the average per capita income in the State and whose denominator is the average per capita income in the United States, according to the latest available United States Department of Commerce figures; or

        (B) such total amount as may be determined by the State but in no event less than $15,000;

(c) may provide reasonable exclusions from or monthly or total limitations on basic restoration benefits for replacement services loss;

(d) may provide reasonable exclusions from or monthly or total limitations on basic restoration benefits for survivor's loss;

(e) may provide that any contract of insurance for no-fault benefits allow an insurer to offer—

(1) a deductible not to exceed $100 for each individual; or
(2) a waiting period not to exceed one week. Deductibles and waiting periods shall be applicable only to claims of insureds and, in the case of the death of an insured, to the claims of his survivors; . . .[20]

Allowable expenses included:

(2) "Allowable expense" means reasonable charges incurred for, or the reasonable value of (where no charges are incurred), reasonably needed and used products, services, and accommodations for—
   (A) professional medical treatment and care;
   (B) emergency health services;
   (C) medical and vocational rehabilitation services; and
   (D) expenses directly related to the funeral, burial, cremation, or other form of disposition of the remains of a deceased victim, not to exceed $1,000.

The term does not include—

(i) that portion of a charge for a room in a hospital, clinic, convalescent, or nursing home, or any other institution engaged in providing nursing care and related services, in excess of a reasonable and customary charge for semiprivate accommodations, unless more intensive care is medically required; or
(ii) any amount includable in work loss, replacement services loss, or survivor's loss.[21]

The public's attitude will have an impact on the progress of no-fault legislation on either a state or federal level. A study released in 1975 by the Insurance Information Institute found that individuals in states with no-fault legislation were divided on the desirability of the law. Table 2-6 gives the results of the Insurance Information Institute's study. While the figures in the table indicate that people in both Florida and New Jersey are strongly supportive of no-fault legislation, the results in Massachusetts and Michigan indicate that no-fault is not always well received. Ohio and Tennessee are states that currently do not have no-fault legislation.

Societal Impact

The proponents of a no-fault system contend that the virtues of no-fault outweigh the disadvantages. There are many points to be considered when evaluating this assertion. Following is a discussion of some of the advantages and disadvantages of no-fault plans.

Safety (Deterrence) The advisability of a given no-fault system is partially dependent on the extent that it will encourge safety. A no-fault system where no one individual or individuals can have a direct

Table 2-5

Provisions of State "No-Fault" Laws*

State	No-Fault Benefits	Limitation on Damages for Pain and Suffering	Vehicle Damage	Effective Date
Massachusetts	$2,000 in benefits for medical, funeral, wage loss, and substitute service expenses. Wage loss and substitute service benefits are limited to 75% of actual loss.	Can recover only if medical costs exceed $500, or in case of death, loss of all or part of body member, permanent and serious disfigurement, loss of sight or hearing, or a fracture.	Stays under tort system after Jan. 1, 1977. Prior to then, no tort liability for vehicle damage.	Jan. 1, 1971.
Delaware	$10,000 per person and $20,000 per accident. Covers medical costs, loss of income, loss of services, and funeral expenses (limited to $2,000).	None. But amount of no-fault benefits received can't be used as evidence in suits for general damages.	Stays under tort system.	Jan. 1, 1972.
Florida	$5,000 per person for medical costs, wage loss, replacement services, and funeral costs (limited to $1,000). Deductibles of $250, $500, $1,000, and $2,000 available.	Cannot recover unless accident results in: serious non-permanent injury materially affecting normal activity and life-style during substantially all of 90 days after accident, and is medically or scientifically demonstrable at end of 90 days; loss of body member; permanent loss of body function; permanent injury other than disfigurement; significant permanent disfigurement; or death.	Stays under tort system.	Jan. 1, 1972, for original law. This version effective Oct. 1, 1976.

State	No-Fault Benefits	Limitation on Damages for Pain and Suffering	Vehicle Damage	Effective Date
Oregon	$5,000 medical benefits. 70% of wage loss up to $750 month. $18 a day substitute services. Wage loss and substitute services paid from first day if disability lasts 14 days; are limited to 52 weeks.	None.	Stays under tort system.	Jan. 1, 1972. Jan. 1, 1974, for benefits at left.
South Dakota	Purchase is optional. $2,000 in medical expense. $60 week for wage loss, starting 14 days after injury, for up to 52 weeks. $10,000 death benefit.	None.	Stays under tort system.	Jan. 1, 1972.
Virginia	Purchase is optional. $2,000 for medical and funeral costs. $100 week for wage loss with limit of 52 weeks.	None.	Stays under tort system.	July 1, 1972.
Connecticut	$5,000 benefits for medical, hospital, funeral (limit $2,000), lost wages, survivors' loss, and substitute service expenses. Wage loss, substitute service, and survivors' benefits limited to 85% of actual loss.	Cannot recover unless economic loss exceeds $400, or there is permanent injury, bone fracture, disfigurement, dismemberment, or death.	Stays under tort system.	Jan. 1, 1973.
Maryland	$2,500 in benefits for medical, hospital, funeral, wage loss, and substitute service expenses.	None.	Stays under tort system.	Jan. 1, 1973.

Continued on next page

State	No-Fault Benefits	Limitation on Damages for Pain and Suffering	Vehicle Damage	Effective Date
New Jersey	Unlimited benefits for medical and hospital costs. Wage loss up to $100 a week for one year. Substitute services up to $12 a day up to $4,380 per person. Funeral expenses to $1,000. Survivors' benefits equal to amount victim would have received if he had not died.	Cannot recover if injuries are confined to soft tissue and medical expenses excluding hospital costs are less than $200.	Stays under tort system.	Jan. 1, 1973.
Michigan	Unlimited medical and hospital benefits. Funeral benefits up to $1,000. Lost wages up to $1,000 per month, adjusted annually to keep up with cost of living, and substitute services of $20 a day payable to victim or survivor.	Cannot recover unless injuries result in death, serious impairment of body function, or permanent serious disfigurement.	Tort liability abolished.	Oct. 1, 1973.
New York	Aggregate limit of $50,000 for medical, wage loss, and substitute service benefits. Wage loss limited to 80% of actual loss up to $1,000 per month for three years. Substitute service benefits limited to $25 a day for one year.	Cannot recover unless medical expenses exceed $500, or injury results in death, dismemberment, significant disfigurement, a compound or comminuted fracture, or permanent loss of use of a body organ, member, function, or system.	Stays under tort system.	Feb. 1, 1974.

State	No-Fault Benefits	Limitation on Damages for Pain and Suffering	Vehicle Damage	Effective Date
Arkansas	Purchase is optional. $2,000 per person for medical and hospital expenses. Wage loss: 70% of lost wages up to $140 a week, beginning 8 days after accident, for up to 52 weeks. Essential services: up to $70 a week for up to 52 weeks, subject to 8-day waiting period. Death benefit: $5,000.	None.	Stays under tort system.	July 1, 1974.
Utah	$2,000 per person for medical and hospital expenses. 85% of gross income loss, up to $150 a week, for up to 52 weeks. $12 a day for loss of services for up to 365 days. Both wage loss and service loss coverages subject to 3-day waiting periods that disappear if disability lasts longer than two weeks. $1,000 funeral benefit. $2,000 survivors' benefit.	Cannot recover unless medical expenses exceed $500, or injury results in dismemberment or fracture, permanent disfigurement, permanent disability, or death.	Stays under tort system.	Jan. 1, 1974.
Kansas	$2,000 per person for medical expenses. Wage loss: up to $650 a month for one year. $2,000 for rehabilitation costs. Substitute service benefits of $12 a day for 365 days. Survivors' benefits; up to	Cannot recover unless medical costs exceed $500, or injury results in permanent disfigurement, fracture to a weight-bearing bone, a compound, comminuted, displaced or	Stays under tort system.	Jan. 1, 1974.

Continued on next page

State	No-Fault Benefits	Limitation on Damages for Pain and Suffering	Vehicle Damage	Effective Date
Kansas	$650 a month for lost income, $12 a day for substitution benefits, for not over one year after death, minus any disability benefits victim received before death. Funeral benefit: $1,000.	compressed fracture, loss of a body member, permanent injury, permanent loss of a body function, or death.		
Texas	$2,500 per person overall limit. Covers medical and funeral expenses, lost income, and loss of services. Purchase optional.	None.	Stays under tort system.	90 days after adjournment of 1973 regular session.
Nevada	Aggregate limit of $10,000. Pays for medical and rehabilitation expenses; up to $175 a week for loss of income; up to $18 a day for 104 weeks for replacement services; survivors' benefits of not less than $5,000 and not more than victim would have gotten in disability benefits for 1 year; and $1,000 for death.	Cannot recover unless medical benefits exceed $750 or injury causes chronic or permanent injury, permanent partial or permanent total disability, disfigurement, more than 180 days of inability to work at occupation, fracture of a major bone, dismemberment, permanent loss of a body function, or death.	Stays under tort system.	Feb. 1, 1974.
Colorado	$25,000 for medical expenses. $25,000 for rehabilitation. Lost income: up to $125 a week for up to 52	Cannot recover unless medical and rehabilitation services have reasonable value of more than $500, or injury causes	Stays under tort system.	April 1, 1974.

State	No-Fault Benefits	Limitation on Damages for Pain and Suffering	Vehicle Damage	Effective Date
Colorado	weeks. Services: up to $15 a day for up to 52 weeks. Death benefit: $1,000.	permanent disfigurement, permanent disability, dismemberment, loss of earnings for more than 52 weeks, or death.		
Hawaii	Aggregate limit of $15,000. Pays for medical and hospital services; rehabilitation; occupational, psychiatric, and physical therapy; up to $800 monthly for income loss, substitute services and survivors' loss; and up to $1,500 for funeral expenses.	Cannot recover from 9-1-74 to 8-31-76, unless medical and rehabilitation expenses exceed $1,500. Thereafter, must exceed a floating threshold established annually by the insurance commissioner. Can also recover if injury results in death; significant, permanent loss of use of body part or function; or permanent and serious disfigurement that subjects injured person to mental or emotional suffering.	Stays under tort system.	Sept. 1, 1974.
Georgia	Aggregate limit of $5,000. Up to $2,500 for medical costs. 85% of lost income with maximum $200 week. $20 day for necessary services. Survivors' benefits same as lost income benefits had victim lived. $1,500 funeral benefit.	Cannot recover unless medical costs exceed $500, disability lasts 10 days, or injury results in death, fractured bone, permanent disfigurement, dismemberment, permanent loss of body function, permanent, partial or total loss of sight or hearing.	Stays under tort system.	Mar. 1, 1975.

Continued on next page

State	No-Fault Benefits	Limitation on Damages for Pain and Suffering	Vehicle Damage	Effective Date
Kentucky	Aggregate limit of $10,000. Covers medical expense; funeral expense up to $1,000; income loss up to $200 weekly, with as much as 15% deducted for income tax savings; up to $200 a week each for replacement services loss, survivors' economic loss, and survivors' replacement services loss. Motorist has right to reject no-fault.	Cannot recover unless medical expenses exceed $1,000, or injury results in permanent disfigurement; fracture of weight-bearing bone; a compound, comminuted, displaced or compressed fracture; loss of a body member; permanent injury; permanent loss of a body function; or death. But limitation does not apply to those who reject no-fault system or to those injured by driver who has rejected it.	Stays under tort system.	July 1, 1975.
Minnesota	$20,000 for medical expense. $10,000 for other benefits, including 85% of lost income up to $200 weekly; $15 a day for replacement services, with 7-day waiting period; up to $200 weekly in survivors' economic loss benefits; up to $200 weekly for survivors' replacement service loss; and $1,250 for funeral benefits.	Cannot recover unless medical expenses (not including x-rays and rehabilitation) exceed $2,000; or disability exceeds 60 days; or the injury results in permanent disfigurement; permanent injury; or death.	Stays under tort system.	Jan. 1, 1975.
South Carolina	Aggregate limit of $1,000. Covers medical and funeral costs, loss of earnings, and loss of essential services.	None.	Stays under tort system.	Oct. 1, 1974.

State	No-Fault Benefits	Limitation on Damages for Pain and Suffering	Vehicle Damage	Effective Date
Pennsylvania	Unlimited medical and rehabilitation benefits. Up to $15,000 for income loss, with monthly maximum determined by relationship of state's per capita income to nation's per capita income. Up to $25 daily for one year for replacement services. Up to $5,000 for survivors' loss. Up to $1,500 for funeral costs.	Cannot recover unless accident results in more than $750 worth of medical and dental services (excluding diagnostic x-ray and rehabilitation costs above $100); more than 60 days continuous disability; permanent, severe, cosmetic disfigurement; serious and permanent injury; or death.	Stays under tort system.	July 19, 1975.
North Dakota	Overall limit of $15,000 per person. Covers medical and rehabilitation costs, up to $150 a week for income loss, up to $15 a day for replacement services, up to $150 a week for survivors' income loss, up to $15 a day for survivors' replacement services loss, and up to $1,000 for funeral expenses.	Cannot recover from insured person unless injury results in more than $1,000 in medical expenses, more than 60 days of disability, serious and permanent disfigurement, dismemberment, or death.	Stays under tort system.	Jan. 1, 1976.

Table 2-6

Desirability of a No-Fault Law*

	Massachusetts	Florida	New Jersey	Michigan	Ohio	Tennessee
No-Fault Law Is:						
Desirable	48%	50%	57%	30%	38%	39%
Not desirable	24	18	17	45	17	13
Don't know/no opinion	17	28	22	23	29	24

*Reprinted with permission from *Does No-Fault Make a Difference?* (New York: Insurance Information Institute, 1975), p. 27.

impact may result in a reduction in safety. Guido Calabresi in *The Costs of Accidents* examined this concept as it relates to workers' compensation. He stated that the concept is best seen:

> ... by considering why workmen's compensation brought about such a change in industrial accident cost avoidance. In theory it should have made no difference whether the workers as a group or the employers as a group were held liable. As I have explained elsewhere, the same accident cost would have become a part of the employment contract no matter who bore the loss. In reality it made an enormous difference because employees consistently underestimated the likelihood of injury and therefore did not take or demand safety precautions.... To employers that same risk was a cold cost figure which could easily be compared with the cost of safety devices. The result was that many safety devices were adopted.[22]

In effect, workers' compensation was able to internalize the cost of workers' safety into the pricing system, while the fault system had failed to achieve this objective. However, the impact of this cost internalization has been eroded. The *Annual Report of the Council of Economic Advisers* for 1977 claimed that workers' compensation, as a means for internalizing cost, is not efficient if the cost of added safety devices exceeds the savings gained from reduced worker injury. The report went on to state:

> If employers confronted the full costs of illness and injury from poor working conditions by having to pay higher wages, or incurred other costs that varied directly with the dangers to health and safety in workplaces, they would tend to operate at an efficient level of occupationally related health and safety. For a number of reasons, however, employers do not actually face the full costs of injuries and illnesses....[23]

The report also expressed the opinion that the best method for handling worker-related exposures was a set of constraints devised by the Occupational Safety and Health Administration.

The same type of problem could arise in many areas if a no-fault type of environment were established. For example, there are a few physicians who are not qualified to practice medicine. Some type of monitoring system would be necessary to prevent abuses under a no-fault system. A no-fault system, per se, would be inadequate to handle the occurrence of an excessive number of claims or a gross negligence claim against a single physician. A special regulatory panel might be necessary to monitor such a situation. (A no-fault system could have a positive effect in the medical area, however. Some critics of the current medical system contend that overutilization of facilities and tests by physicians is directly related to the increasing amount of malpractice litigation. If this assumption is true, a no-fault system could reduce unnecessary medical services and medical costs.)

A similar problem could arise if manufacturers were given the option of selecting no-fault coverage. They might be less inclined to maintain product safety and quality control if no substantial threat of litigation were present.

The problem of safety is not equally relevant to all areas. Some opponents of no-fault have suggested that the elimination of the automobile tort system would discourage safety. This argument appears weak. While it might have some application in small property damage cases, e.g., parking lot accidents, it is unlikely that drivers would be careless on public roads because of no-fault.

Costs Proponents of no-fault programs have claimed that implementation of no-fault plans should result in lower costs to the consumer. The cost question has been particularly important in the debate over the implementation of a federal no-fault automobile system.

Experience, however, does not indicate that substantial savings accrue from a partial no-fault system. Furthermore, any reduction in total cost that occurs under a partial no-fault system appears to be short run rather than long run.

The disparity between the cost increases under no-fault and the savings that were predicted probably is a function of two factors. First, savings projections are based on data gathered under the tort system. Thus, the data is not an appropriate base for making projections. Second, since only limited no-fault plans have been promulgated, the cost problem is compounded with both a system of guaranteed payments and a tort option.

Even with the establishment of a complete no-fault system in automobile insurance, some question exists as to the impact on rates.

The amount of any claim would be limited by the maximum schedule contained in a complete no-fault system; depending on the limits, the average claim could be lower under a complete no-fault system than under the current tort system. However, more people would be paid under a no-fault system. With a lower average claim but higher frequency, a complete no-fault system could be very expensive.

The rates under a complete no-fault system may be relatively stable. Major rate fluctuations should occur only when the benefit schedule is changed.

Economic Impact The full economic impact of no-fault systems is difficult to ascertain. Consequently, only a few areas certain to be affected by a no-fault plan are discussed in this section.

Some members of the tort bar would face a declining demand for their services. These individuals would be forced to seek other areas of legal practice or obtain other forms of employment. From the perspective of the individual lawyer, this economic displacement could be financially devastating. However, the long-run impact could be beneficial to society. If no-fault systems are established in only a few areas of tort law, the legal profession will be better able to handle the economic displacement than if an entirely comprehensive no-fault system were instituted.

A second important segment of the economy which would be affected is the insurance industry. The method for handling claims would be substantially modified. While claim settlement still would be a very significant function of an insurance company, the importance of the claims procedure would be reduced. If states or the federal government decided to insure no-fault benefits themselves, a large portion of the industry would have to seek alternative uses for its capital and surplus.

Governmental programs might benefit from a no-fault system if the system were compulsory. Some benefit payments which now have to be made from programs such as social security, Medicaid, and state assistance would be unnecessary.

Unfortunately, many economically disadvantaged people are unable to afford insurance protection. If, for example, a complete no-fault system were established in the automobile area, many citizens in the United States could not afford this protection just as they cannot afford tort coverage. The financial demands of these individuals on society could increase further. Of course, society could choose to subsidize these people directly through income tax refunds, direct payments, or insurance stamps that would be used to purchase no-fault benefits. If a federal- or state-operated no-fault program were established, however, no direct subsidies would be necessary since some part or all of the program costs would come from general tax revenues.

Who Pays First   Although society as a whole will be responsible for paying for a no-fault system, there are a number of ways to distribute the initial financial impact. Accident costs, for example, could be:

> ...(1) borne by particular victims; (2) paid on a one-to-one basis by those who injure a particular victim; (3) borne by those broad categories of people who are likely to be victims; (4) paid by those broad categories of people who are likely to be injurers; (5) paid by those who in some sense violate our moral codes (in some sense are at fault) according to the degree of their wrongdoing, whether or not they are involved in accidents; (6) paid by those who in some actuarial sense are most likely to violate our moral codes; (7) paid from the general coffers of the state or by particular industry groups in accordance with criteria (such as wealth) that may be totally unrelated to accident involvement; or (8) paid by some combination of these methods.[24]

In workers' compensation, the costs are borne by the employer and in turn, the consumers of products. The problem has not been resolved under other potential no-fault systems. Whatever system is developed, the insurance industry should attempt to have an impact on the decision. Because of its experience and available data in the tort areas, the insurance industry ought to have substantial input into the design of new programs.

No-Fault and Individual Exposures

The following section of this chapter and other chapters in this book examine liability coverages. It is important to be aware of the provisions of these coverages. The liability coverages presented should be examined to ascertain how they might be improved under the current tort law system and under a no-fault system. Whatever changes may be made in the future are likely to have a significant impact on individuals as well as on individual insurance coverage.

INSURING INDIVIDUAL PROPERTY AND LIABILITY EXPOSURES—HOMEOWNERS POLICIES

Development of Homeowners Coverage

The increasing need for efficiency and the desire of insurers to underwrite several lines of insurance coverage forced changes in multiple-line underwriting in the 1940s and 1950s. Beginning in the early 1940s, insurance companies began to write contracts covering several lines. The National Association of Insurance Commissioners, realizing the changing nature of underwriting, established a committee to investigate the necessity for making "multiple-line underwriting power universally available to insurance companies."[25]

After a detailed study, the committee did not recommend the immediate abandonment of the American system of single or classified fields of insurance. In the opinion of the committee, a dramatic shift would not have been in the public interest. The committee did suggest the implementation of five changes that it felt would bring insurance laws into line with underwriting practices. The five recommendations included: (1) granting multiple-line underwriting powers to United States companies operating abroad; (2) permitting any fire, marine, casualty, or surety company to reinsure all types of insurance other than life insurance and annuities; (3) allowing any fire or marine insurer, or any casualty or surety company licensed to write liability insurance, to write automobile liability and physical damage insurance, provided certain financial requirements are met; (4) allowing any fire or marine insurance company, or any casualty or surety company licensed to write liability insurance, to write aircraft liability and physical damage coverages, provided certain financial requirements are met; and (5) permitting fire, marine, casualty, and surety companies to write personal property floater policies. All of these recommendations were based on the assumption that no insurer would be permitted to write multiple-line coverage without substantial policyholders surplus.[26]

In commenting on the recommendations, the committee recognized the need for insurance companies to write a single contract for householders; however, it skirted the issue by suggesting that this area be given further consideration.[27]

During its mid-winter meeting in 1947, the multiple-lines committee made an additional recommendation of major importance. The committee proposed that the:

> ...commissioners severally and the industry seek the enactment of legislation in all states providing for full multiple underwriting powers for insurance companies provided however that adequate financial standards be included in such legislation.[28]

The insurance commisioners did press for new laws pertaining to underwriting powers, and all states now permit multiple-line underwriting.[29]

Because of the multiple-line underwriting movement, it became very easy for insurers to develop the homeowners series of protection.

For the insured, the new policies facilitated the process of obtaining the full amount of desired insurance protection.

Homeowners contracts have several desirable features and have thus become very popular. They avoid gaps in coverages that might exist if individual policies were purchased. (This problem still arises in situations where an individual is not eligible for homeowners coverage and must purchase individual policies.) Second, a homeowners contract is less expensive than several separate individual contracts. An insurance company can issue one policy covering several lines with less cost than it can issue several policies covering those same lines. The savings in administrative expense can be passed on to the consumer in the form of a lower premium. Third, by having one insurance policy instead of several, an insured pays only one insurance premium and renews one insurance contract. Fourth, since the homeowners contract contains a broad range of coverages, it serves as a risk management tool for individual consumers who have neither the time nor the expertise to ascertain their insurance needs. While the contract may result in excess coverage in a few cases, many individuals would rather overinsure than underinsure.

In 1950 when the homeowners program was initiated it constituted only a small segment of the insurance market. Today it is a mainstay in the personal insurance portfolio of many individuals. Because of its importance the homeowners contract is discussed in detail in the remainder of this chapter and in the following chapter.

Types of Homeowners Coverage

There are six homeowners insurance contracts, hereafter referred to as HO-1, HO-2, HO-3, HO-4, HO-5, and HO-6. HO-1, HO-2, HO-3, and HO-5 are designed for owner-occupants of a dwelling. HO-4 is designed for individuals renting a residence or living in a condominium. If HO-4 is used for condomium coverage, it must be endorsed to indicate that the coverage is afforded for property in a condominium. HO-6 is a new form of coverage similar to an HO-4 policy but specifically designed for individuals occupying condomiums. There are other types of homeowners coverage for special groups. For example, there are series of policies available for owner-occupants of farms and mobile homes. "Homeowners '76" (HO-76) is an entirely new series of policy forms developed by the Insurance Services Office and is in effect in a few states. Its major emphasis is on more readable and understandable policy language.

Each homeowners contract is composed of a liability section, a property section, a policy jacket, and a declarations page. Although the forms described in this and the following chapter are not necessarily those utilized by all insurance companies, they are deemed to be representative of those used in the industry.

Liability coverage, section II, is the same for HO-1 through HO-6 and HO-76 and is similar to the coverage in farmowners and mobile-home owners contracts. The property coverage is different in each form.

An individual purchasing a homeowners policy must buy an entire package of coverage, i.e., coverage cannot be restricted to property or liability coverage. In addition, certain types of exposures must be insured under section II (liability) coverage. The following exposures have to be covered at an additional premium:

(1) All additional residence premises where the Named Insured or spouse maintain a residence other than business or farm property;

(2) All residence employees of the Named Insured or spouse not covered or not required to be covered by Workmen's Compensation Insurance (charge required for residence employees in excess of two); and

(3) Incidental office, professional, private school or studio occupancies by the insured and residential premises of the insured.[30]

Eligibility

HO-1, HO-2, HO-3, and HO-5 can be issued only to an owner-occupant of a dwelling not housing more than two families. Each family can have up to two boarders. Prospective owner-occupants can purchase one of these policies for a residence which is under construction.[31]

Normally HO-4 is issued to an occupant who does not own the residence that he or she is occupying. However, sometimes an owner-occupant who is not eligible for HO-1, HO-2, HO-3, or HO-5 still may be eligible for an HO-4.

If two families own and occupy a residence with separate living areas:

...a Homeowners Policy providing building coverage may be issued to only one of the co-owner occupants of the dwelling. The policy may be endorsed to cover the interest of the other co-owners in the building(s) and for premises liability.[32]

Premium Calculations

Homeowners contracts normally are issued for a period of one year. However, many insurance companies issue the policy for a three-year period with the premium being paid in three annual installments. In the past, insurers wanted to utilize the latter approach because it cut down on the administrative costs associated with issuing a new policy every year. As the costs associated with the homeowners insurance product have increased rapidly, some companies have begun issuing policies for one year. By doing so, an insurer maintains greater flexibility in controlling rates—rates can be increased annually instead of every three years. In the automobile insurance area, cost instability has become so severe that some insurers have reduced the policy period to six months.

If an insurer decides to cancel a homeowners policy, the premium refund is calculated on a pro rata basis. Thus, if a one-year policy is canceled after six months, the policyholder would receive a refund equal to 50 percent of the premium. If the insured cancels the policy, the premium generally is refunded in accordance with a schedule such as that shown in Table 2-7. If an insured cancels a policy after six months, for example, he or she would receive only a 40 percent refund of premium.

Although there are six homeowners forms, HO-3 is becoming the one most widely used, and therefore it should be studied carefully.

Persons Insured

The liability coverage extends to the named insured and his or her spouse, if a resident of the named insured's household. Resident relatives of either the named insured or his or her spouse as well as "any other person under the age of twenty-one in the care of any Insured" are covered. In addition:

> (a) with respect to animals or watercraft to which this insurance applies, owned by any Insured, any person or organization legally responsible therefor except a person or organization using or having custody or possession of any such animal or watercraft in the course of his business or without the permission of the owner; and
> (b) with respect to any vehicle to which this insurance applies, any employee of any Insured while engaged in the employment of the Insured [are covered].

Coverage applies separately to any insured under the policy.

Acts Covered and Amount Insured

The homeowners liability coverage acts as comprehensive personal liability protection for an insured. The coverages afforded are discussed in this section.

Personal Liability   Section II, coverage E, of the homeowners policy stipulates that the insurer will pay all bodily injury or property damages for which an insured is legally liable, i.e., the contract provides personal liability coverage. Coverage is subject to the limitations of the policy. The insured is protected not only against bodily injury or

Table 2-7
Short Rate Cancellation Table

Days Policy in Force	Percent of One-Year Premium	Days Policy in Force	Percent of One-Year Premium	Days Policy in Force	Percent of One-Year Premium	Days Policy in Force	Percent of One-Year Premium
1	5%	66- 69	29	154-156	53%	256-260	77
2	6	70- 73	30	157-160	54	261-264	78
3- 4	7	74- 76	31	161-164	55	265-269	79
5- 6	8	77- 80	32	165-167	56	270-273 (9 mos.)	80
7- 8	9	81- 83	33	168-171	57	274-278	81
9- 10	10	84- 87	34	172-175	58	279-282	82
11- 12	11	88- 91 (3 mos.)	35	176-178	59	283-287	83
13- 14	12	92- 94	36	179-182 (6 mos.)	60	288-291	84
15- 16	13	95- 98	37	183-187	61	292-296	85
17- 18	14	99-102	38	188-191	62	297-301	86
19- 20	15	103-105	39	192-196	63	302-305 (10 mos.)	87
21- 22	16	106-109	40	197-200	64	306-310	88
23- 25	17	110-113	41	201-205	65	311-314	89
26- 29	18	114-116	42	206-209	66	315-319	90
30- 32 (1 mo.)	19	117-120	43	210-214 (7 mos.)	67	320-323	91
33- 36	20	121-124 (4 mos.)	44	215-218	68	324-328	92
37- 40	21	125-127	45	219-223	69	329-332	93
41- 43	22	128-131	46	224-228	70	333-337 (11 mos.)	94
44- 47	23	132-135	47	229-232	71	338-342	95
48- 51	24	136-138	48	233-237	72	343-346	96
52- 54	25	139-142	49	238-241	73	347-351	97
55- 58	26	143-146	50	242-246 (8 mos.)	74	352-355	98
59- 62 (2 mos.)	27	147-149	51	247-250	75	356-360	99
63- 65	28	150-153 (5 mos.)	52	251-255	76	361-365 (12 mos.)	100

property damage that he or she might cause but also against actions over which the individual has no control.

In addition to providing personal liability protection, the insurer under a homeowners policy agrees to defend an insured against any suit even if there is no basis for the suit. The cost of this defense of an insured is excess coverage above the policy limit, as illustrated in the following example.

Harry Cathcart was sued by an associate. The cost to defend Harry was $25,000. The plaintiff obtained a judgment for $50,000. Harry has $50,000 of liability coverage under his homeowners policy.

The $25,000 in court costs is excess coverage and is not subtracted from the policy limits. Since the policy limits are equal to the amount of the loss, all costs would be paid.

Sometimes an insurer will not have to pay a direct charge for legal services because it will provide its own legal staff. The insurance carrier has no responsibility to pay any claim or defend any suit if the policy limits have been "exhausted by payment of judgments or settlements." Occasionally an insured should retain his or her lawyer even if a lawyer is provided by the insurer. Obtaining an outside lawyer is very important for an insured when the amount of a suit exceeds the policy limits.

Bodily injury means "bodily injury, sickness or disease, including care, loss of services and death resulting therefrom." While not specifically stated, the term bodily injury is broad enough to cover pain and suffering (the noneconomic loss claimed). Property damage means "injury to or destruction of tangible property, including loss of use thereof."

Coverage for property damage includes loss of use which, as the following example illustrates, is very important.

Mark Hatkins was burning leaves in his yard. The grass around the leaves caught fire, and the fire spread to the house of Mark's neighbor. The house was severely damaged and the neighbors had to move into a motel for three weeks. The liability coverage in Mark's policy paid for the damage to the neighbor's home and the living expenses encountered by that family.

A single limit of liability is stated in the policy declaration for bodily injury and property damage. This limit applies on a per-occurrence basis (the loss-causing event may occur over time) rather than per-accident basis (the loss-causing event must be sudden and both unforeseen and unintended). The former provides broader coverage for the insured as the next example illustrates.

Edward Rutherford has a home in the suburbs of Philadelphia. One of the water pipes under Edward's basement developed a leak two years ago. Since then the leak resulted in the ground shifting slowly, the shift damaged the residence of Edward and his next door neighbor. Edward's homeowners liability coverage would protect him since an occurrence basis is utilized. If the policy were written on an accident basis, no coverage would have been available in this example because the damage was not caused by a sudden event.

The amount of liability insurance protection that a company will sell varies among insurance companies. However, $25,000 or $50,000 frequently is used as the aggregate limit. When an individual has an umbrella liability policy (a personal catastrophe liability policy offering broad coverage over and above certain basic underlying coverages that are required for automobile liability and personal liability), the coverage in the homeowners policy should at least equal the minimum limits required by the umbrella policy. If the limits required in the umbrella policy are not maintained, there will be a gap in coverage.

While an insurer's liability is restricted to the limits stated in the policy declarations, the "insurance afforded . . . applies separately to each Insured against whom claim is made or suit is brought except with respect to the Company's limit of liability." The following example illustrates this concept of severability of insurance.

Thomas Bigelow, age sixteen, deliberately destroyed a neighbor's tool shed. Tom's father, Harold, was sued by the neighbor. The courts awarded the neighbor $1,500 in damages and court costs. Since the damage done by Thomas Bigelow was deliberate, he would not be covered under the liability section of the homeowners policy. However, since his father was the one found liable for the damages, the policy would pay for Harold Bigelow's liability. The coverage applied separately to each of the individuals and the father's coverage was not negated because the destruction of the neighbor's property was deliberate. While coverage applies separately, an insurer will never pay more for an occurrence than the policy limit.

Medical Payments Coverage F under section II of a homeowners policy affords coverage for medical payments to others. Medical expenses are "expenses for necessary medical, surgical, X-ray, dental services, including prosthetic devices, ambulance, hospital, professional nursing and funeral services." Normally coverage is written with a $500 or $1,000 limit per person and an aggregate limit of $25,000 per accident. The medical payments coverage is written on an accident, not an occurrence, basis.

The insurer pays all reasonable medical expenses for bodily injury resulting from an accident if they are incurred within one year of the accident. Payments for these medical expenses are made either to the injured party or on his or her behalf. Medical payments are made for an individual injured as a result of an accident if the individual is:

1. on an insured premises with the permission of any Insured; or
2. elsewhere, if such bodily injury
   a. arises out of a condition in the insured premises or the ways immediately adjoining,
   b. is caused by the activities of any Insured, or by a residence employee in the course of his employment by any Insured,
   c. is caused by an animal owned by or in the care of any Insured, or
   d. is sustained by any residence employee and arises out of and in the course of his employment by any Insured.

Examples of each of these situations are as follows:

- a neighbor visiting in an insured's yard could stumble on a rake (1),
- building supplies stacked on an insured's lot could collapse and injure someone in another yard (2)(a),
- while playing tennis, an individual could accidentally strike an opponent (2)(b),
- the insured's dog could bite a visitor (2)(c),
- a household employee could slip and fall at a shopping center while shopping for the named insured (2)(d).

Some insurance companies will pay only one section (2)(c) claim per animal. The insurer could then cancel coverage for the animal. The company's philosophy is that if an animal is or is becoming vicious, adverse selection is being introduced into the insuring process and, therefore, no further coverage should be provided.

One of the medical payments provisions (2)(b) provides a very broad coverage. Notice that payments are made for an accident caused by the activities of an insured. Activities could be anything from having a party to going to work. The major problem under this provision is determining if an action is caused by an insured or someone else.

Insured Premises

The residence described in the policy declarations is considered the insured premises. In addition, under section II the following additional locations are considered insured premises:

(a) any other residence premises specifically named in this policy;

(b) any residence premises acquired by the Named Insured or his spouse during the term of this policy;

(c) any residence premises which are not owned by any Insured but where an Insured may be temporarily residing;

(d) vacant land, other than farm land, owned by or rented to any Insured; and

(e) individual or family cemetery plots or burial vaults.

Exclusions

Exclusions Applicable to Coverage E and Coverage F The liability section of the homeowners policy has several exclusions. Some of the exclusions apply to both coverage E (personal liability) and coverage F (medical payments). Other exclusions apply to only one of the coverages. The joint exclusions are presented first.

Aircraft and Vehicles. Coverage is not available under coverage E or F for losses arising from the ownership, operation, use, loading, or unloading of:

(1) any aircraft; or

(2) any motor vehicle owned or operated by, or rented or loaned to any Insured; but this subdivision (2) does not apply to bodily injury or property damage occurring on the residence premises if the motor vehicle is not subject to motor vehicle registration because it is used exclusively on the residence premises or kept in dead storage on the residence premises; or

(3) any recreational motor vehicle owned by any Insured, if the bodily injury or property damage occurs away from the residence premises; but this subdivision (3) does not apply to golf carts while used for golf purposes.

The primary purpose of the exclusion is not to provide aviation liability or automobile liability (similar to the FAP) coverage.

A motor vehicle as defined in this exclusion includes "a land motor vehicle, trailer, or semitrailer designed for travel on public roads (including any machinery or apparatus attached thereto)." The term motor vehicle does not include (1) utility, boat, camp or home trailer, (2) recreational motor vehicle, (3) crawler or farm type tractor, (4) farm implement, or (5) equipment designed for use off roads unless these vehicles are being towed by or carried on some motor vehicle, i.e., these items would be covered when they are not being towed or carried.

The policy exclusion is not designed to eliminate coverage for vehicles not designed for road use, as indicated in the definition of motor vehicle cited above. This fact is emphasized in provisions (2) and (3). Provision (2) stipulates the exclusion does not apply to motor vehicles which do not have to be licensed. Provision (3) excludes recreational vehicles, but the definition of recreational vehicle does not include vehicles designed for off-road use if they are not subject to registration.

The coverage for vehicles which do not have to be registered is very important. If this coverage were not available, protection for riding lawn mowers, small tractors, and similar vehicles would have to be purchased separately. The exclusions under provisions (1), (2), and (3) do not apply to residence employees if they are acting within the scope of their employment "except while such employee is engaged in the operation or maintenance of aircraft."

Watercraft. Bodily injury or property damage resulting from the ownership, maintenance, operation, use, loading, or unloading of watercraft is excluded under coverages E and F. However, this exclusion applies only to watercraft which an insured owned or rented if the watercraft has an inboard or inboard-outboard motor with more than fifty horsepower. Coverage also is not afforded for sailing vessels longer than twenty-five feet.

A third group of watercraft is excluded. Watercraft

... powered by any outboard motor(s), singly or in combination of more than 25 total horsepower, if such outboard motor(s) is owned by any Insured at the inception of this policy and not endorsed hereon, unless the Insured reports in writing to this Company within 45 days after acquisition his intention to insure the outboard motor or combination of outboard motors, ownership of which was acquired prior to the policy term.

This exclusion differs significantly from the one described previously. First, rental boats are not excluded. Second, boats with outboard motor(s) having more than twenty-five horsepower are excluded only if they are owned at the beginning of the policy period and not specifically covered by the insured in the policy. Watercraft purchased before a policy becomes effective are covered if reported within forty-five days after purchase. Watercraft purchased after the policy becomes effective are covered until the next policy renewal. The following example illustrates how coverage would apply.

Kristy Powell purchased a homeowners policy on June 1. When Kristy applied for coverage on May 1, she owned a watercraft that had an outboard motor with thirty horsepower. The insurer was informed about the watercraft and coverage was afforded for the watercraft. On May 15, Kristy purchased a second watercraft with a sixty horsepower outboard motor. To obtain coverage for the second watercraft, Kristy must notify her insurer of the purchase by June 29. If on August 1 Kristy traded in her two watercraft for another watercraft with an eighty horsepower outboard motor, coverage would be provided automatically until the policy was renewed.

Professional Services. Neither coverage E nor coverage F covers losses arising when an individual provides or fails to provide professional services. This exclusion is aimed primarily at physicians, lawyers, and accountants.

Business Pursuits. In the homeowners policy, business is defined as "a trade, profession or occupation, including farming, and the use of any premises or portion of residence premises for any such purposes." Renting the home is considered a business except a business does not include:

(a) the occasional rental or holding for rental of the residence premises for dwelling purposes;

(b) the rental or holding for rental of a portion of the residence premises for dwelling purposes unless for the accommodation of three or more roomers or boarders;

(c) the rental or holding for rental of a portion of the residence premises for private garage purposes; or

(d) the rental or holding for rental of a portion of the residence premises as an office, school or studio.

Section II of the homeowners policy contains a specific limitation for business pursuits. However, business pursuits are not excluded when they are "ordinarily incident to non-business pursuits." Business appears to be well-defined, but numerous coverage questions have arisen under the pursuits exclusion. Several cases illustrate the types of coverage questions that can develop.

Corrace Hollier and Alphonse Pitre were employees of Colton Products Company.

> In preparing to operate the company's equipment, Hollier instructed Pitre to close the "truck chute" and open the two corn bin chutes. To do this Pitre had to climb a 65-foot ladder and work on a catwalk. Hollier then walked to the sample room with a plant official and discussed business. When Hollier returned, he looked for Pitre and "hollered" for him, to no avail. He then went to the starter buttons and first started the elevator, then the auger.

Pitre, who was in the auger attempting to clean it, was severely injured when the auger was started by Hollier. Pitre contended that he was eligible for benefits under Hollier's homeowners policy. The company raised the business pursuits exclusion as its defense, but Pitre claimed that pushing the starter button was an activity which was ordinarily incident to nonbusiness pursuits. The appeals courts agreed with the insurer.[33]

A second case involving the business exclusion occurred on a farm. Jasper Burroughs was aiding his stepfather-in-law, Luther Juban, in rounding up some cattle. Both men picked up sticks to prod the cattle. Juban tossed his stick at one of the cattle but inadvertently hit Burroughs in the mouth. Burroughs contended that he was covered under Juban's personal liability insurance coverage since they were off Juban's farm and the activity engaged in was not related to the business of the farm. The insurer contended that the activity was business related. The appeals court agreed with the insurer and declared that there was no coverage.[34]

A third case involved child care. Janet Chamberlain agreed to keep Norma Crane's two children every day while the latter worked. For this service, Mrs. Chamberlain was paid $25 per week and was provided with some groceries. Mrs. Chamberlain had two children, and she watched over the Crane children at the same time that she took care of her own. Mrs. Chamberlain did not have any outside business activities. While in Mrs. Chamberlain's care one of the Crane children, Andrea Crane, suffered burns to her left hand, wrist, and fingers. Mrs. Chamberlain's insurance carrier declined to pay medical expenses for the child. The court eliminated the question of negligence raised by the insurer since negligence is not excluded in the policy; however, the court did examine the business exclusion.

> It seems clear to us that at the time of the accident Mrs. Chamberlain was engaged in an activity which is "ordinarily incident to non-business pursuits." Andrea was being cared for in the home while Mrs. Chamberlain simultaneously cared for her own children. She testified that even if Andrea had not been left in her charge, she would have been caring for her own children at the time of the accident, that she provided lunch for her own children as well as for Andrea, and that she prepared no special diet for Andrea. Assuming that the care of the child constituted a business pursuit, such duties under the circumstances *presented here were clearly incident to Mrs. Chamberlain's non-business regimen of maintaining a household and supervising her own children.* Indeed, it is difficult to conceive of an activity more ordinarily incident to a non-commercial pursuit than home care of children.[35]

For individuals who need coverage for business activity, a limited form of business pursuits coverage can be endorsed as additional coverage to a homeowners policy. The endorsement is very important for an individual with an umbrella liability policy that covers business activities only if they are included in underlying coverage.

Premises and Intentional Injury. Two other exclusions apply to coverages E and F. Bodily injury or property damage "arising out of any premises, other than an insured premises, owned, rented, or controlled by any insured" is excluded. This is not applicable to residence employees in the course of their employment. Finally, losses that either can be expected or are intentional from the insured's perspective are not covered.

Coverage E Exclusions One set of exclusions applies only to coverage E (personal liability).

Contracts. Personal liability coverage does not extend to any contracts related to an insured's business. Other written contracts are covered; this provision is designed to permit coverage for incidental contracts such as leases.

The policy does not apply under coverage E to bodily injury:

> . . . to any person, including a residence employee, if the Insured has a policy providing workmen's compensation or occupational disease benefits for such bodily injury or if benefits for such bodily injury are in whole or in part either payable or required to be provided by the Insured under any workmen's compensation or occupational disease law.

However, workers' compensation coverage can be added to a policy. For example, in California an endorsement (HO-90) is used to afford coverage for all benefits under the workers' compensation law for private residence employees. The endorsement also provides a form of employers' liability coverage for these employees.

Property Owned by an Insured. Coverage E protection does not apply to property owned by an insured. Thus, if one family member damaged the personal property of another member, the homeowners insurance would not provide liability protection. If the insurance company provided such coverage it would be subject to considerable adverse selection.

Property in Care, Custody, or Control. No liability protection is afforded for property occupied or used by an insured or for property rented to or in the care, custody, or control of an insured. This exclusion does not apply to fire legal liability because this coverage is provided in the supplementary coverage section of the policy.

Employee Claims. Any claim by a residence employee is invalid unless the claim is brought against the insured within thirty-six months after expiration of a homeowners policy. Any claim brought after thirty-six months would be the responsibility of the employer.

Nuclear. One exclusion applicable to coverage E, the nuclear exclusion, is found in the general conditions section of the policy. No personal liability coverage is available under a homeowners policy if an insured also has a nuclear energy liability policy "or would be an Insured under any such policy for its termination upon exhaustion of its limit of liability."

Coverage F Exclusions Like the personal liability coverage, medical payments benefits are subject to a workers' compensation exclusion. The exclusion, however, in the medical payments coverage is more restrictive. No payment is made if any person or organization is required to make workers' compensation payments or has a workers' compensation policy. The next two examples illustrate the difference between the two workers' compensation exclusions.

Charles Mall has a housekeeper who works full time. Charles has elected to cover her under workers' compensation. The housekeeper slipped and fell while cleaning the house. Charles' homeowners policy would not provide either personal liability or medical payments coverage because of the existence of the workers' compensation policy.

Charles Mall's sink was clogged. As a result, he had to call a plumber. In the process of fixing the sink the plumber fell and hurt his back. Charles' personal liability coverage would protect him against a suit by the plumber because Charles does not carry workers' compensation on the plumber. If the plumber is self-employed, he is not required to carry a workers' compensation policy; therefore, medical payment coverage would be afforded by Charles' policy. However, if the plumber works for a firm which carries workers' compensation coverage, medical payments would not be provided by Charles' homeowners insurance.

Medical payments for several classes of individuals are excluded. Payments are not available for the named insured, his or her spouse, "the relatives of either, and any other person under the age of twenty-one in the care of any Insured." Individuals who regularly live on any part of the insured premises are not eligible for medical payments. This not only includes the residence described in the policy but also newly acquired and temporary residences. If a business is operated on the insured premises, individuals who are on the premises because of the business will not receive medical payments. This exclusion can be eliminated by use of an endorsement.

Limitations on Payments for Coverage E

The homeowners policy is designed to avoid duplication of coverage. The standard apportionment clause applicable to section II coverage states that in the case of multiple coverage, each insurer will share in a loss on either an equal share contribution or a contribution by-limits basis. Specifically the two provisions state:

(1) Contribution by Equal Shares:
If all of such other insurance includes a provision for contribution by equal shares, this Company shall not be liable for a greater proportion of such loss than would be payable if each insurer contributes an equal share until the share of each insurer equals the lowest applicable limit of liability under any one policy or the full amount of the loss is paid. With respect to any amount of loss not so paid the remaining insurers then continue to contribute equal shares of the remaining amount of loss until each such insurer has paid its limit in full or the full amount of the loss is paid.
(2) Contribution by Limits:
If any of such other insurance does not include a provision for contribution by equal shares, this Company shall not be liable for a greater proportion of such loss than the applicable limit of liability under this policy for such loss bears to the total applicable limit of liability of all valid and collectible insurance against such loss.

Two examples will aid substantially in understanding how each of these provisions function.

Maggie Horne has three liability contracts which contain equal shares clauses. One policy has a $25,000 limit. The second policy provides $35,000 of coverage, and the third affords $40,000. Recently, while visiting Maggie's home, a guest ate some sandwiches, became ill, and required substantial medical treatment. The guest was out of work for several months. The guest sued Maggie and was awarded $50,000 in damages by the courts. Each liability carrier paid an equal share of the

Table 2-8
Division of Losses on an Equal Shares Basis

Insurer 1	(⅓ x 90,000)	$30,000
	Subject to policy limits of $25,000	$25,000
Insurer 2	(⅓ x 75,000) + (½ x 15,000)	32,500
Insurer 3	(⅓ x 75,000) + (½ x 15,000)	32,500
Total		$90,000

loss, i.e., one-third of the loss. (Since one-third of $50,000 is less than the policy limits of any one policy the equal shares did not change.) If the guest had obtained a $90,000 settlement instead of the $50,000 settlement, the payout would have been as shown in Table 2-8.

Whitley Evans has four liability policies—a homeowners contract and three individual liability policies. None of the three individual policies has a contribution by equal shares provision. The homeowners policy has a $50,000 liability limit; the other policies each have $10,000 limits. Whitley is sued and the plaintiff obtains a $20,000 judgment. The homeowners insurer would pay $12,500 of the loss ($50,000/$80,000 × $20,000) and each of the other insurers would pay $2,500 (1/8 × $20,000).

The equal shares and by-limits rules do not apply to bodily injury or property damage that arises "out of the ownership, maintenance, operations, use, loading or unloading of any motor vehicle, recreational motor vehicle or watercraft." If there is other valid and collectible coverage on these items, the homeowners coverage is excess.

Extensions and Supplements

The liability coverage under a homeowners policy contains several coverage supplements and extensions, each of which is designed for a special area of liability.

No-Fault Property Damage Coverage Minor property damage claims are handled without requiring the injured party to obtain a judgment. The insurer agrees to repair or replace damaged property on a no-fault basis subject to a maximum benefit of $250.

The coverage does not apply to damage or destruction caused deliberately by an insured unless the insured is under the age of thirteen. This solves the coverage gap that arises from the mischievous acts of children. These acts are not covered under the liability coverage.

Also excluded is any property:

... owned by or rented to any Insured, any tenant of any Insured or any resident of Named Insured's household; arising out of (1) any act or omission in connection with premises (other than insured premises) owned, rented or controlled by any Insured, (2) business pursuits or professional services or (3) the ownership, maintenance, operation, use, loading or unloading, of any land motor vehicle, trailer or semi-trailer, farm machinery or equipment, aircraft or watercraft.

Property covered under the property section (section I) of the homeowners policy is excluded from the no-fault coverage. This avoids a double payment by the insurer for property damage.

Personal Liability Claim Expense In addition to paying the costs incurred in defending a suit, an insurer will pay premiums on appeal bonds and premiums on bonds to release attachments (providing the bond limit does not exceed the limits of the policy). The cost of bail bonds up to $250 for accident and traffic violations also are paid.

Any interest costs arising after a judgment and before the insurer has paid, tendered, or deposited the amount necessary to cover the judgment are borne by the insurer. The insurer's payment is limited to the lesser of the amount of the judgment or the policy limits. Finally,

... reasonable expenses incurred by the Insured at this Company's request, including actual loss of earnings (but not loss of other income) not to exceed $25 per day because of his attendance at hearings in trials at such request, are paid by the insurer.

All expenses paid by the insurer under the personal claims expense section are additional benefits and do not reduce the limit of liability.

First Aid Expenses The medical payments coverage section of the homeowners policy includes payment for emergency first aid expenses. However, a first aid expense provision exists in the supplementary coverages as well. The first aid expense provision has two principal advantages. First, if a person does not have medical payments coverage, the cost of emergency medical treatment will still be borne by the insurer. Second, the first aid expense benefit is in addition to the medical payments coverage. Thus, emergency first aid expenses can be paid under the supplementary coverage; the full medical payments benefit would still be available for other medical expenses.

Property in Control of Insured The personal liability section of the homeowners policy excludes coverage for damage to property rented to or in the care, custody, and control of the insured. Protection for property occupied or used by the insured also is excluded. This exclusion is partially overcome by the supplementary coverages. The supplementary coverage provision extends coverage E to "property damage to any insured premises and to house furnishings" if the damage is caused by "fire, explosion, or smoke or smudge caused by sudden, unusual, and faulty operation of any heating or cooking unit." The supplementary coverage is basically a legal liability benefit.

Construction of New Residence The supplementary section extends both coverage E and coverage F to vacant land on which a one- or two-unit family residence is being constructed for use by an insured.

Extensions of Coverage by Endorsement

Several endorsements can be used to broaden the liability coverage under a homeowners policy. Form HO-70 adds liability coverage for residence premises rented to other people. Coverage E (personal liability) must be added, but coverage F (medical payments) is optional. If an appurtenant structure is being rented out, HO-40 can be used to extend coverage E and F by including the appurtenant structure as an insured premises. Medical payments coverage is optional.

Business pursuits can be added under the section II coverage by means of HO-71. Like the two endorsements mentioned above, coverage for medical payments to others is optional. Liability for corporal punishment also is optional.

The coverage does not extend to:

1. bodily injury or property damage arising out of the business pursuits of the insured in connection with a business owned or financially controlled by such insured or by a partnership or joint venture of which such insured is a partner or member;
2. bodily injury or property damage arising out of the rendering of or failure to render professional services of any nature (other than teaching), including but not limited to any architectural, engineering or industrial design services, any medical, surgical, dental, or other services or treatment conducive to the health of persons or animals and any cosmetic or tonsorial services or treatment; or
3. bodily injury to a fellow employee of the insured in the course of his or her employment.

Two exclusions apply specifically to teachers. The exclusions stipulate that coverage is not provided:

> when the Insured is a member of the faculty or teaching staff of any school or college;
> a. to bodily injury or property damage arising out of the mainte-nance, operation, use, loading or unloading of draft or saddle animals, vehicles for use therewith, aircraft, motor vehicle, recreational motor vehicle or watercraft owned or operated, or hired by or for the Insured or his employer or used by the Insured for the purpose of instruction in the use thereof; or

b. to bodily injury to any pupil arising out of corporal punishment administered by or at the direction of the Insured, but this exclusion does not apply under Coverage E—Personal Liability if liability for corporal punishment is ... included.

The first exclusion is necessary because most businesses have liability coverage. HO-71 is intended to cover company employees, not owners, for their business pursuits. The second exclusion keeps the business pursuits endorsement from being a professional liability contract, which is available under another policy. The third exclusion applies to an incident covered under workers' compensation although the insured still may be liable.

The liability coverage under the homeowners policy can be converted to farmowners comprehensive liability coverage by the use of endorsement HO-72. The named insured can be an owner or tenant. The special form is very similar to the standard section II. However, the farmers' form allows coverage for employees and includes animal collision coverage. Under the latter coverage, a farmer is paid a fixed amount for any cattle, horse, hog, sheep, or goat killed by collision with a vehicle on a public highway unless the vehicle is owned or operated by the insured or an employee of the insured.

Not all farms can be covered. Farms where "the principal purpose of the farm is to supply commodities for manufacturing or processing by the insured for sale are not eligible."[36] Also ineligible are farms which are incorporated or where racing horses are raised.

HO-74 can be used to extend liability coverage and medical payments "for the owner-occupant of a 3 or 4 family dwelling ... to ... include that portion of the ... premises used for residential purposes not occupied by the Named Insured."[37] This endorsement can be used only with homeowners form 4 (HO-4). HO-74 is used to expand the definition of residence premises to include a three- or four-family dwelling.

HO-75 adds liability and medical payments coverage to watercraft excluded under section II. The watercraft must be listed in the endorsement. Coverage is available even if the named insured is not the owner of the watercraft. Employee injuries are excluded as is coverage for a watercraft used for hire. Another recreational vehicle, the snowmobile, can be insured under the homeowners policy by adding HO-164.

Finally, HO-42 modifies the exclusions under section II so that a residence is not considered a business property if a part of the home is utilized as an office, school, or studio. The endorsement does not add professional liability coverage. Instead, it extends coverage to a residence which ordinarily would not be covered because of the business occupancy.

Insured's Duties in the Event of a Claim

When an event occurs that could result in a loss, the insured is required to aid the insurer in handling the claim. The insured must notify the insurer in writing about an accident or occurrence. The notice must describe the accident or occurrence (including time, place, and circumstances), list witnesses, identify the insured, and identify any injured parties.

In the event of a claim or suit the insured is required to notify the insurer. He or she also must assist in making a settlement, handling a suit, and enforcing third-party rights. The insured must also attend hearings and trials and assist in securing and giving evidence and obtaining the attendance of witnesses.

An insured is not allowed to make voluntarily any payment to or for an injured party except for first aid payments. Any payments made by the insured are at his or her own expense.

If a loss arises under the damage to property of others provision under the supplementary coverages, the insured again must give written notice to the insurer. He or she also has to "file sworn proof of loss with [the] Company within sixty days after the occurrence of loss." If feasible, the insured must show the damaged property to the insurer.

Injured Party's Duty Under Medical Payments

An injured party eligible for medical payments must give written proof of loss claim to the insurer as soon as practicable. The injured individual must give the insurer the right to obtain medical records and, if necessary, must submit to a physical examination by a physician selected by the insurer.

Suit Against the Insurer

An insurer cannot be sued under the homeowners contract until the policy provisions have been met and the insured's obligation has been ascertained by trial or "by written agreement of the Insured, the claimant and this Company." The policy also stipulates that no person or organization has the right to "join the Company as a party to any action against the Insured."

The bankruptcy or insolvency of an insured does not release the insurer from its responsibility under the homeowners liability coverage. Thus, even if a person has no assets and is judgment-proof the insurer would still be required to pay any claim up to the policy limits.

Chapter Notes

1. Morris Mandel, *A Complete Treasury of Stories for Public Speakers* (Middle Village, NY: Jonathan David Publishers, 1974), p. 55.
2. United States Department of Commerce, *Statistical Abstract of the United States 1976* (Washington: Superintendent of Documents, 1976), p. 25.
3. Ibid., p. 29.
4. Fuller's discussions of the causes and effects of inflation are contained in CPCU 9, Economics, and in one of the monographs assigned in CPCU 10, *Issues in Insurance.*
5. Northern California Chapter of The Society of CPCU, "Insuring of Condominiums, Cooperatives and Planned Unit Developments," *CPCU Annals* 28:1 (1975), p. 14.
6. John D. Long, "Future Changes in American Insurance," *CPCU Annals* 29:2 (1976), pp. 159-160.
7. William G. Pritchard, Jr., "Social Responsibility in the Insurance Marketplace," *CPCU Annals,* 27:1 (March 1974), p. 46.
8. Ibid.
9. *Webster's New Twentieth Century Dictionary of the English Language* (New York: Publishers Guild, 1963), p. 688.
10. Robert L. Rabin, *Perspectives on Tort Law* (Boston: Little, Brown and Company, 1976), p. 1.
11. *Automobile Insurance . . . For Whose Benefit?* (New York: New York Insurance Department, 1970), pp. 18-41.
12. Robert E. Keeton and Jeffrey O'Connell, *Basic Protection for the Traffic Victim* (Boston: Little, Brown and Company, 1965), pp. 125-128.
13. Ibid., pp. 323-324.
14. Bernard Webb, "Summaries of Automobile Accident Reparations Reform Proposals and Enacted Legislation," prepared for No-Fault Automobile Insurance Conference, Georgia State University, Atlanta, Georgia, August 10, 1971.
15. Ibid., p. 32.
16. Jeffrey O'Connell, "Elective No-Fault Liability Insurance for All Kinds of Accidents: A Proposal," *Insurance Law Journal* 608 (September 1973), p. 506.
17. Ibid.
18. Clark C. Havighurst and Lawrence R. Tancredi, "Medical Adversity Insurance," *Insurance Law Journal* 613 (February 1974), p. 76.
19. The United States Senate hearings on S.354 (national no-fault law) frequently have centered on the cost question. Individuals interested in the question of cost should find the hearings good background material.
20. U.S. Congress, Senate, Committee on the Judiciary, A Bill to Establish a Nationwide System of Adequate and Uniform Motor Vehicle Accident Reparation Acts and to Require No-Fault Motor Vehicle Insurance as a

Condition Precedent to Using a Motor Vehicle on Public Roads in Order to Promote and Regulate Interstate Commerce, 93rd Cong., 1st and 2nd sess., 1973-1974, pp. 107-109.
21. Ibid., pp. 66-67.
22. Guido Calabresi, *The Costs of Accidents* (New Haven: Yale University Press, 1970), p. 245.
23. Gerald Ford, *Economic Report of the President* (Washington: Superintendent of Documents, 1977), p. 154.
24. Calabresi, p. 22.
25. *Proceedings of the National Association of Insurance Commissioners* (1944), p. 125.
26. Ibid., pp. 125-126.
27. Ibid., p. 128.
28. Ibid., (1948), p. 221.
29. The material for the first part of the section was taken from: Claude C. Lilly, "A History of Insurance Regulation in the United States," *CPCU Annals* 30:2 (June 1976), pp. 110-111.
30. Insurance Services Office, "Homeowners Policy Program," Rev. (New York: Insurance Services Office), p. GR-3.
31. Ibid., p. GR-2.
32. Ibid.
33. *Pitre* v. *Pennsylvania Millers Mutual Insurance Company*, 236 So. 2d 921 (1970).
34. *Burroughs* v. *Employers Liability Assurance Corporation*, 198 So. 2d 202 (1967).
35. *Crane* v. *State Farm Fire and Casualty*, 485 P 2d 1131 (1971).
36. Insurance Services Office, p. GR-7.
37. Ibid., p. GR-8.

CHAPTER 3

Homeowners Coverage

This chapter continues the discussion of homeowners coverages. The first major section of this chapter covers property coverage under various homeowners forms while later sections cover other specialized residential coverages.

PROPERTY COVERAGE
UNDER A HOMEOWNERS POLICY

The personal liability coverage, section II, of the homeowners form is identical for all homeowners policies (HO-1 through HO-6). While the type of property covered in section I of HO-1 through HO-6 is similar, the perils insured against, the limitations, and the exclusions do exhibit some differences. This chapter will concentrate on the differences and the similarities in property coverages among the various homeowners forms HO-1 through HO-5. Because of its specialized nature in protecting condominiums, HO-6 is discussed separately later in this chapter as is HO-76, due to its relatively new approach.

Persons Insured

All homeowners programs protect the named insured and his or her spouse if both inhabit the same household. Relatives of the named insured and his or her spouse, as well as individuals under the age of twenty-one who are in the care of an insured are also covered. The term "insured" includes both the named insured and the other individuals cited above.

In addition, other individuals may be protected under the homeowners policy. For example, the named insured has the option of providing coverage on the personal property of guests and residence employees.

Another interest that can be protected under the homeowners policy is that of the mortgagee. When more than one mortgage exists, all mortgagees may be covered by a single homeowners policy. The coverage afforded a mortgagee is restricted to its interest in the residence and any appurtenant structures.

The mortgagee has broader coverage than the named insured or property owner. Certain acts of the mortgagor or owner of the dwelling may eliminate the named insured's protection, but these actions do not reduce coverage for the mortgagee. In addition, foreclosure of an insured dwelling, an increase in hazard, or changes in ownership do not adversely affect the mortgagee's coverage. The mortgagee is required to report to the insurer any changes in ownership and occupancy as well as any known increase in hazard.

The mortgagee will have to pay the premium to prevent a lapse in homeowners coverage when the named insured fails to pay the regular premium payment or the additional premium required because of an increase in hazard. Consider the following example. Dorothy Jones has a $20,000 mortgage on her $25,000 home. To protect herself, and the mortgagee, she buys a $25,000 homeowners policy. Unknown to the insurer and the mortgagee, Dorothy starts manufacturing fireworks in her basement. While making rockets, she ignites some gunpowder and damages the home. The insurer will pay the mortgagee even though the nature of the exposure has changed. Dorothy will not be paid since the increase in hazard was not reported.

The mortgagee can be designated a loss payee under the homeowners contract instead of being protected under the mortgagee clause. As a loss payee, the mortgagee has the same rights as the insured policyholder and is not entitled to the special protection found in the mortgagee clause. Therefore, mortgagees generally want to be covered under the mortgagee clause not under the loss payee provision.

Property Covered

Dwelling (Coverage A) Section I of the homeowners policies sets forth the amount and type of property coverage. All of the homeowners policies, with the exception of HO-4 and HO-6, cover special types of property including the dwelling (coverage A), appurtenant structures (coverage B), and unscheduled personal property (coverage C). Consequential coverage (coverage D) to insure against the loss of rental value and additional living expenses is also provided under section I. Tenants' form HO-4 provides coverage only for unscheduled personal property and consequential losses, since the insured does not own a residence.

The major property coverage under HO-1, HO-2, HO-3, and HO-5 is coverage A, protection for the dwelling. The contract covers the dwelling described in the policy declarations when occupied as a private residence. Other insurance on the dwelling is not permitted, but, by means of an endorsement, several insurers jointly can write coverage on a dwelling. In cases where several contracts apply, coverage is apportioned among the insurers.

Some types of business activity may occur at a dwelling without endangering the residence's classification as a private dwelling. The term "business" is defined as:

1. a trade, profession, or occupation, including farming, and the use of any premises or portion of residence premises for any such purposes; and
2. the rental or holding for rental of the whole or any portion of the premises by an insured; but business shall not include: (a) the occasional rental or holding for rental of a portion of the residence premises for dwelling purposes; (b) the rental or holding for rental of a portion of the residence premises for dwelling purposes unless for the accomodation of three or more roomers or boarders; (c) the rental or holding for rental of a portion of the residence premises for private garage purposes; or (d) the rental or holding for rental of a portion of the residence premises as an office, school, or studio.

Although the term "business" appears to be well defined, ambiguities exist. It is open to question whether certain business activities constitute the practice of a trade, profession, or occupation. What may be an occasional activity for one individual may be an occupation for another.

In addition to the described dwelling, the policy provides insurance on two other types of property under coverage A. First, any building equipment, fixtures, and outdoor equipment on the premises will be protected as long as they pertain to the service of the premises. If the items were located temporarily at another site, they still would be protected. The items are not covered under the homeowners policy if other coverage is applicable to them. The dwelling coverage also extends to materials and supplies when these items are (1) located on the insured's premises or adjacent thereto; and (2) intended for use in construction, alteration, or repair of the described dwelling.

The homeowners forms are designed for use with a single dwelling.[1] However, an individual may need coverage for a secondary dwelling. Instead of writing a separate policy, an insurer can endorse the homeowners form to include the secondary residence if it is located in the same state as the primary dwelling. Form HO-67, the *secondary residence premises endorsement* provides separate amounts of additional coverage not only for the dwelling, appurtenant structures, and unscheduled personal property but also for consequential losses.

Another endorsement available for use with section I deserves brief mention. A policy may be issued so that several insurers participate in providing property coverage. When this occurs, HO-178, the *contributing insurance endorsement,* is attached to the policy.

Each insurer under the contributing insurance endorsement prepares a declarations page indicating the amount of coverage for which it is liable. The endorsement is then attached to the policy specifying the percentage of the total coverage insured under each policy and the total limit of liability.

Appurtenant Structures (Coverage B) Appurtenant structures are buildings located on the insured premises which are separate from the dwelling described in the policy. Like coverage A, coverage B includes insurance for materials and supplies. These items are covered if they are located on or adjacent to the premises and if they are to be utilized in the construction, alteration, or repair of an appurtenant structure.

The homeowners policy lists two situations where appurtenant structures are not insured. If an appurtenant structure is used partially or completely for business purposes, or if it is rented or leased, it is not covered. The only exceptions to this exclusion are (1) property rented or leased to a tenant of the described dwelling, or (2) an appurtenant structure rented for use solely as a private garage. If the named insured wishes to rent or lease an appurtenant structure to a person not a tenant of the described dwelling, protection can be obtained by using endorsement HO-40. This endorsement adds coverage for an appurtenant structure if it is rented or leased for dwelling purposes only.

The amount of coverage provided for appurtenant structures is a function of the protection on the described dwelling. Normally, coverage on the appurtenant structure is an amount equal to 10 percent of the insurance on the dwelling. This coverage is in addition to coverage A, not a part of it.

When a named insured owns appurtenant structures worth more than 10 percent of the dwelling coverage, that person might want to purchase additional protection. Endorsement HO-48 can be used to purchase additional coverage. This endorsement provides coverage above the 10 percent limit without replacing the 10 percent limit. For example, John Aker purchases $30,000 of coverage on a dwelling under a homeowners policy. Thus, he has $3,000 of protection on all appurtenant structures. If an appurtenant structure is valued at $5,000, he would not be adequately protected. HO-48 could be used to provide the additional $2,000 protection.

Unscheduled Personal Property (Coverage C) Personal property of an insured (which is usual or incidental to the occupancy of the described dwelling and is used or owned by the insured) is covered both on and off premises. The unscheduled personal property coverage can extend to the property of others used by an insured. As an example, a named insured had a homeowners policy on a log cabin in Aspen, Colorado. While the named insured was on a trip, a fire loss occurred. Personal property of both the named insured and a caretaker who lived in the cabin was destroyed. According to the Colorado Court of Appeals, the personal property of the caretaker was insured. Citing the provision of the homeowners policy which states: "This policy covers unscheduled personal property usual or incidental to the occupancy of the premises as a dwelling and owned or used by an insured . . . ," the court found that the ". . . caretaker's stereo equipment was covered under that provision even though the insured had not been occupying the premises at the time of the fire since the insured used the equipment when occupying the premises."[2]

The amount of protection for unscheduled personal property is determined as a percentage of the described dwelling protection. On-premises protection under coverage C of HO-1, HO-2, HO-3, and HO-5 is usually 50 percent of the dwelling coverage. Off-premises protection under HO-1, HO-2, and HO-3 is the greater of $1,000 or 10 percent of coverage C.

HO-5 provides equal amounts of coverage for personal property on and off the premises, except for personal property at a secondary residence, which is limited to 10 percent of coverage C. This restriction can be eliminated from HO-5 by use of endorsements HO-50 or HO-67. Under HO-50, the named insured is permitted to obtain separate section I unscheduled property coverage on a secondary residence. This form can be used only with HO-5. HO-67, which can be utilized with HO-1, HO-2, and HO-3, as well as HO-5, provides separate unscheduled personal property coverages at a secondary residence and separate protection for coverages A, B, and D at a secondary residence.

The coverage in HO-4 is a stated dollar amount since HO-4 does not provide coverages A or B. Off-premises coverage normally is 10 percent of coverage C but never less than $1,000. The following example illustrates how coverage limits would be determined for coverage C on and off the premises under HO-1, HO-2, HO-3, and HO-5. The coverage under John Aker's homeowners policy is $30,000 for coverage A and $3,000 for coverage B. If he has an HO-1, HO-2, or HO-3 policy, the unscheduled on-premises personal property protection is $15,000. The off-premises coverage is the greater of 10 percent (0.10 × 0.50) of coverage C, or $1,000. In this case, 10 percent of coverage C is $1,500; therefore, John will have $1,500 of off-premises unscheduled personal property coverage. If John has an HO-5 contract, the unscheduled personal property limit is $15,000 both on and off the premises except at a secondary residence.

In addition to providing protection for the personal property of an insured, forms HO-1 through HO-4 cover personal property of others. At the option of the named insured, property of others is protected while on the portion of the premises occupied exclusively by the insured. Off-premises protection also may be provided for guests and residence employees if the property of a guest is in a residence occupied by an insured. Unscheduled personal property of a residence employee is protected off the premises only if it is in the custody of the employee or in a residence occupied by an insured.

HO-5 covers the property owned by others located at any residence premises occupied by an insured. Residence employee coverage is available when the employee has custody of property away from the premises. In effect, HO-5 covers the personal property of individuals located in a residence occupied by an insured. HO-1 through HO-4 provide this coverage only at the described dwelling, i.e., off-premises coverage is restricted to guests or residence employees.

The limits of the insurer's liability under coverage C can be changed by one of several methods. The coverage C limit can be increased by providing higher limits in the policy. An insured might not want to increase the limits for all of coverage C. For example, due to a large amount of unscheduled property off the insured premises, a named insured might need to increase only the off-premises protection. HO-66 can be utilized to achieve this goal. This endorsement does not apply to HO-5 since it does not limit off-premises protection.

The amount of insurance applicable to coverage C may be reduced if an individual wants it lowered. Under the first three homeowners forms, coverage C can be reduced to 40 percent of coverage A. When the limit is lowered there is a small premium reduction. The reduction of coverage option is not available under HO-5.

When a homeowners policy is endorsed (HO-42) to cover the use of a portion of the described dwelling as an office, professional facility, private school, or studio, the unscheduled personal property limits must be increased. The 50 percent minimum requirement is raised to 60 percent.

Additional Living Expenses and Rental Value (Coverage D)

Section I of the homeowners policy not only provides property coverages but also time element or consequential loss coverage. Under coverage D of section I, two consequential forms of protection are provided. These are (1) additional living expense, and (2) fair rental value.

If the dwelling described in the policy is damaged by an insured peril and becomes uninhabitable, the named insured and the insured's family will be reimbursed under coverage D for any necessary additional living expenses incurred when suitable living accommodations are maintained elsewhere. The limit for coverage D, like the limits for coverages B and C, is a percentage of the described dwelling protection (coverage A) for HO-1 to HO-3 and HO-5 and a stated percentage of the unscheduled personal property (coverage C) for HO-4. The percentage is usually 10 (HO-1) or 20 (HO-2 to HO-5) percent. The additional living expense is paid only for the length of time necessary to repair or replace the damaged residence. If permanent housing can be found in a shorter period of time, then the shorter period of time will be the benefit pay-out period. The following example demonstrates how this coverage aids a named insured. After Susan Marian's home is damaged by fire, she and her family have to move into temporary quarters. The repairs to the home take sixty days. During this time, Susan rents a duplex at a cost of $395 per month. The utilities for the duplex are (1) water—$17 per month, (2) electricity—$90 per month, (3) gas—$25 per month, and (4) telephone—$12.50 per month plus an installation charge of $15. Susan's laundry bill increases from $15 per month to $40 per month because she cannot use her washer. All utilities in Susan's damaged home have been shut off resulting in the following savings: (1) water—$15 per month, (2) electricity—$140 per month, and (3) telephone—$12.50 per month. Although utility costs were eliminated, Susan still is required to pay the monthly mortgage payment of $360. The expenses paid by the insurer are calculated as shown in Table 3-1.

If the named insured has rented a portion of the described dwelling or an appurtenant structure, the fair rental value of the rented space is reimbursed by the insurer under coverage D. Like the additional living expense protection, noncontinuing expenses are excluded, and coverage is restricted by the overall limit of coverage D. The fair rental value is paid only for the length of time necessary to restore the rented portion.

Both the additional living expenses and the fair rental values may apply even when a direct loss has not occurred to the described dwelling or appurtenant structures. When access to the described premises is barred by order of a civil authority, both the time element coverages are applicable. However, the action taken by any civil authority must be the result of damage to neighboring premises caused by a peril covered in the policy.

Table 3-1

Additional Living Expenses Paid by the Insurer

	Actual Expenditures While Located in Temporary Quarters	What Normal Living Expenditures Would Have Otherwise Been	Covered Costs
Rent	$ 790.00	($ 0)†	$790.00
Water	34.00	(30.00)	4.00
Electricity	180.00	(280.00)	−(100.00)
Gas	50.00	(0)	50.00
Telephone	40.00	(25.00)	15.00
Laundry	40.00	(15.00)	25.00
	$1,134.00	($350.00)	$784.00

† Since the mortgage payments continued, there is no savings. The insurer would pay the named insured $784 in additional living expenses under coverage D.

Minimum Limits. Table 3-2 provides a summary of the standard minimum limits applicable to the various coverages under section I, HO-1 through HO-5. The limits for HO-6 are discussed later in this chapter.

Perils Insured Against

Generally, the same property is covered under the various homeowners contracts, but there is a major difference in the perils insured against in each policy. Two approaches are utilized in covering property. The approaches are (1) named perils, and (2) "all-risks." Named perils protection covers property against losses caused by a list of specified perils, e.g., fire, windstorm, hail, riot, and so on. In addition to restricting coverage to losses arising from a list of named perils, exclusions are contained in the policy. With "all-risks" coverage, every peril not specifically excluded is covered, helping to avoid the possibility of losses from unexpected perils.

When a loss arises under named perils coverage, the loss is covered only if one of the named perils is the *proximate* cause of the loss. According to *Black's Law Dictionary*, proximate cause is "that which, in a natural and continuous sequence, unbroken by any efficient intervening cause, produces . . . [the loss]."[3] Thus, proximate cause is not the same as immediate cause. Immediate cause is the peril closest to the loss.

Table 3-2
Standard Minimum Coverage Limits Under Section I of HO-1 Through HO-5

	HO-1	HO-2	HO-3	HO-4	HO-5
A. Dwelling, building equipment, fixtures, outdoor equipment, materials, and supplies	$8,000	$8,000	$8,000	N/A	$15,000
B. Appurtenant structures	10% of dwelling limit	10% of dwelling limit	10% of dwelling limit	N/A	10% of dwelling limit
C. (1) Unscheduled personal property (on premises)	50% of dwelling limit	50% of dwelling limit	50% of dwelling limit	$4,000 minimum	50% of dwelling limit
(2) Unscheduled personal property (off premises)	10% of coverage C(1) subject to a minimum of $1,000	10% of coverage C(1) subject to a minimum of $1,000	10% of coverage C(1) subject to a minimum of $1,000	10% of coverage C(1) subject to a minimum of $1,000	No restriction except at secondary residence where only 10% of coverage C(1) applies
D. Additional living expense and rental value	10% of dwelling limit	20% of dwelling limit	20% of dwelling limit	20% of coverage C(1)	20% of dwelling limit

Something else may have resulted in the immediate cause and is the proximate cause of the loss. For example, a fire may cause a building to collapse damaging another building. Any fire coverage on the second building would be applicable because the proximate cause of the loss was fire, not collapse. Excluded perils, like covered perils, must be the proximate cause of loss for protection not to be provided.

HO-1 offers the most restrictive coverage. Protection is written on a named perils basis with the following perils insured against: (1) fire, (2) lightning, (3) removal, (4) windstorm, (5) hail, (6) explosion, (7) riot, (8) civil commotion, (9) vehicles, (10) aircraft, (11) smoke, (12) vandalism, (13) malicious mischief, (14) glass breakage, and (15) theft. The coverage under HO-1 is similar to the protection afforded under the standard fire policy with an extended coverage endorsement. However, some differences exist.

The HO-1 protection against losses arising from the perils of vandalism, malicious mischief, glass breakage, and theft are not afforded by a fire policy with an extended coverage endorsement. Vandalism and malicious mischief are the willful and malicious destruction of insured property. The glass breakage peril covers only glass which is a part of the home and excludes glass items in the house, such as a glass vase.

The theft peril is applicable to losses arising from an attempt to steal or the actual stealing of property. The importance of the point should be obvious. First, property damaged during an attempted theft is covered even though it may not have been taken. Second, a theft or an attempted theft must occur for coverage to be activated. A presumption of theft is not sufficient to establish coverage. Unscheduled personal property which has been placed at some location other than the described dwelling for safekeeping is insured as if it were on the insured premises.

HO-2 also covers all property on a named perils basis. It contains the named perils found in HO-1 plus the following additional perils: (1) falling objects; (2) weight of ice, snow, or sleet; (3) collapse of buildings or any part thereof; (4) sudden and accidental tearing asunder, cracking, burning, or bulging of a steam or hot water heating system or of appliances for heating water; (5) accidental discharge or overflow of water or steam; (6) freezing of plumbing, heating, and air conditioning systems and domestic appliances; and (7) sudden and accidental injury from electrical currents artificially generated.

Most of these added perils are self-explanatory, but the collapse peril, which is not well defined, requires further discussion. Some courts have ruled that for this form of coverage to be applicable, a portion of the dwelling must totally collapse. Other courts have found some types of sinking, bulging, or cracking constitute collapse.[4]

In addition to containing more named perils than HO-1, HO-2 expands the definition of the named perils found in HO-1, e.g., fire or lightning, explosion, aircraft, vehicles, breakage of glass, theft, and smoke. The definition of fire or lightning used in HO-2 does not exclude artificially generated electric current as is the case in HO-1. Also, substantive differences exist in the definition of the explosion peril. The definition of explosion in HO-1 excludes:

> . . . loss by explosion of steam boilers, steam pipes, steam turbines or steam engines, if owned by, leased by or operated under the control of the insured.
>
> The following are not explosions within the intent or meaning of this peril (explosion):
> a. shock waves caused by aircraft, generally known as "sonic boom,"
> b. electric arcing, c. rupture or bursting of rotating or moving parts of machinery caused by centrifugal force or mechanical breakdown, d. water hammer, e. rupture or bursting of water pipes, or f. rupture, bursting, or operation of pressure relief devices.

These explosion exclusions do not appear in HO-2.

The vehicle and aircraft peril in HO-1 extends only to damage caused by a vehicle or aircraft coming in contact with insured property. Vehicle damage caused by a vehicle owned or operated by an occupant of the premises is excluded. Vehicle damage to fences, driveways, or walks is excluded as is damage to a vehicle or trailer. In HO-2, all aircraft damage is covered, and all damage caused by a vehicle is subject to the same restrictions as HO-1.

The amount of coverage for glass breakage is not limited in HO-2, while a $50 maximum is imposed in HO-1.

The smoke peril in HO-1 protects against sudden and accidental smoke losses from a cooking or heating unit at the insured residence; HO-2, against sudden and accidental smoke damage from almost any source, except that caused by agricultural smudging or industrial operations.

Finally, theft coverage under HO-2 covers losses that arise not only from stealing and attempts at stealing, but also from the disappearance of property ". . . from a known place under circumstances when a probability of theft exists." This protection is much broader than the theft protection in HO-1.

In HO-3, the dwelling described in the policy and any appurtenant structures are protected against all risks. Since additional living expenses are based on a loss to a described dwelling or appurtenant structure, the additional living expense benefit is also on an "all-risks" basis. Unscheduled personal property, however, is insured only for the named perils listed in HO-2. Form HO-3 does not contain an explicit

Table 3-3

Perils Insured Against in HO-1 through HO-5

	Described Dwelling and Appurtenant Structures	Unscheduled Personal Property
HO-1	*Basic perils* includes: fire, lightning, removal, windstorm, hail, explosion, riot, civil commotion, vehicles, aircraft, smoke, vandalism, malicious mischief, breakage of glass, and theft.	Basic perils
HO-2	*Broad form perils* includes the basic perils plus: falling objects, weight of ice, snow, or sleet, collapse of buildings or any part thereof, sudden and accidental tearing asunder, cracking, burning, or bulging of a steam or hot water heating system or of appliances for heating water, accidental discharge or overflow of water or steam, freezing of plumbing, heating, and air conditioning systems and appliances, and sudden and accidental injury from electrical currents artificially generated.	Broad form perils
HO-3	"All-risks"	Broad form perils
HO-4	N/A	Broad form perils
HO-5	"All-risks"	"All-risks"

breakage of glass peril like that in HO-1. Since this peril applies to the building, the "all-risks" coverage of HO-3 eliminates the need for this protection.

The tenant policy, HO-4, covers only unscheduled personal property for the same named perils found in HO-2. Additional living expense losses are also on a named perils basis in HO-4.

The most comprehensive coverage is provided in HO-5. All property, including the described dwelling, appurtenant structures, and unscheduled personal property, are insured against all risks not specifically excluded in the policy. Since the described dwelling and appurtenant structure coverages are written on an "all-risks" approach, the additional living expense coverage is on an "all-risks" basis.

Table 3-3 summarizes the basis for coverage provided in each homeowners form. Remember that different limitations and exclusions apply under each policy, and that two policies covering the same peril do not necessarily provide the same coverage.

Amount of Coverage

Although it is important to know what property and perils are insured in a homeowners policy, many other factors affect the amount paid to the insured. The actual cash value and replacement cost of property have a bearing on the amount of recovery. Exclusions, limitations, and deductibles can reduce the amount paid. Finally, valued policy statutes and inflation can have a bearing on the amount of insurance coverage. Each of these factors should be analyzed carefully when the amount of coverage is being considered.

Actual Cash Value and Replacement Cost The unscheduled personal property covered under a homeowners policy is insured for its actual cash value. Generally, the actual cash value is equal to the replacement cost less reductions resulting from depreciation and/or obsolescence. Conceivably, the actual cash value of a residence could be greater than the original purchase price.[5] In cases where there is a loss of an item that is part of a pair or set, the basis for settling the claim is not the value of the item. Instead, the ". . . measure of loss shall be a reasonable and fair proportion of the total value of the pair or set. . . ."

Losses to a dwelling and appurtenant structures are covered on an actual cash value or replacement cost basis. Replacement cost coverage is not extended to outdoor radio and television antennae and aerials, carpeting, awnings, domestic appliances, and outdoor equipment even though they may be part of a dwelling or appurtenant structure.

If the named insured purchases coverage equal to 80 percent (or more) of the replacement cost of the structure, then the replacement cost value of any loss will be paid in the following manner:

$$\begin{matrix} \text{Amount of Loss} \\ \text{(Based on Replacement Cost)} \end{matrix} \times \frac{\text{Amount of Insurance in the Policy}}{(0.80)(\text{Replacement Cost of Structure})} =$$

$$\begin{matrix} \text{Amount of Loss} \\ \text{Paid by Insurer} \end{matrix}$$

Obviously, if the named insured does not carry coverage equal to 80 percent of the replacement cost, then he or she is penalized. However, the homeowners contract stipulates that the named insured will receive the actual cash value of the loss if such an amount is greater than the result obtained utilizing the 80 percent replacement cost formula. Under no circumstances, however, will the contract pay more than the lesser of (1) the limits of the policy, (2) the amount necessary to actually effect repair, or (3) the replacement cost.

When calculating the replacement cost base, the named insured can exclude (1) excavations, (2) underground flues and pipes, (3) underground wiring and drains, (4) foundations, (5) piers, and (6) other supports, as described. These exclusions reduce the amount of coverage that must be carried in order to qualify for the replacement cost coverage. Since the price of land on which a home is built is not included in the replacement cost calculation, insurance coverage can be significantly lower than the purchase price of a residence, without the named insured being penalized. The following examples illustrate how losses under a homeowners policy are calculated.

1. Carol Adams owns a home purchased in 1969 for a total purchase price of $30,000. When the home was purchased, Carol obtained an HO-3 policy for $20,000. At the time of the purchase, the land on which the house was located was valued at $7,000, and the foundation and excavation work were worth $3,000.

   Recently, Carol's home was damaged by fire. The replacement cost of the loss is estimated at $7,000, but the actual cash value of the loss is only $4,000. The replacement cost of the home, excluding land, is now $40,000. The foundation and excavation work is currently valued at $4,000. Using the replacement cost formula, the insurance company will pay $4,861 toward the loss. The calculation is shown below.

$$(\text{Loss}) \times \frac{(\text{Amount of Coverage in the Policy})}{(0.80)(\text{Replacement Cost})} =$$

$$\text{Amount of Loss}$$
$$\text{Paid by Insurer}$$

$$\$7,000 \times \frac{\$20,000}{(0.80)(\$40,000 - \$4,000)} = \$4,861$$

   If the actual cash value of the loss had been $5,000 instead of $4,000, then the insurer would not have paid $4,861. Rather, the insurer would have paid the actual cash value of $5,000.

2. Tom Williams owns a home which has a replacement cost value of $60,000 exclusive of the land and any foundations and supports. Tom's agent sold Tom a $30,000 HO-5 policy in 1958 which has never been updated. Recently, Tom's home was damaged by lightning and an ensuing fire. The damage is estimated at $50,000 on a replacement cost basis and $40,000 on an actual cash value basis.

   Utilizing the replacement cost formula, the amount to be paid by the insurer can be calculated. The amount under this approach would be $31,250.

$$\$50,000 \times \frac{\$30,000}{(0.80)(\$60,000)} = \$31,250$$

The actual cash value of the loss is greater than the amount using the formula; so, normally the insurer would pay the actual cash value. Unfortunately, Tom only has $30,000 of coverage. Therefore, the amount actually paid by the insurance company is $30,000.

Homeowners contracts stipulate that when a loss exceeds $1,000 or 5 percent of the coverage applicable to a structure, the replacement cost will not be paid until actual repair or replacement is accomplished.

Limitations Nearly every insurance policy contains limitations and exclusions to meet one or more of several objectives. First, the inclusion of these items allows a company to reduce its premiums. Second, the insured has control over some of the items excluded; if coverage were allowed, extreme adverse selection could be introduced. Third, exclusions and limitations can be used to reduce a company's exposure for perils it cannot profitably cover due to the catastrophic nature of the peril. Flood is an example. Since catastrophic perils are not faced by all insureds, a company could face severe adverse selection if it covered these perils on an optional basis.

Finally, some exposures are covered under particular forms designed to handle specialized exposures. For example, theft coverage on furs is available under a personal property floater; the same protection in a homeowners policy is limited to $500.

Although limitations and exclusions are used by insurers to restrict an insured's coverage, they are significantly different. An exclusion bars coverage. A limitation permits coverage but in some way restricts the peril or the amount of coverage provided.

Every homeowners policy contains special limits on certain kinds of unscheduled personal property. In HO-1 there is a limit of $100 per occurrence on the combined losses of money, bullion, numismatic property, and bank notes. A $500 limitation per occurrence is applicable to all losses arising from securities, accounts, bills, deeds, evidences of debt, letters of credit, notes (other than bank notes), passports, railroad and other tickets, and stamps (including stamp collections). Another $500 limitation per occurrence applies to theft of jewelry, watches, necklaces, bracelets, gems, precious and semiprecious stones, gold, platinum, and furs. It should be noted that the $500 limitation is applicable only if the peril causing the loss is theft.

Manuscripts are covered for losses up to $1,000. Watercraft and their furnishings, equipment, and outboard motors including their trailers are insured for up to $500. Trailers by themselves are insured for

Table 3-4

Hypothetical Theft Loss:
Items Taken and Amount Paid

Loss	Amount Paid by Insurer [†]	Amount Paid by Insured
$ 200 (money)	$100	$ 100
1,900 (bullion)	(no additional coverage since money and bullion are in the same category)	1,900
250 (jewelry)	250	0
500 (watch)	250 (balance of $500 limit)	250
Total $2,850	$600	$2,250

[†]Any deductible in the policy would be subtracted from the amount paid by the insurer.

up to $500. Note, however, that this latter addition does not mean that the named insured can collect $500 for a damaged boat and $500 for the boat's damaged trailer. The named insured can collect under only one of these options. The following example illustrates how these limitations function.

While she was sleeping, Sarah Edward's home was burglarized. The list of items taken and the amount paid by the insurer are shown in Table 3-4.

Homeowners forms HO-2 through HO-4 contain the same special property limitations found in HO-1. HO-5 basically has the same type of limitations in the other forms; however, the limitations are presented differently in HO-5 because it is not a named peril policy.

Fifty dollars is the maximum amount payable for a glass breakage loss in HO-1. This limitation is not found in the other homeowners policies.

Trees, shrubs, plants, and lawns are insured under each of the homeowners forms. A loss is not covered unless it results from (1) fire, (2) lightning, (3) explosion, (4) riot, (5) civil commotion, (6) vandalism, (7) malicious mischief, (8) theft, (9) aircraft, or (10) vehicles not covered or operated by an occupant of the premises. Under HO-1, HO-2, HO-3, and HO-5, the maximum amount payable for all losses to trees, shrubs, plants, and lawns for one occurrence is 5 percent of coverage A. The 5 percent coverage is subject to a maximum internal limit of $250 for any one tree, shrub, or plant which includes the cost of removal, if any. HO-4 has the same internal limit, but aggregate coverage per occurrence is 10 percent of the unscheduled personal property coverage (coverage C).

Exclusions and Restrictions   Under either a named perils or an "all-risks" policy, exclusions and restrictions reduce the situations where insurance coverage is applicable.

All of the homeowners forms have numerous exclusions. The conditions section of a homeowners policy contains exclusions for nuclear reaction or radiation, radioactive contamination, and warlike action. Also found in the general conditions section is an exclusion for:

> . . . insurrection, rebellion, revolution, civil war, usurped power, or action taken by governmental authority in hindering, combating, or defending against such an occurrence; seizure or destruction under quarantine or customs regulations, confiscation by order of any government or public authority; or risks of contraband or illegal transportation or trade.

The contract exclusions in each form, other than those found in the conditions section, are presented in order from HO-1 through HO-5.

Exclusions and restrictions in HO-1, HO-2, and HO-4 can be grouped into three categories: (1) those applicable to all property, (2) those applicable to a specific coverage such as coverage A, and (3) those related to specific perils. HO-3 and HO-5 are difficult to group because of the "all-risks" nature of their coverage. As nearly as possible, however, the groupings will be maintained throughout the presentation of the exclusions in these two policies.

HO-1.   Several of the exclusions and restrictions found in HO-1 can be categorized as additional exclusions and restrictions. The first exclusion pertains to governmental actions and frequently is called the demolition exclusion. When a state or local law results in the destruction or demolition of an insured's building, the insurer is not liable for the loss. An example illustrates how this might occur.

Assume that 60 percent of a home is destroyed by fire. If the house is repaired, it will not meet the current local building standards. The city has an ordinance stipulating that when more than 50 percent of a building is damaged, it cannot be repaired unless it meets the current building code. The owner is forced to tear down the house and incur a total loss although the fire only damaged 60 percent of the house. The insurer's liability is limited to 60 percent of the value of the home.

Losses caused by, resulting from, or aggravated by earth movement, including earthquake; volcanic eruption; landslide; mudflow; and sinking, rising, or shifting of the earth are covered only if loss by fire or explosion ensues. The insurer is liable only for such ensuing loss.

Exclusion number three relates to damage by water. Floods, surface water, tidal waves, waves, tidal water, and overflow of streams or other bodies of water are excluded perils. Neither water that backs up through sewers or drains nor water below the surface of the ground is covered. However, fires and explosions following any of these events are insured. The earth movement and water below the ground exclusions do not bar recovery if the earth movement or water was caused by leaking plumbing. In the case of Koncilja v. Trinity Universal Insurance Company, a state's Court of Appeals:

> . . . held that where accidental leakage and discharge of water upon and into ground from within a plumbing system of a house was properly found to be the efficient proximate cause of the loss, exclusions from policy, which included losses caused by water below the surface of the ground and caused by any earth movement, were not applicable. . . .[6]

In this situation, leaking pipes in the concrete floor of a home discharged water into the ground below the home. As a result, the earth shifted and the house settled and cracked.

In another case, an insurer was required to pay for damages to the foundation of the insured residence after water escaping from a sewer line caused sagging and cracking of the foundation. The insurer had attempted to deny liability based on the below surface water exclusion; however, the court held that the exclusion applied ". . . only to water which was below the surface of the ground as the result of natural causes."[7]

The accidental discharge of water exclusion is not important in HO-1 because the accidental discharge of water is not a covered peril. It is covered in the other policies.

Power, heating, and cooling failures are insured if they result from damage to power, heating, and cooling units on the insured premises. The damage must be the direct result of a named peril insured in the policy. Other power, heating, and cooling failures are not insured. Thus, damage resulting from a failure at a power plant cutting off a named insured's electricity would not be covered.

As well as the additional exclusions, there are specific exclusions and restrictions applicable to each type of coverage. The only restriction in coverage A relates to the use of the insured's dwelling: the principal function must be residential. Appurtenant structures used for business purposes or rented to someone other than a tenant of the described dwelling are not covered. However, an appurtenant structure rented solely as a private garage is not excluded from coverage.

There are nine exclusions found in coverage C. Under the HO-1 policy, unscheduled personal property does not encompass (1) animals, birds, or fish; (2) motorized vehicles, except those used only on the premises and not licensed for road use; (3) aircraft; (4) the property of roomers or boarders not related to the insured; (5) property carried or held as a sample or for sale or delivery after sale; (6) property rented or held for rental to others; (7) business property away from premises; (8) any device or instrument for the recording, reproduction, or recording and reproduction of sound which may be operated by power from the electrical system of a motor vehicle, or any tape, wire, record disc, or other medium for use with any such device or instrument while the property is in or upon a motor vehicle; and (9) property separately described and specifically insured, i.e., property insured under a separate policy or in another section of the homeowners policy.

The business property exclusion is not sufficiently broad to include personal property taken to work for the convenience of the insured. As an example, in Riddle v. Allstate Insurance Company, the insured contended that personal property, e.g., a lamp, plastic flowers, a pen and pencil set, and books at his office, were intended to enhance the appearance of his office. The insured wanted the insurer to pay for these items when they were damaged by water from a hurricane. The insurer claimed that these items were personal property pertaining to business and, therefore, not covered because of the off-premises business personal property exclusion. The Louisiana court ruling on the case stated that it found, ". . . it difficult to comprehend . . ." how these items, ". . . are necessary in the management of a retail merchandising business . . ." and, therefore, the items were not business property.[8]

Coverage D only has one exclusion. It does not reimburse the insured for costs that result if a lease or other written or oral agreement must be canceled.

Fifteen perils are insured against under HO-1. However, all losses resulting from a peril listed in the policy may not be reimbursed by the insurer. In the following paragraphs, the covered perils with their exclusions, if any, are considered.

Fire and lightning are both covered perils; however, damage done by artificially generated current is excluded under HO-1. The exclusion is applicable whether the current damages or destroys electrical appliances, devices, fixtures, or wiring. If a fire occurs as a result of artificial current, the loss created by the fire would be insured, but the initial loss due to the current would not be insured.

Excluded under the perils of windstorm and hail are loss by (1) frost, (2) cold weather, and (3) ice, snow, and sleet even if driven by the wind. Damage by rain, snow, sand, or dust to the inside of a building or the property in the building is not covered unless wind or hail first damages the roof or walls of the building.

Most watercraft on the insured premises are not protected. Generally, only watercraft that are inside an enclosed area are insured. Rowboats and canoes are not subject to the indoor requirement.

Sonic boom, electric arcing, rupture or bursting of machinery caused by centrifugal force, water hammers, rupture or bursting of water pipes, or the rupture, bursting, or operation of pressure relief devices are not considered explosions in HO-1. Therefore, any losses arising from these would not be insured under the explosion peril. Explosions of steam boilers, pipes, turbines, or engines are not classified as explosions in the policy.

Vehicle and aircraft perils contained in HO-1 cover damage done by vehicles and aircraft by physical contact. Coverage is not applicable to vehicular damage to fences, driveways, and walks, nor to damage to or caused by vehicles owned or operated by an occupant of the insured premises.

Smoke from a fireplace is not covered. However, the accidental discharge of smoke from any heating or cooking unit is insured.

Under the standard fire policy, which may be a part of the homeowners policy in some states, coverage lapses if a building is vacant or unoccupied for sixty consecutive days. This limitation is modified in all homeowners forms.

The conditions section applicable to the property coverage states that the insurer grants the named insured permission:

> . . . for the premises to be vacant or unoccupied without limit of time, except as otherwise provided in this policy for certain specified perils; however, a building in the course of construction shall not be deemed vacant; . . . .

In HO-1, losses from vandalism or malicious mischief and glass breakage are not insured if the dwelling is vacant for more than thirty consecutive days.

The named peril of theft contains three types of general exclusions: (1) the general theft exclusions applicable to all property, (2) exclusions applicable while the described dwelling is rented, and (3) exclusions applicable to property away from the described premises.

The general theft exclusion lists four types of losses that are not insured. Protection is neither available for any theft committed by an insured, nor for a theft in or to a dwelling under construction. For coverage to be in effect, the dwelling must be completed and occupied. Materials and supplies located at a building site come under this exclusion. Credit card losses as well as forgery or alterations of negotiable instruments, such as checks, drafts, promissory notes, and bills of exchange are excluded. Finally, the loss of a precious or semi-precious stone from its setting is uninsured.

Exclusions applicable while the insured dwelling is being rented are (1) loss of money, bullion, numismatic property (coin collections), and bank notes; (2) loss of securities, accounts, bills, deeds, evidences of debts, letters of credit, notes (other than bank notes), passports, tickets, stamps, and stamp collections; and (3) loss of jewelry, watches, necklaces, bracelets, gems, precious and semiprecious stones, articles of gold and platinum, or furs. Losses resulting from the actions of a tenant, the tenant's employees, or members of the tenant's household are not covered.

The third category of exclusions applies to property away from the described premises. When an insured temporarily resides at a location other than the dwelling described in the policy, theft coverage is available. If an insured owns, rents, or occupies a dwelling on a regular basis, he or she would not have coverage on property at the secondary residence unless staying at the secondary residence at the time of the loss. This distinction was the focal point in Bryan v. Granite State Insurance Company. A couple rented an attic apartment in a city as a place to stay when they were in town for social activities. Personal property was kept at the temporary residence when the couple returned to their permanent residence. While the couple was at their permanent dwelling, personal property was stolen from the temporary residence. The couple contended that the property was insured since it had been stolen from a temporary residence. The court held that the coverage would have been in effect only if the couple resided at the apartment at the time of the loss. If the couple had been in town at a party with plans to stay at the apartment at the time of the loss, the insurer would have been liable.[9]

Loss of personal property in an unattended, locked, motorized vehicle or trailer is insured if there are signs of forcible entry on the exterior of the vehicle or trailer. If a locked door were opened with a coat hanger, leaving no marks, the insurer would not pay for the loss. However, if the thief broke a window, the personal property in the car would be insured. When a vehicle has to be turned over to a bailee, personal property coverage is not limited even if the vehicle is not locked. Coverage is also available if the personal property is on a public conveyance.

Personal property in an unattended watercraft is insured on the same basis as property in an unattended vehicle or trailer. Coverage is extended only to property in a locked area, and when property is missing, signs of forcible entry into the locked area must be present. Also excluded are the watercraft themselves, their furnishings, equipment, outboard motors, and trailers. The exclusions relative to HO-1 are presented in Table 3-5.

HO-2. The additional and property-related exclusions are very similar in HO-1 and HO-2. The major difference occurs in the additional exclusions relating to earth movement. HO-1 does not cover losses ". . . contributed to or aggravated by any earth movement . . . ; unless loss by

Table 3-5

Major Exclusions and Restrictions Found in HO-1*

Additional:
  "Demolition" (structure)
  Flood, surface water, tidal water, overflow of bodies of water, etc.
  Earth movement, including but not limited to earthquake, landslide, volcanic eruption, etc.
  Power, heating, or cooling failure
Coverages:
  Coverage A:
    Nonresidential dwellings
  Coverage B:
    Structures used for business
    Structures rented or leased (unless structure is used as a private garage or is rented to a tenant of the dwelling)
  Coverage C:
    Animals, fish, or birds
    Motorized vehicles
    Aircraft
    Property of roomers or boarders not related to the insured
    Business samples, property held for sale, or property rented or held for rental
    Business property off premises
    Recording or reproduction equipment for use in a vehicle
    Property separately described and insured by other coverage
  Coverage D:
    Cancellation of lease or written or oral agreement
Perils:
  Fire or Lightning:
    Artificially generated current
  Windstorm or Hail:
    Frost or cold weather or ice (other than hail), snow, or sleet
    Rain, snow, sand, or dust to the interior or property inside (unless these elements enter through an opening made by windstorm or hail)
    Watercraft and related equipment not fully enclosed in a building (except rowboats and canoes)
  Explosion:
    Steam boilers, pipes, turbines, or engines
    Excluded as not being included in the definition of an explosion are: sonic boom, electric arcing, rupture or bursting of machinery, water hammer, rupture or bursting of pipes, rupture or bursting or operation of pressure relief valves
  Aircraft:
    Only physical contact
  Vehicles:
    Only physical contact
    Fences, driveways, and walks damaged by any vehicle
    Any damage by vehicle owned or operated by an occupant of the residence
    Any damage to any motor vehicle or trailer

Smoke:
All smoke except from cooking or heating units in or on premises (Smoke from fireplaces is not covered.)
Vandalism, Malicious Mischief, and Glass Breakage:
Coverage voided if premises left vacant for 30 days prior to loss
Theft:
General:
Committed by an insured
Dwelling under construction
Credit card theft, loss by forgery, or alteration of documents
Precious or semi-precious stone(s) from its setting
While Described Dwelling Is Being Rented:
Money, bullion, numismatic property, bank notes
Negotiable paper, including tickets and stamps
Jewelry, watches, necklaces, and similar items
Furs
Caused by a tenant, a tenant's employees, or members of a tenant's household
Property Away from Premises:
Property in a dwelling that is not a temporary residence for an insured
Property in unlocked car (other than a public conveyance) or boat or locked car or boat unless there are signs of forcible entry
Watercraft and their furnishings
Trailers

---

*The general conditions exclusions relating to nuclear reaction, war, and insurrection are also applicable.

fire or explosion ensues. . . ." In HO-2 glass breakage is added to the ensuing losses that are insured, and the entire exclusion does not apply to loss by theft. The exclusions relating to the perils named in both HO-1 and HO-2 are similar.

The fire or lightning perils in HO-2 do not contain an exclusion for artificially generated electrical currents. In fact, one of the additional named perils found in HO-2 and not in HO-1 is "sudden and accidental injury from electrical currents artificially generated." The only exceptions to the additional named peril in HO-2 are tubes, transistors, and electronic components.

Explosion, as a named peril in HO-2, is not restricted by definition or specific exclusion. Therefore, all explosions that are not excluded by some other portion of the policy are covered automatically. The aircraft and vehicle perils, like the peril of explosion, are expanded under HO-2 in two ways. First, physical contact between the vehicle or aircraft and the property is not required and second, vehicle damage to fences, driveways, and walks is covered. The only exclusion for the latter item relates to damage caused by a vehicle owned or operated by occupants of the premises. Under HO-1, the same damage is excluded if it is accomplished by any vehicle, rather than a vehicle owned or operated by an occupant of the premises. As previously noted, smoke coverage is not as restricted in HO-2. Only smoke from agricultural smudging or industrial operations is not insured. This broader definition of smoke damage is found throughout the other homeowners forms wherever insurance against smoke damage is available.

The theft exclusions diverge in only one area—the exclusions relative to property away from the premises. Under HO-2 property left in an unattended car may be covered even if forcible entry cannot be proven. Unscheduled personal property is covered if it is located in a vehicle when the vehicle is stolen and the vehicle is not recovered within thirty days.

The additional provisions relating to named perils found in HO-2 also contain exclusions. Damage inflicted by falling objects is insured. However, the interior of a building or the personal property contained in the building is not insured against loss from falling objects unless the exterior of the building is first damaged by the falling object. Since many falling objects will not damage the interior of a building without first damaging the exterior, this exclusion has a limited impact on claims. Outdoor equipment, awnings, and fences damaged by falling objects also are not covered.

Like the falling objects peril, the named peril of the weight of ice, snow, or sleet excludes loss arising from damage to outdoor equipment, awnings, and fences. In addition, damage from freezing, thawing, or the pressure of ice or water to (1) fences, (2) pavements, (3) patios, (4) swimming pools, (5) foundations, (6) retaining walls, (7) bulkheads, (8) piers, (9) wharves, or (10) docks is excluded.

Buildings, as well as any portion of a building, are covered against collapse. Damage done by the portion of the building that collapses is likewise insured, but collapse of the following items independently is not covered: (1) outdoor equipment, (2) awnings, (3) fences, (4) pavements, (5) patios, (6) swimming pools, (7) underground pipes, (8) flues, (9) drains, (10) cesspools, (11) septic tanks, (12) foundations, (13) retaining walls, (14) bulkheads, (15) piers, (16) wharves, or (17) docks. Collapse is further restricted to situations not involving settling, cracking, shrinkage, bulging, or expansion.

Loss from accidental discharge or overflow of water or steam from within plumbing, heating, or air conditioning systems or domestic appliances is not covered if (1) it is caused by repeated seepage or leakage over a long period of time, or (2) if the building covered had been vacant for at least thirty days immediately preceding the loss. Damage to the subsystem or appliance itself is excluded.

Freezing is also excluded under the peril covering sudden and accidental tearing asunder, cracking, burning, or bulging of a steam or hot water system, or appliances for heating water. The freezing exclusions are partially compensated by another peril that protects against the freezing of plumbing, heating, and air conditioning systems and domestic appliances. The exclusions for HO-2 are summarized in Table 3-6.

HO-3 and HO-4. The additional exclusions found in HO-2 are contained in HO-3. However, since HO-3 provides "all-risks" coverage, some exclusions found under the named perils section of HO-1 and HO-2 are contained in the additional exclusions section of HO-3. For example, the exclusion relating to losses to fences, pavements, patios, and so on from freezing, thawing, or from the pressure or weight of ice or water is found in the general section.

Exclusions relating to specific coverages are slightly different. Coverages A, B, and D, the "all-risks" coverages, do not cover (1) wear and tear; (2) marring or scratching; (3) deterioration; (4) inherent vice; (5) latent defects; (6) mechanical breakdown; (7) rust; (8) mold; (9) wet or dry rot; (10) contamination; (11) smog; (12) smoke from agricultural smudging or industrial operations; (13) settling, cracking, shrinkage, bulging, or expansion of pavements, patios, foundations, walls, floors, roofs, or ceilings; (14) birds; (15) vermin; (16) rodents; (17) insects; or (18) domestic animals. If any of these result in fire, smoke, explosion, collapse of a building, glass breakage, or water loss that is covered in the policy, the ensuing loss is covered. As an illustration, assume that a dog knocked over a lamp, damaging a wall. As a result, the lamp bulb shorts and starts a fire. The damage to the wall by the lamp is not covered; however, the fire loss is covered. Other exclusions under coverages A, B, and D are (1) theft losses in or to a dwelling that is not completed and occupied; (2) loss from the continuous leakage of water or steam from within a plumbing, heating, or air conditioning system or from within a domestic appliance; and (3) loss from vandalism or glass breakage if vacant more than thirty days immediately preceding the loss.

Since only unscheduled personal property is covered on a named perils basis under HO-3, a comparison on a named perils basis is difficult. Basically, the exclusions and the named perils found in HO-2 are applicable to coverage C in HO-3. The major differences lie in the exclusions relating to (1) falling objects; (2) the weight of ice, snow, or sleet; (3) collapse of buildings; and (4) the accidental discharge, leakage, or overflow of water or steam.

The exclusions found in the named perils coverage of HO-4 are similar to those found in HO-3. The similarity results because both contracts cover unscheduled personal property on a named perils basis. The exclusions in HO-3 and HO-4 are summarized in Table 3-7.

Table 3-6

Major Exclusions Found in HO-2*

Additional:
　Basically the same exclusions except for the additional coverage for glass breakage under the earth movement exclusion
Coverages:
　Coverage A:
　　Same as HO-1
　Coverage B:
　　Same as HO-1
　Coverage C:
　　Same as HO-1
　Coverage D:
　　Same as HO-1
Perils:
　Fire or Lightning:
　　No exclusion for artificially generated current since it is an insured peril in HO-2
　　Artificially generated current losses except those to tubes, transistors, and electronic components are insured
　Windstorm or Hail:
　　Same as HO-1
　Explosion:
　　No exclusions
　Aircraft:
　　No exclusions
　Vehicles:
　　Damage to fences, driveways, and walks by vehicle owned or operated by an occupant
　Smoke:
　　Agricultural smudging and industrial operations
　Theft:
　　General:
　　　Same as HO-1
　　While Described Dwelling Is Being Rented:
　　　Same as HO-1
　　Property Away From Premises:
　　　Same as HO-1 except unscheduled personal property is not excluded if it is in a vehicle when the vehicle is stolen (assumes vehicle is not recovered in thirty days)
　Falling Objects:
　　Outdoor equipment, awnings, fences
　　Interior of residence or property on the inside of the dwelling unless falling object first damages exterior
　Weight of Ice, Snow, or Sleet:
　　Outdoor equipment, awnings, fences
　　Freezing, thawing, or pressure of ice or water to fences, pavements, patios, swimming pools, foundations, retaining walls, bulkheads, piers, wharves, or docks

No coverage for property contained in the building unless building
   damaged first
Collapse:
   Outdoor equipment, awnings, fences, pavements, patios, swimming
      pools, underground flues, drains, cesspools, septic tanks, founda-
      tions, retaining walls, bulkheads, piers, wharves, or docks unless
      the direct result of a collapse of a building
   Settling, shrinkage, bulging, or expansion
Accidental Discharge or Overflow of Water or Steam:
   Dwelling leaks over long periods of time
   System from which water or steam escapes
   Freezing
   Vacancy for more than 30 days immediately preceding the loss
Accidental Tearing Asunder, Cracking, Burning, Bulging of Steam or
      Hot Water System or of Appliances for Hot Water:
   Freezing
Freezing of Plumbing, Heating, and Air Conditioning Systems and
      Domestic Appliances:
   Vacancy restriction

---

*The general conditions exclusions relating to nuclear reaction, war, and insurrection also
are applicable.

HO-5. In HO-5, as in HO-3, the additional exclusions section
includes items that were named peril exclusions under HO-1 and HO-2.
Again, this situation arises because of the "all-risks" nature of the
coverages in HO-5. The coverage exclusions in HO-1, HO-2, and HO-3
are repeated in HO-5.

The wear and tear exclusion found in HO-3 is also found in HO-5
but is applicable to all coverages rather than just to coverages A, B, and
D. The additional exclusions in HO-5 also contain three of the four
standard exclusions, specifically flood, demolition, and power failure.
Other exclusions applicable to all coverages in HO-5 include (1) loss of
fences, pavements, patios, etc., caused by freezing, thawing, or by the
pressure or weight of ice or water; (2) loss of or to a dwelling under
construction; and (3) loss to plumbing, heating, air conditioning systems,
or domestic appliances.

Coverages A, B, and D have three other exclusions. One of these is
the earth movement exception found in all homeowners forms. The
second is the leakage of water or steam over a long period of time.
Finally, vandalism and malicious mischief and glass breakage are
excluded if the dwelling has been vacant for at least thirty days.

Coverage C has four exclusions applicable only to personal property.
Credit card thefts and forgery losses are exempted from coverage.
Likewise, humidity and temperature changes are excluded unless rain,
snow, sleet, or hail is the direct cause of loss. In addition, property that is
being repaired or refinished is not insured against damage occurring

Table 3-7

Major Exclusions and Restrictions Found in HO-3 and HO-4*

HO-3

Additional:
  Demolition
  Flood, surface water, tidal water, overflow of bodies of water, etc.
  Water backup, water below surface of ground
  Earth movement, including but not limited to earthquake, volcanic eruption, landslide, etc.
  Power, heating, or cooling failure
  Fences, pavements, patios, swimming pools, foundations, retaining walls, bulkheads, or docks if loss caused by freezing, thawing, or pressure or weight of ice or water
Coverages:
  Coverage A:
    Nonresidential dwellings
  Coverage C:
    Animals, fish, or birds
    Motorized vehicles, except those pertaining to the service of the premises and not licensed for road use; aircraft; property of roomers or boarders not related to the insured
    Business property held for sale or samples
    Property rented or held for rental
    Business property off premises
    Recording or reproduction equipment for use in a vehicle
    Property insured by other insurer
  Coverages A, B, and D:
    Wear and tear, marring or scratching, deterioration, inherent vice, latent defects, mechanical breakdown, rust, mold, wet or dry rot, contamination, smog, smoke from agricultural smudging or industrial operations, settling, cracking, shrinkage, bulging or expansion of pavements, patios, foundations, walls, floors, roofs or ceilings, birds, vermin, rodents, insects, domestic animals (unless insured peril ensues)
    Theft to dwelling under construction
    Continuous leakage of water or steam
    Vandalism or malicious mischief if dwelling vacant
Perils:
  (Coverage C only)
  All the named peril exclusions in HO-2 are found in HO-3.

*The general conditions exclusions relating to nuclear reaction, war, and insurrection are also applicable. HO-4 has the same additional exclusions and the same exclusions for unscheduled personal property as HO-3.

during the repairing or refinishing process. This exclusion does not apply to watches, jewelry, or furs.

The final unscheduled personal property exclusion relates to breakage. When any of the following items are broken, they are not covered under the policy: (1) eyeglasses, (2) glassware, (3) statues, (4) marble, (5) bric-a-brac, (6) porcelains, and (7) other fragile articles. "Other fragile articles" do not include jewelry, watches, bronzes, cameras, or photographic lenses.

The objective of the insurer under the breakage exclusion is to eliminate the common or expected accidents. Therefore, breakage is covered if it is caused by (1) fire; (2) lightning; (3) windstorm; (4) hail; (5) smoke (other than smoke from agricultural smudging or industrial operations); (6) explosion; (7) riot; (8) civil commotion; (9) falling aircraft; (10) vehicle collision; (11) vandalism; (12) malicious mischief; (13) collapse of a building; (14) earthquake; (15) water damage (not otherwise excluded); (16) theft or attempted theft; and (17) sudden and accidental tearing asunder, cracking, burning, or bulging of a steam or hot water system. Table 3-8 contains a summary of the exclusions for HO-5.

Handling Exclusions and Limitations Many of the exclusions and limitations found in the homeowners policy can be amended by endorsement. A brief presentation of some of the endorsements utilized to amend the exclusions and limitations will convey the amount of flexibility available under a homeowners policy.

Amendment of Exclusions. A federal law restricting a credit card owner's liability to $50 for the unauthorized use of a card has caused people to question the value of credit card coverage. However, an individual with five to ten credit cards can still suffer a substantial loss. Also, it should be remembered that the endorsement attached to a homeowners policy to provide credit card coverage provides protection against depositors forgery in addition to credit card forgery. The endorsement is extremely inexpensive relative to the total homeowners premium, and is not subject to the deductible otherwise applicable to property losses under the policy.

Credit card and depositors coverage can be added to a homeowners policy by attaching endorsement HO-53, the credit card and depositors forgery coverage endorsement. The insurer's limit of liability stated in the endorsement is ascertained independently of the other coverages in a homeowners policy. The endorsement protects the insured against losses as a result of the unauthorized use of a lost or stolen credit card. The insurer has the duty to defend the insured against suits attempting to hold the insured responsible for a loss covered by the endorsement even if the suits are groundless, false, or fraudulent. As in most defense

Table 3-8

Major Exclusions and Restrictions Found in HO-5*

Coverages:
 Coverages A, B, C, and D:
  Wear and tear; marring or scratching; deterioration; inherent vice; latent defect; mechanical breakdown; rust; mold; dry or wet rot; contamination; smog; smoke from agricultural smudging or industrial operations; settling, cracking, shrinkage, bulging, or expansion of pavements, patios, foundations, walls, floors, roofs, or ceilings; birds, vermin, rodents, insects, domestic animals
  Theft to dwelling under construction
  Flood, surface water, tidal water, overflow of bodies of water, etc.
  Fences, pavements, patios, swimming pools, foundations, retaining walls, bulkheads, piers, wharves, or docks by freezing, thawing, or by pressure or weight of ice or water whether driven by the wind or not
  Demolition
  Power failure
 Coverages A, B, and D:
  Earth movement
  Continuous leakage of water or steam
  Vandalism, malicious mischief, and glass breakage if building is vacant for 30 days
 Coverage C:
  Breakage of eyeglasses, glassware, statuary, marble, bric-a-brac, porcelain, and similar fragile articles (unless caused by certain named perils)
  Dampness or temperature extremes (unless directly caused by rain, snow, sleet, or hail)
  Damage resulting from property being refurbished, renovated, or repaired (except watches, jewelry, and furs)
  Credit card losses
  Forgery or alterations of checks, drafts, etc.

---

*The general conditions exclusions relating to nuclear reaction, war, and insurrection also are applicable.

provisions, the amount spent to defend the insured does not reduce the limit of liability. The depositors forgery section of the endorsement sets forth the coverage for the insured and the insured's bank to be:

> ... forgery or alteration of, on or in any check, draft, promissory note, bill of exchange or similar written promise, order or direction to pay a sum certain in money, made or drawn by or drawn upon the Insured or made or drawn by one acting as agent of the Insured, or purporting to have been made or drawn as hereinbefore set forth. ...

Legal expenses incurred by the insured or his or her bank in defense of a suit to enforce payment of a forged document are covered. Counterfeit money coverage also is afforded. The insurer restricts its liability in counterfeit cases to $50 per transaction and $100 in total.

There are several important exclusions in this endorsement. The depository forgery and counterfeit money coverages do not extend to business transactions. The credit card coverage does not apply to use of a card by a resident of the named insured's household or to an individual to whom a credit card has been entrusted.

HO-54 and HO-55, when attached to a homeowners form, delete exclusions for earthquake damage and volcanic eruption found in section I of the homeowners policy. HO-54 is used with HO-1, HO-2, HO-3, and HO-4 while HO-55 is utilized to amend section I of HO-5.

An earthquake is defined as all shocks occurring within seventy-two hours of an initial shock. If one shock occurs on Wednesday and another on Thursday, both shocks would be considered the same earthquake. If the two shocks took place ten days apart, then they would be considered two separate occurrences. A flood or tidal wave created by an earthquake or volcanic eruption is not covered.

A flat deductible of 2 percent is included in these endorsements. Property insured on an actual cash value basis is subject to a deductible equal to 2 percent of the actual cash value. If replacement cost is the basis of a claim, then the deductible applies to the replacement cost. Regardless of which basis is applicable, the deductible applies separately to coverages A, B, and C.

Use of HO-55 basically gives the same effect as HO-54. The major difference between the endorsements is that in HO-55 only coverages A and B are amended to cover the perils of earthquake and volcanoes. Coverage C does not need to be amended since the earthquake exclusion in HO-5 does not apply to coverage C.

Under HO-2, HO-3, and HO-4, property in unattended vehicles or watercraft is insured only if the vehicles or watercraft are locked. Additionally, there must be signs of forcible entry on the exterior of the vehicle or watercraft compartment. By utilizing HO-46, the theft coverage extension endorsement, these two theft exclusions can be eliminated.

Amendment of Limitations. Several endorsements are available for changing the limitations in a homeowners form. For example, the insurer's aggregate limits of liability for money, bullion, numismatic property, and bank notes can be increased by implementation of endorsement HO-65. The same endorsement can provide additional coverage limits for securities, accounts, bills, deeds, evidences of debt, letters of credit, notes other than bank notes, passports, railroad and other tickets, and stamps including philatelic property.

Glass coverage is afforded under all homeowners policies except

HO-4. Scheduled glass coverage can be provided by using HO-68. Glass shown in the schedule of the endorsement is insured against loss resulting from breakage or the application of chemicals. The removal and replacement of obstructions because of a glass loss are insured, as are any temporary installations made to cover openings. Thus, if an insured installs a plate glass window and the window is broken, the insurer, under HO-68, is responsible for the cost of removing any debris in the window frame, boarding up the window, and replacing the glass. Homeowners holding HO-1 policies have only $50 of glass breakage coverage. The use of HO-68 would allow them to increase this limit.

The coverage in the homeowners policy for the theft of unscheduled jewelry, watches, and furs is limited to $500. To expand this protection to $1,000, endorsement HO-171 may be added to HO-1 through HO-4, and HO-172 may be attached to HO-5. In HO-172, the $1,000 limitation does not apply if the loss is caused by (1) fire, (2) lightning, (3) windstorm, (4) hail, (5) smoke, (6) explosion, (7) riot, (8) civil commotion, (9) falling aircraft, (10) falling objects, (11) vehicle collision, (12) vandalism, (13) malicious mischief, or (14) collapse of buildings.

HO-210 and HO-211 also provide unscheduled jewelry, watch, and fur coverage for HO-1 through HO-4 and HO-5, respectively. Like HO-171 and HO-172, these forms provide for an aggregate $1,000 limit, but only $500 of coverage is provided for any one item. Table 3-9 lists some of the endorsements that can be utilized to restrict the exclusions or the limitations in a homeowners policy.

Deductibles Numerous deductibles can be utilized with the various homeowners forms. These deductibles apply to section I but not to additional living expense or fire department services. Coverages A, B, and C in HO-1 through HO-4 sometimes contain a "disappearing deductible." To determine the amount of insurance to be paid by the insurer, the deductible is subtracted from the amount of loss. The result is then multiplied by 111 percent. As the size of the loss increases, the amount of the deductible decreases. For example, Jane Weatherford has an HO-3 policy which includes $30,000 of insurance (the replacement cost) on the described dwelling under coverage A of section I. (Since the amount of the deductible is never lower than $50, this figure is used in this example.) During a hail storm, the roof of Ms. Weatherford's home incurs $300 of damage. The insurance company pays the insured $277.50 which is determined as follows:

$$(\$300 - \$50) \times 111\% = \$277.50$$

Figure 3-1 illustrates the impact of a $50 disappearing deductible with a 111 percent multiplier. Losses above $500 are paid in full because applying the 111 percent above $500 would result in payment of more

Table 3-9
Endorsements for Handling Exclusions and Limitations

Number of Endorsement	Utilize With	Coverage
HO-53	All homeowners policies	Protects against credit card and depositors forgery and counterfeit money
HO-54	HO-1, HO-2, HO-3, and HO-4	Earthquake damage
HO-55	HO-5	Earthquake damage
HO-46	HO-2, HO-3, and HO-4	Eliminates exclusion that restricts coverage on personal property in vehicles and watercraft unless locked, and signs of forcible entry are present (i.e., theft coverage extension)
HO-65	All homeowners policies	Provides additional coverage for money and securities
HO-68	HO-1, HO-2, HO-3, and HO-5	Scheduled glass coverage
HO-171	HO-1, HO-2, HO-3, and HO-4	Increases limit of liability for theft of unscheduled jewelry, watches, and furs up to $1,000
HO-172	HO-5	Increases limit of liability for theft of unscheduled jewelry, watches, and furs up to $1,000
HO-210	HO-1, HO-2, HO-3, and HO-4	Increases aggregate limit of liability for theft of unscheduled jewelry, watches, furs up to $1,000 (limit of $500 for one item)
HO-211	HO-5	Increases aggregate limit of liability for theft of unscheduled jewelry, watches, and furs for up to $1,000 (limit of $500 for one item)

Figure 3-1

Loss Payments Under a $50 and 111 Percent Disappearing Deductible

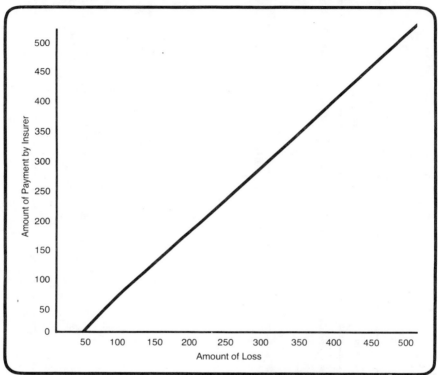

than the amount of loss. The disappearing deductible does have the effect of eliminating small nuisance claims; yet, it still prevents an insured from having to absorb a deductible when a large loss occurs.

HO-5 also may be written with a disappearing deductible; the amount of the deductible is $100 instead of $50, and the multiplier applied to each loss is 125 percent.

The standard deductibles can be modified. Endorsements to modify the deductibles fall into one of three classes: (1) those applicable to HO-1 through HO-4, (2) those applicable to HO-5, and (3) those applicable to all forms. While there are numerous endorsements, not all of these can be used in every state.

The deductibles under forms HO-1 through HO-4 can be amended in several ways. First, HO-56, the $100 special loss deductible clause, can be used to provide a flat $100 deductible. No percentage is applied to losses in excess of $100; thus, the named insured is responsible for the first $100 of loss.

A deductible applicable only to losses resulting from windstorm and hail may be added to HO-1, HO-2, HO-3, and HO-4. As an example, endorsement HO-122 provides a $50 disappearing deductible with 111 percent multiplier for windstorm and hail losses. To increase the disappearing deductible to $100 and a 125 percent multiplier, HO-175 can be used.

Raising the disappearing deductible in HO-1 through HO-4 from $50 and 111 percent to $100 and 125 percent for all the perils covered can be achieved by utilizing endorsement HO-174. Form HO-202 will allow a named insured to obtain a flat $50 deductible, and HO-177 provides a special deductible of $250 for loss of unscheduled personal property by theft.

Two endorsements generally can be used with any of the homeowners forms. These endorsements are HO-58 and HO-59, which provide flat deductibles of $250 and $500, respectively.

There are two endorsements used specifically with HO-5. HO-57 reduces the disappearing deductible in HO-5 to $50 and 111 percent. A flat $50 deductible is available under HO-232. Table 3-10 summarizes the endorsements cited above.

Utilizing different deductibles has an impact on the premium paid by an insured. Obviously, the lower the deductible the greater the cost per dollar of coverage for an insured. For example, conversion from a $50 disappearing deductible to a $100 disappearing deductible results in a 10 percent premium savings to the insured. Moving from a $100 disappearing deductible to a $250 flat deductible results in an additional 10 percent savings subject to a maximum savings of $30. Replacing a $250 flat deductible by a $500 flat deductible yields another 10 percent of credit subject to a maximum of $60. Use of flat deductibles for all perils is increasing in popularity.

Valued Policy Statutes In some states, coverage under the homeowners policy will be affected by valued policy laws. The insurer is required to pay the full face amount of the policy on total losses arising from fire, lightning, and other perils, even if the insured has coverage in excess of the value of the property. Theoretically, this prevents the insurer from selling the insured unnecessary coverage and benefiting from the excess premium. Some states also require that partial losses be paid by the insurer without a deduction for depreciation. The Florida statute exemplifies the latter type of state law, and the Nebraska statute the former.

Florida's statute states the following:

1. In the event of total loss by fire or lightning of any building or structure located in this state and insured by any insurer as to such perils, in the absence of any change increasing the risk without the

Table 3-10

Endorsements Used to Modify Deductibles

Number of Endorsements	Utilized With	Purpose
HO-56	HO-1, HO-2, HO-3, and HO-4	Provides a flat $100 deductible for all perils
HO-122	HO-1, HO-2, HO-3, and HO-4	Allows a $50 disappearing deductible for windstorm and hail
HO-175	HO-1, HO-2, HO-3, and HO-4	Allows a $100 disappearing deductible for windstorm and hail
HO-220	HO-1, HO-2, HO-3, and HO-4	Provides a flat $50 deductible for windstorm and hail
HO-174	HO-1, HO-2, HO-3, and HO-4	Raises disappearing deductible for all covered perils from $50 to $100
HO-177	HO-1, HO-2 HO-3, and HO-4	Establishes a special deductible of $250 for loss of unscheduled personal property by theft
HO-58	All homeowners policies	Allows a flat deductible for all perils of $250
HO-59	All homeowners policies	Allows a flat deductible for all perils of $500
HO-57	HO-5	Establishes a $50 disappearing deductible for all perils
HO-232	HO-5	Provides a flat deductible of $50 for all perils

insurer's consent, the insurer's liability, if any, under the policy for such total loss shall be in the amount of money for which such property was so insured as specified in the policy and for which premium has been charged and paid.

2. In the case of partial loss by fire or lightning of any such property the insurer's liability, if any, under the policy shall be for the actual amount of such loss, but not to exceed the amount of insurance specified in the policy as to such property and such perils.[10]

Nebraska's statutes state:

Wherever any policy of insurance shall be written to insure any real property in this state against loss by fire, tornado, or lightning, and the property insured shall be wholly destroyed, without criminal fault on the part of the insured or his assignee, the amount of the insurance written on such policy shall be taken conclusively to be the true value of the property insured and the true amount of loss and measure of damages.[11]

Other states require that the premium for the excess coverage be returned to the insured with interest accumulated from the date the policy is issued.[12]

Inflation During periods of inflation, the replacement cost of a home increases. The unwary policyholder who does not increase his or her insurance limit in a homeowners policy may be penalized by inflationary trends; thus, the homeowner desiring full replacement cost coverage must continually ascertain the accuracy of the policy limits.

Figure 3-2 shows the increase in residential building costs for the period from 1955 to 1975. While the cost of constructing a home increased steadily from 1955 to 1967, the increase has been dramatic since 1967. Obviously, as the cost of new construction increases, the replacement cost of older dwellings rises.

To avoid inadequate coverage, a homeowner can use one of several approaches. These approaches are designed to make sure that an insured is carrying insurance at least equal to the 80 percent replacement cost requirement.

One approach is to have a dwelling appraised every two to six months. The homeowner purchases additional coverage according to the increase in value of the home. This approach has two major drawbacks: (1) the homeowner periodically incurs the expense of hiring an appraiser, and (2) a portion of the homeowner's time is absorbed in determining the proper time to have the home appraised and seeing that the policy limits are increased appropriately. Thus, it is not a realistic approach.

A second approach is the purchase of more insurance than is necessary. If a home is valued at $40,000, the homeowner might purchase $42,500 of coverage hoping that the value of the home would not be more than $42,500 at any time during the policy period. Ideally, the home would be worth exactly $42,500 at the end of the policy period. The problem with this method is that it requires the insured to purchase unnecessary coverage. In addition, accurately estimating the cost of the dwelling at the end of the policy period is extremely difficult.

Insurers have devised a procedure for helping the insured maintain adequate protection. Instead of requiring the homeowner to continually estimate the value of a home, an inflation guard endorsement specifying periodic increases in the policy limit is attached to a policy. Only by chance will these increases exactly match the increasing building cost. However, if they are a close approximation, the insured probably will have adequate coverage.

Inflation guard protection for HO-1, HO-2, HO-3, and HO-5 is

Figure 3-2

Building Costs Index for Residential Construction—1955–1973*

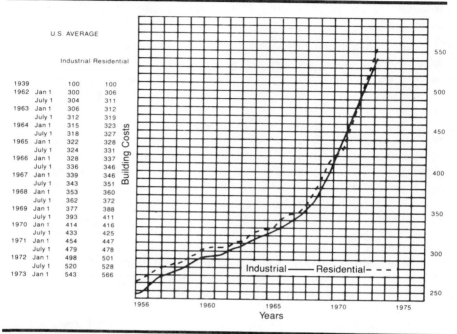

		Industrial	Residential
1939		100	100
1962	Jan 1	300	306
	July 1	304	311
1963	Jan 1	306	312
	July 1	312	319
1964	Jan 1	315	323
	July 1	318	327
1965	Jan 1	322	328
	July 1	324	331
1966	Jan 1	328	337
	July 1	336	346
1967	Jan 1	339	346
	July 1	343	351
1968	Jan 1	353	360
	July 1	362	372
1969	Jan 1	377	388
	July 1	393	411
1970	Jan 1	414	416
	July 1	433	425
1971	Jan 1	454	447
	July 1	479	478
1972	Jan 1	498	501
	July 1	520	528
1973	Jan 1	543	566

U.S. AVERAGE

*Reprinted with permission of the Factory Mutual System. The Factory Mutual Building-Cost Index is obtained from periodic checks on current costs of labor in the primary building trades and in the cost of major materials that go into construction of typical buildings. These checks are made in key locations in the various sections of the United States and Canada and are compiled to show direction of costs since the base year, 1939.

afforded under HO-47. This endorsement increases the policy limits of all section I coverages every three months. The increases, which are not cumulative, are 1 percent every three months except for the last increase which is 2 percent. Table 3-11 lists the increases and the impact of these increases on a coverage A limit. Although coverages B, C, and D are not listed, the impact would be the same. It is obvious from Table 3-11 that HO-47 is designed for use on a three-year policy.

Four other inflation guard endorsements are available for use with HO-1, HO-2, HO-3, and HO-5. HO-184 increases section I limits by 1 percent at the end of every three months of the policy period. Normally, it is used with one-year policies, but the 1 percent increase is applicable during any policy extension. HO-242 and HO-243 are similar to HO-184; the differences are that under HO-242 there is a 2 percent increase every three months and under HO-243 the increase can be selected by the

Table 3-11

Coverage A Limit Increases Under Inflation Guard
Endorsement HO-47 (Ed. 11-68)

Policy Period (Months)	Percent of Increase	Impact of Increase on a $20,000 Coverage A Limit
3	1%	$20,200
6	2	20,400
9	3	20,600
12	4	20,800
15	5	21,000
18	6	21,200
21	7	21,400
24	8	21,600
27	9	21,800
30	10	22,000
33	12	22,400

insured. HO-184 is also like HO-242 but the rate of increase is 1.5 percent.

Apportionment When a homeowners policy is issued, the insurer generally assumes that the named insured has no other such policy. However, if a named insured has several policies, he or she could make a profit in the event of a loss. To prevent this occurrence, a homeowners policy contains pro rata or apportionment clauses. Under these clauses, the insurer's liability is reduced if other coverage exists. When an insured has more than one policy on a home or appurtenant structure, each insurer pays the proportion that its coverage bears to the entire amount of coverage. The rule applies even if some of the insurance cannot be collected. The homeowner may use endorsement HO-178, which permits several insurers on one exposure.

Coverage C protection, unlike the other coverages, is not shared on a pro rata basis. Instead, it is excess to ". . . other valid and collectible insurance which would apply in the absence of . . ." the homeowners policy. For example, Frank Gormley purchased an HO-2 policy on his home for $24,000 from Insurer 1 and an HO-3 policy for $24,000 from Insurer 2. The replacement cost value of the home is $30,000. Additionally, Gormley maintained a personal property floater purchased from Insurer 3 for $5,000 on the living room furniture. A fire destroyed one-half of the home and $1,000 (actual cash value) of the living room furniture. Insurer 1 and Insurer 2 would each pay:

$$\frac{\$24,000}{\$48,000} \times \$15,000 = \$7,500$$

Insurer 3 would be responsible for the $1,000 furniture loss. (Any deductible would be subtracted.)

Further assume that Gormley purchased a $10,000 HO-2 policy from Insurer 1, a $10,000 HO-2 policy from Insurer 2, and a $10,000 HO-2 policy from Insurer 3. Following the $15,000 replacement cost loss, Insurer 1 becomes insolvent. The actual cash value of the loss is $12,000. Since the coverage does not meet the replacement cost requirement of 80 percent of insurance to value, each insurer would be liable for its share of the actual cash value of the loss. Insurer 2 would pay:

$$\frac{\$10,000}{\$30,000} \times \$12,000 = \$4,000$$

Insurer 3 would pay:

$$\frac{\$10,000}{\$30,000} \times \$12,000 = \$4,000$$

Insurer 1 would not pay anything.

Extensions of Coverage All of the homeowners policies contain supplemental benefits which expand the insurance protection. These benefits expand only the types of losses insured, not the coverage limits.

Automatic Removal. Occasionally, the named insured will purchase another residence within the United States. If this new residence is to serve as the principal residence, the named insured will be transferring unscheduled personal property to it. The automatic removal provision allows the named insured coverage on all unscheduled personal property in the new residence. There are, however, several conditions. First, the amount of coverage on the property at the new residence is equal to the amount of insurance multiplied by the ratio of the value of the unscheduled personal property at the new location to the total unscheduled personal property value at both residences. Second, the coverage extension is not available when the homeowners policy has been canceled. Third, coverage begins when any unscheduled personal property is first removed from the home insured in the policy; cessation of coverage occurs thirty days later. Finally, unscheduled personal property in transit between the two locations is covered only for the usual amount afforded unscheduled personal property away from home (i.e., 10 percent of coverage C or $1,000, whichever is greater).

For example, Lauri Frohling has $5,000 of insurance on her unscheduled personal property under her current homeowners policy. If she purchased a new home to serve as her principal residence and moved

$2,000 out of $14,000 of unscheduled personal property to the new home, her coverage on unscheduled personal property at the new home would be:

$$\text{Total Coverage} \times \frac{\text{Amount at new location}}{\begin{array}{c}\text{Total amount at old and}\\ \text{new locations}\end{array}} = \begin{array}{c}\text{Coverage at}\\ \text{new location}\end{array}$$

$$\$5,000 \times \frac{\$2,000}{\$14,000} = \$714.29$$

The automatic removal provision is not found in HO-5 since unscheduled personal property is covered on a worldwide basis (with one exception—there is a 10 percent limit on property at a secondary residence).

Debris Removal. All homeowners policies provide some coverage for the cost of removing debris following a loss to the property covered by the policy. However, the cause of loss must be insured under the policy.

Fire Department Service Charge. An insured may not live within any city, municipality, or fire district that provides fire service. Or, an insured may live in one fire territory or district but be closer to a fire station in another territory or district. When an insured utilizes the fire services of a territory or district in which he or she does not live, the insured may have to pay a service charge. Under the supplemental coverages of all homeowners policies, the insurer will pay up to $250 of this service charge.

Building Additions and Alterations. Both HO-4 and HO-5 include coverage for additions and alterations up to a maximum amount of 10 percent of coverage C. HO-5 covers additions and alterations in or on residences occupied but not owned by the insured. HO-4 is limited to alterations of an addition to the building occupied by the insured. In both cases, the additions or alterations must be located in the area occupied by the named insured. Thus, alterations to the inside of an apartment would be covered, but alterations to the joint areas of an apartment building would not be covered.

The 10 percent limit of liability can be increased by endorsement HO-49 under an HO-5 policy and by HO-51 under an HO-4 policy.

OTHER RESIDENTIAL COVERAGES

While homeowners policies are both broad and flexible, they do not meet the residential insurance needs of some individuals. There are three types of dwellings for which specialized policies have been developed. These three are (1) condominiums, (2) mobile homes, and (3) farms. In spite of the differences among these types of dwellings, many provisions of the policies for these dwellings are identical to those found in homeowners policies.

Condominiums

Individuals owning condominiums insure their interest in the building by means of either a standard fire policy with endorsements or a special multi-peril policy with the condominium endorsement. Insurance for the individual's personal property and legal liability must be obtained under an HO-4 policy with endorsement HO-192, or an HO-6 policy—the homeowners policy for condominium unit owners. Generally, HO-4 is used only when HO-6 is not available.

The protection afforded by HO-6 is distinguished from that provided under the HO-4 policy in two principal areas. The alterations and additions coverage under HO-4 applies only to changes made to a nonowned residence. In the case of a condominium, the insured owns the unit. The alterations and additions coverage under HO-4, therefore, does not apply to improvements made to a condominium. HO-6 corrects this weakness by covering a unit owner's additions and alterations. A second difference is the deductible. HO-4 has a $50 disappearing deductible while HO-6 has a straight $100 deductible applicable to all property losses except additional living expenses and the fire department service charge.

These differences are not as substantial as they might appear. HO-4 can be endorsed to provide a straight $100 deductible. In addition, by attaching endorsement HO-192 to HO-4, additions and alterations insurance can be provided for unit owners.

To make adjustments to HO-6, a multi-purpose endorsement HO-CO is used. Six different changes can be made using this form: (1) increased limits for additions and alterations, (2) "all-risks" coverage for additions and alterations, (3) coverage while the condominium is rented to others (this includes coverage for the unit and loss of rent), (4) protection for appurtenant structures, (5) additional living expense limits, and (6) protection against loss assessments. Item (6) requires special attention.

Under most condominium arrangements, unit owners comprise an association controlled or governed by a set of rules. Generally, under these rules, the association has the right to assess each unit owner for uninsured property or liability losses relative to the association.

The loss assessment coverage provided under HO-CO will cover these assessments for the condominium owner. However, the assessments must arise either from a loss of the unit owner's property from either a peril covered in the additions and alterations section, section I, or a liability loss covered under section II. The deductible for this coverage is $250, and there is a special maximum limit of $1,000 applicable only to assessments paid by the unit owner because of deductibles in the insurance coverage of the association.

Mobile Homes

To meet the needs of mobile home owners, insurers have developed MP-1. The types of property coverage in the mobile home policy are similar to those in the homeowners policies. Coverage is provided for the mobile home if it is located on land owned or leased by the named insured and occupied principally as a private residence. Parts, equipment, and accessories that are permanent parts of the mobile home as well as steps and heating or cooling tanks are covered under coverage A. Appliances, furniture, and equipment which are sold with the home and listed in the certificate of origin or sales invoice also are included under coverage A. Since homes can be resold and additional equipment added by a used mobile home dealer, the appliances, furniture, and equipment insured can vary among owners. Awnings, shelters, cabanas, porches, other additions, carports, water pumps, air conditioners, or other structures are excluded.

Unscheduled personal property coverage (coverage B) in MP-1 is different in four major ways from the unscheduled personal property coverage in the homeowners series. Unscheduled personal property away from home is 10 percent of the limit for coverage B or $300, whichever is greater. Remember that in the homeowners series, the minimum limit was $1,000. There are three additional exclusions. Trailers are not covered. In the homeowners policy they are covered unless they are away from the premises. Business property is not insured under MP-1 while the homeowners series covers business property when it is on the premises. Finally, appliances, furniture, and equipment furnished by the manufacturer or dealer as standard equipment and awnings, shelters, cabanas, porches, other additions, carports, water pumps, and air conditioners are excluded. Most of these items can be covered by coverage A, the mobile home section, or coverage C, the additions to mobile homes, appurtenant structures, and equipment section. Coverage C can cover (1) awnings, (2) shelters, (3) cabanas, (4) carports, (5) porches, (6) other additions, (7) water pumps, (8) air conditioners, and (9) structures and equipment attached to or appurtenant to the mobile home. However, these items must be listed in the policy declarations for coverage to exist.

Coverage D, the additional living expenses benefit, restricts benefits to $15 per day. The homeowners policy does not contain this limit. The homeowners policy also pays benefits until the damaged property is repaired or replaced or the named insured has found permanent quarters. Under MP-1, the $15 per day benefit will not be paid for more than forty-five days even if the damage has not been corrected and the named insured still is not settled permanently.

These are not the only differences between the homeowners series and MP-1. The mobile home form promises to reimburse the named insured for expenses incurred in removing the mobile home from an area endangered by an insured peril; the benefit is limited to $100. The fire service charge benefit is $100, not the $250 found in all homeowners forms. A flat $100 deductible is applied to each property loss except additional living expense, the fire department charge, and the emergency removal expense.

The special limits of liability are slightly different under the mobile home policy. Coverage for trees, shrubs, plants, and lawns is only $200, and recovery for the destruction of a lawn or a tree is restricted to $100. Recovery on plants and shrubs is limited to $25 for any one item. MP-1 does not contain the special limit on manuscripts, watercraft, or trailers, but it does contain the other special limits found in the homeowners series.

Three additional exclusions are contained in MP-1:

1. No coverage is provided for losses ". . . due to conversion, embezzlement or secretion by any person in possession of the mobile home under a bailment lease, conditional sale, purchase agreement, mortgage, or other encumbrance."
2. All damage caused by a vehicle owned or operated by an occupant of the mobile home is not insured. This exclusion is similar only to the exception in HO-1.
3. Theft of tires or wheels is excluded unless the tires are attached to the mobile home or are located inside an enclosed area when they are stolen. This exception to the theft peril is not found in any policy in the homeowners series.

MP-1 contains liability protection. The liability coverage is like the liability section of all the homeowners policies.

Numerous endorsements are available for use with MP-1 to make it more responsive to the needs of the insured. Counterparts to most of these endorsements can be found in the homeowners series. Several representative examples are given here. MP-80 allows an additional insured to be added under the policy. Collision coverage while a vehicle is in transit is afforded under MP-82. MP-85 deletes the exclusion for conversion, embezzlement, and secretion and adds collision coverage. MP-85 can only be utilized to protect the interest of a vendor. Protection for the perils of earthquakes and volcanoes can be added by utilizing endorsement MP-87. Other endorsements permit the insured to (1) increase the limits on money and securities, (2) increase unscheduled personal property coverage away from home, (3) add unscheduled glass coverage, (4) change the deductible, and (5) add credit card and depositors' forgery coverage.

Farms

Farms reflect a unique combination of personal (basically residential) and business (farming operations) loss exposures. This fact is just as true of corporate farming operations, which usually involve a manager and his or her family residing on the premises, as it is of family-owned and operated-farms. The farmowners-ranchowners (FR) program has been designed specifically to meet these specialized insurance needs. The FR program is a modified and extended version of the homeowners package policy concept. The essential differences between the two programs reflect the different nature and characteristics of farm property and operations as contrasted with city or suburban dwellings.

The format of the FR program resembles that of older standard package policies:

- the declarations page,
- the 165 numbered lines of the standard fire policy,
- a section concerned with general conditions,
- a section affecting section I (property) coverage, and
- a section dealing with section II (liability) coverage.

Of course, appropriate endorsements may be added.

The farmowners-ranchowners section I (property) coverages include:

A. Dwelling
B. Unscheduled Personal Property (Household)
C. Additional Living Expense
D. Farm Personal Property (Scheduled Coverage)
E. Farm Personal Property (Blanket Coverage)
F. Barns, Buildings, Structures and Additional Dwellings (Scheduled)

Farmowners-ranchowners section II (liability) coverage combines comprehensive personal liability insurance and the business liability protection required for farm operations, products, and premises. This coverage is discussed in some detail in CPCU 3.

The major differences between the FR program and homeowners program are summarized below:

1. There is no automatic coverage for appurtenant private structures under the FR policy. This coverage, if desired, must be scheduled and a separate premium charge levied.

2. The FR program offers two basic options for coverage on residential property, i.e., dwelling and unscheduled personal (nonfarm) property: (1) basic form FR-1, which is the equivalent of homeowners basic form HO-1, or (2) broad form FR-2, the equivalent of homeowners broad form HO-2. The tenants broad form FR-4 has its counterpart in homeowners form HO-4. The special and comprehensive forms (HO-3 and HO-5 respectively) are not, generally, duplicated in the FR program. However, supplemental "all-risks" coverage in the form of various floaters—personal, agricultural machinery, livestock, and so on—may be attached.

3. The additional living expense limit of liability is the same under form FR-1 as under form FR-2—10 percent of the amount of coverage on the farm dwelling.

4. FR policies are written on an actual cash value basis. Replacement cost coverage generally may be added but it is not a feature of the FR forms.

5. Owner-occupancy is not required. An FR policy may be written on a farm operated by a tenant, though it is required that the owner manage the operation or that a management contractor does.

6. If the policy is written for an owner-*non*occupant, coverage of unscheduled personal property—household goods, clothing, and so on—must be omitted. When coverage is desired, it may be included in the schedule of farm personal property or it may be added by means of the scheduled personal property endorsement.

7. Trees, shrubs, plants, and lawns are specifically excluded from coverage in the FR forms.

HOMEOWNERS 76

Consumerism, as a concept and as a movement, has expanded rapidly in recent years. One concern of many insureds is that they cannot understand their policies. The Insurance Services Office has therefore devised the homeowners 76 policy program which is supposedly easier to understand than the old homeowners policy program.

To illustrate the differences in the language in the old program and the new program, two examples are presented. In each example, the new policy's provision is presented first.

New Policy

We will provide the insurance described in this policy in return for the premium and compliance with all applicable provisions of this policy.[13]

Old Policy

In Consideration of the Provisions and Stipulations Herein or Added Thereto and of the premium above specified (or specified in endorsement(s) made a party hereof), this Company, for the term shown above from inception date shown above at noon (Standard Time) to expiration date shown above at noon (Standard Time) at location of property involved, to an amount not exceeding the limit of liability above specified, does insure the insured named in the declarations above and legal representatives, to the extent of the actual cash value of the property at the time of loss, but not exceeding the amount which it would cost to repair or replace the property with material of like kind and quality within a reasonable time after such loss, without allowance for any increased cost of repair or reconstruction by reason of any ordinance or law regulating construction or repair, and without compensation for loss resulting from interruption of business or manufacture, nor in any event for more than the interest of the Insured, against all DIRECT LOSS BY FIRE, LIGHTNING AND OTHER PERILS INSURED AGAINST IN THIS POLICY INCLUDING REMOVAL FROM PREMISES ENDANGERED BY THE PERILS INSURED AGAINST IN THIS POLICY, EXCEPT AS HEREINAFTER PROVIDED, to the property described herein while located or contained as described in this policy, or pro rata for five days at each proper place to which any of the property shall necessarily be removed for preservation from the perils insured against in this policy, but not elsewhere.

Assignment of this policy shall not be valid except with the written consent of this Company.

This policy is made and accepted subject to the foregoing provisions and stipulations and those hereinafter stated, which are hereby made a part of this policy, together with such other provisions, stipulations and agreements as may be added hereto, as provided in this policy.

New Policy

Coverage A—Dwelling
We cover: a. the dwelling on the residence premises shown in the declarations used principally as a private residence, including structures attached to the dwelling; and b. materials and supplies located on or adjacent to the residence premises for use in the construction, alteration or repair of the dwelling or other structures on the residence premises.[14]

Old Policy

Coverage A—Dwelling
This policy covers the described dwelling building, including additions in contact therewith, occupied principally as a private residence. This coverage also includes:
1. if the property of the insured and when not otherwise covered, building equipment, fixtures and outdoor equipment all pertaining to the service of the premises and while located thereon or temporarily elsewhere; and
2. materials and supplies located on the premises or adjacent thereto, intended for use in construction, alteration or repair of such dwelling.[15]

The new homeowners 76 program, in addition to containing different language, has different coverage. The expanded features of the new program include (1) credit card, forgery, and counterfeit money coverage up to $500; (2) sound reproduction equipment protection if the equipment is not installed permanently in an automobile; (3) coverage up to $500 on any tree, shrub, or plant; (4) no limitation on coverage (other than the coverage C limit) for personal property off premises unless the property is located at a residence of the insured, in which case there is a 10 percent limit; (5) an additional 5 percent limit to cover debris removal; (6) medical payments coverage extending to three years instead of one year; (7) reasonable expenses of $50 incurred by the insured at the request of the company; (8) coverage for personal property of a student at school if the student has been at the residence away from home fifteen days; (9) loss for broken glass is settled on the basis of replacement with safety glazing materials when required by law; and (10) residence employee coverage for injuries arising out of ownership, maintenance, use, loading, or unloading of an aircraft.

The new coverage in some areas is more restrictive than the old program. Less coverage is a result of (1) a $1,000 limitation on all silverware, silver-plated ware, goldware, gold-plated ware, and pewterware; (2) a $1,000 limitation on all guns; (3) a $100 limit on gold, silver, and platinum; (4) the application of deductibles to the loss of use coverages; (5) a $500 limitation on manuscripts rather than the old limit of $1,000; and (6) a loss by theft from any portion of a residence rented by the insured to someone who is not an insured.

Chapter Notes

1. In some states a dwelling can be covered if it is part of a one, two, three, or four family residence under a homeowners policy. The general rule, however, is that a homeowners policy cannot cover a dwelling that houses more than two families.
2. Langford, Garrett v. Allstate Insurance Company, 1975 C.C.H. (Fire and Casualty) 690.
3. Henry Campbell Black, *Black's Law Dictionary* (St. Paul: West Publishing Co., 1968), p. 1391.
4. For a thorough discussion of cases on collapse, see: J. Kenneth Duff, ed., *Fire, Casualty and Surety Bulletins*, Fire and Marine Section (Cincinnati: National Underwriter Company, 1975), pp. Dwelling Col-1 - Col-9.
5. Many types of value relate to a residence. Book value, market value, replacement cost, and actual cash value are just a few. However, homeowners policies only deal with replacement cost and actual cash value. These values may not be of importance to an insured except in relation to his or her insurance coverage.
6. Koncilja v. Trinity Universal Insurance Company, 528 P. 2d 939 (1974).
7. Cantanucci v. Reliance Insurance Company, 1975 C.C.H. (Fire and Casualty) 704.
8. Riddle v. Allstate Insurance Company, 203 So. 2d 823 (1968).
9. Bryan v. Granite State Insurance Company, 185 So. 2d 310 (1966).
10. West's F.S.A. Sec. 627-702 (1) and (2): For an example of how a partial loss is handled in Florida, see: Sperling v. Liberty Mutual Insurance Company, 281 So. 2d 297 (1973).
11. Nebraska Reissue Revised Statutes of 1943, Ch. 48, Sec. 380.
12. For an example, see: General Statutes of North Carolina Ch. 58, Subc. 3, Art. 18, Sec. 58159.
13. Insurance Services Office, Homeowners 76 policy.
14. Ibid.
15. In the current series, this type of coverage is assumed to exist, but the policies do not specify that the coverage is available.

CHAPTER 4

Automobile Coverages

THE FAMILY AUTOMOBILE POLICY

The Development of Automobile Coverage

Automobile insurance coverage attracted the attention of most insurers and regulators in the first decade of the 1900s. In 1907, New York amended its insurance laws to include automobile insurance. The New York law permitted the writing of coverage:

> ... against loss or damage to an automobile resulting from collision, and against loss by legal liability for damage to property resulting from collision of an automobile with another automobile, or vehicle, or object.[1]

Coverage on automobiles had been offered by insurers before the New York law was passed even though a specific automobile policy had not been developed. The Travelers Insurance Company first issued coverage on automobiles in 1897 to a Massachusetts resident at a price of $7.50 per $1,000 of liability coverage.[2]

However, in the first part of the twentieth century, the main question concerning insurers was not if automobile coverage should be written, but who should write it. Multiple-line coverage was still not acceptable to regulators, and both property and liability companies vied for the opportunity to write complete coverage on automobiles. Regulators in most states decided that:

> A fire and marine insurance company can write all types of automobile insurance except the public liability coverages; a casualty company can write all types of automobile insurance except coverage against

155

loss or damage by fire or while being transported in any conveyance by land or water.[3]

There were some areas in which both types of insurers could write policies, but this apparently did not create a substantial problem. Sometimes a single policy was issued, and a property insurer and liability insurer shared the coverage. Which company actually was responsible for providing a particular type of coverage was irrelevant to the insured. In other cases, however, separate contracts were issued for liability and property coverages.

Not until the late 1940s and the early 1950s did combination automobile coverage become widely accepted. During this period, multiple-line underwriting became an accepted procedure, and individual insurers became eligible to write liability and physical damage coverages pertaining to an automobile.

Early automobile contracts did not provide coverage for many situations covered automatically today under certain automobile forms such as the family automobile policy (FAP). In the early 1940s, an individual purchasing an automobile policy could only obtain liability protection for the operation of nonowned vehicles by use of a special endorsement. C. A. Kulp, discussing this situation in his book *Casualty Insurance*, stated:

> Two principal classes of persons or organizations run the chance of liability for the operation of private passenger automobiles they do not own. All persons occasionally drive other persons' cars which may or may not be insured or whose insurance may or may not include an omnibus clause.[4] For them are provided the so-called named operator and drive-other-cars forms. The first is issued to non-car owners to protect them when driving other cars; the second to owners of insured cars driving other cars. Both may be used for private passenger automobiles only or for any type of automobile. Named operator extended cover is contributing; drive-other-car is excess.[5]

The stock and mutual casualty insurers designed a national standard basic liability policy for private passenger, commercial, and public hazards which became effective January 1, 1936. This form was liberalized in 1936, 1940, and 1941. Individual hazard property insurance for the automobile was standardized in 1941 following an agreement by the stock and mutual conferences.

The basic automobile policy was developed in 1955, and the FAP was introduced in 1956. The FAP underwent numerous revisions including a major revision in 1963. The special automobile policy (SAP), sometimes called the special package automobile policy (SPAP) was introduced in September of 1959. More recently, a personal automobile policy (PAP) has been developed as a simplified, more readable policy. It was approved for implementation in three states in January 1977.

Ultimately, the PAP is expected to replace the FAP and the SPAP as its use is gradually extended to other states.

This chapter will discuss primarily the FAP since it currently is used to meet the needs of most families.[6] However, since some families purchase the SAP, a comparison between the FAP and the SAP will be made.

Liability Coverage Under the Family Automobile Policy

Persons Insured There are two categories of persons insured under Part 1 (the liability section) of the FAP: individuals who are insured under the policy when driving the owned automobile, and individuals insured by the policy while driving a nonowned automobile.

Owned Automobiles. Three classes of individuals are insured when they are driving an owned automobile. First, the named insured and any resident of the named insured's household are covered. The spouse of the person named in the policy is considered a named insured if both live in the same residence.

The second class of insured individuals consists of persons who use an owned automobile with the permission of the named insured. Insureds other than the named insured, e.g., residents of the household, cannot grant this permission. The actual operation or use of the vehicle by other persons must be within the scope of the permission granted. For example, if the named insured authorized his or her next door neighbor to go to the store and purchase some groceries, that neighbor would be insured. However, if the neighbor, instead of going to the store, had left town for six hours, the policy would not have provided coverage.

The two extremes, cited above, are fairly simple; however, there are a number of cases where the person using the car only deviates slightly from the granted permission. Expanding the example above, if the neighbor had stopped by the hardware store on the way to the grocery store, coverage may or may not have been in effect. The circumstances surrounding permission would dictate whether or not coverage was applicable.

The court cases concerning permissive use are diverse, and interpretations and practices vary by state. In Muzichuk v. Liberty Mutual Insurance Company, the problem of defining the term "permission" was discussed thoroughly by the Massachusetts Appeals Court. Because of the numerous aspects of this case, portions of the case are reproduced here as an example of what might constitute permissive use.

At all times material to this case, Henry [Lappin] lived with his wife, Regina, and their two sons, Leonard and Barry, at 117 Bay State Road, Boston. Henry owned two cars, a Pontiac and an Austin-Healy. Both were registered in his name. On the date of the accident, which involved the Pontiac, there was in force a "Massachusetts Combination Motor Vehicle Policy," issued by the defendant with respect to the Pontiac. The policy included "Coverage B" with "limits of liability" of $100,000 as to each person and $300,000 as to each accident.

Shortly after the purchase of the Pontiac in 1965, Henry gave duplicate sets of car keys to his wife and to Leonard. Henry, a licensed physician, was unable to operate a motor vehicle because of an eye condition. As he could not drive, his wife or Leonard would drive him whenever a need arose. From the time the Pontiac was purchased until March 10, 1966, it was used by Leonard at least once a week. Henry never restricted Leonard's use of the Pontiac except when he needed the car and a driver to visit a patient. Henry knew that Paul Muzichuk and others rode with Leonard. He never objected.

At approximately 3:00 P.M. on March 10, 1966, Leonard was at [Paul] Muzichuk's house when he was summoned home by his mother. When he arrived there Henry told him to take his brother Barry to a garage in Wellesley Hills (Crandall-Hicks) in order for Barry to pick up the Austin-Healy, which was being repaired. Henry told Leonard to take the Pontiac and to return home. Henry did not set a time before which the Pontiac was to be returned.

Barry, with Leonard as a passenger, drove the Pontiac to Muzichuk's house where they picked up Muzichuk and [Robert] Petrillo. At about 3:30 P.M. Barry drove to Crandall-Hicks. The drive took about twenty minutes. Barry left the car, and Leonard drove back to Boston with his two passengers. In Boston he drove to an ice cream shop and met [Allen] Oi at a pool parlor next door. All except Leonard went into the ice cream shop seeking employment. When they came out Leonard, with Muzichuk, Petrillo, and Oi as passengers, drove to Storrow Drive, over the Harvard Bridge, onto Memorial Drive, and then to Harvard Square to another ice cream shop. It was then about 5:00 P.M. At that point Leonard was about three miles from his home on Bay State Road. After leaving the ice cream shop in Harvard Square with his passengers, Leonard drove to Memorial Drive, where the accident happened at 5:22 P.M.

Leonard's use of the vehicle at the time of the accident was beyond what was needed to carry out his father's request to convey Barry to Crandall-Hicks and to return home. It is clear that Leonard's use of the car that day to drive his friends to Cambridge was within the scope of the broad general permission Henry had given him to use the vehicle for his own business and pleasure. Thus, in making such use of the car, Leonard would have been an "insured" within the terms of the policy unless (as the defendant argues and as we assume without deciding) Henry had imposed a limitation on that permission by telling Leonard to return home as soon as he dropped Barry off in Wellesley Hills.

We are of the opinion that Henry's statement to that effect was not such a limitation on the general permission given to Leonard. Henry did not state any time for his son's return. Any need for the car for his own transportation was not clearly stated. Leonard was permitted to use the car on weekdays as well as on weekends. On some occasions prior to using the car he had asked his mother or father if either had need of it. He used his own judgment as to the use of the car. We are impressed by the facts that this car was available to Henry, to his wife and to Leonard, and that on the occasions when Leonard had questioned his parents as to their need for the car his purpose had been to avoid conflicts between his use of the car and that of his parents. Upon all of the evidence we find that the permission granted Leonard was general and uninterrupted. It was not a series of permissions interspersed with periods of no permission.[7]

The third class of insureds with respect to the owned automobile is "... any other person or organization but only with respect to his or its liability because of any acts or omissions of an insured ..." as defined under the first two classes.

To understand the operation of the owned automobile liability coverage, an individual must be familiar with the meaning of an owned automobile. The policy defines an owned automobile in four ways. An owned automobile means:

1. a private passenger, farm, or utility automobile described in this policy for which a specific premium charge indicates that coverage is afforded;
2. a trailer owned by the named insured;
3. a private passenger, farm, or utility automobile ownership of which is acquired by the named insured during the policy period ..., or
4. a temporary substitute automobile.

A private passenger automobile is defined as a "... four wheel private passenger, station wagon or jeep type ..." vehicle. Therefore, scooters, motorized tricycles, motorcycles, and similar vehicles would not be insured as owned automobiles. The term farm automobile means "... an automobile of the truck type with a load capacity of fifteen hundred pounds or less...." However, a farm vehicle used for business purposes other than farming is not included. Utility automobiles are defined as vehicles which have a pickup body, sedan delivery, or paneltruck style. Like farm automobiles, utility automobiles cannot have a load capacity of more than 1,500 pounds or be utilized for business purposes.

The term trailer means:

... a trailer designed for use with a private passenger automobile, if not being used for business or commercial purposes with other than a private passenger, farm or utility automobile or a farm wagon or farm implement while used with a farm automobile.

This definition includes farm wagons or farm implements, but not farm machinery.

Private passenger automobiles frequently are acquired during the term of the FAP. If the named insured were required to obtain an additional automobile policy, the procedure would be costly and inconvenient. To assist individuals with this problem, insurance companies, under the FAP, permit some new vehicles to be classified as owned automobiles. For example, an automobile which replaces a private passenger, farm, or utility automobile is covered automatically. In addition, if the company insures *all* private passenger, farm, or utility automobiles owned by the named insured, then any additional private passenger, farm, or utility automobiles purchased can be covered. To extend coverage to these automobiles, the named insured "... notifies the company during the policy period or within 30 days after the date of such acquisition of his election to make this and no other policy issued by the company applicable to such automobile. . . ."

A temporary substitute vehicle is any automobile or trailer not owned by the named insured which is provided as a temporary substitute for the owned automobile(s) or trailer(s). The substitution must result, however, because the owned automobile has had a breakdown, is being repaired, is being serviced, is lost, or has been destroyed.

Nonowned Automobiles. The coverage for owned automobiles focuses on the vehicle or vehicles listed in the policy. Coverage for nonowned automobiles tends to follow persons and not vehicles. The persons insured with respect to nonowned automobiles or trailers are the named insured and any relatives living with the named insured if they are driving private passenger automobiles or trailers. The operation of a nonowned or private passenger automobile or trailer must be with the permission of the owner of the vehicle and the actual operation or use of the vehicle must be within the scope of such permission. However, if the relative reasonably could be believed to have the permission of the owner, coverage also is available. The policy states that "... any other person or organization not owning or hiring the automobile, but only with respect to his or its liability because of the acts or omissions of an insured ..." listed above is insured. Table 4-1 summarizes the types of owned or nonowned automobiles that are insured as well as who is insured while driving.

Acts Covered and Amount Insured Under the FAP, the insurance company provides bodily injury and property damage protection for losses that result because of the ownership, maintenance, or use of the owned or any nonowned automobile. "Use" in the context of the FAP includes the loading or unloading of an automobile.

Bodily injury coverage includes "bodily injury, sickness or disease including death resulting therefrom" and property damage is defined as "injury to or destruction of property including loss of use thereof." The

Table 4-1

Coverage for Owned and Nonowned Automobiles Under the Family Automobile Policy

Type of Automobile	Definition of Automobile	Interests Covered
Owned:	Private passenger, farm, or utility automobile, trailers, replacement automobiles, additional automobiles (if insurer covers all automobiles), temporary substitute automobiles	Named insured, any resident of named insured's household, persons using an owned automobile with permission of named insured, anyone else liable because of the actions of the drivers listed above
Nonowned:	Not owned by or furnished for the regular use of the named insured or any relative	Named insured, any relatives living with the named insured, anyone else liable because of the actions of the drivers listed above

company promises to defend an insured against any suit involving bodily injury or property damages covered under the policy. The insurer's obligation to defend suits extends even to groundless, false, or fraudulent actions. However, the insurer has the right to settle a claim or suit in any manner which it deems necessary; this often works to the detriment of the insured, as shown in the following example.

Anita Johnson is involved in a two-car collision. Anita is sued by the driver of the other car for $5,000, but she contends that she was not responsible for the accident. The facts surrounding the case support Anita's contention. However, her insurance company does not want the case to go to trial. Therefore, it offers the driver of the other car a $1,000 settlement. This is done because the adjuster feels that it will cost between $2,000 and $3,000 to win the case. The other driver accepts the settlement, but Anita is upset because she was not negligent.

There are individual limits of liability in the FAP for bodily injury and property damage liability. Nearly always, the bodily injury liability limits are higher than the property damage liability limits. Bodily injury liability limits are stated in two ways: a limit for each person injured in an occurrence and a limit for each occurrence.[8] For example, a policy might provide $100,000 of coverage for each person who is injured and $300,000 for all injured parties for each occurrence.

Property damage liability is written with a single limit, but, like the bodily injury limit, is stated in thousands of dollars of coverage per occurrence. Typically, liability coverage limits are stated per person per occurrence for bodily injury, for all persons per occurrence for bodily injury, and per occurrence for property damage liability. That is, liability limits of 10/20/5 indicate that a policy has $10,000 of bodily injury coverage per person per occurrence, $20,000 of bodily injury coverage for all persons per occurrence, and $5,000 of property damage coverage per occurrence. Two examples serve to illustrate how the limits of liability affect the insured's coverage.

1. Don Oakes owns an FAP policy with 50/100/10 limits of liability. While driving to work, Don fails to yield the right of way and collides with another automobile, severely damaging the other automobile and injuring its two occupants. The two occupants of the other car sustained $10,000 and $15,000 in medical expenses, respectively. The damage to the other car was $2,200. Don's insurance carrier will pay all the damages under the FAP because none of the losses exceeds the policy limits.

2. Roberta Miller owns an FAP with 10/20/5 limits. While driving under the influence of alcohol, Roberta crossed a median on an interstate highway and collided with an oncoming automobile. The three occupants of the other automobile were severely injured and sustained $5,000, $16,000, and $6,000 in medical expenses, respectively. The occupants filed suit against Roberta in sequence, starting with occupant 1. The other automobile was a total loss and was valued at $4,700. The car was owned by the brother of one of the occupants.

   Roberta's FAP will pay the $4,700 property damage because the amount is below the policy limit of $5,000. However, the FAP will not cover all of the medical expenses. The first occupant, who incurred $5,000 in medical expenses, obtains a settlement for $10,000. The second occupant obtains a settlement of $26,000. The policy imposes a $10,000 limit per person; therefore, the FAP covers the suit filed by the first occupant and $10,000 of the suit filed by the second occupant. The balance of the settlement will have to be paid by Roberta. The third occupant, who obtained a settlement of $10,000, will not be paid by the insurer under the FAP because the coverage limits of $20,000 have been reached. Thus, Roberta is responsible for a total of $26,000. (($26,000 − $10,000) + $10,000)) The insurer is responsible for $20,000 in medical claims and $4,700 in damages to the other vehicle. (The settlements are larger than the medical bills because they include other economic and noneconomic costs as well as attorney's fees.)

The increasing size of bodily injury and property damage claim settlements has caused some insureds to increase the limits for these

Table 4-2

Bodily Injury and Property Damage Liability Rate Factors*

Bodily Injury (Increased limits table applicable to 10/20 rates only)		Property Damage (Increased limits table applicable to $5,000 property damage liability rates)	
Bodily Injury Limit	Factor	Property Damage Limit	Factor
10/20	1.00	$ 5,000	1.00
20/20	1.20	10,000	1.05
15/30	1.18	15,000	1.06
20/40	1.30	25,000	1.08
25/50	1.39	35,000	1.10
35/35	1.41	50,000	1.13
50/100	1.63	100,000	1.18
100/200	1.82		
100/300	1.89		

*Adapted from *Private Passenger Automobile Manual* (New York: Insurance Services Office, 1976), pp. 23, 24.

types of potential losses. While increasing liability limits increases the premium, the increase is not linear. For example, the premium for 100/200 bodily injury liability limits is less than ten times the rate for 10/20 limits. Table 4-2 lists the rate factors in one state for bodily and property damage liability coverage, as of 1976.

Extensions of Coverage Under Part 1 of the FAP, the insurer agrees to provide types of supplemental benefits in addition to the bodily injury and property damage limits stated in the policy. First, the company promises to pay all expenses that it incurs, all suit costs taxed against the insured, and all interest on any judgment. These costs are paid only if they accrue "... after entry of the judgment and before the company has paid or tendered or deposited in court that part of the judgment which does not exceed the limit of the company's liability...."

The insurer also agrees to pay premiums for appeal bonds, bonds to release attached property, and bail bonds. The bonds to release attachments must be within the limits of liability of the policy. Payment is made for bail bonds only in the case of an accident or traffic law violation which arises out of the use of an automobile insured in the policy. The insurer will not pay more than $100 per bail bond. The insurer has no obligation other than to pay for the bond. The insured is required to make application for bonds.

Emergency medical and surgical expenses incurred at the time of the accident are another form of supplemental coverage. These expenses are not covered if the loss is due to war, however. The emergency medical and surgical expense coverage has broader protection for injured persons than the medical payments coverage does.

The fourth supplementary benefit pays all reasonable expenses other than loss of earnings incurred by the insured at the request of the insurer. Thus, if an insurer requested that an insured testify in a case, the insurer would be liable for the reasonable expenses incurred by the insured because of such testimony, e.g., taxis, hotel bills, and food, but not for wages lost by the insured because of time away from his or her employment.

Exclusions The liability section of the FAP contains ten major exclusions.

1. There is no coverage for an automobile used as a public or livery conveyance. For example, if the named insured uses a vehicle to provide limousine service, he or she would not be covered. This exclusion does not always apply, however. Bodily injury or property damage is covered if the named insured is a passenger in a nonowned taxi.
2. Bodily injury or property damage caused intentionally by or at the direction of the insured is excluded.
3. If an insured has a nuclear energy liability policy issued by the Nuclear Energy Liability Insurance Association, the Mutual Atomic Energy Liability Underwriters, or the Nuclear Insurance Association of Canada, then any bodily injury or property damage liability which is covered under the nuclear energy liability policy is not covered under the FAP. This is a limited exclusion. The bodily injury or property damage is not covered if a nuclear energy liability policy exists. However, if an insured did not carry nuclear energy liability coverage, the FAP would still pay for any nuclear exposures. In most cases, however, an individual who is subject to nuclear loss exposures will carry or otherwise be covered by a special nuclear energy liability policy because of the catastrophic nature of the exposure.
4. Bodily injury or property damage arising from the use of farm machinery is excluded.
5. Bodily injury to any employee of the insured other than a domestic employee is excluded. Domestic employees are excluded only if benefits are required to be provided under a

workers' compensation law. Bodily injury for the domestic employee would be covered in all other cases.

6. Bodily injury to fellow employees of the insured is not covered if the injury results from the insured's use of an automobile in the business of his or her employer. This exclusion does not apply to the named insured.

7. A seventh exclusion eliminates coverage for all owned automobiles when used by any person employed or engaged in the selling, repairing, servicing, storing, and parking of automobiles. There are some exceptions to this exclusion. The exclusion does not apply to:

> ... the named insured, a resident of the same household as the named insured, a partnership in which the named insured or such resident is a partner, or any partner, agent or employee of the named insured, such resident or partnership.

The intent of this exclusion is not to bar the named insured or the other parties listed from coverage if they are engaged in the automobile business. For example, the named insured or his partner could utilize an owned automobile in conducting their automobile business and still have coverage. However, if the named insured and partner took the owned automobile to a garage for servicing, the policy would not extend coverage to the garage owner. The garage owner could obtain liability coverage only under his or her own contract.

8. Exclusion eight applies to nonowned automobiles maintained or used by any person while engaged in "... the automobile business of the insured or any other person or organization, and ... any other business or occupation of the insured...." The second segment of this exclusion is not applicable to private passenger automobiles or trailers operated or occupied by the named insured or his or her private chauffeur or domestic servant.

9. Neither liability for property owned or transported by the insured nor liability for property rented to or in the care, custody, and control of the insured, unless property in a residence or private garage, is covered.

10. The final exclusion relates to an automobile obtained during the policy period or a temporary substitute automobile. Liability coverage under the FAP does not extend to these vehicles if the named insured has purchased other automobile liability insurance applicable to these classes of automobiles.

Other Insurance The FAP makes specific provision for cases where a named insured has several policies that provide liability coverage. The FAP states that it will pay only that proportion of each loss that its applicable limit of liability bears to the total applicable limit of liability of all valid and collectible insurance against such loss. The policy also stipulates that the insurance provided under the FAP is excess coverage over all other valid and collectible insurance with respect to temporary substitute automobiles or nonowned automobiles. Two examples illustrate how these provisions function.

1. Kim Holston obtains two FAPs on his 1978 Chevrolet Impala. One contract provides limits of 10/20/5 and the other limits of 50/100/50. Kim is at fault in an accident in which the driver of the other car sustains substantial injuries. The total value of pain and suffering and medical expenses for the other driver's injuries is determined by a jury to be $30,000. Insurer I would pay $5,000 of the loss, and Insurer II would pay $25,000 of the loss. The calculations for determining each insurer's responsibility are shown below:

$$\frac{\$10,000}{\$60,000} \times \$30,000 = \$5,000$$

$$\frac{\$50,000}{\$60,000} \times \$30,000 = \$25,000$$

2. JoAnne Haigh's mother comes to visit her, bringing her car. One afternoon JoAnne needs to go shopping, but her husband has taken their car to the garage for repair. Therefore, JoAnne borrows her mother's car.

On the way to the store, JoAnne has an accident which is her fault resulting in an award against her of $15,000. JoAnne and her mother have FAPs with 10/20/5 limits. The mother's policy would contribute first towards the loss and JoAnne's contract would be excess coverage.

Financial Responsibility Laws

The development of financial responsibility laws has already been discussed. To meet the financial responsibility laws, an individual can purchase an FAP. In cases where an individual was not insured at the time of an accident, he or she is required to provide proof of financial responsibility. The insurer certifies to the state through the use of a form known as an "SR-22" that an FAP policy has been issued to the insured; thus, the insured has met the requirements of the financial responsibility law. This certification automatically brings the policy into compliance with the provision of the financial responsibility law. This does not mean, however, that the insurer is responsible for an amount in excess of the limits of liability stated in the policy. If the insurer makes payments because of the certification which it would not make otherwise, the insured agrees to reimburse the company. A summary of current state financial responsibility laws can be found in Table 4-3.

Medical Expense Coverage

Subject to the limits stated in the policy, the insurer will make medical payments for the named insured, relatives of the named insured, and other individuals. Medical payments are made for:

> ... all reasonable expenses incurred within one year from the date of accident, for necessary medical, surgical, X-ray and dental services, including prosthetic devices, and necessary ambulance, hospital, professional nursing and funeral services. . . .

These medical payments are made regardless of who is at fault. There are two divisions of coverage.

In division one, the named insured and each relative are covered if they are occupying (including entering or alighting from) an owned automobile or a nonowned automobile with the permission of the owner. Additionally, they are covered as pedestrians against injury inflicted by an automobile or trailer.

The second division provides coverage for other individuals who are injured in an accident in either an owned or nonowned automobile. Any person, other than the named insured and relatives occupying an owned automobile being used by the named insured, a resident of the named insured's household, or some other individual with permission of the named insured is covered. Coverage for the other individuals also extends to nonowned automobiles. Coverage is available for individuals in nonowned automobiles operated or occupied by the named insured or a relative of the named insured. When a relative is operating or occupying a nonowned automobile, medical payments coverage applies only if the automobile is operated as a private passenger automobile or trailer. In the event that the named insured's private chauffeur or domestic servant is operating the nonowned automobile, the coverage would be as if the nonowned vehicle were being operated by the named insured. The assumption is made that any nonowned automobile is being operated with the permission of the owner and that the use of the vehicle is within the scope of the owner's permission.

The medical payments coverage (Part II of the FAP) includes an insurance provision similar in nature to the other insurance clause found in Part I, the liability section. In the event of duplicate coverage, the medical expense benefit will pay the proportion of the loss that its limit

Table 4-3
State Financial Responsibility Laws*

State	Required Limits	Scope of Law† Accidents / Years	Convictions / Years	Judgments Years	Minimum Reportable Property Damage
Alabama	10/20/5	S	P—3	Sat. & P—3	$ 50
Alaska	25/50/10	S & P—3	P—3	Sat. & P—3	200
Arizona	15/30/10	S & P—3	P—3	Sat. & P—3	300
Arkansas	10/20/5	S	P—3	Sat. & P—3	250
California	15/30/5	P—3	P—3	Sat. & P—3	250
Colorado	15/30/5	S	P—3	Sat. & P—3	100
Connecticut	20/40/5	S	P—3	Sat.	400
Delaware	10/20/5	S	P—3	Sat. & P—3	250
D.C.	10/20/5	S	P—3	Sat. & P—3	100
Florida	15/30/5 (optional $500 property damage deductible)	S & P—3	P—3	Sat. & P—3	200
Georgia	10/20/5	S & P—1	P—1	Sat.	100 ($300 for nonresidents)
Hawaii	25/no limit/10	S	P—3	Sat. & P—3	100
Idaho	10/20/5	S	P—3	Sat. & P—3	$100
Illinois	10/20/5	S	P—3	Sat. & P—3	250
Indiana	15/30/10	S & P—2	P—3	Sat. & P—3	200
Iowa	10/20/5	S	P—3	Sat. & P—3	250
Kansas	15/30/5				
Kentucky	10/20/5		P—3	Sat. & P—3	200
Louisiana	5/10/1	S	P—3	Sat. & P—3	200
Maine	20/40/10	S & P—3	P—3	Sat. & P—3	200
Maryland	20/40/5			Sat.	
Massachusetts	5/10/5			Sat. & P—3	
Michigan	20/40/10		P—3		
Minnesota	25/50/10				
Mississippi	10/20/5	S & P—3	P—3	Sat. & P—3	100

State	Financial Responsibility Limits	Security	Future Proof	Satisfaction	Accident Reporting
Missouri	10/20/2	S	P—2	Sat. & P—2	100
Montana	10/20/5		P—3	Sat. & P—3	250
Nebraska	15/30/10	S & P—3	P—3	Sat. & P—3	250
Nevada	15/30/5	S	P—3	Sat. & P—3	$250
New Hampshire	20/40/5	S & P—3	P—3	Sat. & P—3	300
New Jersey	15/30/5	S	P—3	Sat. & P—3	200
New Mexico	15/30/5			Sat.	100
New York	10/20/5	S		Sat.	200
North Carolina	15/30/5 (deductible for property damage allowed)	S			200
North Dakota	10/20/5	S & P—3	P—3	Sat. & P—3	200
Ohio	12.5/25/7.5	S	P—3	Sat. & P—3	150
Oklahoma	5/10/5	S & P—3	P—3	Sat. & P—3	100
Oregon	15/30/5	P—5	P—5	Sat. & P—5	200
Pennsylvania	15/30/5	S	P—3	Sat. & P—3	200
Rhode Island	10/20/5	S	P—1	Sat. & P—1	200
South Carolina	15/30/5	S & P—3 Min. 5 Max.	P—3 Min. 5 Max.	Sat. & P—3 Min. 5 Max.	100
South Dakota	15/30/10	S & P—3	P—3	Sat. & P—3	250
Tennessee	10/20/5	S & P—3	P—3	Sat. & P—3	$200
Texas	10/20/5	S & P—5	P—5	Sat. & P—5	250
Utah	15/30/5	S	P—3	Sat. & P—3	100
Vermont	10/20/5	P—3	P—3	Sat. & P—3	100
Virginia	25/50/5		P—3	Sat. & P—3	200
Washington	15/30/5	S	P—3	Sat. & P—3	200
West Virginia	10/20/5	S	P—3	Sat. & P—3	100
Wisconsin	15/30/5	S	P—3	Sat. & P—3	200
Wyoming	10/20/5	S	P—3	Sat. & P—3	250

†S = Security, P = Future Proof, Sat. = Satisfaction.

*Reprinted with permission from American Mutual Insurance Alliance, *Compendium of Insurance Charts* (Chicago: American Mutual Insurance Alliance, 1976), section entitled "Financial Responsibility Laws."

of coverage bears to the total coverage. Like the liability section, medical payment insurance coverage is excess to other valid and collectible medical payment insurance on nonowned or temporary substitute automobiles.

The medical expense coverage contains several exclusions. Bodily injury sustained while occupying either an owned automobile used as a public conveyance or a vehicle used as a residence is not covered. Also excluded are injuries sustained by the named insured or a relative when occupying or struck by a farm vehicle, equipment designed for use off public roads, or a vehicle operated on rails or crawler-treads.

Individuals other than the named insured or a relative are not covered when they are occupying a nonowned automobile used as a public conveyance. They also are not covered if the injury results from "... the maintenance or use of a nonowned automobile by such person while employed or otherwise engaged in the automobile business ..." or if the injury results from:

> ... the maintenance or use of a non-owned automobile by such person while employed or otherwise engaged in any other business or occupation, unless the bodily injury results from the operation or occupancy of a private passenger automobile by the named insured or by his private chauffeur or domestic servant, or of a trailer used therewith or with an owned automobile.

There are exclusions for war and for injuries sustained by individuals working in the automobile business. In the latter case, the accident is excluded only if benefits are paid or required to be paid partially or totally under a workers' compensation law.

For example, Kay Bool was driving the members of her car pool to work. Kay's automobile tire blew out. The car ran off a bridge and struck a tree. Kay received minor injuries and her medical bill was $112. Two of the passengers of the car were injured seriously—one incurred $1,700 in medical expenses, and the other sustained $2,633 in injuries.

Kay's medical expense limit was $1,000. Since this limit is on a per person basis, Kay's expenses would be paid in full. The other two individuals that were injured would receive $1,000 each. While the injured parties would not be reimbursed in full under the medical expense benefits section of Kay's FAP for their losses, they might be able to collect the balance under the medical expense segment of their own FAP. If Kay had been negligent, then the injured parties could seek compensation under the liability section of Kay's FAP.

Medical payments limits are available up to $100,000.[9] The medical expenses payment coverage applies to the medical expenses actually incurred.

Property Coverage Under the Family Automobile Policy

Part III of the FAP contains two types of physical damage coverage: comprehensive and collision. Comprehensive coverage can be written without the collision protection, but an insured who purchases both coverages obtains much broader protection. There are situations in which the insured is better off not to purchase any physical damage coverage. If the value of the insured owned automobile is extremely low, the coverage may be expensive relative to the amount that can be recovered. As a rule of thumb, the property risk probably should be retained by the individual when the premium is more than 20 percent of the actual cash value of the vehicle less any deductible.

Many individuals feel that physical damage coverage is designed only to cover the interest of the owner of an automobile, but this is not the case. The following section examines who is covered against loss under the physical damage coverage, Part III of the FAP.

Interests Insured The physical damage section of the FAP protects the interests of three different parties. The contract is designed primarily to protect the interest(s) of the named insured, but he or she may not be the only individual with an interest in the automobiles or trailers described in the policy declarations. The most common example of this situation arises when the named insured makes a loan at a bank and utilizes the borrowed funds to purchase an automobile described in the policy declarations. The bank has an interest in the automobile to the extent of the loan. To protect the interest of the bank, there is a loss payee clause in the FAP. In this section of the declarations, the insurance company states that any loss payable under the physical damage section will be made to the named loss payee and the named insured as their interests appear. In effect, the named insured is purchasing coverage for the benefit of the lending institution. The following example illustrates the impact of the loss payee clause.

Susie Tiernan purchased a 1977 Chevrolet Impala from a local Chevrolet dealer for $6,332. Of this amount, she borrowed $5,000 from the First National Bank of Briarcreek. Two days after purchasing the automobile, Susie demolished it during a heavy rain storm when the car slid off a highway.

Susie had obtained an FAP on her new automobile. Following the loss, the insurance company paid off the $5,000 loan to the bank and reimbursed Susie for the balance of the actual cash value.

One other interest is also covered under the physical damage section of the FAP. Coverage for nonowned automobiles (as defined in the contract) is provided if the named insured or a relative is operating or is using the nonowned automobile with the permission of the owner when it is damaged. This coverage is provided on an excess basis (excess to the owner's coverage).

Persons Insured   The term "insured" under the physical damage portion of the FAP is different from the definition as applicable to the liability coverage. With respect to the owned automobile, there are two categories of insured. The first is the named insured. The second is:

> ... any person or organization (other than a person or organization employed or otherwise engaged in the automobile business or as a carrier or other bailee for hire) maintaining, using or having custody of said automobile with the permission of the named insured and within the scope of such permission.

With respect to the nonowned automobile, the insured is defined as the named insured and any relative while using the nonowned automobile. As is true throughout the FAP, the use of the nonowned automobile must be with the actual or implied permission of the owner and within the scope of the granted or implied permission.

Property Covered   Both the comprehensive and collision coverages provide protection on owned or nonowned automobiles. In either case, what is being insured is a private passenger automobile or trailer. The same definition of "owned automobile" applies in both the liability and physical damage sections of the FAP, except that under the physical damage coverage, the term "owned automobile" does not include:

> ... (1) a trailer owned by the named insured on the effective date of this policy and not described herein, or (2) a trailer, ownership of which is acquired during the policy period, unless the company insures all private passenger, farm and utility automobiles and trailers owned by the named insured on the date of such acquisition and the named insured notifies the company during the policy period or within 30 days. . . .

A trailer is defined as a trailer for use with a private passenger automobile. A trailer is not covered, however, if it is being used for business purposes with other than a private passenger, farm, or utility automobile or as a home, office, store, display, or passenger trailer. The definition for a nonowned automobile in both Parts I and III of the FAP is similar.

The comprehensive coverage provides limited protection for personal effects. Personal effects are covered up to $100 for any loss due to fire or lightning. Personal effects include ". . . robes, wearing apparel, and other personal effects which are the property of the named insured or a relative, while such effects are in or upon the owned automobile." Coverage on personal effects is duplicative for many individuals since the homeowners policy provides extended coverage for losses to property away from premises caused by fire or lightning.

Perils Insured Against For the individual who purchases both comprehensive and collision coverage, basically "all-risks" protection is afforded. The collision protection covers owned and nonowned automobiles against collision with other objects, collision with attached vehicles, or upset. Normally, insureds tend to think of collision coverage as applying to collisions between an insured automobile and some other vehicle. This perception is too limited. For example, if an insured automobile strikes a wheel that is rolling down the highway, that would constitute collision. Hitting a fixed object, such as a house, or running into a highway sign would also constitute collision.

Another misconception is that an insured automobile must be moving at the time that the collision occurs. A parked automobile hit by another car would be protected by collision coverage. The following example illustrates how the collision coverage operates.

Jim Wilbur was driving his automobile down an old country road. Over the years, rain had washed away a segment of the road's foundation. When Jim drove over the weakened area, the road buckled but did not collapse. The car was thrown off the road and turned over several times. The damage to the car would be covered under the collision section of the FAP instead of the comprehensive section because the car was upset.

The comprehensive section under the FAP promises to pay for loss caused other than by collision. The contract further stipulates that certain types of losses are covered under the comprehensive section of the policy rather than the collision section. The collision coverage may have a deductible that differs from that of the comprehensive coverage. Thus, placing a particular type of loss under one category may reduce or increase the amount of payment that an individual receives.

The types of losses that are considered comprehensive risks and not collision risks are (1) breakage of glass, (2) loss caused by missiles, (3) falling objects, (4) fire, (5) theft, (6) larceny, (7) explosion, (8) earthquake, (9) windstorm, (10) hail, (11) water, (12) flood, (13) malicious mischief, (14) vandalism, (15) riot, (16) civil commotion, and (17) collision with a bird or animal.

Amount of Coverage Generally coverage on the insured automobile(s) is written on an actual cash value basis. In some instances, however, the insurance company will write coverage on the insured automobile for a stated value. Most insurers do not issue the stated amount policy contract on a regular basis; usually it is utilized for coverage of antique automobiles. Actual cash value is the price that the market sets on an automobile. The adjuster has numerous sources of information available to aid him or her in ascertaining the value. However, from the insured's perspective, the actual cash value frequently appears to be a function of random guessing. Most insureds accept the loss adjuster's determination of the actual cash value. If the insured and company do not agree on the amount of the loss, either may demand an appraisal. Under the policy, both the insured and the insurance company would select an appraiser; these appraisers in turn would select a disinterested umpire. The insured's and the insurer's appraisers would each state his estimate of the actual cash value of the loss and attempt to agree on a settlement. If the two appraisers did not agree, their differences would be submitted to the umpire for a decision. An award determined by two of the three individuals would constitute the amount of the loss. The insured and the insurance company pay the expenses of their own appraisers and share equally in the expenses of the appraisal and the umpire. The procedure would work as shown in the following example.

Betsy Van Dorn, while driving an automobile during a recent outing in the country with her family, struck a horse with her automobile. Severe damage was done to her car. The vehicle, which was extremely old, was worth less than the amount necessary to repair it. In the process of settling the claim, the loss adjuster ascertained that the value of the automobile was $1,450. Betsy thought that the automobile was worth at least $2,600. After an extended period of time, Betsy and the adjuster failed to reach an agreement. Thus, Betsy hired an appraiser to work with the company's loss adjuster. The appraiser hired by Betsy valued the car not at $2,600 but $2,700. The company adjuster, however, continued to contend that the vehicle was worth only $1,450. The dispute was submitted to a third appraiser who had been selected by the company's adjuster and Betsy's appraiser. The umpire, after examining all the facts, came to the conclusion that the vehicle was worth $2,200. Betsy's appraiser felt that this was a valid compromise and agreed with the umpire. Thus, the insurance company was obligated to pay the $2,200 less any deductible in the contract.

While the limit on the automobile is the actual cash value, there is a separate limit of $500 for any trailer not owned by the named insured. The insurance company has several options available to it under the FAP other than paying the actual cash value for damage. In lieu of paying for a loss, the insurance company has the right to repair or replace any property that is damaged or stolen. When property has been stolen, the insurance company has the right, if the property is found, to return it to the insured rather than paying for a total loss. However, if the property has been damaged, the insurance company is obligated to pay for such damage.

The insurance company can take all or part of the property and pay the insured the actual cash value of the property. This option is unilateral. The insurance company has the right to accept property that the insured wants to give it and pay for the loss, but it is not required to do so. The insured may not abandon property to the company.

The insurance company always reduces the amount of payment by the amount of the deductible stated in the contract. In the FAP, a flat deductible generally applies to collision coverage. A deductible may or may not apply to the comprehensive coverage. With the spiraling cost of automobile insurance, some insurers now require a deductible on both collision coverage and comprehensive coverage.

The amount of the deductible has an impact on the amount of the premium. Where a low deductible is being utilized in the FAP, the insurer knows that it will have a large number of relatively small, so-called nuisance claims. As a result, as the size of the deductible increases, the size of the premium decreases. The FAP physical damage coverage premium exemplifies this situation. Figure 4-1 illustrates the impact of the deductible on the cost of collision coverage. A rise in the deductible in a collision policy from $200 to $250 produces a reduction in premium of 10 percent. Raising the deductible another $250 to $500 reduces the basic collision premium for a $200 deductible by 40 percent. Raising the deductible to $1,000 decreases the premium 65 percent. Savings also accrue under comprehensive coverage if the deductible is raised.

Many state insurance commissioners have been suggesting that one method of keeping insurance costs low is to increase deductibles. It is obvious from Figure 4-1 that raising the deductible on physical damage types of coverages would have a tremendous impact on costs. However, this approach does not solve the long-range problems related to insurance costs.

Changing a deductible does lower cost temporarily, but it does not have any impact on the factors which are forcing insurance premiums to rise. The primary causes of increasing premiums are the rising cost of automobile repairs, litigation, and other services insurers purchase.

The deductible that is applicable to collision losses is not always utilized by the insurance company. When an insured automobile collides with another automobile and the same insurer has the coverage on both automobiles, then the collision deductible does not apply. The contract requires only that both cars be insured by the same company, regardless of whether or not both cars have collision coverage. The following example demonstrates how the deductible would be applied.

Exclusions The physical damage section of the FAP contains numerous exclusions. Some of these exclusions are similar to other exclusions found in the FAP. Coverage does not apply:

Figure 4-1

Impact of Deductible on Collision Coverage Costs*

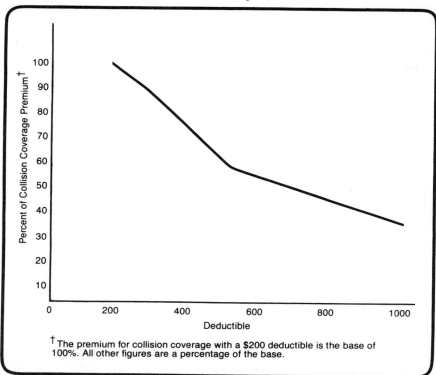

† The premium for collision coverage with a $200 deductible is the base of 100%. All other figures are a percentage of the base.

*Reprinted with permission from *Private Passenger Automobile Manual* (New York: Insurance Services Office, 1976), notice.

(a) to any automobile while used as a public or livery conveyance; (b) to loss due to war; (c) to loss to a non-owned automobile arising out of its use by the insured while he is employed or otherwise engaged in the automobile business; (d) to loss to a private passenger, farm or utility automobile or trailer owned by the named insured and not described in this policy or to any temporary substitute automobile therefor, if the insured has other valid and collectible insurance against such loss; (e) to damage which is due and confined to wear and tear, freezing, mechanical or electrical breakdown or failure, unless such damage results from a theft covered by this policy; (f) to tires, unless damaged by fire, malicious mischief or vandalism, or stolen or unless the loss be coincident with and from the same cause as other loss covered by this policy; (g) to loss due to radioactive contamination; (h) under coverage E (collision coverage), to breakage of glass if insurance with respect to such breakage is otherwise afforded.

The contract also contains another insurance provision which makes the FAP proportional coverage for owned automobiles and excess coverage for nonowned or temporary substitute automobiles. This other insurance clause is almost identical to the one found in Part I of the policy, the liability section.

Other Benefits The insured may purchase coverage for towing and labor costs necessitated by disablement of an owned or nonowned automobile. Labor costs are restricted to those expenses incurred at the location where the vehicle is disabled. The FAP has a limit, normally $25, on towing and labor expenses.

In addition, the physical damage coverage contains two supplementary payments. Beginning forty-eight hours after the theft of an insured automobile has been reported, the insurer will reimburse the insured for transportation expenses. The maximum amount that the insurer will pay under the FAP is $10 per day up to an aggregate amount of $300. Thus, if the insured, forty-eight hours after his or her car was stolen, rented a car for fifteen days at $20 per day, the insurance company would pay the insured $150.

The other supplementary payment available under the physical damage coverage is payment of general average and salvage charges which arise when an automobile is being transported by a public carrier.[10] However, the insured must be liable for the charges in order to be covered under the FAP.

Uninsured Motorists Coverage

Basic Coverage An individual should be concerned about his or her liability to the operator of other vehicles. Unfortunately, many motorists, for a variety of reasons, are not able to pay for damages they may cause, and they do not carry insurance. To protect an innocent party against a loss caused by an uninsured motorist, insurance companies have provided uninsured motorists protection under Part IV of the FAP. The coverage is designed to pay for bodily injury damages caused by an uninsured motorist. Thus, if an insured's car is struck by a vehicle driven by an uninsured motorist, the insured's loss would be paid by his or her insurer under the FAP.

In a few states, both property damage and bodily injury liability coverage are made available under the uninsured motorists protection, but a majority of the states do not permit property damage coverage under the uninsured motorists protection. Instead, it is covered under the collision section of the FAP. Since most states only permit uninsured motorists protection for bodily injury damages, this section will concentrate on bodily injury protection.

The uninsured motorists coverage in the FAP states that it will:

> . . . pay all sums which the insured or his legal representative shall be legally entitled to recover as damages from the owner or operator of an uninsured automobile because of bodily injury, sickness or disease, including death resulting therefrom, hereinafter called "bodily injury," sustained by the insured, caused by accident and arising out of the ownership, maintenance or use of such uninsured automobile; provided, for the purposes of this coverage, determination as to whether the insured or such representative is legally entitled to recover such damages, and if so the amount thereof, shall be made by agreement between the insured or such representative and the company or, if they fail to agree, by arbitration.
>
> No judgment against any person or organization alleged to be legally responsible for the bodily injury shall be conclusive, as between the insured and the company, of the issues of liability of such person or organization or of the amount of damages to which the insured is legally entitled unless such judgment is entered pursuant to an action prosecuted by the insured with the written consent of the company.

While the provision appears straightforward, a thorough understanding of the terms and the case law relating to the coverage is necessary to appreciate the protection afforded under this section of the FAP.

The policy states that it covers damages that are caused by bodily injury resulting from an accident. The term "accident" is viewed from the perspective of the insured. In the event that an uninsured motorist intentionally injures or causes the injury of an insured, coverage still is available provided that the occurrence is an accident from the perspective of the injured party. In Leatherby v. Willoughby, Plitz, who was uninsured, deliberately drove his truck into the insured, Willoughby. Willoughby had uninsured motorists protection under his automobile policy. The insurer, Leatherby Insurance Company, contended that the incident was not an accident as stated in the policy. According to the company, the deliberate actions of the truck driver barred the incident from being an accident. The Florida District Court of Appeals, ruling on the case, indicated that since the injured insured did not contemplate being intentionally hit by the tortfeasor, the incident was an accident from the standpoint of the insured, and the uninsured motorists coverage was applicable.[11]

An accident must arise from the ownership, maintenance, or use of an uninsured automobile. The terms "ownership," "maintenance," and "use" encompass a broad range of activities. For example, an insured is covered as either a passenger or as a pedestrian. The insured also is covered while entering or leaving or while loading or unloading an automobile.

An uninsured automobile is an automobile or trailer for which there is no bodily injury liability bond or insurance policy applicable at the time of the loss. However, if such a bond or insurance policy is in effect at the time of the loss and the company writing the bond or insurance policy denies coverage, then the automobile still is classified as an uninsured automobile.

A hit-and-run automobile also is classified as an uninsured automobile. An automobile is a hit-and-run vehicle if the insured is unable to ascertain the identity of either the owner or operator of the automobile. In addition, the insured or the insured's representative must inform the authorities about an accident within twenty-four hours of its occurrence and also must file with the insurance company within thirty days after an accident a statement asserting that the insured has a cause of action against some unknown party.

The term "uninsured automobile" does not include the following:

1. an insured automobile or an automobile furnished for the regular use of the named insured or a relative;
2. an automobile or trailer owned or operated by a self-insurer within the meaning of any motor vehicle financial responsibility law, motor carrier law or any similar law;
3. an automobile or trailer owned by the United States of America, Canada, a state, a political subdivision of any such government or an agency of the foregoing;
4. a land motor vehicle or trailer if operated on rails or crawler-treads or while located for use as a residence or premises and not as a vehicle; or
5. a farm type tractor or equipment designed for use principally off public roads, except while actually upon public roads.

The individuals insured against damage caused by an uninsured motorist include not only the named insured but also any relatives of the named insured. Other persons who are occupying an insured automobile are covered. The term "insured automobile" encompasses not only the automobile described in the policy but also replacement vehicles, temporary substitute automobiles, and nonowned automobiles operated by the named insured. A nonowned automobile does not include an automobile utilized as a public conveyance, an automobile which is not being used with the permission of the owner, or an automobile or trailer which belongs to a resident of the household of the named insured.

Uninsured motorists coverage is applicable only when the insured or the insured's legal representative has a legal right to recover damages from the owner or operator of an uninsured automobile. If this right against the uninsured motorist lapses, then the insured loses his protection under the uninsured motorist coverage in the FAP. Two cases illustrate the importance of having a right against an uninsured tortfeasor. In Crenshaw v. Great Central Insurance Company, a Missouri Court of Appeals ruled that an insured may be entitled to bring action against the insurance company under the uninsured motorists coverage, but if the insured's legal right to recover from the tortfeasor has expired, then the insurance company is not liable.

In this case, Columbus and Fae Frances Crenshaw, the parents of Dale Crenshaw, brought an action against Great Central Insurance Company. In the action, the parents contended that their son was killed due to the negligence of an uninsured motorist, one Gail Martin. The Crenshaws further contended that their son was provided coverage under the uninsured motorists provision of their policy. Great Central Insurance Company agreed that the Crenshaws had had a cause of action against Gail Martin pursuant to section 537.100 of the Wrongful Death Statutes of Missouri. However, the company claimed that that section of the Missouri Code stipulated that if legal action was not commenced within two years after the cause of action, then the cause of action lapsed. Since the Crenshaws sued the company more than two years after the accident, the company contended that there was no coverage because the Crenshaws no longer had a cause of action against Martin.

The court found in favor of the insurance company. In its decision, the court noted that the insureds had ten years under the contract statutes of Missouri to take action against an insurance company. However, the court went on to state that coverage depended on the insured having a legal right against the tortfeasor. Any action against the insurance company was forfeited when action was not brought against the company within two years.[12]

In Associate Indemnity Corporation v. Cannon, the question of suing a tortfeasor was again considered. In this case, which was decided by the Oklahoma Supreme Court, the court considered whether or not an insured had to first sue a known uninsured tortfeasor before action could be brought against an insurance company under the uninsured motorists coverage. The Oklahoma Supreme Court decided that the insured was not required to first bring action against a known tortfeasor. In addressing this question, the court cited an earlier case in which a Kansas court stated that:

> A requirement that an insured must first proceed to judgment against the uninsured tortfeasor will present multiple problems. Where the uninsured motorist was killed in the accident insured will be required to have an administrator appointed to represent the uninsured motorist; if the uninsured motorist is a "hit-and-run" driver additional problems will be presented; and if uninsured refuses to let the insurance company defend or participate in the action, questions of due process will arise. Such a procedure will require vexatious and fruitless actions against indigent and bankrupt motorists; it will encourage insurance companies and their attorneys to solicit the defense of uninsured motorists; and it will put the insured plaintiff to

the expense and delay of trying two lawsuits in order to collect one judgment.[13]

The Kansas case indicates that an insured may have the right to sue an uninsured motorist, but a suit is not a prerequisite to having the right to proceed against an insurer. The following example illustrates how uninsured motorists coverage functions.

Ruth Helmetag has an FAP with uninsured motorists coverage. The policy limits for this coverage are $5,000 per person and $10,000 per accident. While Ruth was driving to the grocery store to purchase groceries, her car was struck by another car driven by a hit-and-run driver. Ruth received numerous cuts and a broken arm. Her medical expenses were $500; her economic loss from being out of work was $1,000; and the damage to her car was $1,790.

Under Ruth's uninsured motorists coverage, her insurer would pay for the medical expenses. The damage to the car would be paid under Ruth's collision coverage, if any. Even if Ruth had been hit by an insured driver, her medical payments coverage would have provided some medical expense protection. In some states the property damage would also be covered under the uninsured motorists coverage. Ruth's economic loss ($1,000) would also be covered by her uninsured motorists benefits, since the total sum of her losses does not exceed the $5,000 per person limitation.

Exclusions The uninsured motorists coverage contains three exclusions. First, the coverage excludes payment for bodily injury sustained ". . . while occupying an automobile . . . owned by the named insured or a relative, or through being struck by such an automobile." Obviously, this exclusion is not applicable to an insured automobile; if it were, coverage virtually would be eliminated.

The second exclusion pertains to settlements by the insured with a liable party. If the insured or his or her legal representative makes a settlement without the consent of the insurer, then the insurer is not responsible for bodily injury damages.

The third exclusion relates to workers' compensation. The benefits under the uninsured motorists coverage cannot inure "to the benefit of any workers' compensation or disability benefits carrier or any person or organization qualifying as a self-insurer under any workmen's compensation or disability benefits law or similar law."

Limits of Liability Uninsured motorists protection has a limit per person and per accident. These limits are contained in the policy declarations. Generally, the limits are equal to those required in the financial responsibility laws in each state. In most states, an individual can purchase higher limits if he or she feels that they are necessary.

The limits paid to the insured are subject to reduction. Payments which are made by an uninsured motorist, the owner of an uninsured automobile, or other party liable for the operation of the uninsured automobile are deducted from the uninsured motorists benefits. Benefits paid under workers' compensation, disability benefits, or similar laws also serve to reduce the coverage provided.

Two other limiting factors are important. Payments made under the uninsured motorists coverage are ". . . applied in reduction of the amount of damages which he may be entitled to recover from any person insured under Coverage A . . ." (the bodily injury liability coverage). Second, the insurer is not liable for medical expense payments that can be recovered from the owner or operator of an uninsured automobile and which are payable under Part II, expenses for medical services.

Other Insurance   The other insurance clause in the uninsured motorists coverage of the FAP is designed to prevent the insured from stacking benefits, that is, profiting by collecting benefits from several sources. When an insured is in an automobile not owned by the named insured, his or her uninsured motorists coverage is excess only to the extent it exceeds the limits of the primary coverage. The following example illustrates how this provision would affect coverage.

Jerry Risser made it a regular practice to ride to work every day with his next door neighbor, Ruth Pierce. One afternoon when Ruth was driving home, her car was struck by another automobile driven by a negligent uninsured motorist. Ruth's policy had uninsured motorists limits of $15,000 per person and $30,000 per accident. The limits for uninsured motorists coverage on Jerry's policy were $5,000 and $10,000, respectively. Jerry sustained severe internal injuries as a result of the wreck and required several operations. Jerry's hospital bills amounted to $17,834. Ruth's insurer paid $15,000 to Jerry. Jerry's insurer paid nothing under the uninsured motorists coverage because (1) its coverage was excess to the coverage provided in Ruth's policy, and (2) its limits were less than the limits of Ruth's policy.

In the previous example, if the limits under the policy had been reversed, i.e., Jerry's policy had had $15,000 and $30,000 limits and Ruth's policy had had $5,000 and $10,000 limits, Ruth's insurance would only have paid $5,000, the limits of her policy. Jerry's policy would have paid $10,000, the amount by which the limit of his policy exceeded the limit of the primary insurance.

The portion of the other insurance clause cited above refers to nonowned automobiles. In other cases, only the uninsured motorists coverage with the highest limits is available to the insured. All insurers contribute to these limits based on the proportion that their limits bear to the total limits.

In spite of the other insurance clause, courts in some recent decisions have allowed the insured to collect twice. An examination of one recent case serves as an illustration of the direction that some courts have taken in reducing the impact of the other insurance provision in uninsured motorists coverage.[14]

The Wyoming Supreme Court heard the case of Ramsour v. Grange Insurance Association and Liberty Mutual Insurance Company. The plaintiff in this case had rented an automobile from Ford Rent-a-Car. The rental car dealer was covered by a policy issued by Liberty Mutual Insurance Company with uninsured motorists coverage for $10,000. The policy covered the plaintiff. The plaintiff was the named insured in a policy issued to her by the Grange Insurance Association. This policy, like the Liberty Mutual contract, contained uninsured motorists coverage for $10,000.

While driving the rental car, the plaintiff was injured in a collision with an uninsured motorist. The insurance companies involved contended that the plaintiff was not entitled to collect twice. Instead, the insurers felt that she was entitled to $10,000. Each insurer was to be responsible for 50 percent of this amount.

Basing its decision on the Wyoming statute on uninsured motorists coverage, which reads in part:

> No policy . . . shall be delivered or issued . . . unless coverage is provided . . . in limits for bodily injury . . . under provisions approved by the insurance commissioner, for the protection of persons insured thereunder . . . from owners or operators of uninsured motor vehicles . . .[15]

The court found for the plaintiff. The court's decision for the plaintiff was based on three points. These points, and the court's comments on each, follow.

> The statute states that every policy of insurance that is issued shall be in the amount of the statutory minimum. It does not say that if there is more than one policy covering the insured, that the maximum to be paid would be the minimum limit of one policy. We cannot stretch, extend, enlarge nor amend what the legislature has clearly said.
>
> As to the second point, the only answer is that there is no reason to conjecture about how much insurance the uninsured might have had, had he had any at all, by assuming that he would have had only $10,000. The only inequity that there could be would be to permit "stacking" of coverage in order to permit the insured to recover more than his damage and thus gain a windfall. We do not approve such "stacking." On the other hand, to not permit "stacking" to result in a sum equal to or less than the insured's damage will result in a windfall to the insurer. "Stacking" to that extent is approved. Here again, we see no such intent as that urged upon us in the language of the pertinent statute.

We see no significance to the fact that the Wyoming Insurance Commissioner has approved the "other insurance" provisions. He has no authority to approve any policy that eliminates the required coverage because our statute cannot be ignored when it says that "No policy" shall be delivered without uninsured motorists coverage. "No policy" means every policy issued in the context of the statute. There is not coverage in every policy if one of two, as here, does not, in fact, give coverage. The defendant tells us, if we do as we intend to do in this case, insurance rates will go up because the plaintiff got what she bargained for—a policy with an escape clause—and they cost less. The ordinary policyholder has not the knowledge, skill nor strength to bargain with an insurance company. It was a take-it-or-leave-it proposition for her.

For the reasons stated, we are fully satisfied and hold that the excess-escape-paragraph of the "other insurance" provision of the Grange endorsement is repugnant to the statute, and is, as applied to the facts here presented, invalid and ineffective.[16]

However, other courts have not permitted stacking. In fact, a United States District Court has ruled in an Alabama case that uninsured motorists limits cannot be stacked.

Passenger in automobile which collided with one driven by an allegedly uninsured motorist brought action against uninsured motorist insurer of passenger's father and uninsured motorist insurer of owner of the automobile in which passenger was riding. The Senior District Judge held that, under Alabama law, a passenger could not stack uninsured motorist coverage of the owner of the automobile in which she was riding even though the policy listed two automobiles, in one of which passenger was riding at the time of the accident, and even though a separate and specific premium had been paid for uninsured coverage on each vehicle; and that, under Alabama law, coverage of passenger's father's insurer was secondary and excess to coverage of automobile owner's insurer.[17]

Arbitration and Trust Agreements Two other clauses in the uninsured motorists coverage require brief examination. As in many property and liability insurance contracts, there is an arbitration clause. Under this clause, if the parties do not agree on the amount that should be recovered, or if they do not agree that the insured is legally entitled to recover damages from the owner or operator of an uninsured automobile, then either party can demand that the matter be settled by arbitration. The arbitration is guided by the rules of the American Arbitration Association and is binding on the participating parties.

The second clause, the trust agreement, states that anyone receiving benefits under the uninsured motorists coverage agrees to protect the right of the insurer to subrogate against liable parties. The party receiving benefits also agrees to remit to the insurer any funds received in a settlement or judgment up to the limit of the coverage provided under the uninsured motorists protection.

Summary   A summary of the state uninsured motorists provisions can be found in Table 4-4. This table presents the limits that normally are provided under uninsured motorists coverage in each state as well as other pertinent information.

General Conditions

Notification of Insurer   There are several conditions found in the FAP with which every insured should be familiar. When an accident, occurrence, or loss has taken place, the insured is required to notify the insurer as soon as possible. The notification should be in writing and should provide a detailed description of the circumstances surrounding the event, including the time and place as well as the names and addresses of parties injured and witnesses. Further, the contract requires the insured to notify the police promptly in the event of a theft.

Action Against Company   The insured is not permitted to bring action against the insurance company under Part I, the liability coverage unless the insured has complied with the terms of the policy. In addition, a judgment must have been rendered against the insured through the process of a trial or by written agreement between the insured, the claimant, and the insurance company.

The insured cannot bring action against the insurance company under Parts II, III, or IV of the contract unless the insured has complied with all the terms of the contract. With reference to Part III, there is a further proviso that the insured must wait thirty days after proof of loss is filed and the amount of loss is determined as provided in the policy.

Medical Claims   Under Parts II and IV of the FAP, the insured is eligible for payments for medical expenses. The contract requires that the insured provide proof of any medical claim. This includes providing statements under oath, if required, regarding the nature and extent of the claim. The proof must be filed as soon as is practicable. However, the contract does not establish what is "as soon as practicable."

Effective Date of Coverage   All the coverages of the standard FAP become effective at 12:01 A.M., standard time, at the address of the named insured. If the named insured is on daylight savings time, then daylight savings time would be the standard time. Or, if the insured lived in California, then the contract would go into effect at 12:01 A.M. standard time in California, not at 12:01 A.M. where the insurer is located. The 12:01 A.M. time frame, however, is becoming less important because many family automobile insurance policies are bound before the policy is physically issued. Under such circumstances, the insured is covered from the time the coverage is bound.

Table 4-4
Summary of State Uninsured Motorist Coverage as of January, 1976*

State	Limits	Right to Reject Coverage	Required Deviations from Standard Wording	Insolvency Provision Included	/Cut-off Period
Alabama	10/20	Yes		No	
Alaska	25/50	Yes		No	
Arizona	15/30 up to 45/90	No		Yes	
Arkansas	10/20	Yes	(a)	Yes	1 Year
California	15/30	Yes	(b)	Yes	1 Year
Colorado	15/30	Yes		No	
Connecticut	20/40 up to B/I limits	No	Arbitration is optional	Yes	
Delaware	10/20/5 ($250 property damage deductible)	Yes		Yes	1 Year
Florida	15/30 up to B/I limits	Yes	(b) (a)	Yes	1 Year
Georgia[1]	10/20/5 up to 25/50/10 ($250 property damage deductible)	Yes	(c) (b)	Yes	
Hawaii	10/20	Yes		No	
Idaho	10/20	Yes		Yes	1 Year
Illinois	10/20	No		Yes	
Indiana	15/30	Yes		Yes	2 Years
Iowa	10/20	Yes		Yes	1 Year
Kansas	15/30	Yes	Arbitration is optional	Yes	2 Years
Kentucky[2]	10/20	Yes		Yes	1 Year
Louisiana[2]	Not less than policy BI limits	Yes	Arbitration is optional	Yes	1 Year
Maine[2]	20/40 up to BI limits	No			
Maryland	20/40/5[3] ($100 property damage deductible)	Yes	(c)	Yes	1 Year

Has a state fund which pays for losses as the result of death, injury, or damage caused by an unidentified vehicle or driver.

State	Limits	Notes			
Massachusetts	5/10 up to 15/40		No	Yes	1 Year
Michigan				No	
Minnesota[2]	25/50 up to BI limits		No	Yes	
Mississippi	10/20 up to BI limits		Yes	Yes	1 Year
Missouri	10/20	(c) Arbitration is optional	No	Yes	2 Years
Montana	25/50		Yes	No	
Nebraska	15/30		Yes	Yes	
Nevada	15/30 up to B/I limits	(b) (a)	Yes	Yes	1 Year
New Hampshire	20/40 up to B/I limits ($5,000 property damage claims because of insolvency covered, if no other insurance available)	(c)	No	Yes	3 Years
New Jersey	15/30/5 ($100 property damage deductible)		No	No	
New Mexico	15/30/5 ($250 property damage deductible)		Yes	[4]	
New York	10/20	Administered by MVAIC	No	No	
North Carolina	15/30/5 ($100 property damage deductible)		Yes	Yes	3 Years
North Dakota	10/20		No	Yes	
Ohio	12.5/25		Yes	Yes	
Oklahoma	5/10—but larger amounts may be offered and purchased if desired	(b) Arbitration is optional	Yes	Yes	1 Year
Oregon	15/30 up to 50/100	(b)	No	Yes	2 Years
Pennsylvania	15/30		No	Yes	6 Years
Rhode Island	10/20	(b)	Yes	Yes	
South Carolina	15/30/5 ($200 property damage deductible)	(c)	No	Yes	

Continued on the next page

State	Coverage limits				
South Dakota²	15/30 up to BI limits	No			Yes
Tennessee¹	10/20/5 ($200 property damage deductible)³ up to policy limits	Yes	(c)		Yes
Texas	10/20	Yes			Yes
Utah	15/30	Yes			No
Vermont	10/20	No			Yes — 1 Year
Virginia	25/50/5 ($200 property damage deductible) up to policy limits	No	(c)	(b)	**
Washington	15/30	Yes	(c)		Yes — 3 Years
West Virginia	10/20/5 ($300 property damage deductible)	No	(c)		Yes
Wisconsin	15/30 up to BI limits	No			Yes
Wyoming	10/20	Yes			Yes

(a)—Medical Payments Coverage benefits are not allowed to be set off.

(b)—Workmen's Compensation benefits are not allowed to be set off or uninsured motorist payment excluded because of such benefits.

(c)—Arbitration not permitted.

Absent a specific statutory prohibition of subrogation, the insurer has the contractual rights afforded by the Trust Agreement in the uninsured motorist coverage.

1—Uninsured Motorist Coverage—Extends uninsured motorist coverage to include tortfeasors whose bodily injury liability limits are less than insured victims uninsured motorist coverage limits.—maximum recovery subject to insureds uninsured motorist coverage limits.

2—Underinsured Motorist Coverage—Extends uninsured motorist coverage to include tortfeasors whose bodily injury liability limits are less than insured victims bodily injury liability limits.—maximum recovery subject to insureds bodily injury liability limits.

3—May be reduced after policy issuance.

4—There is no statutory insolvency provision. However, the prescribed encorsement for the state contemplates such coverage.

Territorial Restrictions   Regardless of when coverage becomes effective, an automobile is not covered if it is outside the boundaries of the United States, its possessions or territories, or Canada. However, coverage is available for automobiles being transported between ports thereof. This is true for both physical damage and liability coverages. An insured entering a foreign country can be covered only by purchasing additional automobile insurance protection. What often is overlooked by an insured is that the coverage under the FAP provides protection in Canada but *not* in Mexico.

Cancellation   The named insured has the option of canceling the FAP at any time. The insurer, however, does not have this flexibility. The insurer must give the named insured a minimum of ten days' notice before it can cancel the contract. Notice is effected by mailing to the address shown on the policy a written notice stating when the contract is to be canceled. Like most policies, if the insured cancels, earned premium is calculated on a short-rate basis, but if the company cancels, earned premium is calculated on a pro rata basis.

A special cancellation provision relates to Part I (the liability coverge) under the FAP. If a new policy has been in effect sixty days or if the policy is renewed, the company cannot exercise its right to cancel the liability coverage unless (1) the named insured fails to pay the premium; (2) the insurance was obtained through fraudulent misrepresentation; (3) the insured violates the terms and conditions of the policy; or (4) the named insured or any other operator, who is a resident in the same household with the named insured or who customarily operates an automobile insured under the policy:

> (a) has had his driver's license suspended or revoked during the policy period, or (b) is or becomes subject to epilepsy or heart attacks, and such individual cannot produce a certificate from a physician testifying to his unqualified ability to operate a motor vehicle, or (c) is or has been convicted of or forfeits bail, during the 36 months immediately preceding the effective date of the policy or during the policy period, for: (1) any felony, or (2) criminal negligence resulting in death, homicide or assault, arising out of the operation of a motor vehicle, or (3) operating a motor vehicle while in an intoxicated condition or while under the influence of drugs, or (4) leaving the scene of an accident without stopping to report, or (5) theft of a motor vehicle, or (6) making false statements in an application for a driver's license, or (7) a third violation, committed within a period of 18 months, of (i) any ordinance or regulation limiting the speed of motor vehicles, of (ii) any of the provisions in the motor vehicle laws of any state, the violation of which constitutes a misdemeanor, whether or not the violations were repetitions of the same offense or were different offenses.

(These same provisions are not found in the policies of all states.)

Some states have placed further restrictions on the insurer's right to cancel or deny renewal of coverage. Table 4-5 contains a list of state automobile insurance termination laws, but these laws are highly susceptible to change.

Policy Readability

The previous chapter contained information on the new homeowners policy which is designed to be easier for the insured to understand. To policyholders, the FAP is as difficult to comprehend as any of the homeowners contracts. Developing a policy consumers can understand has been a goal of insurers for many years. However, many insurers have avoided designing a new policy fearing legal complications. Legal complications would arise because the language in the new policy would have to be tested in the courts. The FAP already has been tested in the courts and therefore its policy language is less likely to be the source of litigation.

Several insurers have decided that changing the policy is worth the risk and have designed their own specialized forms of personal automobile coverage. One such contract is called the "Plain Talk Car Policy" while another contract carries the subheading "Auto Insurance Protection You Can Count On In A Policy You Can Understand."

A comparison of a few of the provisions of these contracts with the corresponding provisions in the FAP will show the change in style that has taken place. In the example that follows, some of the supplementary payments afforded under the liability section of the FAP are compared with their counterparts in one of the new policies.

Old Policy (FAP)

Supplementary Payments: To pay in addition to the applicable limits of liability:
(a) all expenses incurred by the company, all costs taxed against the insured in any such suit and all interest on the entire amount of any judgment therein which accrues after entry of the judgment and before the company has paid or tendered or deposited in court that part of the judgment which does not exceed the limit of the company's liability thereon;
(b) premiums on appeal bonds required in any such suit, premiums on bonds to release attachments for an amount not in excess of the applicable limit of liability of this policy, and the cost of bail bonds required of the insured because of accident or traffic law violation arising out of the use of an automobile insured hereunder, not to exceed $100 per bail bond, but without any obligation to apply for or furnish any such bonds;
(c) expenses incurred by the insured for such immediate medical and surgical relief to others as shall be imperative at the time of an

accident involving an automobile insured hereunder and not due to war;

(d) all reasonable expenses, other than loss of earnings, incurred by the insured at the company's request.

New Policy One insurance company has reworded this section as follows:

Additional benefits
In addition to the amount we'll pay for Damages, we'll also pay for the cost of investigating the Car Accident and arranging for the settlement of any claim against You.

If You're sued by someone for Damages because of a Car Accident—even if the accusations aren't true—we'll defend You, hire and pay a lawyer, and pay all defense costs.

If the person who sues You tries to tie up Your property by an attachment, we'll pay for a bond to release the attachment. We have to limit this, though. You'll have to pay the cost of the additional amount of the bond if the bond required is more than the limits of liability You selected.

If You lose a lawsuit that we're defending, we'll pay the court costs. We'll also pay interest on the full amount of the judgment even if the judgment is higher than the limit of liability. And we'll pay this interest from the day the judgment is entered until we've offered the other party the amount of the judgment up to the full limits of liability available under this insurance.

We'll pay any reasonable expenses You might have for attending hearings or a trial at our request because of a lawsuit against You. We'll also pay You for any actual loss of wages up to $35 a day when You lose time from work to attend these hearings or trial.

We'll pay up to $300 for the cost of any bail bond required of You because of a Car Accident or traffic law violation.

We'll pay Your expense for first aid to others at the scene of a Car Accident.[18]

A second insurance carrier has chosen another approach which is shown below:

Auto Liability
We will pay property damage and bodily injury liability losses up to the limits as stated in the attached Declarations. Also, in connection with any covered liability loss: a) we will defend at our expense, with attorneys of our choice, any suit against the insured, even if the suit is groundless, false, or fraudulent. We may investigate, negotiate, and settle any claim or suit as we think appropriate.

b) we will pay all expenses incurred by us, and all costs levied against the insured in any such suit.

c) we will pay all premiums on appeal bonds in defended suits, and on bonds to release property that has been attached. We also will pay a premium of not more than $250 for bail bond required because of an accident or traffic violation. Although paying such premiums, we have no obligation to apply for or furnish such bonds.

d) we will pay interest accruing on all damages awarded, until such

Table 4-5
Automobile Insurance Termination Laws as of January 1976*

	Applicable To	Advance Notice of Cancellation	Advance Notice of Nonrenewal	Only Allowable Reasons for Cancellation	Initial Period When Insurer Not Restricted
Alabama	Private passenger automobile liability	20 Days	20 Days	Several per statute	60 Days
Alaska	Private passenger automobile	20 Days	20 Days	Nonpayment, suspension or revocation of license	60 Days
Arizona	Private passenger automobile	10 Days	10 Days	Several per statute	60 Days
Arkansas	Private passenger automobile	20 Days (Concurrent notice to financial institution which is lienholder) (30 Days to servicing agent)	20 Days	Several per statute	60 Days
California	Private passenger automobile	20 Days (10 days during first 60 days)	20 Days	Nonpayment, suspension or revocation of drivers license or registration	60 Days

	Applicable To	Advance Notice of Cancellation	Advance Notice of Nonrenewal	Only Allowable Reasons for Cancellation	Initial Period When Insurer Not Restricted
Colorado	Private passenger automobile	20 Days	20 Days	False statements, nonpayment, suspensions or revocation of drivers license or registration	60 Days
Connecticut	Private passenger automobile liability	20 Days (certified mail)	20 Days	Nonpayment, revocation of license or registration	60 Days
Delaware	Private passenger automobile	30 Days	30 Days	Several per statute	60 Days
D.C.	All automobile	30 Days (35 Days for agent)	30 Days (35 Days for agent)	Nonpayment, misrepresentation in the application or claim, suspension of registration	30 Days
Florida	Private passenger automobile liability	60 Days	45 Days (Registered or certified mail)	Nonpayment, suspension or revocation of license or registration and fraud	60 Days
Georgia	Private passenger automobile	30 Days (10 days during initial 60 days)	30 Days	Several per statute (5 days subsequent notice to Department of Public Safety)	60 Days

Continued on next page

	Applicable To	Advance Notice of Cancellation	Advance Notice of Nonrenewal	Only Allowable Reasons for Cancellation	Initial Period When Insurer Not Restricted
Hawaii	Automobile liability	30 Days (Notice also to Chief of Police and County Finance Director) (Registered or Certified Mail)	30 Days	Nonpayment, or suspension or revocation of license of principal	None
Idaho	Private passenger automobile	20 Days	30 Days	Several per statute	60 Days
Illinois	Private passenger automobile liability	20 Days (Registered or Certified Mail)	30 Days (Registered or Certified Mail)	Several per statute	60 Days
Indiana	Private passenger automobile liability	20 Days	20 Days (Insured) 30 Days Indiana Agents	Several per statute	60 Days
Iowa	Private passenger automobile	20 Days	30 Days	Nonpayment, suspension or revocation of drivers license or registration, fraud or material misrepresentation, violation of policy conditions	60 Days
Kansas	Automobile liability	30 Days (Registered or certified mail) (copy to Division of Vehicles—Department of Revenue)	30 Days	Several per statute	60 Days

	Applicable To	Advance Notice of Cancellation	Advance Notice of Nonrenewal	Only Allowable Reasons for Cancellation	Initial Period When Insurer Not Restricted
Kentucky	Private passenger automobile	20 Days	20 Days	Nonpayment, suspension or revocation of drivers license or registration	60 Days
Louisiana	Private passenger automobile	20 Days	20 Days	Nonpayment, suspension or revocation of drivers license or registration, fraud or material misrepresentation in the presentation of a claim	60 days
Maine	Private passenger automobile	20 Days	30 Days	Nonpayment, suspension or revocation of drivers license or registration, fraud or material misrepresentation in the presentation of a claim and violation of the policy's terms or conditions	60 Days
Maryland	All automobile	45 Days "Prompt notice also to Motor Vehicle Administration" (Certified Mail)	45 Days	Not restricted	N/A

Continued on next page

	Applicable To	Advance Notice of Cancellation	Advance Notice of Nonrenewal	Only Allowable Reasons for Cancellation	Initial Period When Insurer Not Restricted
Massachusetts	All automobile	20 Days (Registered Mail or Certified Mail)	45 Days	Nonpayment, suspension or revocation of drivers license or registration, fraud or material misrepresentation	90 Days
Michigan	Private passenger automobile liability	20 Days (Certified Mail)	20 Days	Nonpayment, suspension or revocation of drivers license or registration	55 Days
Minnesota	Automobile liability	30 Days (Certified Mail) Subsequent 30-day notice Commissioner of Public Safety	60 Days	Several per statute	60 Days
Mississippi	Private passenger automobile	20 Days	30 Days	Nonpayment, suspension or revocation of drivers license or registration, or operation by excluded driver	60 Days
Missouri	Private passenger automobile	30 Days	30 Days	Nonpayment, suspension or revocation of license of all named insureds	60 Days

	Applicable To	Advance Notice of Cancellation	Advance Notice of Nonrenewal	Only Allowable Reasons for Cancellation	Initial Period When Insurer Not Restricted
Montana	All automobile	30 Days	30 Days	Nonpayment, suspension or revocation of license	60 Days
Nebraska	Private passenger automobile liability	30 Days (Certified Mail)	20 Days	Nonpayment, license suspension or revocation, fraud, or auto theft	60 Days
Nevada	Private passenger automobile	30 Days	30 Days	Nonpayment or grounds specified in policy	70 days
New Hampshire	Private passenger automobile	45 Days	45 Days	Nonpayment, or nonresidency, or suspension or revocation of drivers license or registration	None
New Jersey	Private passenger automobile	20 Days	60 Days	Nonpayment, suspension or revocation of drivers license or registration	60 Days
New Mexico					
New York	Private passenger automobile	20 Days (Copy of Notice to Motor Vehicle Commissioner 30 days after cancellation)	45 Days But not more than 60 days (Copy of Notice to Motor Vehicle Commissioner)	Nonpayment, suspension or revocation of drivers license or registration	60 days

Continued on next page

	Applicable To	Advance Notice of Cancellation	Advance Notice of Nonrenewal	Only Allowable Reasons for Cancellation	Initial Period When Insurer Not Restricted
North Carolina	Automobile liability	60 Days (Notice to Department of Vehicles "forthwith")	60 Days	Nonpayment and nonresidency of insured	None
North Dakota	Private passenger automobile liability	20 Days (Certified Mail)	20 Days	Not applicable	60 Days
Ohio	Private passenger automobile liability	30 Days	30 Days	Several per statute	90 Days
Oklahoma Oregon	Private passenger automobile	20 Days (Expiration notice 20 days prior to expiration date obviates requirement of nonrenewal notice)	20 Days	Nonpayment, suspension	60 Days
Pennsylvania	Private passenger automobile	30 Days	30 Days	Nonpayment, suspension or revocation of drivers license or registration	60 Days
Rhode Island	Private passenger automobile	30 Days	30 Days	Nonpayment, suspension or revocation of drivers license or registration	60 Days
South Carolina	Private passenger automobile	60 Days (Must immediately notify the Chief Highway Commissioner)	60 Days	Nonpayment, suspension or revocation of drivers license or registration	None

	Applicable To	Advance Notice of Cancellation	Advance Notice of Nonrenewal	Only Allowable Reasons for Cancellation	Initial Period When Insurer Not Restricted
South Dakota	Private passenger automobile	20 Days	60 Days	Nonpayment, suspension or revocation of drivers license or registration	60 Days
Tennessee	Private passenger automobile liability	20 Days	20 Days	Several per statute	60 Days
Texas	All vehicles written on the Family Automobile Policy	30 Days (10 days during first 60 days)	30 Days	Nonpayment, license suspension or revocation	60 Days
Utah	Private passenger automobile	20 Days	30 Days	Nonpayment, license suspension or revocation and false statement on application	60 Days
Vermont	Private passenger automobile liability	20 Days (Certified Mail)	20 Days (Certified Mail)	Nonpayment, license suspension or revocation, fraud, or violation of policy conditions	60 Days

Continued on next page

	Applicable To	Advance Notice of Cancellation	Advance Notice of Nonrenewal	Only Allowable Reasons for Cancellation	Initial Period When Insurer Not Restricted
Virginia	Private passenger automobile liability	45 Days (Insurer must retain copy of Notice certifying original was mailed)	45 Days	Nonpayment and license suspension or revocation	60 Days
Washington	Private passenger automobile	20 Days	20 Days (Certified Mail)	Nonpayment, suspension or revocation of drivers license or registration	60 Days
West Virginia	Private passenger automobile liability	Silent	45 Days	Several per statute	60 Days
Wisconsin	All automobile	30 Days	30 Days	Nonpayment on grounds set forth in policy	70 Days
Wyoming	Private passenger automobile	20 Days	30 Days	Nonpayment, fraud in the application, and suspension of driver's license or registration	60 Days

*Reprinted with permission from American Mutual Insurance Alliance, *Compendium of Insurance Charts* (Chicago: American Mutual Insurance Alliance, 1976), section entitled "Automobile Insurance Termination Laws."

time as we have paid, formally offered, or deposited in court the amount for which we are liable under this policy.

e) we will pay emergency expenses incurred by the insured for imperative medical and surgical aid to others at the time of accident.

f) we will pay all reasonable expenses incurred by the insured at our request, but not more than $25 per day for loss of earnings.

After the liability limits of this policy have been exhausted by payment, we will not be obligated to defend any suit or pay any claim or judgment.[19]

The structure of the contract, as well as the language, is different in the revised policies. Both of the contracts cited above contain a table of contents which aids the insured in finding those areas of the policy that discuss a particular type of coverage. Important definitions are displayed prominently in the policy and placed next to the items to which they apply. For example, the FAP promises to "pay for loss caused by collision to the owned automobile or to a nonowned automobile." The definition of a collision is found in a separate part of the insurance contract. The two more "readable" policies incorporate the definition of collision into the collision coverage proviso. One of these policies reads: "Under this coverage, we will pay for direct and accidental loss of or damage to, your auto and its equipment caused by collision or upset."[20]

The idea of a more readable policy obviously is desirable from the insurer's perspective. An easy to read policy is a good marketing tool and reduces the consumer's distrust of insurance companies. One new simplified policy has been accepted by some insurers, and probably it eventually will be adopted by a large segment of the industry.

All automobile policies contain a lot of detailed information, and while the policies that have been discussed are easier to read, they still must be read carefully. Unfortunately, many consumers will purchase a contract because it is easier to read and yet never read it. This is a problem insurance companies cannot overcome.

Discounts

In addition to the individual company rate deviations, many insurers offer certain discounts that benefit consumers. For example, a policyholder can obtain a bumper discount which reduces this collision premium.

In some states, a good student discount is available. A student qualifies for this discount if in the preceding school semester he or she was under a specified age limit and:

1. ranked among the upper 20% of his class scholastically, or

2. in schools using letter grades, had a grade average of "B" or its equivalent or, if the system of letter grading cannot be averaged, no grade shall be below "B," or
3. in schools using numerical grade point, had an equivalent of "B," such as at least 3 in a 4, 3, 2, 1 point system, or
4. was included in the "Dean's List," "Honor Roll" or comparable list indicating scholastic achievement.[21]

Supposedly, good students will be more cautious and mature. In addition, since they are studying, they will not be using an automobile as much as students who do not study. This combined effect should make good students better exposures.

Driver's training courses afford young drivers another method for reducing the premiums that they pay. To receive a premium discount, the youthful driver must have completed a driver training program in a secondary school, college, or university. The program and the instructors must be approved by the appropriate state education units. Generally, there are insurance company limitations on the minimum number of hours contained in the driver education program.

An individual can be given discounts both for being a good student and for taking driver education. A comparison of the rate factors found in the Insurance Services Office's *Private Passenger Automobile Manual* for an unmarried female youthful driver with and without a good student or driver education discount is shown in Table 4-6. The factors shown in the table are multiplied by the base premium. Thus, the higher the value of the factor, the higher the premium cost.

The female driver who uses a car for pleasure and who is eligible for the driver training and good student discounts would pay a premium equal to 135 percent of the base rate. Without these discounts, the premium would be 175 percent of the base rate, an increase of 30 percent.

Some insurers allow a premium discount on policies when the principal driver has had a defensive driving course. There is no age limitation or correlation between age and the size of the discount.

For the owners of two or more automobiles, insurers have designed a multi-car discount. Savings supposedly exist under a multi-car policy because of the reduced administrative costs resulting from issuing a single policy and the reduced amount of utilization of each car.

Effect of Driving Record

One of the most important cost considerations from the perspective of both the insurer and the insured is the insured's driving record. In

Table 4-6

Rates Factors for Youthful, Unmarried Female Drivers*

Age	Youthful Driver Not Eligible for Good Student Discount		Youthful Driver Eligible for Good Student Discount	
	Pleasure Use	Drive to Work	Pleasure Use	Drive to Work
Without Driver Training 17	1.75	2.00	1.50	1.75
18	1.60	1.85	1.35	1.60
19	1.50	1.75	1.25	1.50
20	1.25	1.50	1.10	1.35
With Driver Training 17	1.60	1.85	1.35	1.60
18	1.50	1.75	1.25	1.50
19	1.40	1.65	1.15	1.40
20	1.20	1.45	1.05	1.30

*Reprinted with permission from *Private Passenger Automobile Manual* (New York: Insurance Services Office, 1976), pp. 6, 8.

some states, premiums are increased because of traffic violations and certain accidents. In these states, a merit rating system or safe driving plan is used.

When a company uses an individual's driving record as a basis for determining the individual's rates, some type of point system normally is involved. The Insurance Services Office's manual on private passenger automobile coverages includes a chapter on the Safe Driver Insurance Plan. Under this system, an individual is given points when he or she is involved in an accident or is convicted of certain traffic violations. The more points an individual accumulates, the poorer the driving record and the higher the premium costs. As an example, the Insurance Services Office's manual assigns three points for conviction of:

(a) driving while intoxicated or under the influence of drugs; or
(b) failure to stop and report when involved in an accident; or
(c) homicide or assault arising out of the operation of a motor vehicle; or
(d) driving during a period while license is suspended or revoked.[22]

Lesser violations carry reduced point debits. For example, a moving violation, ". . . as a result of which (a) an operator's license was suspended or revoked; or (b) the filing of evidence of Financial Responsibility Law is required. . . ." If a policyholder collects an excessive number of points, the insurance company can cancel the policyholder's coverage. However, a single three-point violation is normally adequate grounds for cancellation.

SPECIAL AUTOMOBILE POLICY

In addition to the FAP, many insurers offer a special automobile policy (SAP). The SAP contains some provisions which, from the consumer's viewpoint, are more liberal than the FAP counterparts and other provisions which are less liberal. Overall, the two contracts are similar, and a detailed analysis of the SAP would be repetitious. Only the differences between the SAP and the FAP are presented in this section.

Liability Coverage

Under the FAP, the insured has the option of selecting liability coverage with or without the other benefits. The SAP can be sold to an insured only if he or she is willing to purchase medical expense benefits, uninsured motorists' protection, and accidental death benefits in addition to liability coverage. All of these coverages, except accidental death, are found in the FAP, but they are not mandatory. Although the accidental death coverage is not an integral part of the FAP, it can be added to the FAP by endorsement; this coverage is broader than that included in the SAP.

The bodily injury liability coverage in the FAP is stated in terms of coverage per person and is subject to a maximum per occurrence. There is a separate limitation on property damage liability in the FAP. The SAP has only one limit for both bodily injury and property damage liability. The most common limits are $25,000, $50,000, $100,000, $200,000, and $300,000. A single limit under the SAP can provide additional protection for the policyholder in some cases. The following example illustrates such a case.

Recently Martha Covers drove Jane Fenster and Carol Mailer to the shopping center. Because they started later than they anticipated, Martha drove at an excessive rate of speed. As a result, she lost control of her car and collided with a bridge abutment. Jane Fenster sustained extensive injuries and sued Martha, obtaining a judgment for $120,000 for medical expenses and pain and suffering. Carol was paralyzed permanently as a result of the wreck and required continual medical attention. Like Jane, Carol sued Martha, and a jury awarded her $375,000.

If Martha had had an FAP with $100,000 coverage limit per person and a $300,000 limit per occurrence, her insurance company would have been required to pay $200,000—$100,000 to Jane and $100,000 to Carol. If Martha had had an SAP with a $300,000 limit, the insurer would have been obligated to pay $300,000. Assuming that Jane filed suit first, the insurer would have paid her $120,000 and $180,000 to Carol. Therefore, under the FAP, Martha would have had to pay $295,000 in excess of the insurer's payment. Under the SAP, however, she would have been responsible for an additional $195,000.

This example does not prove that an SAP policy always provides more coverage, but only indicates that in certain circumstances, it may provide more coverage than the FAP.

Liability limits are not the only difference between the liability sections of the FAP and the SAP. The FAP covers the named insured and includes as "persons insured" any resident of the same household and other persons using the vehicle with permission. The SAP covers household residents only if they have permission. However, anyone with residents other than the named insured and his or her spouse might find this coverage unduly restrictive. While coverage can be extended to residents of the same household under the SAP with permission of the named insured, this places a burden on the resident to obtain such permission every time an automobile is used.

One other distinction is important. The term relative in the FAP means "a relative of the named insured who is a resident of the same household." In the SAP, a relative means "a person related to the named insured by blood, marriage or adoption who is a resident of the same household, provided neither such relative nor his spouse owns a private passenger automobile." Obviously, the latter definition is more restrictive.

Another difference between the two contracts centers around the term "trailer." The SAP covers only utility trailers, which do not include trailers designed for use as a home, office, store, display, or passenger trailer. These types of trailers are covered automatically under the FAP. Also, under the FAP, a trailer can be considered a temporary substitute automobile; this is not the case under the SAP.

The FAP, under the supplemental payments section of liability coverage, promises to pay premiums for certain types of bonds mentioned earlier in this chapter. A limit of $100 applies to bail bonds. The SAP offers the same bond coverage and a higher limit of $250 on bail bonds.

The supplementary payments section of the FAP includes coverage for reasonable expenses that a policyholder incurs at the company's request. Loss of earnings is not included in this coverage. The SAP provides a supplemental benefit, which includes coverage for wage or salary losses subject to a maximum of $25 a day.

The FAP states that "relative" means "a relative of the named insured who is a resident of the same household." This is particularly important with respect to nonowned automobiles where specific reference is made to coverage for any relative. The SAP contains nearly the same definition of "relative" as the FAP, but stipulates that if the relative owns a private passenger automobile, he or she is not covered. Consequently, a relative could end up without any coverage if he or she did not have separate protection.

When a policyholder purchases a new automobile, coverage for that vehicle can be automatic under the FAP. Coverage on a new car is automatic if the car replaces an owned automobile insured under the policy or if it is an additional automobile and the insurance company insures all the automobiles owned by the policyholder. The policyholder's responsibility is to notify the company during the policy period of a new automobile or within thirty days, whichever is longer. The SAP requires the insured to notify the insurer within thirty days after purchasing a new car in order to have coverage. So, new automobiles are covered automatically only for a short period under the SAP.

The other insurance provision is also different in the SAP. The FAP states that the policy will prorate its coverage with other valid and collectible coverage for temporary substitute or nonowned automobiles, except in those cases where it is treated as excess coverage. The basis for prorating coverage is the policy limit.

The SAP has the additional provision that:

> . . . if the insured has other excess or contingent insurance applicable to loss arising out of the use of a temporary substitute or non-owned automobile, the company shall not be liable under this policy for a greater proportion of such loss than the amount which would have been payable under this policy, had no such other insurance existed, bears to the sum of said amount and the amounts which would have been payable under each other policy applicable to such loss, had each policy been the only policy so applicable.

Uninsured Motorists Coverage

There are only two major distinctions between the uninsured motorists coverage under the SAP and FAP. First, the uninsured highway vehicle under the SAP would include motorcycles and other two-wheeled motorized vehicles. The FAP restricts uninsured automobile coverage to four-wheeled vehicles.

The limit of liability under the SAP is stated as a single amount. The amount is adequate to meet the Financial Responsibility Laws of most states.

Medical Payments

The SAP does not cover the named insured's resident relatives if struck by a car if the relative has his or her own automobile. The FAP provides this coverage.

Comparison of Medical Expense Coverage The insurance company providing the protection under the SAP will not pay medical expenses to an individual unless that person agrees in writing that any payments made under the medical expense coverage will be deducted from any liability settlement that may be made at a later date. Coverage for medical expenses under the SAP range from $1,000 to $5,000 with increments of $1,000. Since these limits are utilized to offset any liability claims, this coverage actually has the impact of expanding the liability coverage. The provisions of the FAP do not require that medical expense benefits be used to offset future liability claims.

The SAP excludes certain items which are not excluded from the FAP. There is no coverage for medical expenses arising from intentional acts of the insured. Also, the medical expense benefits are not paid under the SAP for any coverage available from:

... any (1) premises insurance affording benefits for medical expenses, (2) individual, blanket or group accident, disability or hospitalization insurance, (3) medical, surgical, hospital or funeral service, benefit or reimbursement plan, or (4) workmen's compensation or disability benefits law or any similar law. ...

Physical Damage Coverage

Under the comprehensive portion of the FAP, robes, wearing apparel, and other personal effects are covered for up to $100 against losses arising from fire or lightning subject to a limit of $100 per occurrence. Under the SAP, $200 of protection per occurrence is provided for losses caused by (1) fire; (2) lightning; (3) flood; (4) falling objects; (5) explosion; (6) earthquake; (7) theft of the automobile; or (8) collision for robes, wearing apparel, and personal luggage. Collision coverage is available only if collision is purchased separately. The items covered are robes, wearing apparel, and personal luggage. The items are covered only if they belong to the named insured or a relative of the named insured.

Another difference relates to the definition of the insured. The FAP provides coverage for the insured and any relative of the named insured while using a nonowned automobile:

... provided his actual operation or (if he is not operating) the other actual use thereof is with the permission, or reasonably believed to be with permission, of the owner and is within the scope of such permission. ...

Coverage is not based on fault.

In the SAP, coverage is not afforded for damage to nonowned automobiles unless the named insured or relative is legally responsible for the damage done to the nonowned automobile. Finally, the FAP contains $500 of coverage for physical damage to any trailer not owned by the named insured. This same coverage is not afforded under the SAP.

Liberalization Clause

Finally, the SAP contains the following liberalization clause which does not have a counterpart in the FAP:

If the company revises this policy form with respect to policy provisions, endorsements or rules by which the insurance hereunder could be extended or broadened without additional premium charge, such insurance as is afforded hereunder shall be so extended or broadened effective immediately upon approval or acceptance of such during the policy period by the appropriate insurance supervisory authority.

Chapter Notes

1. Laws of New York 1907, Ch. 206, Sec. 1.
2. Travelers Insurance Company, *The Travelers 100 Years* (Kansas City: R. M. Rigby Printing Company, Inc., 1964), p. 67.
3. *Proceedings of the National Convention of Insurance Commissioners* (1920), p. 160.
4. The omnibus clause is that portion of the liability section of the automobile policy which extends coverage to persons using the owned automobile including persons or organizations legally liable for the use of the owned automobile.
5. C. A. Kulp, *Casualty Insurance* rev. ed. (New York: Ronald Press Company, 1942), p. 181.
6. A copy of the family automobile policy can be found in the Policy Kit.
7. Muzichuk v. Liberty Mutual Insurance Company, 311 N.E. 2d. 560, 561.
8. An occurrence is different from an accident. An occurrence can take place over a period of time while an accident is sudden.
9. Insurance Services Office, *Private Passenger Automobile Manual* (New York: Insurance Services Office, 1976), p. 24.
10. A general average loss occurs when the captain of a vessel jettisons cargo to save the vessel. All those that have an interest in the vessel and the vessel's cargo share in the loss. To illustrate this, consider a vessel worth $1 million which is carrying two cargoes (A and B), each worth $500,000. If the captain has to throw cargo A overboard to save the vessel and cargo B, each party shares in the loss. The vessel owner would be responsible for 50 percent of the loss of cargo A. The owner of cargo B would pay for 25 percent of cargo A, and the owner of cargo A would assume 25 percent of his or her own loss.
11. Leatherby Insurance Company v. Willoughby, 315 So. 2d 553.
12. Crenshaw v. Great Central Insurance Company, 527 S.W. 2d 1.
13. Associate Indemnity Corporation v. Cannon, 536 P. 2d 922-23.
14. A number of cases on this topic have been adjudicated. For examples, see: Clayton v. Alliance Mutual Casualty Company, 512 P. 2d 507; Van Tassel v. Horace Mann Insurance Company, 207 N.W. 2d 348; Hartford Accident and Indemnity Company v. Turner, 498 S.W. 2d 8; Motor Club of America Insurance Company v. Phillips, 330 A. 2d 360; and Walton v. State Farm Mutual Automobile Insurance Company, 518 P. 2d 1399.
15. Ramsour v. Grange Insurance Association, 541 P. 2d 37.
16. Ibid., pp. 37-39.
17. Long v. United States Fidelity and Guaranty Company, 396 F. Supp. 966.
18. Sentry Insurance, "Your Plain Talk Car Policy."
19. Nationwide Mutual Insurance Company, "Nationwide's Century II Auto Policy."
20. Ibid.

21. Insurance Services Office, *Private Passenger Automobile Manual* (New York: Insurance Services Office, 1976), p. 4.
22. Ibid.

CHAPTER 5

Other Personal Property and Liability Insurance Coverages

COVERAGE LIMITATIONS OF THE HOMEOWNERS AND FAMILY AUTOMOBILE POLICIES

Coverage provided under personal package policies (e.g., the family automobile and homeowners policies) is designed to protect an insured against a broad spectrum of exposures. No insurance policy provides protection for all exposures though, and policy limitations and exclusions may preclude an insured from recovering for a particular loss. Additionally, an individual may not be eligible to purchase a family package policy, and may, therefore, seek coverage under some other contract. The following sections review the reasons why an individual may not be covered adequately, even if he or she has a personal package policy. Many of the insurance coverages available to fill the gaps in the protection under the homeowners and family automobile policies are then presented.

Eligibility

In many cases, an individual is not eligible to purchase a personal package policy. For example, a nonoriginal owner of a residence is not eligible to purchase a homeowners contract on a rented dwelling. An individual with a bad driving record may be forced to seek automobile insurance protection from an automobile insurance plan (assigned risk plan). The family automobile policy has not been approved in a few states; therefore, any individual not eligible for coverage in the regular

213

market cannot obtain the family automobile policy. While most assigned risk plans have approved the family automobile policy, the insured must pay a higher premium under the automobile insurance plan than if it is obtained in the regular insurance market.

Exclusions

Within a personal package policy, some coverages may not be written on an "all-risks" basis. Even where "all-risks" coverage is afforded, exclusions may prevent an insured from collecting in the event of a specific loss. Personal package policies contain several exclusions. The liability section of the family automobile policy excludes liability when an automobile is used as a public livery conveyance or when the bodily injury or property damage is caused intentionally by the insured. The homeowners policy excludes, for example, damage relating to flood, water backed up in sewers, or earthquakes.

An individual who does not have adequate coverage may seek protection under some other policy. If this option is not available, then he or she can either attempt to have a package policy amended to cover the exclusion, retain the exposure and accept the exclusion, seek governmental insurance protection, or attempt to use some other risk management device. As an example, a homeowner temporarily renting a dwelling might transfer all of his or her jewelry to a safe deposit box since jewelry is not covered against theft while an insured dwelling is rented. Unfortunately, insureds often are not aware of exactly what coverages are provided in their policies. As a result, they may not take adequate steps to protect their interests. Therefore, periodic review of exposures is very important.

Reductions in Coverage (Internal Limits)

Another gap in personal package policies relates to the question of adequate protection. As an example, the homeowners contract, in some cases, provides coverage for jewelry which is stolen. However, there is a $500 limitation per occurrence which may be insufficient to cover jewelry exposures. Handling all the special problems with insurance is not possible, but many problems can be handled with special insurance coverages. Insurance methods for handling the gaps in the personal package policies follow.

AUTOMOBILE COVERAGE

Residual Automobile Markets

Insurance underwriting has improved substantially since the early 1900s when a desirable subject of insurance included:

(1) cars driven only by the owner, if he is a man of responsible and good habits, (2) cars owned by high class concerns and kept in a splendid state of repair and cleanliness, (3) cars driven by better class chauffeurs—particularly where the chauffeur holds a more responsible position in addition to the duties of driving a car.[1]

However, today many drivers still cannot obtain insurance in the standard marketplace and are forced to utilize the substandard or residual insurance market. The residual insurance market is composed of companies who offer coverage to drivers who cannot get coverage through normal channels. Some companies specialize in writing coverage for drivers with bad records. Others write coverage in the residual market as part of their total book of business. The public knows the mechanism designed to handle the residual market as an "assigned risk plan" while the insurance industry is more familiar with the phrase "automobile insurance plans." The latter will be used in this discussion.

As the number of drivers has increased, use of automobile insurance plans has grown. In some states this growth is partially because of the denial of adequate rate increases by insurance commissioners. The result has been the nonrenewal of policies by insurance companies in an effort to have these same policies rewritten in the automobile insurance plan at an adequate premium.

This section discusses methods and types of coverage provided for drivers in the residual market. The plans of two states, New York and Iowa, are examined. Types of coverage, commissions, assignment provisions, and eligibility are discussed. While these state plans are representative of many of the plans operating in the United States, summaries of the plans in each state can also be found in the material that follows.

Automobile Insurance Plan Operation

Purpose The primary purpose of automobile insurance plans is to provide insurance coverage for those individuals who cannot obtain protection in the regular market. Although this material deals with private passenger automobile exposures, other types of motor vehicles can be covered under a state insurance plan. The second purpose of a state insurance plan is "to establish procedures for the equitable distribution of risks assigned to insurance companies."[2]

Distribution of Risks   Individual private passenger automobiles covered under an automobile insurance plan are divided among the insurers in the state that writes private passenger automobile coverage. Normally, each insurer writing private passenger coverage is assigned a proportionate share of the residual market. This share is obtained by multiplying the automobile insurance plan premium by the ratio of the direct car years of coverage that an insurer writes in a state to the total car years of coverage written. If the insurer voluntarily writes certain exposures, it can credit these against this share. A division exists between liability and physical damage coverages. Since an insurer may write one or both of these coverages, it receives only automobile insurance plan premiums in the lines of coverage that it writes. For example, the New York automobile insurance plan states under the bodily injury liability, property damage liability, medical payments, and personal injury protection coverage section that:

> The plan shall distribute the risks which are eligible for coverage (a) [coverages cited above] so that each insurer will receive the same proportion of "private passenger non-fleet Automobile Insurance Plan premiums" that its respective "voluntary private passenger non-fleet direct written car years" bear to the statewide total of the "voluntary private passenger non-fleet net direct written car years" of all insurers in the state . . . .[3] (brackets added)

Most automobile insurance plans are similar to the New York plan.

Automobile Insurance Plan Coverage

Eligibility   An individual is eligible to participate in most state automobile insurance plans if he or she has attempted unsuccessfully to obtain coverage sixty days prior to making application to the plan. If the insured has been able to obtain coverage, but the rate is higher than the rate available under the plan, he or she still can participate in the plan. An applicant is not entitled to coverage if any person who will be driving the automobile does not have a valid driver's license. Also, if an individual applying for insurance or anyone who will be driving the automobile has not paid his or her insurance premium during the twelve months preceding the application for admission to the plan, coverage is not afforded.

Additional restrictions may apply to physical damage coverage. For example, in the Iowa plan coverage may not be provided to an applicant owning an antique automobile (one which is twenty-five years or older) or for vehicles with an actual cash value in excess of $10,000. The New York plan also prohibits antique automobiles, but does not prohibit automobiles with an actual cash value in excess of $10,000. The New York plan does have a maximum limit on physical damage of $10,000.

Table 5-1 shows the number of private passenger vehicles and the percentage of all registered vehicles in the individual state plans in the year 1974. Examination of the data indicates that there is a wide disparity in the need for automobile insurance plans among the states.

If an individual is eligible for a state automobile insurance plan, he or she is assigned to an insurer for three years. At the end of this period, the individual can reapply to the state plan if coverage cannot be obtained through regular market channels.

Limits of Coverage and Types of Policies The bodily injury and property damage liability coverage(s) afforded under automobile insurance plans have limits at least equal to the minimum required limits set forth in a state's financial responsibility law. However, most states make it possible for an individual to obtain higher limits. Normally, there are several options of increased limits of liability coverage. In New York an individual can obtain limits of $10,000/$20,000/$5,000; $25,000/$50,000/$10,000; $50,000/$100,000/$10,000; or $100,000/$300,000/$50,000. The excess coverage can be written under the primary policy or a separate excess policy.

Medical payments coverage on private passenger automobiles is available in most states. Normally, there is some choice of payment limits. Another option available in many state plans is physical damage coverage wth a $100 deductible. The physical damage coverage normally includes both comprehensive and collision coverages. Table 5-2 contains a summary of the optional coverages available under state automobile insurance plans.

The standard policy coverage for private passenger automobiles in most state automobile insurance plans is the family automobile policy. Only New Hampshire and Ohio have not approved the family automobile policy for use under their automobile insurance plans. The policy used in an automobile insurance plan is not necessarily identical to that used in the standard market. The liability and physical damage coverages may be amended to exclude newly acquired automobiles unless the named insured notifies the insurance company of the new automobile within thirty days of acquiring the vehicle. The physical damage coverage may be amended to exclude protection for "any prearranged racing or competitive speed contest or (b) ... the business of transporting flammables or similar hazardous material."[4]

Table 5-1

Drivers in Automobile Insurance Plans*

	1974 Number of Private Passenger Vehicles in Plan[1]	1974 Percent of Registered Vehicles in Plan[1,2]
Alabama	14,290	0.79
Alaska	409	0.30
Arizona	508	0.05
Arkansas	7,684	0.79
California	165,354	1.23
Colorado	2,726	0.20
Connecticut	43,446	2.67
Delaware	23,848	8.45
District of Columbia	8,117	3.40
Florida	Florida Joint Underwriting Association became operational October 1, 1973.	
Georgia	27,242	1.02
Hawaii	Hawaii Joint Underwriting Association became operational September 1, 1974.	
Idaho	387	0.07
Illinois	20,148	0.38
Indiana	3,017	0.12
Iowa	734	0.05
Kansas	24,572	1.89
Kentucky	17,295	1.06
Louisiana	27,162	1.63
Maine	10,898	2.27
Maryland	State Fund became operational January 1, 1973.	
Massachusetts	Reinsurance Facility became operational January 1, 1974.	
Michigan	91,140	1.97
Minnesota	1,358	0.07
Mississippi	26,652	2.61
Missouri	Missouri Joint Underwriting Association became operational January 1, 1975.	
Montana	336	0.09
Nebraska	860	0.11
Nevada	114	0.03
New Hampshire	Not applicable	Not applicable
New Jersey	303,338	8.20
New Mexico	895	0.17
New York	479,644	7.13
North Carolina	North Carolina Reinsurance Facility became operational October 9, 1973.	
North Dakota	253	0.08
Ohio	11,321	0.20
Oklahoma	1,777	0.13
Oregon	3,569	0.25

	1974 Number of Private Passenger Vehicles in Plan[1]	1974 Percent of Registered Vehicles in Plan[1,2]
Pennsylvania	74,655	1.18
Rhode Island	8,800	1.71
South Carolina	South Carolina Reinsurance Facility became operational October 1, 1974.	
South Dakota	476	0.14
Tennessee	52,677	2.59
Texas	244,722	4.20
Utah	315	0.05
Vermont	5,351	2.34
Virginia	192,973	7.18
Washington	4,591	0.25
West Virginia	4,242	0.61
Wisconsin	3,760	0.18
Wyoming	644	0.34

1. Written car years.
2. Includes all categories.

*Reprinted with permission from Automobile Insurance Plans Service Office, "Chart Analysis—Automobile Insurance Plans, Corrections March, 1976."

Application An individual must make application to an automobile insurance plan on the forms prescribed or established by the plan. An application will not be processed without an accompanying deposit. In New York, the amount of the required deposit is 30 percent of the annual premium, while in Iowa it is 25 percent of the annual premium or $25, whichever is greater. If an individual is eligible for coverage under the plan, insurance usually becomes effective at 12:01 A.M. on the day after the application is mailed to the plan or to a participating company. This varies by state.

Some states require the insured to pay the balance of the premium when the coverage is issued. Other states permit payments to be made in installments. An installment service charge is made if an installment plan is utilized. The installment provision in the Iowa automobile insurance plan, in addition to requiring that a minimum deposit accompany the application, provides that the balance of the premium is paid:

One-fifth of the remainder of the premium, subject to a minimum premium of $20 (to which any outstanding balance of less than $20 is to be added) plus an installment charge of $2 on each installment, due as follows: (1) 1st installment—2 months after effective date of the policy; (2) 2nd installment—3 months after effective date of the policy; (3) 3rd installment—4 months after effective date of the policy; (4) 4th installment—5 months after effective date of the policy; (5) 5th installment—6 months after effective date of the policy.[5]

Table 5-2
Optional Coverages Under Automobile Insurance Plans*

	Extent of Coverage		Optional Physical Damage $100 Deductible Comprehensive and Collision Combined
	Optional Increased Limits	Optional Medical Payment on Private Passenger	
Alabama	No	$1,000	No
Alaska	25/ 50/10 50/100/10 100/300/50	1,000 5,000	Yes
Arizona	25/ 50/10 50/100/10 100/300/50	1,000 2,000 5,000	Yes
Arkansas	No	500 and no-fault	Yes
California	No	1,000	No
Colorado	25/ 50/10 50/100/10 100/300/50	(Personal injury protection effective 4-1-74)	Yes
Connecticut	25/ 50/10 50/100/10 100/300/50	5,000	Yes
Delaware	25/ 50/ 5 50/100/ 5 100/300/ 5	Personal injury protection all risks 10/20/5; accidental death and dismemberment	Yes

	Private passenger only	personal injury protection 100/300/100 (private passenger only)	
District of Columbia	25/ 50/10 50/100/10	1,000	Yes
Florida	Florida Joint Underwriting Association became operational October 1, 1973		
Georgia	Optional including limits for additional personal injury protection of $10,000, $25,000, or $50,000 per insured injured person	No	Yes; $100 deductible private passenger only; $250, $500 or $1,000 deductible for other vehicle
Hawaii	Hawaii Joint Underwriting Association became operational September 1, 1974		
Idaho	25/ 50/10 50/100/10 100/300/50	1,000 5,000	Yes
Illinois	25/ 50/10 50/100/10 100/300/10	1,000 2,000 3,000	Yes
Indiana	No	1,000	Yes
Iowa	25/ 50/10 50/100/10 100/300/50	1,000 2,000 5,000	Yes

	Extent of Coverage		
	Optional Increased Limits	Optional Medical Payment on Private Passenger	Optional Physical Damage $100 Deductible Comprehensive and Collision Combined
Kansas	20/ 40/10 25/ 50/10 50/100/10	500 or 1,000	Yes; also $250 or $500 deductible at request of insured, collision only
Kentucky	25/ 50/10 Private passenger only	1,000 available only if no-fault is rejected	No
Louisiana	10/ 20/10 25/ 50/10 50/100/10 100/300/50	1,000 2,000 5,000	Yes
Maine	25/ 50/10 50/100/25 100/300/50 100/300/100	500 1,000 2,000 5,000	Yes, comprehensive only; full coverage optional
Maryland	State Fund became operational January 1, 1973		
Massachusetts	Reinsurance Facility became operational January 1, 1974		
Michigan	20/ 40/10 or 25 25/ 50/10 or 25 50/100/10 or 25	Full no-fault since 10-1-73 Coordination of benefits since 6-3-74	Yes

State	Limits	Personal injury protection	$50 deductible, comprehensive; Collision $100 deductible
Minnesota	25/ 50/10 50/100/10	Personal injury protection basic—20/10 Options—30/10, 40/10, 50/10 Deductible—$100, $200, both Uninsured motorist Underinsured	250 500
Mississippi	15/ 30/10 25/ 50/10 50/100/10	500 or 1,000	No
Missouri	Missouri Joint Underwriting Association became operational January 1, 1975		
Montana	25/ 50/10 50/100/10 100/300/50	1,000 2,000 5,000	Yes
Nebraska	25/ 50/10 50/100/10 100/300/50	500 or 1,000	No
Nevada	25/ 50/10 50/100/10 100/300/50	Personal injury protection	Yes
New Hampshire	25/ 50/10 30/ 60/10	1,000	Yes
New Jersey	Up to 100/300/100	1,000 and 10,000; also personal injury protection Up to $5,000	Yes (but not combined)
New Mexico	Up to 100/300/50 effective 7-1-75		Yes

		Extent of Coverage	
	Optional Increased Limits	Optional Medical Payment on Private Passenger	Optional Physical Damage $100 Deductible Comprehensive and Collision Combined
New York	25/ 50/10 50/100/10 100/300/50	1,000, 5,000; personal injury protection $50,000; additional personal injury protection $100,000	Yes
North Carolina	North Carolina Reinsurance Facility became operational October 9, 1973		
North Dakota	10/ 20/ 5 25/ 50/10 50/100/25 100/300/50	Personal injury protection basic $15,000: additional $25,000	Yes
Ohio	25/ 50/10 50/100/25 100/300/50	500 or 1,000	Yes
Oklahoma	10/ 20/ 5 15/ 30/ 5	1,000 2,000	No
Oregon	25/ 50/10 50/100/10 100/300/50	Personal injury protection	Yes
Pennsylvania	25/ 50/10 50/100/10 100/300/50	Basic and added personal injury protection	Yes
Rhode Island	25/ 50/10 50/100/10	500 or	Yes
South Carolina	South Carolina Reinsurance Facility became operational October 1, 1974		
South Dakota	15/ 30/10 25/ 50/10	1,000 2,000	Yes

State			
Tennessee	50/100/10 100/300/50	5,000 and supplemental coverage 1,000	Yes
Texas	No	No	No
Utah	25/ 50/10 50/100/10 100/300/50	Personal injury protection	Yes
Vermont	25/ 50/10 50/100/10 100/300/50	1,000 2,000 5,000	Yes
Virginia	Private passenger only 100/300/50	Private passenger and non-owned risks only 1,000 2,000 5,000	Yes
Washington	Private passenger only 25/ 50/10 50/100/10 100/300/50	5,000	Yes
West Virginia	25/ 50/10 50/100/10 100/300/10	1,000	Yes; also comprehensive with liability coverage
Wisconsin	No		No
Wyoming	25/ 50/10 50/100/10 100/300/50	1,000 2,000 5,000	Yes

*Reprinted with permission from Automobile Insurance Plans Service Office, "Chart Analysis—Automobile Insurance Plans Corrections, March 1976."

New York does not have a program for the installment payment of insurance premiums under its automobile insurance plan. Table 5-3 indicates the type of premium payment option, if any, available to the insured in each state.

Cost of Plan Participation Each state with an automobile insurance plan has rates, rules, premiums, and classifications which have been determined by the Automobile Insurance Plans Service Office on file. A driver is rated on the basis of his or her driving record. Under most plans, an individual is assigned points based on the number of moving traffic violations or accidents for which the individual is responsible. Under New York's plan, one penalty point results in no additional surcharge. Two points produces a 20 percent additional charge. Three, four, five and six points develop additional surcharges of 30, 40, 50 and 75 percent, respectively. An individual who has seven or more penalty points pays a 100 percent surcharge. All the percentages are a function of the base premium.

Most state plans allow a surcharge above 100 percent. When the potential for loss is much greater than can be represented by the point system, an insurer can request that the automobile insurance plan committee permit an increase in the rate for that particular applicant. The committee evaluates the exposure and decides whether an additional surcharge should be imposed.

The agent of record is paid a percentage of the premium charged under the automobile insurance plan. In most states the percentage paid the producer is less than that which the producer would receive if he or she wrote coverage in the regular market. The commission paid the producer for private passenger automobiles, other than long haul and public vehicles, ranges from 8 to 15 percent. Most states permit a maximum of 10 percent.

Cancellations As with most insurance contracts, the insured always has the option to cancel. When the insured cancels, the amount of premium to be returned is calculated on a short rate basis. The insurer, however, also has the option of canceling an assigned risk policy in some cases. For example, Iowa's automobile insurance plan sets forth four conditions under which the insurer can cancel a contract. Coverage can be canceled if the individual that is insured (1) is not or ceases to be eligible or in good faith entitled to insurance, (2) has violated any of the terms or conditions upon the basis of which the insurance was issued, (3) has obtained the insurance through fraud or misrepresentation, or (4) has failed to pay any premiums due on the policy.[6] New York has an additional provision that the insurer can cancel if the insured's automobile does not meet the standards set forth in the state's vehicle inspection law.

Table 5-3

Premium Payment Plans*

| | Premium Payment Plans | |
	Number of Payments	Installment Charges
Alabama	No	No
Alaska	5	$2 per installment
Arizona	5	$2 per installment
Arkansas	No	No
California	5	$2 per installment
Colorado	5	$2 per installment
Connecticut	5	$2 per installment
Delaware	2	$2 per installment
	35% down 50% of remainder for each payment effective 8/15/75	
District of Columbia	No	No
Florida	Florida Joint Underwriting Association became operational October 1, 1973.	
Georgia	3 (40%, 30%, 30%)	$2 per installment
Hawaii	Hawaii Joint Underwriting Association became operational September 1, 1974.	
Idaho	5	$2 per installment
Illinois	5	$2 per installment
Indiana	3 (40%, 30%, 30%)	$2 per installment
Iowa	5	$2 per installment
Kansas	3 (40%, 30%, 30%)	$6 total
Kentucky	No	No
Louisiana	No	No
Maine	5	$2 per installment (effective 6/15/75)
Maryland	State Fund became operational January 1, 1973.	
Massachusetts	Reinsurance Facility became operational January 1, 1974.	
Michigan	3 equal payments after 25% deposit	$8 total
Minnesota	3 (40%, 30%, 30%)	$6 total
Mississippi	No	No
Missouri	Missouri Joint Underwriting Association became operational January 1, 1975.	
Montana	5	$2 per installment
Nebraska	5	$2 per installment
Nevada	5	$2 per installment
New Hampshire	No	—
New Jersey	3 (40%, 30%, 30%)	$2 per installment
New Mexico	5	$2 per installment
New York	No	—

	Premium Payment Plans	
	Number of Payments	Installment Charg :s
North Carolina	North Carolina Reinsurance Facility became operational October 9, 1973.	
North Dakota	3 (40%, 30%, 30%)	$6 total
Ohio	No	No
Oklahoma	No	No
Oregon	5	$2 per installment
Pennsylvania	3 (40%, 30%, 30%)	$2 per installment
Rhode Island	3 (40%, 30%, 30%)	$6 total
South Carolina	South Carolina Reinsurance Facility became operational October 1, 1974.	
South Dakota	3 (40%, 30%, 30%)	$6 total
Tennessee	5	$2 per installment
Texas	No	No
Utah	5	$2 per installment
Vermont	5	$2 per installment
Virginia	3 (40%, 30%, 30%)	$6 total
Washington	5	$2 per installment
West Virginia	3 (40%, 30%, 30%)	$2 per installment
Wisconsin	5	$2 per installment (effective 9/1/75)
Wyoming	5	$2 per installment

*Reprinted with permission from Automobile Insurance Plans Service Office. "Chart Analysis—Automobile Insurance Plans, Corrections March, 1976."

The insured has the right to appeal the insurer's decision through the state's automobile insurance plan committee. The committee can reverse the decision of the insurer if it feels the insurer's decision is improper. If the committee sustains the cancellation by the insurer, then the applicant has the right to reapply for coverage at a later date.

Reinsurance and Joint Underwriting Facilities for Residual Markets

Not all states have an assigned risk type of automobile insurance plan. Two other methods have been adopted in a few states. One method is an automobile reinsurance facility, under which an insurer accepts all exposures instead of placing some in an assigned risk plan. The insurer then has the option of reinsuring part or all of any undesirable exposure in the state reinsurance pool. The insurers participating in the plan share in the underwriting results of the pool.

A few states have adopted joint underwriting associations. Like the reinsurance facility, joint underwriting associations require the participation of all insurers writing automobile insurance coverage. Coverage is issued by the underwriting association and is underwritten by the plan insurers.

OTHER AUTOMOBILE COVERAGES

Land Vehicles

The expanding demand by the public for recreational vehicles has created a need for special coverage. Sometimes recreational vehicles may not be covered under either the automobile or homeowners policy.

The family automobile policy only provides limited coverage for recreational vehicles. Trailers, while used in conjunction with a private passenger automobile, are covered under the liability, medical payments, and uninsured motorists sections of the family automobile policy. The trailer also is insured under the physical damage portion of the policy, but coverage is limited to $500. Most self-propelled recreational vehicles cannot be insured under the family automobile policy because they do not meet the definition of a private passenger automobile. The definition states that a private passenger automobile "means a four wheel private passenger, station wagon or jeep type automobile."

The homeowners policy, like the family automobile policy, has limited coverage for recreational vehicles. Liability and medical payment coverages are afforded for recreational vehicles on premises but not off premises. There is one exception. Liability and medical payments protection for golf carts off premises is available if the cart is being utilized for golf.

Since the recreational vehicle coverage is restricted in both the family automobile and the homeowners policies, an individual may need added protection. Protection for liability and physical damage can be purchased under a recreational vehicle policy. This policy can be written to cover registered recreational vehicles, nonregistered recreational vehicles, and recreational camping vehicles.

The recreational vehicle policy is issued to cover vehicles used for recreational activities owned by an individual or a husband and wife living in the same household. The following types of vehicles can be insured under a recreational vehicle policy: (1) all-terrain vehicle, (2) antique automobile (over twenty-five years old), (3) dune buggy, (4) go-cart, (5) golf cart, (6) minibike, (7) motorcycle, (8) motor home, (9) recreational camping vehicle, (10) snowmobile, and (11) trail bike.

Definitions for a few of these terms are necessary to clarify what can be insured under the policy. An all-terrain vehicle is a four or six wheel vehicle designed for rugged terrain. A motor home is "(a) a truck or van type motor vehicle equipped with a self contained living compartment that is an integral part of the vehicle chassis, or (b) a pick-up truck to which is attached either permanently or temporarily, a unit commonly referred to as a camper body, designed and constructed so as to provide living quarters consisting of at least facilities for cooking and sleeping."[7] A recreational camping vehicle is "a non-self propelled land vehicle, under 40 feet in length equipped with living facilities, designed to be towed by a motor vehicle, and not used as a permanent residence."[8]

Liability, medical payments, and uninsured motorists coverage are available under the FAP or SAP covering a towing vehicle. Therefore, these coverages cannot be purchased under the recreational vehicle policy for a recreational camping vehicle; i.e., the recreational vehicle policy covers only physical damage. Some recreational vehicle owners could purchase liability and physical damage coverage under a basic automobile policy.

An amphibious type of automobile cannot be insured under the recreational vehicle policy. It can be insured under an automobile policy by endorsing the contract.

Excess Indemnity Coverage

Insureds who cannot obtain adequate automobile liability coverage under their primary contracts can purchase an excess indemnity policy. The contract, while available to all insured owners of private passenger automobiles, generally is sold to individuals in state automobile insurance plans (assigned risk plans) to allow them limits of protection above the basic coverage.

The excess limits can be purchased separately. However, if the insured desires, he or she can add medical payments and uninsured motorists coverage to the excess indemnity policy.

Sound Reproducing and Transmitting Equipment

During the 1960s many individuals had stereo tape players installed in their automobiles. These tape players were easily stolen. As a result of high losses, most insurers have eliminated insurance protection for car stereos that are not permanently installed. Since stereos are excluded under the personal property section of a homeowners contract, insureds have not been able to obtain adequate coverage in this area.

Recently, a similar problem has arisen with citizen band radios and mobile telephones not permanently attached to an automobile. They are easy to steal, and the citizen band antenna makes it easy for a would-be thief to spot a car with a radio. To solve this problem, some insurers have raised their rates for automobile policies covering citizen band radios, and required that the units be permanently installed in the automobile.

UMBRELLA LIABILITY POLICY[9]

Although available liability coverages, such as automobile and comprehensive personal liability, may provide substantial protection, an individual often needs additional liability insurance because of increased public awareness of the ability to bring suit. For example, the increasing settlements provided by juries in automobile cases illustrate why an individual needs automobile liability protection above the $100,000/$300,000 limits that might be provided in a family automobile policy. In addition, there are many areas of liability which are not covered under package policies. An individual may obtain excess liability coverage and protection for uninsured liability for personal exposures which are not covered by the underlying coverage under an umbrella liability policy. The intent of this contract is to provide the same type of coverage for the individual that is made available to companies under the commercial umbrella liability policy.

Persons Insured

The personal umbrella liability contract, like the homeowners and family automobile coverages, is designed to protect a broad range of individuals. Like most insurance contracts, there is a named insured who is the owner of the policy. The term "individual named insured" also includes the owner's spouse, but the spouse is covered only if he or she is a resident of the same household as the named insured.

Relatives of the individual named insured are covered. A relative is anyone who is related by blood or marriage to the named insured or who is a ward, adopted child, or other person under the age of twenty-one in the care of and residing with the individual named insured.

There is a special category of insured for individuals operating an automobile or watercraft. An insured in this situation is defined as: (1)

any person (including a relative) while using an automobile or watercraft owned by, loaned to, or hired for use by or on behalf of the individual named insured with permission of the individual named insured, provided his actual operation or (if he is not operating) his other actual use thereof is within the scope of such permission, or (2) any relative while using any other automobile not owned by or furnished for regular use to such relative, provided use of such automobile is with permission, or reasonably believed to be with permission, of the owner.

These definitions restrict the coverage of a relative and other persons while using automobiles or watercraft conditioned on permissive use. This is the same condition contained in the omnibus clause of the FAP.

Under the fourth category, an insured is defined as a person or organization who, with the named insured's permission, "has custody or possession of any animal owned by the individual named insured." This would extend coverage to a varied group of individuals, but the most common application of this coverage is to a veterinarian or other individual having custody of pets.

The final category of insured persons includes any individual or organization which is liable because of the actions of an insured as defined under the previous four categories. As a result of this provision, coverage extends to an individual named insured's employer.

Three categories of individuals are not considered insureds. Anyone who owns an automobile and loans or leases it to the individual named insured is not covered under the policy. The second group of individuals not covered is those persons who, while employed in the automobile or watercraft business, operate an automobile or watercraft. This limitation does not apply if the person engaged in the automobile or watercraft business is the individual named insured. Finally, an insured is not a person or organization involved in the loading or unloading of an automobile or watercraft. This restriction does not apply to the individual named insured, an employee or agent of the individual named insured, or a relative.

Amount of Coverage

The personal umbrella liability policy pays for damages for which an insured is liable because of personal injury or property damage. The insurer's liability is equal to the ultimate net loss, but this is never more than the insurance policy limit per occurrence. The ultimate net loss includes the amount the insured is obligated to pay because of settlement or adjudication. The insured has to have the permission of the insurer to make a settlement. The insurer needs this restriction in order to protect its interest in any settlement.

The ultimate net loss as stated in the policy does not include any recovery or salvage or

> ... loss expenses and legal expenses (including attorneys' fees, court costs and interest on any judgment or award ... [or] salaries of the employees and office expenses of the insured, the company or any underlying insurer so incurred.

The ultimate net loss is payable only after the applicable underlying limit has been exhausted. The applicable underlying limit is either (a) the limit as stated in the policy, or (b) the underlying insurance coverage required in the schedule of the umbrella liability contract. In the former case, the insured is required to pay the retention limit set forth in the contract if no other insurance coverage is applicable. Thus, if the contract has a $250 retention limit and a $20,000 judgment accrued against the insured, the insured pays $250 and the insurer pays $19,750.

An umbrella liability insurer requires that the insured carry minimum limits of automobile liability and comprehensive personal liability insurance. If the insured carries at least the minimum limit and a loss occurs, the insured generally does not have to absorb any of the loss. However, if the insured fails to carry the underlying coverage that is found in the schedule of the personal umbrella liability policy, then he or she is responsible for the difference between what is carried and what is required. The following example illustrates the coverage provided.

Henry Minor was involved in an automobile accident. The court ruled that Henry was responsible for the accident and awarded damages to two plaintiffs. The first plaintiff was awarded $200,000 for bodily injury and $5,000 for property damage. The second plaintiff received $7,000 in property damage and $15,000 for bodily injury. Henry owns a family automobile policy with limits of $100,000/$300,000/$10,000. He has a personal umbrella liability policy with a $1 million aggregate limit that requires that he have automobile liability coverage of $100,000/$300,000/$10,000. The losses would be paid by the insurers as shown in Table 5-4.

If Henry had $25,000/$50,000/$10,000 limits in his family automobile policy, his umbrella liability policy would not have picked up the difference between the required limits and the limits in Henry's policy. Instead, losses would have been distributed as shown in Table 5-5.

Many individuals who purchase a personal umbrella liability policy need only two underlying coverages: (1) automobile liability and (2) comprehensive personal liability. Under these liability policies, the minimum limits that an individual usually would have to carry to be covered would be $100,000/$300,000/$10,000 for automobile liability and

Table 5-4

Illustrative Liability Insurance ($100,000/$300,000/$10,000)

	Plaintiff 1	Plaintiff 2
Family Automobile Policy Insurer	$100,000 Bodily Injury $5,000 Property Damage	$15,000 Bodily Injury $5,000 Property Damage
Umbrella Liability Insurer	$100,000 Bodily Injury	$2,000 Property Damage

Table 5-5

Illustrative Liability Insurance ($25,000/$50,000/$10,000)

	Plaintiff 1	Plaintiff 2
Family Automobile Policy Insurer	$25,000 Bodily Injury $5,000 Property Damage	$15,000 Bodily Injury $5,000 Property Damage
Henry	$75,000 Bodily Injury	——
Umbrella Liability Insurer	$100,000 Bodily Injury	$2,000 Property Damage

$50,000 for comprehensive personal liability. If an individual owned an aircraft, the personal umbrella liability insurer would require an aircraft liability insurance contract. The required limits would probably be $100,000/$300,000/$25,000. And if the insured owned a watercraft over twenty-six feet in length, a liability insurance policy for watercraft would be required. Normally, $100,000 is the minimum amount of coverage an umbrella liability insurer would require. If professional liability or other specific types of liability coverage are afforded under a particular company's personal umbrella liability policy, specified limits of coverage under underlying policies will be required for the specialized areas. A retention limit of $250 for losses not covered by an underlying policy is used frequently. However, higher and lower retained limits can be used.

Exclusions

Although the personal umbrella liability policy provides a broad range of liability protection for an insured, it contains a number of exclusions. Both racing activity and intentionally inflicted acts are not covered. War and civil unrest, unless it takes place inside the United States of America, its territories or possessions, or Canada are excluded. Nuclear energy liability is not covered if the insured has any type of nuclear energy liability policy. This exclusion is similar to the one found in the family automobile policy. Nuclear energy liability coverage is available if the individual does not have separate nuclear energy liability insurance.

Most personal umbrella liability contracts do not cover business pursuits. A few insurers will write coverage for these exposures if there is underlying coverage. One insurer handles the business pursuits exclusion in the following manner:

> This policy does not apply: ...
> 8. to personal injury or property damage arising out of business pursuits of the Insured, but this exclusion does not apply to personal injury or property damage arising out of: (a) activities ordinarily incident to nonbusiness pursuits, (b) business pursuits or the ownership, maintenance or use of professional business property if an underlying liability insurance policy described in the schedule or a renewal or replacement thereof, affords coverage with respect to such personal injury or property damage, or (c) the ownership, maintenance, operation, use loading or unloading of automobiles, or watercraft by the insured ...[10]

Of primary importance is the fact that this exclusion requires not only that underlying coverage be purchased but also that the underlying coverage be listed in the schedule of underlying insurance for business pursuits coverage to be in effect under an umbrella liability policy. But, if the umbrella liability policy schedule lists the homeowners contract, the individual can endorse the homeowners policy to include business pursuits coverage and thereby gain protection for liability arising from business pursuits. The insured must be sure that the homeowners business pursuits liability coverage provides the type of coverage needed since the umbrella policy is excess only to covered business exposures.

Most umbrella liability policies do not provide protection for an insured who is held liable under a workers' compensation, unemployment compensation, disability benefits law, or any similar law. Property damage liability is not available for property owned by the insured. Coverage is not available for aircraft which are "rented to, used by or in the care, custody, or control of the insured" or property rented to, used or occupied by, or in the care, custody, or control of the insured "to the extent that the insured has agreed to provide insurance therefor."

Personal injury and property damage liability arising from the ownership, maintenance, or operation of any aircraft owned or operated by the insured or chartered without crew by or on behalf of the insured is excluded. This exclusion does not apply to injury to employees of the insured in the course of their employment.

Personal injury and property damage liability arising from the operation of owned recreational vehicles or watercraft over twenty-six feet in length are also excluded. This exclusion does not apply to the watercraft on premises owned by, rented to, or controlled by the insured. The insured can delete this exclusion by obtaining underlying insurance for recreational vehicles or watercraft and having them listed in the umbrella liability policy schedule, or by making written request to the umbrella insurer for insurance on such recreational vehicles or watercraft within thirty days after the insured purchases them. Aircraft liability protection can be added under an umbrella liability policy if an underlying policy is obtained and scheduled.

Defense Cost

The personal umbrella liability contract requires the insurer to defend any suit seeking damages against the insured if the damages are not payable under underlying coverages. The legal costs involved in settling a claim are not charged against an insured's policy limits (i.e., the legal expense costs are paid in addition to the policy limits). The defense of suit coverage applies to those situations where the individual insured is obligated for the retention limit and no other insurance coverage is applicable other than the umbrella liability policy. The defense clause in the umbrella liability contract contains many of the standard provisions found in other liability contracts. For example, the insurer is required to defend suits even if they are groundless, false, or fraudulent. The insurance company also has the right to settle any claim or suit as it deems expedient. This protects the insurance company against having to fight claims which would cost more to win than to settle.

The insurer is required to pay all costs and all interest on the amount of any judgment which accrues after entry of the judgment and taxed against the insured before the insurance company has paid its limit of liability. The insurer is responsible for premiums on appeal bonds that may be required as well as premiums on bonds to release attachments and the cost of bail bonds required because of accidents or traffic violations. Further, the insurer is responsible for the reasonable expenses that an insured incurs at the insurance company's request. This does not include loss of earnings, however. The following illustrates the impact of the defense cost benefit under the umbrella liability policy.

Recently, Martha Jefferson was extremely upset about the actions of an associate. Without considering the consequences, Martha made some derogatory remarks about the associate. The associate sued Martha for slander and was awarded $30,000 in damages. The cost of defending the suit was $5,000. Martha has an umbrella liability contract which requires that she carry automobile and comprehensive personal liability. The contract has a retention limit of $1,000 and a limit of liability per occurrence of $1 million.

The umbrella carrier is responsible for $29,000 of the judgment plus the defense cost of $5,000. Martha is responsible for the retained limit of $1,000 since slander is not covered by an underlying contract.

The umbrella liability insurer has the option of appealing a judgment which is not pursued by the insured or an underlying insurer where underlying coverage is required. This option only accrues if the judgment exceeds the underlying liability limit or the retention limit. In the event that the umbrella insurer does elect to appeal a judgment, it is responsible for all the costs related to such an appeal.

General Policy Conditions

Cancellation   The umbrella liability policy can be canceled by the insured at any time. The insurer has the right to cancel the policy by giving the insured at least thirty days' notice prior to the date of cancellation. If the insurance company cancels the contract, the earned premium is calculated on a pro rata basis. If the insured cancels the contract, then the earned premium is calculated on a short rate basis.

Assignment   The insured has the right to assign the umbrella liability policy. The assignment is not valid until the company has endorsed the policy. If the insured should die, or be adjudged, or become bankrupt or insolvent during the policy period, the contract would extend coverage to the insured's legal representative.

Other Insurance   Because of the nature of the umbrella liability contract, it is designed as excess insurance over other valid and collectible coverage. This is true even if the insurance is primary, contributing, excess, or contingent. If such "other insurance" specifically applies only in excess of a stated amount, the two policies apply pro rata. Without this type of other insurance clause, the purpose of the umbrella liability protection to provide capstone coverage would be defeated.

Table 5-6
Illustrative Liability Insurance

	Bodily Injury Including Pain and Suffering	Property Damage
Passenger 1 (owner of other automobile)	$800,000	$5,000
Passenger 2	580,000	
Passenger 3	340,000	

Table 5-7
Illustrative Liability Insurance ($100,000/$300,000/$10,000)

	Bodily Injury	Property Damage
Automobile Liability Insurer	$ 300,000	$5,000
Umbrella Liability Insurer	1,000,000	
Edward	420,000	

Subrogation The subrogation clause of the personal umbrella contract has three stages. Any recovery that occurs as a result of subrogration is paid first to anyone who is liable for coverage in excess of the umbrella liability insurer's limits. If there is any residual, it is paid to the umbrella liability insurer. Lastly, the underlying insurer, or the insured if the retained limit applies, is reimbursed. To illustrate:

Edward Cane, while driving his automobile lost control and struck another vehicle. Three passengers were riding in the other vehicle. A court has determined that Edward is liable for the damages sustained by the passengers as shown in Table 5-6.

If Edward has an umbrella liability contract with an occurrence limit of $1 million and an underlying automobile limit of $100,000/$300,000/$10,000, losses will be paid as shown in Table 5-7.

After extensive testing, an engineer discovered that the wreck was the result of Edward's car having a defective steering column. As a result, Edward sued the manufacturer and received a judgment of $1.5 million. The order of priority for distributing this money would be: Edward, $420,000; umbrella liability insurer, $1 million; and the automobile liability insurer, $80,000.

FEDERAL INSURANCE PROGRAMS

Fair Access to Insurance Requirements Plans (FAIR Plans)

As a result of the riots which took place during the 1960s in many metropolitan areas, insurers suffered substantial underwriting losses. Insurance companies responded to these heavy losses by restricting the writing of business in areas that companies considered to be riot prone— particularly inner city areas. Many homeowners and business owners found it extremely difficult or impossible to obtain insurance coverage.

Congress held hearings on the lack of availability of insurance protection in inner city areas and ascertained that some type of change had to take place. Specifically, Congress found that:

> ... the vitality of many American cities is being threatened by the deterioration of their inner city areas; responsible owners of well maintained residential, business, and other properties in many of these areas are unable to obtain adequate property insurance coverage against fire, crime, and other perils; the lack of such insurance coverage accelerates the deterioration of these areas by discouraging private investment and restricting the availability of credit to repair and improve property therein; and this deterioration poses a serious threat to the national economy ....[11]

To overcome this problem, Congress passed the Urban Property Protection and Reinsurance Act of 1968. The Act was designed to do three things. First, the Act encouraged the states to develop a plan for making property insurance coverages readily available to residential, business, and other properties which met reasonable underwriting standards and which were located in the inner city. Second, the program provided a reinsurance facility for losses resulting from riots and other civil commotion. Finally, the Act established the right of the federal government to offer insurance directly to the public for crime exposures where crime exposure coverage was not made available by the private sector.

Control of the program was placed in the hands of the Secretary of Housing and Urban Development. The program is run by the Federal Insurance Administration, a part of the Department of Housing and Urban Development.

Reinsurance Operation The Urban Property Protection and Reinsurance Act of 1968 has two major parts. Part A sets forth the requirements for a statewide plan to assure fair access to insurance coverage. Part B provides for reinsurance coverage for riots and civil disorder losses. A third part, establishing crime insurance coverage, was added in 1970.

An insurance company is not able to participate under Part B unless it is a member of the state reinsurance coverage plan. Therefore, if an insurer wants to obtain reinsurance coverage for its property lines in the District of Columbia, it must belong to the District of Columbia's FAIR Plan.

Reinsurance can be offered by the Secretary of Housing and Urban Development for riot and civil disorder losses under the following lines of coverage: (1) fire and extended coverage; (2) vandalism and malicious mischief; (3) other allied lines of fire insurance; (4) burglary and theft; (5) portions of multi-peril policies coverage 1, 2, 3, and 4; (6) inland marine; (7) glass; (8) boiler and machinery; (9) ocean marine; and (10) aircraft physical damage.

A state plan has to be approved by its state insurance authority who is responsible for forwarding a description of the plan's operation to the Secretary of Housing and Urban Development. This plan makes standard lines of property insurance available for exposures which are located in undesirable areas. It accomplishes this by affording inspection service for property owners in undesirable areas and placing these exposures with insurance companies. This is handled by means of a pool in each state where each insurer assumes a certain portion of the FAIR Plan exposure. Normally, each insurer's percentage equals the proportion its property premium bears to the property premium written by all insurers in the FAIR Plan.

States also must share in riot and civil disorder losses. A state may have to contribute an amount up to 5 percent of the earned premium of the lines covered by reinsurance in the year preceding the year of a loss. This amount is paid to the federal government if a riot or civil disorder loss exceeds reinsurance premiums and company retention. To illustrate, consider a riot loss above the company retention, of $100 million. If the earned premium for all the applicable lines of insurance reinsured in the state are $200 million then the state would be responsible for reimbursing the government $10 million of the $100 million loss.

Placement FAIR Plans are designed for those individuals who cannot obtain coverage in the regular market. When a property owner is unable to obtain coverage in the standard market, the property owner, authorized representative, insurance agent, broker, or producer can request that the state's FAIR Plan have the property owner's property inspected.

The inspection is provided for the property owner at no cost. Once the inspection report is completed, it normally is forwarded to an all-industry placement facility. Exposures are covered by a joint underwriting association which reinsures its business with all insurance companies participating under the state FAIR Plan.

The facility determines if the exposure "meets reasonable underwriting standards at the applicable premium rate."[12] Three courses of action are possible. The property can be accepted either at standard rates or with a surcharge, if one is authorized. Coverage can be declined with the reasons for the declination given to the property owner. However, protection cannot be refused because of location. Coverage may be issued conditionally. In this case, the facility agrees to write coverage subject to improvements being made. For example, an application may be accepted subject to the elimination of debris in an adjacent alley. If the application is turned down, the property owner has a right to appeal the decision.

FAIR Plans can establish maximum limits of liability and underwriting rules and surcharges. When the exposure exceeds the established limit, the plan must aid the property owner in finding excess coverage.

FAIR Plans are required to have either a deemer or a binder requirement in order to prevent a lapse of coverage for an eligible risk. If the deemer approach is adopted, then:

> ... eligible risks are automatically deemed insured if, (1) through no fault of the applicant, coverage has not been either offered or denied within 20 calendar days after the date the request for inspection was received, and (2) the applicant, at the time of requesting the inspection or any time prior to the receipt of an inspection report indicating that the property is uninsurable, pays either the estimated annual premium or the portion thereof that is appropriate for the period of time for which a coverage is provided.[13]

Under the binder approach, the property owner can obtain temporary coverage from the time that the property owner requests an inspection until the inspection actually is made. The insured must pay a provisional premium for this protection. If the inspection shows that the property is uninsurable, coverage can be dropped or can be continued during the time needed for improvements to be made.

More than half the states have adopted a FAIR Plan program to provide broader coverage and to permit insurers to obtain federal reinsurance for the basic property insurance coverage. The need for state FAIR Plans or the federal reinsurance program has been questioned. Several years have passed since a major riot in the United States has occurred, and this may be part of the reason that there has been some discussion of eliminating FAIR Plans. However, the losses under the various state FAIR Plans have been sizable. Through the first nine months of 1975, state FAIR Plans had underwriting losses of $245,600,000.

Crime Insurance

The Housing and Urban Development Act of 1968 also gave the federal government the responsibility for implementing a crime insurance program for property "for which statewide programs and the federal reinsurance program either do not make crime insurance available or offer such insurance to property owners only at a prohibitive cost."[14] It did not give the federal government the right to subsidize any crime insurance afforded under the law, but the Federal Insurance Administration (FIA) felt that it could not offer federally unsubsidized crime insurance. In 1970, the head of the FIA, George Bernstein, addressing the problem of high burglary and theft losses in most urban areas, stated "that they make insurance prohibitive, if not totally unavailable ... burglary and theft insurance cannot be made available in urban areas on an economic basis without some form of subsidization."[15] Bernstein had made a similar statement before the House Subcommittee on Banking and Currency in 1970. During the Committee hearings, Bernstein stated:

> As I indicated in my testimony, the unavailability of crime coverage is unique because of the cities' horrendous crime loss experience. It may require a determination by government at either the State or Federal level on whether on not to subsidize the cost of crime insurance to make it generally available. This type of approach is not authorized under the existing FAIR Plan legislation, and would require significant departure from the present scope of the program.[16]

Congress passed the Housing and Urban Development Act of 1970 which established a federal insurance program for burglary and theft and placed the operation of the program under the auspices of the Secretary of Housing and Urban Development. However, like the FAIR Plan, crime insurance is controlled by the Federal Insurance Administration.

The crime insurance program was a departure from the FAIR Plan. The FAIR Plan was and is a reinsurance program in which the private insurance industry provides insurance coverage and the Federal Insurance Administration serves as a reinsurer for certain perils. The crime insurance program puts the federal government directly in the insurance business. While insurance companies, agents, brokers, adjustment organizations, and other insurance organizations can be and are used by the Federal Insurance Administration under the crime insurance program, the Federal Insurance Administration is the direct writer of the insurance coverage.

Coverages The Federal Insurance Administration offers both commercial and residential crime coverage. This section covers residential coverage. Residential coverage is available to individuals or families occupying one to four family residences. A tenant's form is available for individuals living in apartments or dormitories.

The owner's or tenant's residential crime insurance policy provided by the Federal Insurance Adminstration is designed for those individuals who cannot obtain coverage at reasonable rates in the regular market. No attempt is made to determine whether an individual is eligible for the plan. All an individual has to do to obtain coverage is complete the application and pay a six-month premium. The next semi-annual premium is billed approximately forty-five days before the due date and is payable on or before the due date. If the insured fails to pay the additional six-month premium, then coverage lapses.

Property Covered and Perils Insured Against. An owner's or tenant's residential crime insurance policy pays for losses to personal property both on the premises of and in the presence of an insured. The insured includes the named insured who is the owner of the contract and "any person while a permanent member of the named insured's household other than (1) a residence employee or (2) a person not related to the named insured or his spouse and who pays board or rent to either."

The perils insured against are burglary and larceny or robbery, including observed theft. A burglary is any unlawful taking of property from the insured premises provided that there are visible marks upon or physical damage to the exterior of the residence at the place where the burglar or burglars entered. This coverage is more limited than some commercial forms of protection which would provide coverage for burglaries where there were visible signs of damage to the building either on the interior or the exterior of the building.

A robbery occurs when an individual is forced to give up property because of violence or fear of violence. Recovery also extends to those cases where an individual is relieved of property after being rendered unconscious or killed.

Robbery includes observed theft. This is an important extension since coverage for personal property only applies when the personal property is located in the residence or is in the presence of an insured. The following illustrates the importance of this coverage.

John Royal and Julia Allen recently attended a business convention together. Upon arriving in the convention city, they obtained their luggage and proceeded to find transportation. In their search for transportation, John and Julia placed their luggage at a door of the airport and walked approximately 200 feet to the counter of a limousine service. When John turned around after paying the limousine fee, he saw an individual stealing both bags; however, because of the distance and the crowd, John was not able to catch the thief.

John has an owner's residential crime insurance policy issued by the Federal Insurance Administration. Since John observed the theft of the luggage, coverage would be afforded under the crime insurance policy. If John had not seen the culprit who had stolen the luggage, no coverage would have been afforded under the crime insurance policy.

Personal property coverage is provided while it is in a locked luggage compartment of a motor vehicle or trailer, but there have to be visible signs of entry upon the exterior of the vehicle for coverage to be applicable. The term "locked luggage compartment" is not defined in the policy, and therefore, it is difficult to ascertain the extent of this insurance protection. Obviously, a trunk would qualify as a locked luggage compartment. However, a problem may arise with vehicles which have hatchbacks or which have a trunk release located inside the vehicle. In the case of the hatchback, there may not be a locked luggage compartment available in the vehicle. This is true particularly if the back seat folds forward in the automobile creating an open passage to the trunk. The Federal Insurance Administration probably would provide coverage in the case of a hatchback where the seat folds forward, although this is not specifically stated in the policy. When the trunk release is located inside the automobile, another problem may arise. Instead of breaking into the trunk, a burglar may break into the front of a car to reach the trunk release. There would be no visible signs of forced entry on the locked luggage compartment. The Federal Insurance Administration should pay for losses where the burglar breaks into the interior of the car to reach the trunk release, but there is no policy provision establishing coverage.

Coverage for damages to the premises and the insured's personal property is afforded under the residential crime insurance policy. Coverage applies to damage caused as the result of a burglary or robbery. This coverage extends beyond damage to the exterior of the building when it is being burglarized to include vandalism and malicious mischief. The following example shows how the vandalism and malicious mischief coverage operates.

Sandra Kent has a residential crime insurance policy. While Sandra was at work, a burglar forced open a rear window of her apartment. Since Sandra kept most of her valuables in a safe deposit box, the burglar was unable to steal anything of substantial value. Apparently, angerd at his or her inability to find anything of value, the burglar proceeded to destroy the furniture in Sandra's living room. The loss would be covered as well as damage to the apartment where the burglar entered.

Table 5-8

Annual Rates for Residential Crime Coverage*

Coverage	Low Crime Areas	Average Crime Areas	High Crime Areas
$ 1,000	$20	$30	$40
3,000	30	40	50
5,000	40	50	60
7,000	50	60	70
10,000	60	70	80

*Reprinted from Department of Housing and Urban Development, "HUD News" No. 75-298, September 15, 1975.

Amount of Insurance Coverage. The residential crime insurance policy offers limits of $1,000, $3,000, $5,000, $7,000 or $10,000. These limits of coverage may be purchased by any individual whether he or she lives in a low, average, or high crime area. Each state has been assigned one of these crime areas based upon crime statistics gathered by the Federal Bureau of Investigation. Individual metropolitan statistical areas may have territory ratings that differ from the state ratings. As a rule, a metropolitan area will have a higher statistical rating than the state as a whole.

Table 5-8 contains a list of the amount of coverages available for purchase under the residential crime insurance coverage and the corresponding rates for low, average, and high crime areas. The table indicates that there is a $10 increment across crime areas and across coverage limits. Losses have not followed the pattern that the rates would indicate. Premium costs are estimates which are not based on loss data. As a result, arbitrary levels of premium cost have been established for varying amounts of coverage in varying crime areas.

Coverage is reduced by the amount of the deductible for residential coverage contained in the crime policy. Initially, the deductible was the greater of $75 or 5 percent of the gross amount of any loss. This has been revised and is now the greater of $50 or 5 percent of the gross amount of any loss. The deductible does not act to reduce the limits of coverage. If an individual has a $5,000 policy, he or she can receive up to $5,000 in loss protection. The next example illustrates how the deductible in the residential crime insurance policy functions.

Exclusions and Restrictions. The residential crime insurance policy contains numerous exclusions. Losses committed by an insured are excluded. Aircraft, motor vehicles, trailers, boats, or any equipment relating to these types of vehicles are not insured. Animals, fish, or birds are also excluded. Business articles which are "carried or held as samples or for sale or for delivery after sale" are not insured.

If the premises are being used as a boarding or lodging house, or for any occupancy which is not primarily a private residence occupancy, then coverage is voided. Even if the premises is being used primarily as a private residence, coverage is not extended to persons who are renting a portion of the insured premises but who are not related to an insured.

The policy contains some of the standard exclusions found in many property policies, such as war, insurrection, rebellion, revolution, or civil war. It also contains a nuclear reaction exclusion as well as a nuclear radiation and radioactive contamination exclusion.

Some of the exclusions in the residential crime insurance policy are unnecessary. For example, "property while in the charge of any laundry, cleaner, dyer, tailor or presser except by robbery or burglary at such premises" is not insured. This exclusion is not necessary since the policy does not cover property away from the premises unless it is in the presence of the insured. For the same reason, the exclusion for property while in the mail is unnecessary.

The policy excludes coverage for losses away from the premises of:

> ... (1) property pertaining to a business of an insured, (2) property while at any dwelling, including grounds, garages, stables, and other outbuildings incidental thereto, owned or occupied by or rented to an insured except while an insured is temporarily residing therein, (3) property of residence employee unless at the time of loss he is engaged in the employment of an insured and the property is in his custody, or the property is at a dwelling as aforesaid while an insured is temporarily residing therein, (4) property while unattended unless in or on any motor vehicle or trailer, other than a public conveyance, unless the loss is the result of forcible entry into a fully enclosed and locked luggage compartment....

This exclusion, like some of the others, is somewhat perplexing. The second part of the exclusion applies to dwellings, grounds, garages, stables, and other buildings unless the insured is temporarily residing therein. This is misleading since coverage is not available even if the insured is residing in these areas unless the property is in the insured's presence. Even then, theft is the only covered peril. The exclusion for losses away from the premises of property of a residence employee also is unnecessary. The term "insured" in the contract specifically excludes such employees. Thus, residence employees are never covered. The fourth part of the exclusion is like the insuring agreement and is not needed.

Apparently, the Federal Insurance Administration, in designing the residential crime insurance policy form, attempted to follow personal theft policies. The result has been that there are some unnecessary exclusions, as cited above. However, these do not detract from the coverage and only reinforce sections of the policy. Since the Federal Insurance Administration relies mainly on the insuring agreement for ascertaining whether or not coverage exists, the additional exclusions should not, but could, create problems for an insured.

The contract contains limitations and restrictions as well as exclusions. The contract stipulates that it covers the actual cash value of a loss or what it will cost to repair or replace the property, with similar quality and type. This is subject to some limitations. No more than $100 is paid for coverage of money, and no more than $500 for securities. There is a $500 limit on personal property stolen from a locked luggage compartment.

If the premises is rented to someone else, the insurance afforded under the residential crime insurance policy is altered. First, loss or damage coverage applies only to the property owned by an insured. Insurance coverage for certain items terminates. These include money, securities, jewelry, watches, necklaces, bracelets, gems, precious and semiprecious stones, articles of gold or platinum, furs, fine arts, antiques, and coin or stamp collections. Coverage for damage caused by the tenant, his or her employees, or members of the tenant's household is excluded.

Another set of restrictions relates to residences in which rooms or space is rented to three or more persons who are not related to the named insured. Coverage is available only for the property owned by the named insured and then coverage does not extend to money, securities, gems, precious and semiprecious stones, gold or platinum, antiques, and coin or stamp collections. There is a $50 limit for loss of any one article of jewelry. Finally, coverage is not provided for a tenant or tenant's employee or household.

Removal. The named insured has coverage for personal property which is being moved from the insured premises under the policy to a new permanent residence. Coverage extends from the time the moving begins for up to thirty days. Protection is avilable for personal property at the original premises, at the new premises, and during transportation between the two locations. Once all personal property is moved to the new permanent location, insurance coverage on the original premises ceases, and the entire coverage is provided on personal property at the new premises. However, after the end of the thirty-day period, which starts at the time that the moving begins, all coverage ceases for all locations.

Appraisal. If the insured and the insurer cannot agree on the actual cash value of the loss, then each party chooses an appraiser to make an evaluation of the extent of the loss. These two appraisers have the responsibility of ascertaining the actual value of the loss. But, if they cannot agree, then the two appraisers are required to select a third appraiser. Any difference of opinion between the insurer's appraiser and the insured's appraiser are submitted to the third appraiser. Agreement between any two of the appraisers, "shall be considered by the Insurer in determining the amount of the loss but shall not be considered binding upon him and shall not be admissible as such in court." The difference between this type of appraisal clause and that found in an insurance contract is obvious. In most contracts, the decision of two of the three appraisers is binding on all parties unless some type of fraud or misconduct is involved. In this appraisal clause, agreement of two of the three appraisers is considered but is not binding in determining the loss.

Other Insurance. If an insured has other valid and collectible insurance, the residential crime insurance policy coverage serves as excess protection. In addition, property which is listed specifically and covered by other insurance is not covered under the crime insurance policy.

Cancellation. The insured, under the federal residential crime insurance policy, has the option of canceling the coverage. If the insured should cancel the contract, the premium is returned on a short rate basis. If the insurer cancels, a short rate basis also is used. This is unlike the private sector where if the insurer cancels the coverage, premium is refunded on a pro rata basis.

The contract does not state specifically the reasons for cancellation. These can be found in Subchapter C, Chapter VII, Title 24 of the *Code of Federal Regulations.* The grounds for cancellation by the insurer include nonpayment of premium, fraud or misrepresentation in either an application or a claim, use of the insured residence for an illegal purpose, or any other failure to comply with the provisions of Subchapter C.

Protective Devices. An applicant, when he applies for insurance protection, is informed that the residence covered by the crime insurance policy must have certain protective devices and if these devices are not on the insured residence at the time of the loss, then coverage is voided. For example:

> ... (a) Each exterior doorway or doorway leading to garage areas, public hallways, terraces, balconies, or other areas affording easy access to the insured premises, shall be protected by a door which, if not a sliding door, shall be equipped with a dead lock using either an interlocking vertical bolt and striker, or a minimum 1/2 inch throw dead bolt, or a minimum 1/2 inch throw self-locking dead latch. (b) All sliding doors, first floor and basement windows, and windows opening onto stairways, fire escapes, porches, terraces, balconies, or other areas

affording easy access to the premises, shall be equipped with a locking device of any kind.

Commission Rates for Agents and Brokers Agents and brokers who sell policies under the federal crime insurance program are entitled to a relatively small commission. The commission for residential policies for the initial year of protection is 16 percent for policies in low crime areas, 15 percent for policies in average crime areas, and 14 percent for policies in high crime areas. However, a minimum commission of five dollars per policy has been established. The commission rate for renewal contracts for all territories is 12 percent. The agent is not allowed to deduct the premium in advance as is the case in the regular insurance market, but must remit the entire premium to the servicing company which then sends a commission check to the agent. If the crime insurance policy is canceled, the agent must pay back any unearned portion of the commission that exceeds the minimum of five dollars.

Organization of the Federal Crime Insurance Program When Congress was considering how crime insurance lines should be written, the former Federal Insurance Administrator, George Bernstein, indicated a preference for utilizing state operations where possible. He stated during testimony on the housing and urban development legislation that:

> ... with respect both to the crime lines problem and the other property insurance availability problems with which we are concerned, we continue to favor the approach so soundly taken in the 1968 Act, which recognized the efficacy of State regulation, which gave the States an opportunity to determine their own needs, and which gave the States and the companies doing business therein a reasonable opportunity to solve these problems once they were formally given the occasion and the incentive to recognize them. Based upon our numerous discussions with the State insurance authorities and industry representatives during recent months, we believe that the outlook for property insurance availability is beginning to improve, and that the States and the industry will make substantial progress in the solution of these problems in the months ahead if we give them the opportunity to do so to avoid preemption of the field by additional regulation.[17]

Congress placed in the Housing and Urban Development Act of 1970 a section which gave the states the option of establishing a crime insurance program in lieu of the federal program. Following the passage of the 1970 Act, the Federal Insurance Administrator informed the insurance commissioners of states in which he felt that there was a high crime rate and that crime insurance must be made available through the states' FAIR Plans or the federal government would begin writing crime insurance in these states. In order for the states' crime insurance programs to qualify, the rates in the state plans had to meet the criterion of affordability. Five states developed a state sponsored crime insurance program before the federal deadline of August 1, 1971, when the Act of 1970 went into effect. Nine states came under the program as of August 1, 1971, since they did not establish a state plan. The number of states in the program since August 1971 has almost doubled. The five states that originally enacted crime insurance programs skirted the issue of insurance affordability by adopting the federal premium rate schedules.[18]

In those states where the Federal Insurance Administration started offering crime insurance coverage, it utilized insurance companies as servicing agents. Coverage was sold by agents and brokers who had the responsibility of explaining the coverage to an applicant and assisting the applicant in completing the application. This included explaining to a prospective applicant the nature of the protective device requirements. The insurance companies which were serving the business found the cost of servicing to be too high. As a result, the Federal Insurance Administration, through the Safety Management Institute, took over the servicing of the business in a majority of the states. The Insurance Company of North America and Aetna Casualty and Surety Insurance Company still service crime insurance in a few of the states.

Growth of the Program The growth of the crime insurance program has been slow. From its inception until the end of 1973, a total of 32,560 policies were written, representing total premium payments of slightly over $2 million. Several factors contributed to this lack of demand for the program in its early stages. First, the initial premium rates were too high. When the Federal Insurance Administration reduced rates in 1972, it noted the fact that high rates had hurt the program. The Federal Insurance Administrator stated:

> The purpose of the Federal crime insurance program is to make needed crime insurance coverage available to both residential and business property owners and tenants at premium rates that they can afford, in States where such insurance is not available either through a State program or the private insurance market. Although the program has now been in effect in 10 major urban States for nearly a year, only 6,000 policies have been sold. Inquiries made by the Federal Insurance Administration and correspondence from Members of Congress, State and local officials, agents and brokers groups, the servicing companies, consumer organizations, and members of the general public have all indicated that a substantial number of those for whom the program is primarily intended, especially commercial risks with low gross receipts believe that the present premium rates are too high ....[19]

The slow start of the program has also been attributed to the lack of enthusiasm of agents and brokers for sale of the coverage. As a result, minimum commission rates have been established to encourage agents and brokers to sell the coverage.

National Flood Insurance Program

Flood insurance coverage was first authorized by Congress under the Federal Flood Insurance Act of 1956. However, Congress failed to provide any funds to implement the act. Efforts to pass additional flood insurance legislation were made in 1962, 1963, and 1965, and in 1965 the Southeastern Hurricane Disaster Relief Act was passed. This act included a provision that a feasibility study be undertaken on flood coverage by the Secretary of Housing and Urban Development. The study revealed that although plans for preventing flood losses had been implemented in many states, the flood hazard was increasing. According to the study, the reason for the increasing hazard was a move by individuals into flood-prone areas in spite of the high flood risk. The study also stated:

> ... that a national flood insurance program was feasible and could provide subsidized premium rates for properties already existing in high-risk areas, but only if actuarial rates were charged for future construction and the program required sound land use and control measures to reduce or avoid future losses.[20]

In response to this study and the general need for flood insurance, Congress passed the National Flood Insurance Act of 1968. The act set forth how the flood insurance program should be operated. It also established the need for the Secretary of Housing and Urban Development to determine what subsidized rates and what actuarial rates should be charged for the flood insurance program. The act provided that strict land use control measures be adopted by public bodies in a flood-prone area for coverage to be available under the plan.

The National Flood Insurance Act of 1968 did not provide coverage for mudslides. This coverage was added later under the Housing and Urban Development Act of 1969.

The program was further amended under the Flood Disaster Protection Act of 1973. This act not only increased the limits of coverage afforded under the National Flood Insurance Program but also changed the procedures for establishing whether an area shall be designated as a flood-prone area. In addition, it put constraints on the use of federal funds for property in flood-prone areas unless the property is protected by flood insurance. This last measure was the most important. Federal agencies cannot lend money on a property in a flood-prone area unless the property is covered by flood insurance. Included in the list of federal agencies affected are the Federal National Mortgage Administration, the Veterans Administration, and the Federal Mortgage and Home Loan Administration.

Organization of the Flood Insurance Program Prior to January 1, 1978, the flood insurance program was underwritten and managed by the National Flood Insurers Association, an organization of more than 100 private insurers, in accordance with policies established by the Federal Insurance Administration.

During 1977, the Department of Housing and Urban Development decided it had the right to issue regulations that superseded provisions in its contract with the National Flood Insurers Association. It proposed regulations which would give HUD management and operational authority over the program. NFIA charged that HUD was violating its contract with the insurance industry and that the new regulations would change the relationship between the Federal Insurance Administration and NFIA from a cooperative venture to one which would reduce the industry pool to a subordinate, mechanical entity. HUD responded that because the purchase of flood insurance is not really voluntary any longer in many cases, the program should not be left in the control of private insurers. NFIA notified HUD that it was terminating its contract as of December 31, 1977; HUD then announced that it was seeking a new administrative agent and invited bids from interested parties.

As a result, in 1978, by authority granted to HUD under the National Flood Insurance Act, national flood insurance became a program in which HUD purchases only administrative services from a private contractor. EDS Federal Corporation, a subsidiary of Dallas-based Electronic Data Systems Corporation, was selected as the administrative services vendor.[21] It is the vendor's responsibility to maintain all policyholder records and funds. Marketing of flood insurance is still performed by independent agents in communities enrolled in the program. The vendor appoints local adjusting firms to assist in loss settlements involving flood damage. Financial and statistical reports on the program's performance are prepared by the contractor and submitted to the FIA. The National Flood Insurance Fund, run by the FIA, is now the sole insurer.

The Department of Housing and Urban Development continues to operate its regional flood insurance specialist offices. These offices are located throughout the United States in major metropolitan areas and are available to assist brokers and prospective insureds in obtaining insurance coverage. In addition, each state has a state coordinating agency for flood insurance which works with the Department of Housing and Urban Development in establishing flood controls and implementing flood prevention measures.

Determination of Flood Insurance Availability For the residents of any area to become eligible for flood insurance, one of two procedures must be followed. Under one approach, the community makes application to the Department of Housing and Urban Development to be included in the flood insurance program. Once an application has been submitted, and all the information has been provided by the community, then a flood hazard boundary map is prepared, if one has not been prepared before. The flood hazard boundary map is a temporary map designed to identify flood-prone areas in the community. The map specifically recognizes special flood hazard areas. A special flood hazard area is any area that is "subject to inundation by the base flood, i.e., a flood that has a one-percent chance of occurrence in any given year."[22] The map is sent to the community and all the participating agencies, the servicing company, any state coordinating agency, any state insurance commissioner, any regional specialist, Housing and Urban Development field offices, and other federal agencies. After this is done, the first layer of insurance is available for buildings and contents at subsidized rates provided the community eligible for coverage has established a flood plain management plan. A flood plain management plan "means the operation of an overall program of corrective and preventive measures for reducing flood damage." Flood plain management is a continual process that is necessary for a community to continue to be eligible for flood insurance coverage.

Once the first layer of insurance coverage has been made available to individuals in a flood-prone area, they cannot obtain federal monies for new construction unless flood insurance is purchased. New construction includes not only new buildings but also:

> ... any repair, reconstruction, or improvement of a structure, the cost of which equals or exceeds 50 percent of the market value of the structure either (a) before the improvement is started, or (b) if the structure has been damaged and is being restored, before the damage occurred.[23]

The program providing the first layer of protection is called the emergency program. After it has been completed, the Department of Housing and Urban Developme. t undertakes the project of ascertaining actuarial rates for the flood-prone insurance area. It attempts to establish an accurate flood insurance map. This second map is called a flood insurance rate map. The second phase is called the regular flood insurance program.

Under the second procedure, the Department of Housing and Urban Development can determine that an area is flood prone and notify the area that it must comply with federal flood standards. The community has the option of either making the appropriate application or contesting its designation as a flood-prone area. If the community cannot prove that it is not a flood-prone area, then it has to go through the procedures mentioned above, including making application to the flood insurance program. Figures 5-1 and 5-2 illustrate the processes the Federal Insurance Administration uses in an emergency program and a regular program, respectively.

Coverage Under the Standard Flood Insurance Policy The dwelling building and contents flood insurance contract policy is designed to protect real and personal property against flood. The term "flood" means:

A. A general and temporary condition of partial or complete inundation of normally dry land areas from: 1. The overflow of inland or tidal waves. 2. The unusual and rapid accumulation of runoff of surface waters from any source. 3. Mudslides (i.e., mudflows) which are approximately caused or precipitated by accumulations of water on or under the ground.

B. The collapse or subsidence of land along the shore of a lake or other body of water as a result of erosion or undermining caused by waves or currents of water exceeding the cyclical levels which result in flooding as defined in A-1 above.

The contract contains exclusions for many of the perils which are found in a homeowners policy. There is a nuclear exclusion as well as a power failure exclusion unless "... such failure results from physical damage to power, heating or cooling equipment situated on premises ... caused by the peril insured against...." Loss caused by the enforcement of any government regulation is not insured, and coverage for theft, fire, windstorm, explosion, earthquake or landslide other than a mudslide is not covered. Losses caused by war or civil disorders do not come under the coverage afforded in the policy.

The insurer is not responsible for losses caused by:

... (1) rain, snow, sleet, hail or water spray; (2) freezing, thawing or by the pressure or weight of ice or water, except when the property covered has been simultaneously damaged by flood; or (3) water, moisture or mudslide damage of any kind resulting primarily from conditions, causes or occurrences which are solely related to described premises or within the control of the insured (including but not limited to design, structural or mechanical defects, failures, stoppages or breakages of water or sewer lines, drains, pumps, fixtures or equipment, seepage or backup of water, or hydrostatic pressure) or any condition which causes flooding which is substantially confined to the described premises or properties immediately adjacent thereto....

Property Covered. The standard flood insurance policy for residences covers both the dwelling and the contents of the dwelling. The contents are covered only if they are contained within an enclosed structure. A dwelling is a single structure which contains living quarters for one to four families. Included in the definition of dwelling would be a new house or a townhouse as long as the units are:

Figure 5-1
National Flood Insurance Program Emergency Program Procedures*

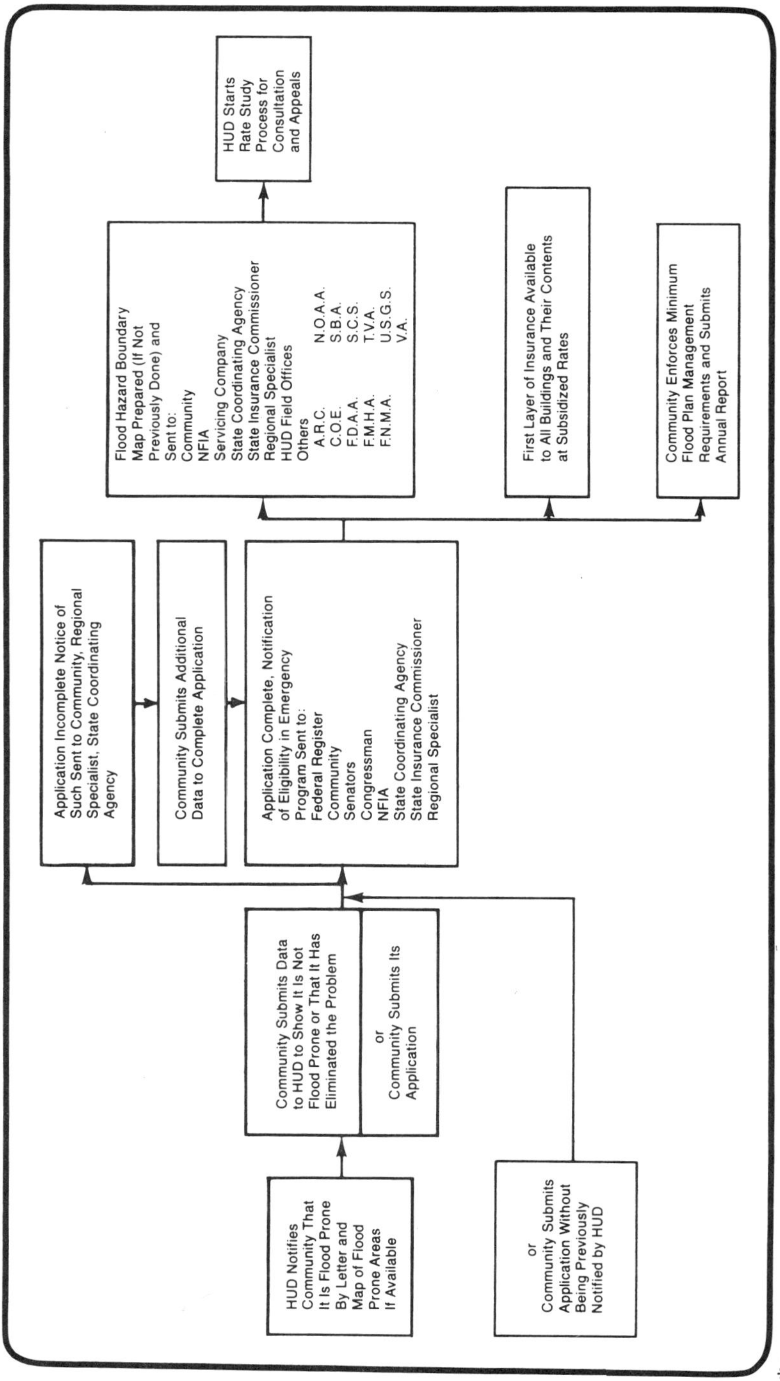

HUD Notifies Community That It Is Flood Prone By Letter and Map of Flood Prone Areas If Available

or
Community Submits Application Without Being Previously Notified by HUD

Community Submits Data to HUD to Show It Is Not Flood Prone or That It Has Eliminated the Problem

or
Community Submits Its Application

Application Incomplete Notice of Such Sent to Community Regional Specialist, State Coordinating Agency

Community Submits Additional Data to Complete Application

Application Complete, Notification of Eligibility in Emergency Program Sent to:
Federal Register
Community
Senators
Congressman
NFIA
State Coordinating Agency
State Insurance Commissioner
Regional Specialist

Flood Hazard Boundary Map Prepared (If Not Previously Done) and Sent to:
Community
NFIA
Servicing Company
State Coordinating Agency
State Insurance Commissioner
Regional Specialist
HUD Field Offices
Others
A.R.C.   N.O.A.A.
C.O.E.   S.B.A.
F.D.A.A.   S.C.S.
F.M.H.A.   T.V.A.
F.N.M.A.   U.S.G.S.
                 V.A.

HUD Starts Rate Study Process for Consultation and Appeals

First Layer of Insurance Available to All Buildings and Their Contents at Subsidized Rates

Community Enforces Minimum Flood Plan Management Requirements and Submits Annual Report

*Reprinted from the Federal Insurance Administration.

Figure 5-2

Consultation and Appeals Procedures Under the Flood Disaster Protection Act of 1973*

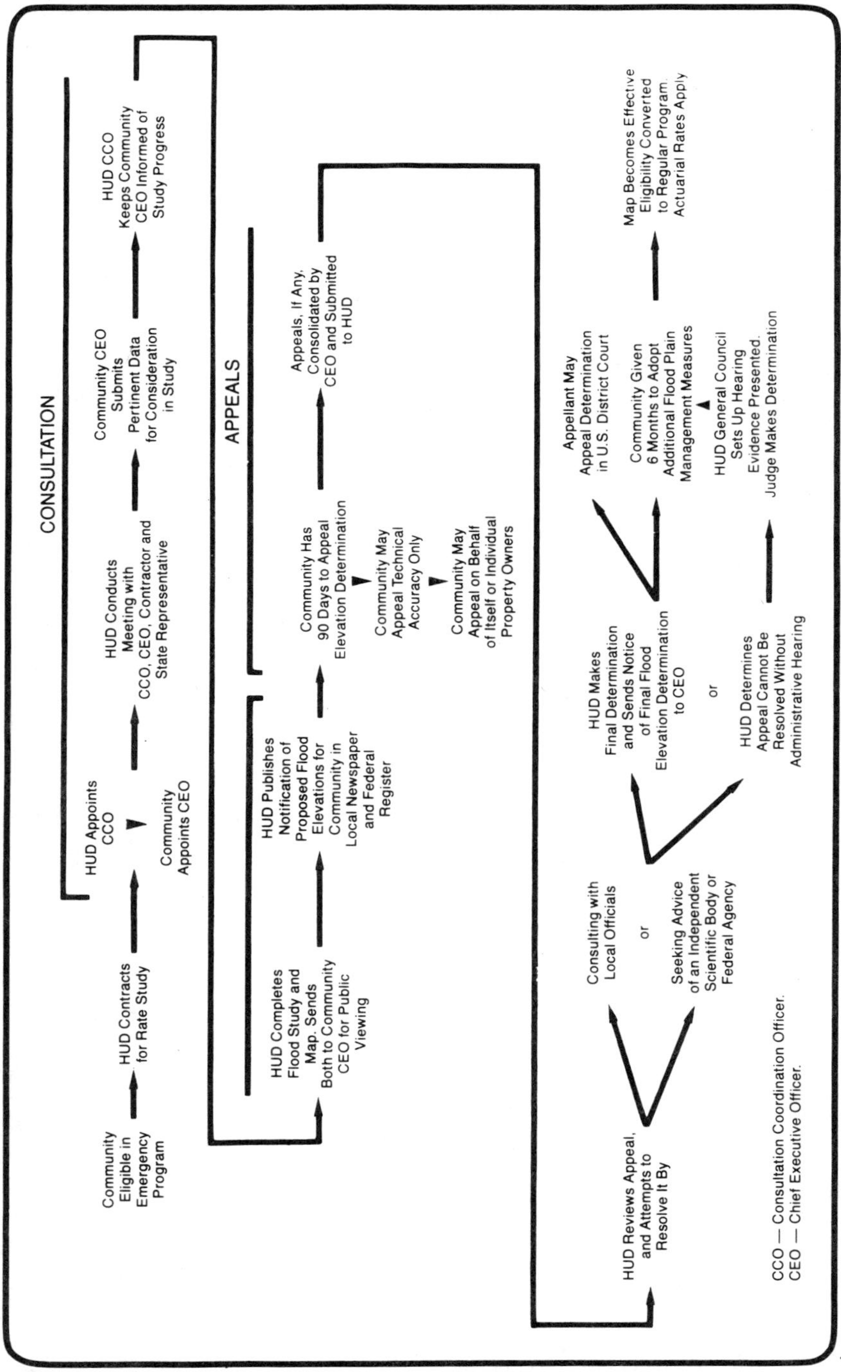

* Reprinted from the Federal Insurance Administration.

... separated from other residential units by intervening clear space or masonry division walls, . . . has a separate legal description and generally is regarded as a separate property for other real estate purposes. . . .[24]

This would not include a condominium in which there is joint ownership and control of certain designated areas other than the living space by all those who are members of the condominium association. However, in the latter case, joint rather than individual coverage can be written for the condominium association. Mobile homes on foundations can be covered as dwellings.

There is a dwelling extension which allows the insured to apply up to 10 percent of the coverage on the dwelling for damage to appurtenant private structures if they are located on the insured premises. This 10 percent extension does not expand the amount of coverage afforded under the policy. It merely gives the insured flexibility in applying the insurance limit.

The dwelling coverage applies to additions which are attached to the dwelling. Building equipment, fixtures, and outdoor equipment used in the service of the premises and which are contained in an enclosed structure on the premises are insured. Building materials and supplies inside an enclosed structure and utilized in the construction, alteration or repair of the dwelling or appurtenant structure come under the protection afforded by the flood insurance policy.

Contents coverage is provided for "all household and personal property usual or incidental to the occupancy of the premises as a dwelling." Contents coverage is reduced by any more specific coverage on personal contents which insures against the peril of flood. Generally, an individual will not have other flood coverage except under floaters.

The property covered has to belong to the insured who owns a flood contract or members of the insured's family who live with the insured. Coverage extends to property for which the insured may be held liable. The property of servants or guests is covered at the insured's option while the property is located in a building on the insured premises.

The contents coverage has a 10 percent benefit extension. Ten percent of the amount of insurance applicable to contents can be applied to improvements, alterations, and additions to the dwelling and appurtenant structures if the insured is not the owner of the premises. When the contract covers an individual condominium unit, 10 percent of the coverage can be applied to the interior walls, floors, and ceilings which are not covered under a condominium association policy.

The 10 percent coverage is not additional protection. As in the case of the dwelling, the extension is an alternative means of using the policy limit.

The cost of removing debris following a loss is covered under the

Table 5-9

Limits of Coverage Under the Flood Insurance Program*

| | Emergency Layer | | Regular Layer | |
	Building	Contents	Building	Contents
Single Family Dwelling				
All states and jurisdictions				
(except below)	$ 35,000	$10,000	$ 35,000	$10,000
Alaska, Hawaii, Guam,				
and Virgin Islands	50,000	10,000	50,000	10,000
Other Residential †				
All states and jurisdictions				
(except below)	100,000	10,000	100,000	10,000
Alaska, Hawaii, Guam,				
and Virgin Islands	150,000	10,000	150,000	10,000

†This coverage would apply to condominiums written as an association.

*Reprinted with permission from *Flood Insurance Manual* (Arlington, VA: National Flood Insurers Association, 1975), p. 1–7.

flood policy. This does not increase the insurer's limit of liability. The liability of the insurer "for both loss to property and debris removal expense shall not exceed the amount of insurance applying under this policy to the property covered."

Excluded from coverage are accounts, bills, currency, deeds, evidences of debt, money, securities, bullion, manuscripts, valuable papers or records, numismatic or philatelic property, fences, retaining walls, sea walls, outdoor swimming pools, bulkheads, wharves, piers, bridges, and docks. Personal property in the open is excluded. Land values, lawn, trees, shrubs, plants, growing crops, and livestock do not come under the protection. Underground structures and equipment are not classified as covered property. Driveways and other paved structures which are not part of the foundation walls of a structure are not afforded insurance. Finally, animals, birds, aircraft, motor vehicles, trailers on wheels, watercraft, and business property are excluded.

Amount of Coverage. The amount of coverage for the building and the contents depends on whether the insured dwelling and contents are located in an area which is under an emergency program or a regular program. The limits for both a subsidized emergency program and a regular program are found in Table 5-9.

Under the emergency program, a single family dwelling can be insured for up to $35,000. Contents can be insured for up to $10,000. An exception is made for Alaska, Hawaii, Guam, and the Virgin Islands where the maximum building coverage is $50,000 instead of $35,000. Other residential dwellings, i.e., condominium coverage, can be insured up to a maximum of $100,000 in all states and jurisdictions except Alaska, Hawaii, Guam, and the Virgin Islands. In the case of Alaska, Hawaii, Guam, and the Virgin Islands, the limit is $150,000. A maximum of $10,000 is available for contents coverage for other residential dwellings. Once a regular program has been established, additional coverage is made available to the insureds. The additional coverage is equal to the amount of coverage provided in the first layer of protection. Therefore, insurance protection is doubled. The rates for the coverage in the regular program are not subsidized but are the actuarial rates. The rates for the first layer of coverage may be the subsidized rates or the actuarial rates depending on when the insured premises was constructed. The following is an example of how the coverage limits function.

Helen Porter owns a home in a flood-prone area. The home is valued at $50,000. The contents of the home are worth $19,000 on an actual cash value basis. The community in which Helen lives has qualified under the emergency flood insurance program. Therefore, Helen can insure the house for $35,000 and the contents for $10,000. Once the community is under the regular program, Helen could apply for full coverage because the maximum available limits under the plan would be $70,000 for dwellings and $20,000 for contents.

Coverage on both the dwelling and the contents is subject to a deductible. The deductible is the greater of either $200 or 2 percent of the amount of loss.

Coverage is reduced by any other insurance which the insured may have against the peril of flood. The contract states that the National Flood Insurance Fund will not pay a greater proportion of the loss than the amount of coverage in the policy bears to all coverage against the peril of flood whether the other coverage is collectible or not.

A $1,000 limitation is placed on aggregate losses of paintings, etchings, pictures, tapestries, or glass windows and other works of art. There is also a $500 aggregate limit on loss to jewelry, watches, necklaces, bracelets, gems, precious and semiprecious stones, articles of gold, silver, platinum and furs or articles which contain fur.

Rating a Flood Policy. The rating procedure applicable to flood insurance is complex. Parts may be written at subsidized rates while the balance may be written at actuarial rates. The actuarial rates are the rates that are needed to cover losses. The subsidized rate is the rate the government sets based on affordability.

When an emergency program becomes effective, subsidized rates are used, that is for the first layer of coverage—$35,000 on the residence and $10,000 on the contents. The subsidized rates apply to structures

Table 5-10

Federal Flood Insurance Rates

Sam			
Residence	0.0025 × 30,000	=	$ 75.00
Contents	0.0035 × 10,000	=	35.00
Total Premium			$110.00
John			
Residence	0.0035 × 30,000	=	$105.00
Contents	0.0090 × 10,000	=	90.00
Total Premium			$195.00

which existed and have not been improved substantially since December 31, 1974, or "before the effective date of the FIRM (Flood Insurance Rate Map), whichever is later."[25] Once the FIRM has been developed, the regular program becomes effective. Individuals whose residences existed before the regular program is initiated continue to pay the subsidized rate for the first layer of coverage or the actuarial rate if it is less than the subsidized rate. The second layer of coverage is written with actuarially determined rates. Residences constructed or substantially modified after December 31, 1974, or the date of the FIRM, whichever is later, pay actuarial rates for both layers of coverage. An example follows.

Both Sam Turner and John Reynolds own one story one family residential structures. Construction on Sam's home was started in June of 1976. John's home was started during the same period in 1977. The homes are located on the same street in a community which is considered to have a severe flood problem. In December of 1976, the Federal Insurance Administration released the FIRM. The subsidized rates per $1.00 of value for coverage of structures and contents are 0.25 percent and 0.35 percent, respectively. Corresponding actuarial rates are 0.35 percent and 0.90 percent. Both Sam and John have homes worth $30,000. Contents in both homes are valued at $10,000. The premium paid by each man is shown in Table 5-10. John's cost is substantially higher.

If the actuarial rates for the building and the contents were 0.20 and 0.25 percent respectively, Sam and John would pay the same premium since Sam could elect the lower actuarial rate.

Replacement Cost. The residential flood insurance policy contains several provisions that are similar to those found in a homeowners policy, e.g., pair and set, other insurance, mortgagee, and replacement cost clauses. The replacement cost clause in the flood insurance policy does have one very important provision not found in a homeowners policy. The insured has to purchase coverage equal to 80 percent of the replacement cost or the maximum insurance available, whichever is less. This flexibility is mandatory since an individual may not be able to purchase flood insurance equal to 80 percent of the value of his or her residence.

AIRCRAFT INSURANCE

Aircraft owners are not covered by any of the personal liability contracts that have been discussed except the umbrella policy. If an insurer covers aircraft under an umbrella liability policy, there still has to be underlying protection. To cope with this problem, an individual has to purchase an aircraft policy. Most insurers do not accept aircraft exposures, but some companies have formed pools which underwrite aircraft protection. As an example, the United States Aircraft Insurance Group is a pool of companies that writes aircraft coverage.

The grouping of insurers to cover aircraft exposures has occurred because of the large potential losses in terms of possible liability claims and hull damage. The crash of a single plane can result in millions of dollars of losses.

Private Passenger Aircraft Coverage[26]

Aircraft protection is available for a broad range of insureds including airport owners and operators, aircraft manufacturers, and aircraft owners.

Several forms of protection are available for both liability and hull exposures. At least one aircraft insurance pool has five liability coverage options: (1) bodily injury excluding passengers, (2) property damage, (3) passenger bodily injury, (4) bodily injury and property damage, and (5) bodily injury (excluding passengers) and property damage. Coverages one and three are written with a per person and per occurrence limit. Coverages two, three, and four are written for a single limit per occurrence.

Like personal lines coverage, an aircraft contract contains medical payments coverage. The medical coverage, stated on a per person basis, applies to expenses incurred by passengers within one year of an accident. Medical coverage for the crew including the pilot can be added if the named insured desires.

Liability and medical payments coverage extends to nonowned aircraft. For example, a temporary substitute vehicle is covered if it is replacing an aircraft being repaired or that has been destroyed. Other aircraft not owned by the named insured but used on an irregular basis by or for the named insured are covered.

Hull coverage can be provided in one of four ways. First, "all-risks" coverage is available. As an alternative, an aircraft owner can buy "all-risks" coverage for an aircraft when it is not in flight and more limited coverage when it is. The limited protection normally covers perils such as robbery, fire, lightning, explosion, vandalism, and theft. The term "in flight" is defined under one contract as

> ... the time commencing when the aircraft (other than a motorcraft) moves forward in attempting to take-off and continuing thereafter until it has completed its landing run.

Therefore, the hull is covered against a limited number of perils from the time it gets to the end of the runway to take off and to land. The two other forms of coverage are "all-risks" protection when not in flight and "all-risks" coverage when not in motion. Motion includes the time when the aircraft is in flight or moving under its own power.

Liability coverage has no deductible. The hull coverage has two deductibles. One applies when an aircraft is in motion; the other is applicable when an aircraft is not in motion.

In the event of a total hull loss, the insurer pays the amount of the policy less the deductible. (Actual cash value policies would not necessarily pay the policy limit.) For partial losses, the cost of materials, labor, and transportation is paid. The transportation expense is the cost incurred in moving the damaged aircraft to the place of repair or in bringing replacement parts to the site of a loss. Once the aircraft is repaired, it is returned to the site of the loss or the named insured's home airport, whichever is closer.

Newly acquired aircraft—whether replacement or additional—are automatically insured for liability, medical, and hull coverage. The insured must notify the insurer within thirty days of the acquisition of the new aircraft for coverage to continue beyond thirty days. Additional aircraft are protected only if the insurer insures all the aircraft of the named insured. Other benefits include payment for defense costs, bonds, and emergency medical expenses.

Exclusions

Several categories of exclusions are found in aircraft coverage. Liability coverage does not apply to liability assumed under contract either caused intentionally or paid under a workers' compensation or similar law. Dollar limitations on liability claims for hangar damage and property in the control of the insured are found in the exclusions section.

Hull coverage for fire losses "other than by theft, vandalism, or malicious mischief, unless such loss is the direct result of other physical damage, covered by this policy, to the aircraft" is not provided. Wear and tear, deterioration, freezing, and mechanical or electrical breakdown are not insured perils under the hull coverage unless they are the result of damage caused by an insured peril. Protection for hull losses while an aircraft is encumbered and the encumbrance is not described in the contract or for loss resulting from "... conversion, embezzlement, or secretion by any person in lawful possession of the aircraft under a lease or rental agreement, conditional sale, (or) mortgage" is not available.

Medical payment coverage has one exclusion. Expenses required because of workers' compensation laws are not insured.

Three exclusions apply to all coverages. Coverage lapses unless aircraft have been registered under a Standard Category Airworthiness Certificate issued by the Federal Aviation Agency. It also lapses if the aircraft is not used for the purpose set out in the policy declarations or if the aircraft is not operated in flight by a pilot listed in the declarations.

Endorsements

Two important endorsements can be purchased for use with a private aircraft policy. One of these endorsements provides protection for nonowned aircraft utilized on a regular basis. This supplements the nonowned aircraft coverage found in the policy.

The other endorsement is a voluntary settlement endorsement. Under this endorsement the insurer agrees "to offer to pay on behalf of the Insured a sum requested by the named Insured to or for each passenger who sustains a loss hereinafter specified, in consideration for a full and final release of all liability...." The endorsement contains limits of settlement per person. The coverage is paid regardless of fault; therefore, it is similar in concept to the medical payments coverage. If an injured party does not accept the settlement, then the insurer provides the liability coverage found in the policy.

ADDITIONAL PERSONAL PROPERTY PROTECTION

The homeowners policy provides protection for unscheduled personal property. For many individuals, this coverage is sufficient to cover most losses. Individuals who have larger amounts of unscheduled personal property may increase their homeowners coverage from 50 percent of the dwelling limit ($4,000 for tenants policies) to higher limits by endorsing their homeowners contract.

However, even increased limits may not provide adequate insurance. Internal limits (e.g., the $500 restriction on jewelry losses by theft) can keep some insureds from having the protection they need. Other individuals who do not have a homeowners contract may need both unscheduled personal property coverage and protection for specific items. To meet the needs of the insuring public, the insurance industry has developed two major forms of personal protection. One form of coverage is the personal articles floater and the other the personal property floater.[27] The personal articles floater is designed to cover specific classes of scheduled properties like jewelry, furs, and cameras. Additional items also can be scheduled. Personal property floaters cover both scheduled and unscheduled personal property. In the latter case, coverage is similar to the protection in the homeowners contract. Floater policies were in use before the homeowners policies were developed and their popularity has declined as homeowners policies have gained acceptance.

Personal Articles Floater

Property Covered The personal articles floater can be purchased as a policy or it can be added to a homeowners contract by utilizing HO-61. Discussion of the endorsement will provide an idea of the coverage under all forms.

Nine specific categories or classes of property are insured under a personal articles floater. These classes are jewelry, furs, cameras, musical instruments, silverware, golfer's equipment, stamp and coin collections, and fine arts. As stated earlier, other items can be scheduled. The property is covered only if it is "owned by or in the custody or control of the insured and members of the insured's family of the same household."

Since the contract uses a schedule, specific amounts of coverage are available under the contract for each classed item of property. Losses may be determined by using the actual cash value or by paying the amount stated in the policy, depending on the contract. The latter approach is known as a valued policy.

Property is covered anywhere in the world against "all-risks" of loss. However, special conditions apply to specific items and many reduce this protection.

Certain types of additionally acquired property can be covered. The insured agrees to notify the insurer within thirty days if additional personal property of the type insured under the floater is purchased and must pay a pro rata premium to cover this additional property from the date of acquisition to the end of the policy period.

During the thirty-day period, the insured has coverage for jewelry, watches, furs, cameras, and musical instruments if that class of property is covered under the contract. The amount of coverage is the lesser of either $10,000 or 25 percent of the amount of the coverage provided on the particular class of property. If the insured fails to notify the insurer within thirty days, coverage ceases. The following example demonstrates how this coverage extension functions.

Betty Hawkins owns a personal articles floater. Under her contract, Betty insures the property classes of jewelry, furs, and cameras for $10,000, $15,000, and $10,000, respectively. Betty's husband gave her a new fur coat valued at $3,000 and her son gave her an organ for her birthday, both of which were destroyed by fire two weeks after Betty received them.

The insurer is obligated to pay up to 25 percent of the class coverage limit or $10,000, whichever is less, for the fur coat. Twenty-five percent of the class limit is $2,500; thus, the insurer would pay Betty $2,500. The insurer would not pay anything for the loss of the organ, since the musical instrument property class is not insured under Betty's policy.

The personal articles floater automatically provides coverage for newly acquired fine arts objects. However, the percentage of coverage extended on new items varies depending on the desires of the insured. There is no dollar limitation similar to the $10,000 limitation cited above. Insureds have ninety days to report the acquisition of new fine arts objects rather than the thirty days afforded for jewelry, watches, furs, cameras, and musical instruments.

Exclusions and Conditions The personal articles floater contains several general exclusions. Specific exclusions and conditions relating to golfer's equipment, musical instruments, stamp and coin collections, and fine arts objects also are included.

The general exclusions include wear and tear, gradual deterioration, insects, vermin, and inherent vice. There are exclusions for war, governmental actions, weapons of war, civil insurrections, and nuclear exposures. The nuclear exclusion does not apply to direct loss by fire resulting "from nuclear reaction or nuclear radiation or radioactive contamination."

The personal articles floater is designed for an individual, not professional groups or organizations. One of the constraints under the special conditions section of the policy is that musical instruments will not "be played for remuneration during the term of this policy" since insurers do not want to provide coverage for individuals who play professionally without receiving an additional premium charge for the increased exposure.

Silverware as a class of property is limited under the special conditions section. Excluded are pens, pencils, flasks, smoking implements, or accessories and articles of personal adornment. The purpose is to cover serving pieces and utensils rather than articles of jewelry.

The special conditions section spells out what constitutes golfer's equipment. The contract states that this insurance covers "... golf clubs, golf clothing and golf equipment (watches, jewelry, and stock for sale excepted) the property of the Named Insured; also on other clothing of the Named Insured while contained in any locker situated in a club house or other building used in connection with the game of golf...."

Golf balls are insured only against loss by fire or burglary. Burglary is defined as the felonious abstraction of the balls from within a building, room, or locker by persons who have feloniously entered the building. Visible marks of the forcible entry have to be present on the exterior of the premises for the loss to be paid.

Several classes of property including collections of stamps, coins, and fine arts, are given special attention under the exclusions section. Stamp and coin collections are not covered against fading, creasing, denting, scratching, tearing, thinning, transfer of colors, inherent defect, dampness, extremes of temperature, gradual depreciation, or damage from handling or while actually worked upon and resulting therefrom. Mysterious disappearance of stamps and coins is not covered unless the lost item(s) is scheduled in the contract or "unless mounted in a volume, and the page to which they are attached is also lost...." Property in the custody of transportation companies is not insured and shipments by mail, except registered mail, are not covered. Another exclusion applies to property in unattended automobiles except while the coins or stamps are being shipped by registered mail.

If a loss does occur, the insurance company pays up to the amount specified in the policy. If there is a partial loss of an item which is part of a set, then the amount of loss is "the cash market value of the whole set, less the cash market value of the remainder at the time of the loss, it being however understood and agreed that in the event of the property being insured for less than the cash market value, the liability of this Company shall not exceed the proportion that the amount insured bears to the cash market value." When items are not scheduled, special internal limits are applicable. There is a $1,000 limitation on unscheduled numismatic property and a $250 limit for any one stamp, coin, or other individual article.

Fine arts objects are not covered against damage sustained by, due to and resulting from being repaired, restored, or retouched. Breakage of art glass windows, statuary, marbles, glassware, bric-a-brac, porcelains, and similar fragile articles is insured only if the loss is the result of fire, lightning, aircraft, theft or attempted theft, cyclone, tornado, windstorm, earthquake, flood, explosion, malicious damage or collision, or derailment or overturn of conveyance. This is done to avoid paying for the breakage that might occur because of everyday handling. As an example, an individual might knock a statue over while dusting it and break it. He or she could make a claim for the loss if the breakage limitation were not in the contract. Property at exhibits, such as fair grounds or national or international expositions, is covered only if these premises are specifically described in the policy.

Two other special conditions apply to fine arts. First, the insured promises that fine arts items will be packed by competent packers when they are being shipped. Secondly, the insured, in the event of a total loss of one or more items in a set, agrees to turn the set over to the company. The company pays the total amount scheduled in the policy and accepts the partial set from the insured.

When other categories of personal property, e.g., wedding presents, bicycles, and contact lenses are covered, additional conditions and exclusions will be found in the personal articles floater. Every form should be reviewed to ascertain specific item provisions.

Personal Property Floater

Property Covered The personal articles floater is designed to cover specific items belonging to an individual. The personal property floater covers not only some specific items on a scheduled basis but also unscheduled personal property on a blanket basis, just as it would be covered in a homeowners contract. The unscheduled personal property covered is all "Personal property owned, used or worn by the person in whose name this policy is issued and members of the insured's family of the same household." Since the property covered is that which is owned, used, or worn by an insured, this protection extends to property which belongs to other individuals not in the named insured's family. As an example, coverage would extend to a lawnmower the insured might borrow from his or her next-door neighbor to cut the insured's grass, or to furniture which the insured was sitting on in the home of a friend. The coverage applies to individuals such as college students who are members of the named insured's household but who are away temporarily.

Covered property is protected on an "all-risks" basis subject to the exclusions contained in the contract. Excluded property includes animals, automobiles, motorcycles, aircraft, boats, or other conveyances or their equipment unless the equipment is at the residence of the insured and is removed from the vehicle. Bicycles, tricycles, baby carriages, wheel chairs and similar conveyances are covered. Property belonging to a governmental body is excluded. Unscheduled personal property which relates to "a business, profession or occupation of the persons whose property is insured hereinunder, excepting professional books, instruments, and other professional equipment owned by the insured while actually within the residence of the insured. . . ." Damage from flood waters, surface water, waves, tidal water or tidal waves, and water backups as well as water below the ground are perils not covered by the policy. These items are covered if fire or explosion ensues but then only to the extent of the damage done by the fire or explosion. The flood and water exclusions do not apply to losses which arise from theft.

Damage or loss caused by animals or birds owned or kept by an insured or residence employee is not covered unless loss by fire, explosion, or smoke ensues and then only for such loss caused by the fire, explosion, or smoke. A breakage exclusion, similar to the one in the personal articles floater, reads:

> This policy does not insure . . . against breakage of eyeglasses, glassware, statuary, marbles, bric-a-brac, porcelains, and similar fragile articles (jewelry, watches, bronzes, cameras and photographic lenses excepted), unless occasioned by theft or an attempt thereat, vandalism or malicious mischief, or by fire, lightning, windstorm, earthquake, explosion, falling aircraft, rioters, strikers, collapse of building, accident to conveyance or other similar casualty, nor unless likewise occasioned, against marring or scratching of any property not specifically scheduled herein. . . .

Mechanical breakdown and loss or damage to electrical apparatus caused by electricity other than lightning are excluded. However, in the latter case, damage or loss is covered if a fire ensues. Losses resulting to property on exhibit from war, civil unrest, and nuclear exposures are also excluded in the personal property floater.

Finally, the contract does not cover losses which arise from wear and tear or:

> . . . caused by dampness of atmosphere or extremes of temperature unless directly caused by rain, snow, sleet, hail, bursting of pipes or apparatus and provided further that such loss or damage is not specifically excluded . . .; against deterioration, insects, vermin, and inherent vice; against damage of property (watches, jewelry, and furs excepted) occasioned by acts or actually resulting from any work thereon in the course of any refinishing, renovating or repairing process. . . .

This last exclusion is extremely important because an insured may not realize no coverage exists when an item is sent out to be refinished, renovated, or repaired. For example, if an individual sends a television out to be repaired and the television is damaged in the process of being repaired, then the television set is not covered.

Amounts of Insurance   The personal property floater contains three coverage limits. There is a limit on unscheduled personal property; there is a limit on personal jewelry, watches, furs, fine arts, and other property which are scheduled, and a limit on unscheduled jewelry, watches, and furs in excess of the basic $250 policy limit on such property. The excess coverage is against loss caused by fire and lightning only. The first limit on unscheduled personal property applies to all of the unscheduled personal property belonging to the insured which is not excluded. There are specific categories of items which are listed in the floater and for which the insured estimates approximate values. These estimates are not limits of coverage, but rather indicate how much of a particular class of property an insured has. Normally, the insured is required to indicate the total amount of property in the category and then the amount situated in some residence other than the principal residence. Categories of properties for which the insured has to declare values are silverware and pewter; linens; clothing; rugs and draperies; books; musical instruments; television sets, radios, record players, and records; paintings, etchings, pictures and other objects of art; china and glassware; cameras and photographic equipment; golf, hunting, fishing, and other sports and hobby equipment; refrigerators, stoves, washing machines, electrical appliances and other kitchen equipment; bedding, furniture; and all other personal property.

The contract permits the insured to apply only 10 percent of the amount of the coverage on unscheduled personal property to unscheduled personal property away from the principal residence.

In addition to the basic $250 limit on jewelry, watches, and furs, money and numismatic property is subject to a $100 limitation. A $500 limitation is placed on loss of notes, securities, stamps, accounts, bills, deeds, evidences of debt, letters of credit, passports, documents, and tickets.

Some personal property items, e.g., jewelry, watches, furs, and fine arts can be scheduled separately under a floater. If an item is scheduled, the amount of loss is the amount stated in the schedule. The following illustrates how the amounts of insurance in a personal property floater would operate in the event of a loss situation.

C. S. Evans has a personal property floater. The amounts of insurance are $5,000 for unscheduled personal property, $1,000 for scheduled jewelry, $2,000 for scheduled furs, and $1,000 on unscheduled personal jewelry, watches, and furs against fire and lightning. Recently, a portion of Evans' home burned, and the losses were:

Clothes	$1,000
Books	500
Scheduled Jewelry	1,000

Television Set	700
Furniture	1,000
TOTAL LOSS	$4,200

The day following the fire, a thief broke into the damaged portion of the Evans' home and stole Mr. and Mrs. Evans' watches', valued at $1,000.

The insurer would pay the $4,200 loss of personal property because the Evans' policy has adequate limits, but would not pay for all the watches' loss. Only $250 is payable since the cause of the loss was neither fire nor lightning.

Extensions of Coverage The personal property floater contains several valuable extensions of coverage. The insured may cover the personal property of other individuals including servants when the property is in the insured's residences. The personal property of servants has to be in the possession of the servant, and the servant has to be engaged in the services of the insured. This would not extend coverage to the personal property of the servant when the servant is not acting or is not engaged in providing a service for the insured (e.g., on a day when the servant is off). The contract also provides coverage for vandalism and malicious mischief to the interior of the residence and protection for the building against damage done when anyone is attempting to break into the structure.

Ten percent of item (A) can be applied to losses caused by fire, lightning, windstorm, cyclone, tornado, hail, explosion, riot, riot attending a strike, smoke, damage by vehicles or aircraft, losses to improvements or betterments made by the insured to buildings occupied by the insured as a residence but not owned by the insured. However, this coverage also can be extended to improvements and betterments made to a condominium. Finally, loss payments for unscheduled personal property in a class do not reduce the amount of coverage for that class.

None of these extensions of coverage work, however, to expand the limits of protection for unscheduled personal property. They provide flexibility but not additional protection.

Other Insurance The personal property floater does not permit "other insurance" unless coverage under the personal property floater is not adequate or is not the primary insurance protection. For example, an individual could have additional vandalism, malicious mischief, improvements or betterments, and jewelry, watches and fur coverage. Additional coverage above the $100 limitation on money and the $500 limitation on securities, stamps, accounts, bills, deeds, etc., also would be permissible. If there is other insurance, the personal property floater becomes excess coverage. It never serves as contributing insurance.

Miscellaneous Coverages

In addition to the personal articles floater (PAF) and the personal property floater (PPF), a number of specific insurance coverages have been developed to provide protection for single categories of personal property. The basic difference between the PAF, and PPF, and the more specific types of personal property coverages is the scope of the property or items covered, not in the method of providing such coverage. A partial list of items for which such coverage is available is provided below:

- furs
- jewelry
- silverware
- golfer's equipment
- cameras
- fine arts and antiques
- stamp and coin collections
- muscial instruments
- wedding presents
- bicycles
- physicians' and surgeons' instruments

WATERCRAFT

The homeowners contract provides limited insurance protection for some types of watercraft. Five hundred dollars in property damage protection is available for a watercraft and its trailer.

Liability coverage is available for watercraft if it has an inboard or inboard-outboard engine with less than fifty horsepower, if it is a sailing watercraft which is less than twenty-six feet long, or if it has an outboard motor with less than twenty-five total horsepower. Liability coverage can be extended to boats which exceed these limitations by using HO-75, the watercraft endorsement.

The HO-75 endorsement provides bodily injury and property damage liability. Coverage does not extend to employees of the insured whose principal duties are related to the watercraft. This is done not only so that the insurer does not become responsible for the employer's tort liability to employees but also so that the insurer does not have to make payments under the Longshoremen's and Harbor Workers' Act. For a broad range of insurance protection including coverage for employees, a boat owner would have to buy either a yacht policy (an ocean marine policy designed primarily for boats with inboard motors) or an outboard motorboat policy (an inland marine coverage).[28]

Chapter Notes

1. Ambrose Ryder, *Automobile Insurance* (New York: Spectator Company, 1924), p. 119.
2. Automobile Insurance Plans Service Office, "New York Automobile Insurance Plan" (New York: Automobile Insurance Plans Service Office, 1976), p. 1.
3. Ibid., p. 2.
4. Ibid., p. 7.
5. Ibid., p. 5.
6. Ibid., p. 7.
7. Insurance Services Office, "Recreational Vehicle Manual" (New York: Insurance Services Office, 1976), p. 1.
8. Ibid.
9. A copy of a representative personal umbrella liability contract can be found in CPCU policy kit.
10. Reliance Insurance Company, "Executive Security Policy."
11. Housing and Urban Development Act of 1968, Public Law 90-448, Approved August 1, 1968, Sec. 1102.
12. Ibid., Sec. 1211b(5).
13. 35 *Federal Register* 12115.
14. Housing and Urban Development Act of 1968, Public Law 90-448, Approved August 1, 1968, Sec. 1102.
15. George Bernstein, "Critical Evaluation of the FAIR Plans," *Journal of Risk and Insurance,* Vol. XXXVIII, 2 (June, 1971), p. 275.
16. U.S., Congress, House, Subcommittee on Housing of the Committee on Banking and Currency, Housing and Urban Development Legislation—1970, 91st Cong., 2d sess., 1970, p. 375.
17. U.S., Congress, House, Subcommittee on Housing of the Committee on Banking and Currency, Housing and Urban Development Legislation, p. 351.
18. Taken from an unpublished paper entitled "The Federal Crime Insurance Program," presented at the 1974 annual American Risk and Insurance Association meeting by James E. Jonish and Claude C. Lilly.
19. 37 *Federal Register* 147.
20. U.S. Department of Housing and Urban Development, "National Flood Insurance Program" (Washington: Superintendent of Documents, 1974), p. 44.
21. *The National Underwriter, Property and Casualty Insurance edition,* December 30, 1977, pp. 1, 6.
22. U.S. Department of Housing and Urban Development, "HUD News," March 10, 1975 (Washington: Superintendent of Documents, 1975), p. 3.
23. U.S. Department of Housing and Urban Development, "Title 24—Revised as of April 1, 1975," reprint (Washington: Superintendent of Documents, 1976), p. 535.

24. National Flood Insurers Association, *Flood Insurance Manual* (Arlington: National Flood Insurers Association, 1975), pp. 1-4.
25. Ibid., pp. 1-8.
26. Most of the material on aircraft insurance is based on coverage offered by the United States Aircraft Insurance Group.
27. A third type, the so-called personal effects floater, is available to cover personal property carried or worn by travelers. This relatively minor type of insurance coverage provides one blanket amount of insurance on an "all-risks" and worldwide basis (except that it does not cover the insured items at home or in storage).
28. For a fuller discussion of pleasure boat insurance coverages, see G. William Glendenning and Robert B. Holtom, *Personal Lines Underwriting* (Malvern, PA.: Insurance Institute of America, 1977), Chapter 10.

CHAPTER 6

The Financial Basis for Life Insurance Planning

INTRODUCTION

Risk management is generally regarded as a method of managing property and liability loss exposures and is not frequently associated with life and health insurance. This is unfortunate, because risk management provides a framework that can be used to analyze almost all types of exposures, including life and health exposures.

The risk management approach enables an individual to identify, evaluate and rank the relative importance of a wide variety of loss exposures. This approach, in turn, permits the individual to select methods of treatment which are appropriate for the different exposures as well as consistent with the individual's broader financial goals and his or her resources.

This chapter focuses primarily on the financial problems caused by premature death (i.e., death prior to retirement). Generally, this corresponds to a study of life insurance since life insurance is by far the most important method of handling this peril. However, this product has many other uses as well. For example, many life insurance contracts provide benefits to living policyowners, such as disability benefits and retirement benefits.

ANALYSIS OF THE DEATH EXPOSURE

Types of Losses

While many types of losses occur when a person dies, this text focuses only upon the financial losses which may be dichotomized as: (1) costs that result from death, and (2) loss of income.

Costs Associated with Death A large number of expenses may be incurred when a person dies, including last illness and burial expenses. Moreover, estate shrinkage involves a variety of expenses, such as taxes, estate administration fees, and other cash outlays and decreased property values resulting from forced liquidation.

Costs associated with death are a function of the wealth of the deceased. At one extreme, if a person has virtually no property, burial expenses might be the only cost. For wealthy individuals, however, the costs associated with death may be enormous. Indeed, often those who own large estates concentrate their financial planning on these costs.

Loss of Income The most valuable asset possessed by most individuals is their ability to earn an income. Except for income which is not dependent upon the continued life of an individual, such as earnings from a savings account, dividends, rent, and royalties, this asset is lost when an individual dies.

Most people go through a period in their lives when others (usually spouses and children) are financially dependent upon them for support. If a person lives until retirement, however, the point is reached when there is no earned future income to be provided to others. Thus, if a retired person dies, there is no income loss.

Chances of Death

The probability of death can be calculated with a high degree of accuracy, and this information is available in published mortality tables. Mortality tables are constructed by collecting data on the number of individuals exposed to death at each age and the number who died at each age. The mortality rate equals the number of deaths at any given age divided by the number of observed lives at that age. One of the more important mortality tables is the Commissioner's 1958 Standard Ordinary Mortality Table (C.S.O. 58) which is reproduced as Table 6-1. Referring to Table 6-1, it can be seen that at age zero, the mortality rate equals 70,800/10,000,000 or 0.00708, which means that roughly 7 out of every 1,000 individuals aged zero are expected to die within a year. (Note that the mortality rates are rather high at age zero, higher than any other age less than forty-nine.)

Mortality rates decline until age 10 and then rise at an increasing rate until age 100, at which point it is assumed that everyone has died. The column showing expectation of life has virtually no usefulness for life insurance since life premiums are based on mortality rates (i.e., the yearly probabilities of dying) and not on life expectancy. While the life expectancy of an infant is sixty-eight years, a person who has reached sixty-eight has a further life expectancy of about eleven years.

Table 6-1 provides worthwhile risk management information since it allows one to calculate the chances of dying during a period of time. An individual's chance of dying from his or her present age until retirement provides a good estimate of the chances of premature death. Assume that Mr. A, age twenty-five, believes he should not buy life insurance because he thinks his changes of dying before age sixty-five are not significant. But, in terms of probabilities, Mr. A's chances of dying before age sixty-five are calculated by dividing the number of people dying from age twenty-five to sixty-five by the number living at age twenty-five. Out of 9,575,636 people living at age twenty-five, 6,800,531 will be alive at age sixty-five, and 2,775,105 will die (9,575,636 – 6,800,531). Expressed as a fraction, the number dying (2,775,105) out of the number living (9,575,636) is 2,775,105/9,575,636, or approximately 29 percent.

The older the person, the less likely that premature death will occur. For example, the probability of a forty-year-old individual dying before attaining age sixty-five is 26 percent. (The number dying between ages forty and sixty-five is 9,241,359–6,800,531 or 2,440,828, and 2,440,828/9,241,357 is approximately 26 percent.) At age sixty there is roughly a 12 percent probability of dying before reaching age sixty-five. Based on the general criteria established in a risk management approach, there is no age at which the chance of death before age sixty-five is so low that the peril may be safely ignored. If a person had a 12 percent chance of, say, a large liability suit, some type of risk management technique surely would be used.

In CPCU 1, it was suggested that the insurance technique may not be realistic when the probability of loss is too high. This principle can be applied to the premature death exposure. At the older ages the mortality rates increase rapidly and, as a result, the insurance approach becomes less effective as an economical risk management technique. Few people past age sixty-five apply for life insurance, since the cost at advanced ages is prohibitive.

Table 6-1
1958 Commissioners' Standard Ordinary Mortality Table

1958 Commissioners' Standard Ordinary Mortality Table

Age	Number Living	Deaths Each Year	Deaths Per 1,000	Expectation of Life-Years
0	10,000,000	70,800	7.08	68.30
1	9,929,200	17,475	1.76	67.78
2	9,911,725	15,066	1.52	66.90
3	9,896,639	14,449	1.46	66.00
4	9,882,210	13,835	1.40	65.10
5	9,868,375	13,322	1.35	64.19
6	9,855,053	12,812	1.30	63.27
7	9,842,241	12,401	1.26	62.35
8	9,829,840	12,091	1.23	61.43
9	9,817,749	11,879	1.21	60.51
10	9,805,870	11,865	1.21	59.58
11	9,794,005	12,047	1.23	58.65
12	9,781,958	12,325	1.26	57.72
13	9,769,633	12,896	1.32	56.80
14	9,756,737	13,562	1.39	55.87
15	9,743,175	14,225	1.46	54.95
16	9,728,950	14,983	1.54	54.03
17	9,713,967	15,737	1.62	53.11
18	9,698,230	16,390	1.69	52.19

1958 Commissioners' Standard Ordinary Mortality Table

Age	Number Living	Deaths Each Year	Deaths Per 1,000	Expectation of Life-Years
50	8,762,306	72,902	8.32	23.63
51	8,689,404	79,160	9.11	22.82
52	8,610,244	85,758	9.96	22.03
53	8,524,486	92,832	10.89	21.25
54	8,431,654	100,337	11.90	20.47
55	8,331,317	108,307	13.00	19.71
56	8,223,010	116,849	14.21	18.97
57	8,106,161	125,970	15.54	18.23
58	7,980,191	135,663	17.00	17.51
59	7,844,528	145,830	18.59	16.81
60	7,698,698	156,592	20.34	16.12
61	7,542,106	167,736	22.24	15.44
62	7,374,370	179,271	24.31	14.78
63	7,195,099	191,174	26.57	14.14
64	7,003,925	203,394	29.04	13.51
65	6,800,531	215,917	31.75	12.90
66	6,584,614	228,749	34.74	12.31
67	6,355,865	241,777	38.04	11.73
68	6,114,088	254,835	41.68	11.17

Age				
69	5,859,253	267,241	45.61	10.64
70	5,592,012	278,426	49.79	10.12
71	5,313,586	287,731	54.15	9.63
72	5,025,855	294,766	58.65	9.15
73	4,731,089	299,289	63.26	8.69
74	4,431,800	301,894	68.12	8.24
75	4,129,906	303,011	73.37	7.81
76	3,826,895	303,014	79.18	7.39
77	3,523,881	301,997	85.70	6.98
78	3,221,884	299,829	93.06	6.59
79	2,922,055	295,683	101.19	6.21
80	2,626,372	288,848	109.98	5.85
81	2,337,524	278,983	119.35	5.51
82	2,058,541	265,902	129.17	5.19
83	1,792,639	249,858	139.38	4.89
84	1,542,781	231,433	150.01	4.60
85	1,311,348	211,311	161.14	4.32
86	1,100,037	190,108	172.82	4.06
87	909,929	168,455	185.13	3.80
88	741,474	146,997	198.25	3.55
89	594,477	126,303	212.46	3.31
90	468,174	106,809	228.14	3.06
91	361,365	88,813	245.77	2.82
92	272,552	72,480	265.93	2.58
93	200,072	57,881	289.30	2.33
94	142,191	45,026	316.66	2.07
95	97,165	34,128	351.24	1.80
96	63,037	25,250	400.56	1.51
97	37,787	18,456	488.42	1.18
98	19,331	12,916	568.15	0.83
99	6,415	6,415	1000.00	0.50

Age				
19	9,681,840	16,846	1.74	51.28
20	9,664,994	17,300	1.79	50.37
21	9,647,694	17,655	1.83	49.46
22	9,630,039	17,912	1.86	48.55
23	9,612,127	18,167	1.89	47.64
24	9,593,960	18,324	1.91	46.73
25	9,575,636	18,481	1.93	45.82
26	9,557,155	18,732	1.96	44.90
27	9,538,423	18,981	1.99	43.99
28	9,519,442	19,324	2.03	43.08
29	9,500,118	19,760	2.08	42.16
30	9,480,358	20,193	2.13	41.25
31	9,460,165	20,718	2.19	40.34
32	9,439,447	21,239	2.25	39.43
33	9,418,208	21,850	2.32	38.51
34	9,396,358	22,551	2.40	37.60
35	9,373,807	23,528	2.51	36.69
36	9,350,279	24,685	2.64	35.78
37	9,325,594	26,112	2.80	34.88
38	9,299,482	27,991	3.01	33.97
39	9,271,491	30,132	3.25	33.07
40	9,241,359	32,622	3.53	32.18
41	9,208,737	35,362	3.84	31.29
42	9,173,375	38,253	4.17	30.41
43	9,135,122	41,382	4.53	29.54
44	9,093,740	44,741	4.92	28.67
45	9,048,999	48,412	5.35	27.81
46	9,000,587	52,473	5.83	26.95
47	8,948,114	56,910	6.36	26.11
48	8,891,204	61,794	6.95	25.27
49	8,829,410	67,104	7.60	24.45

Estimating Loss Severity

After analyzing the chances of loss, the next step in the risk management process is to estimate loss severity, i.e., the dollar amounts that can be lost.

The Human Life Value Concept Dr. S. S. Huebner, a pioneering insurance educator, was largely responsible for promoting the human life value (HLV) concept. According to this concept, an individual's worth is the present value of that person's future income stream that will be allocated to others. The method of calculating the value may be broken down into three steps:

1. Estimate the individual's average annual earned income from the person's present age to the age of retirement.
2. Deduct the amount that is not allocated to others. Money spent for income taxes, life and health insurance premiums, and all other self-maintenance expenses should be deducted.
3. Using a reasonable interest rate, determine the present value of the amounts allocated to others for the working period used in step 1. Table 6-2, a present value table, facilitates these calculations. Present value calculations are explained in the final section of this chapter.

For example, assume that Mr. A is forty years of age and expects to earn $25,000 next year. Although it is difficult for Mr. A to estimate his future earnings, he expects his income to increase at an average rate of 4 percent per year. He allocates about two-thirds of his income to his family, which consists of a wife and three children. Mr. A believes that an average of 5 percent interest can be earned on funds placed in a safe investment or savings vehicle. With these assumptions, one can calculate Mr. A's human life value to his family.

The first step in the HLV calculation is to estimate the average annual earnings to be earned in the future. Mr. A assumed that his earnings would increase at an average of 4 percent each year, and the calculation of his average earnings is shown in Table 6-3.

The second step is to determine the amount allocated to others. In the case of Mr. A, two-thirds of the average earnings is assumed to be devoted to the family. Two-thirds of $41,638 is $27,759.

The present value of $27,759 each year discounted at 5 percent for the next twenty-five years is 14.094 × $27,759 or $391,235, which is Mr. A's human life value.

The calculation of Mr. A's human life value can be summarized as follows:

Table 6-2

Present Value of an Annuity of $1

Period	3%	5%	6%	8%	10%	12%
1	0.971	0.952	0.943	0.926	0.909	0.893
2	1.913	1.859	1.833	1.783	1.736	1.690
3	2.829	2.723	2.673	2.577	2.487	2.402
4	3.717	3.546	3.465	3.312	3.170	3.037
5	4.580	4.329	4.212	3.993	3.791	3.605
6	5.417	5.076	4.917	4.623	4.355	4.111
7	6.230	5.786	5.582	5.206	4.868	4.564
8	7.020	6.463	6.210	5.747	5.335	4.968
9	7.786	7.108	6.802	6.247	5.759	5.328
10	8.530	7.722	7.360	6.710	6.145	5.650
15	11.938	10.380	9.712	8.559	7.606	6.811
20	14.877	12.462	11.470	9.818	8.514	7.469
25	17.413	14.094	12.783	10.675	9.077	7.843
30	19.600	15.373	13.765	11.258	9.427	8.055

Table 6-3

Calculation of Mr. A's Average Annual Earnings
(Assuming an Increase of 4 Percent Each Year)

Age	Expected Earnings	Age	Expected Earnings
41	$25,000	53	$40,020
42	26,000	54	41,620
43	27,040	55	43,284
44	28,121	56	45,015
45	29,245	57	46,815
46	30,414	58	48,687
47	31,630	59	50,634
48	32,895	60	52,659
49	34,210	61	54,765
50	35,578	62	56,955
51	37,001	63	59,233
52	38,481	64	61,602
		65	64,066

Average Annual Earnings = $41,638

Table 6-4

Mr. A's Human Life Value at Selected Ages

(1) Age	(2) Average Annual Remaining Earnings	(3) Amount Devoted to Family [(2) x ⅔]	(4) Present Value Factor	(5) Human Life Value (3) x (4)
40	$41,638	$27,759	14.094	$391,235
45	45,278	30,185	12.462	376,165
50	49,389	32,926	10.380	341,772
55	54,043	36,028	7.722	278,208
60	59,324	39,549	4.329	171,207
65	—0—	—0—	—0—	—0—

1. Number of years until retirement (age sixty-five minus present age forty)   25
2. Average annual earnings (taken from Table 6-3) $41,638
3. Average annual earnings devoted to the family (two-thirds of $41,638) $27,759
4. Present value factor for a stream of income for twenty-five years at 5 percent (taken from Table 6-2)   14.094
5. Mr. A's human life value ($27,759 times 14.094) $391,235

A person's human life value has a strong tendency to decrease as he or she gets older since there is a shorter earnings period as each year passes.

Table 6-4 provides information on Mr. A's human life value at older ages. The same assumptions are used here as were used earlier, except the calculation is made at older ages.

The normal pattern is for the HLV to decrease with the age of the individual, but there are two exceptions to this rule. First, an HLV is not created until other people derive a financial benefit from a person's life. Therefore, in a typical situation there usually will be no human life value until a person is married since earnings usually do not provide a financial benefit to others.

Secondly, if a person recalculates his or her human life value and finds that the original assumptions are incorrect, a new calculation may produce a substantially different human life value. When a person's earnings increase much more than originally estimated, the revised human life value may increase. Still, there is a strong tendency for the human life value to decrease, even with the assumption of higher earnings, because of the shorter period of earnings remaining as a person gets older.

Evaluation of the Human Life Value Concept The HLV concept involves the use of many questionable assumptions. In theory, the concept explains an important part of the insurable values contained in a human life, and without it, it would be difficult to estimate the financial losses that result from death.

There are situations such as in a court case, in which application of the HLV is very useful. The most obvious example is the case of a wrongful death in which a person's negligence is responsible for the death (or disability) of another. The amount of the damages will be influenced by the calculation of the deceased's human life value.

The assumptions required in the HLV calculation frequently are difficult to justify. Estimating future annual earnings for a person is extremely difficult, even under the best conditions. For a person who is just beginning a career, an estimate of future earnings may be nothing more than a sheer guess. The problem may be less troublesome for a person who has an established career, but even in these cases future earnings are difficult to estimate.

Another assumption that may prove to be incorrect is the assumed working period. Although age sixty-five is the most common retirement age, there is a trend toward earlier retirement, but some never retire. Thus, an assumed retirement at any age may not be reliable.

Another problem is the estimate of the amount of earned income that is allocated to others. A common assumption is that one-third of a person's income is needed for self-maintenance, and therefore, two-thirds can be allocated to the family. Realistically, the proportion of income allocated to the family may be higher while children are being raised or may be substantially different in any given situation.

The interest rate used to discount future earnings is a critical assumption in the HLV calculation. A difference of only one percentage point will have a large effect on the value if earnings are discounted over a long period.[1] But there is no accurate method of determining the rate of interest that can be earned on conservative investments or savings accounts for a long period into the future.

In addition to the practical problems involved in the calculation of the human life value, there is an important conceptual error in the calculation as it has been described. The error can be excused only on the basis that it simplifies the calculations. The easiest method of understanding the mistake is to return to the previous example of Mr. A. It was assumed that his earnings would increase 4 percent each year.

Then Mr. A's average earnings were calculated at $41,638. This amount ($41,638) was used as a basis for the HLV and the portion allocated to the family was discounted over the remaining working years. In effect, it was assumed that Mr. A would allocate two-thirds of $41,638 (or $27,759) to his family every year. This is incorrect because Mr. A's gross earnings were only $25,000 at that time! In other words, the error arises from averaging Mr. A's income.

The correct approach involves discounting the appropriate amount each year. Using the figures shown in Table 6-3, the correct procedure would involve $25,000 minus one-third of $25,000 for the first year. The second year's calculation would be $26,000 minus one-third of $26,000 discounted for one year. For the third year, the $27,040 minus one-third of $27,040 should be discounted for two years. The correct total would be attained by continuing the process on a year-by-year basis, and adding the present values for all years.

It is easy to misuse the HLV concept. Often, for example, the human life value is regarded as the amount of life insurance a person should own. Instead, the concept is a measure of maximum possible loss of future earnings only. It does not determine the amount of individual life insurance a person should own for the following reasons:

1. Other Sources of Income. Proceeds from individual life insurance policies may not be the only sources of income available at death. In most cases, a person's survivors will receive funds from social security and group life insurance plans through the employer. Furthermore, other plans (such as pension or profit-sharing plans) may provide death benefits.
2. Costs Associated with Death. The loss of future earnings is only one of the types of losses caused by a person's death, and the HLV concept ignores these other costs. For a young person, the loss of future earnings may be the most important type of loss. For older people, however, the other costs associated with death may be more important than the loss of future income.

METHODS OF MEETING THE DEATH EXPOSURE

Four techniques are used to meet the financial problems caused by death. These are: (1) loss prevention, (2) social insurance, (3) group insurance, and (4) individual insurance. In addition, a variety of social welfare programs are provided by the government (at the federal, state, and local levels) which might be regarded as other techniques for meeting the premature death exposure. For example, public assistance benefits are used in some circumstances to alleviate financial problems

Figure 6-1

Methods of Dealing with Financial Problems Caused by Death

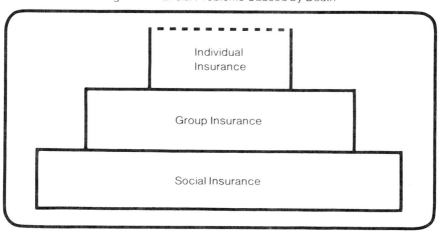

that result from death. However, these types of programs will not be treated in this chapter. While these programs may benefit needy individuals and families, they should not be viewed as an alternative method of planning for financial security. Public assistance benefits are based on demonstrated need; only those who can prove dire financial circumstances may receive benefits. Public assistance programs, therefore, may be regarded as a last-resort method of dealing with financial emergencies. In a sense they are not planning methods at all because they are used only when all other techniques have failed.

Likewise, loss prevention is a technical subject involving medical science and is beyond the scope of this text.

The remaining methods of dealing with the financial problems caused by death (social insurance, group insurance, and individual insurance) can be seen as a three-layered pyramid.

In Figure 6-1, social insurance provides the base, indicating that social insurance programs cover more people than the other methods. It is the newest of the three insurance approaches and is also the fastest growing.

The second layer, group insurance, originated in the early 1900s and has grown rapidly. Individual insurance (the top layer) is owned by over 60 percent of the adult population. Furthermore, individual insurance is the only technique that generally allows individual determination of the amount of protection owned (indicated by the dotted line at the top of the pyramid).

THE SOCIAL INSURANCE TECHNIQUE

The most important social insurance program for dealing with premature death is the Old Age, Survivors, Disability, and Health Insurance program (OASDHI). It is one of several social insurance programs which make up the social security system. This discussion is limited primarily to the OASDHI death and survivor benefits, but other social insurance programs also provide death benefits (workers' compensation, for example). The retirement income, disability income, and health insurance benefits of the OASDHI program will be treated in detail in later chapters.

Characteristics of OASDHI

Compulsory Participation in OASDHI is compulsory for all workers in covered occupations. (Only about 2 percent of the working population does not participate in OASDHI or the comparable programs for federal employees or railroad workers.) A voluntary program would attract a disproportionate number of older or unhealthy individuals and would not meet the social objective of providing benefits to a substantial majority of the population. Furthermore, the compulsory feature makes the program large, thereby providing administrative economies and actuarial advantages.

Minimum Floor of Income OASDHI provides a floor or protection which should be supplemented by effective private pensions as well as individual insurance, personal savings, and other investments. It is difficult to define "floor of protection." At one extreme, it can be argued that benefits should be set at the subsistence level. At the other extreme, it can be argued that OASDHI benefits should provide a reasonable living standard exclusive of other sources of income.

Sacrifice in Individual Equity Private insurance plans are designed to treat individual policyowners fairly. In fact, state insurance laws prohibit insurance rates that are unfairly discriminatory. Each policyowner is placed in a group that comprises individuals who have similar loss producing characteristics, and each pays the same premium rate. There is a close relationship between this rate and the expected losses of the group.

The OASDHI system stresses social adequacy rather than individual equity. Several elements of the program assume the social adequacy of the program.

First, low-paid workers receive benefits that are a higher proportion of past earnings than do higher-paid workers due to the design of the benefit formula. The law also provides a "special" minimum benefit for workers who have worked under the program regularly over the years but at relatively low wage lvels. The statutory minimum benefit is paid even when contributions would otherwise be inadequate to support the benefit.

Second, full benefits are paid to workers already near retirement when the program was established or when their occupations were first covered by the program. If the cash benefits paid in the early years of the program had been no larger than the amounts that could be financed by the contributions paid, the benefit amounts would have been too small to substantially reduce dependency.

Third, the OASDHI program provides benefits for dependents and survivors of insured workers in order to reduce dependency. Thus, workers who have dependents get more protection in relation to their taxes than do workers who have no dependents.

Benefits Based on Earnings   OASDHI benefits are a function of earnings, since the higher a person's earnings, the greater the retirement, disability, or survivors benefits. However, the relationship between earnings and benefits is not based on individual equity. Benefits are subject to certain minimums and maximums and the benefit formula generally favors the lower income workers as discussed later in this chapter.

Contributory Funding   The OASDHI program is financed by taxes levied on employers, employees, and the self-employed under the Federal Insurance Contributions Act of 1939 (and subsequent amendments). These taxes, commonly known as FICA taxes, are based on earnings up to a limit known as the social security earnings base.

The OASDHI program is not fully funded. This concept can be illustrated by explaining briefly how a private life insurer must operate. A private commercial life insurance company must maintain a reserve (which is a liability) on its balance sheet, and the reserve must be at least equal to the difference between the present value of future benefits and the present value of future premiums for all policies in force. If a company maintains this standard, it could discontinue the sale of new contracts and still meet its obligations on existing contracts with continuing premium income and interest earnings. In brief, a private life insurer must maintain full funding to safeguard the rights of policyowners.

The trust funds for the OASDHI program are not nearly as large as full funding would require. However, partial funding is defended on the grounds that participation is compulsory, and the program will never terminate since it is supported by the federal government.

The absence of full funding may result in intergenerational inequities since the benefits paid to each retired generation are financed by the current generation of workers.

The OASDHI system has faced long-term financial problems that arose from two primary sources: (1) demographic changes, and (2) an excessive adjustment for inflation in the present method of automatically adjusting the benefits and earnings base.

The nation's birth rate has dropped sharply in recent years while longevity has been increasing. This combination of longer life and fewer births means that the number of retired people will increase more rapidly than the number of active workers. In 1950 there were approximately fourteen covered workers for each beneficiary receiving retirement or survivor benefits. That is, fourteen taxpayers shared the cost of each beneficiary. By 1977, the ratio had fallen to three workers for each beneficiary. Because of increasing longevity and a decreasing birth rate, the ratio is expected to fal to two workers per beneficiary over the next four decades.

Benefits Prescribed by Law The benefits under the OASDHI program are established, changed, and administered by federal law.

Benefits Related to Presumed Need An individual who meets the requirements for benefits in the OASDHI program is entitled to benefits as a matter of right—demonstration of need is not required. However, *presumed* need is the basis for all benefits. Retirement benefits are not paid automatically at age sixty-five, but rather are paid only upon retirement or when a person reaches age seventy-two—beginning in 1982, age seventy—(when there is a presumed need). A person who continues to be gainfully employed after the OASDHI normal retirement age may not receive retirement benefits or may receive reduced benefits. On the other hand, a wealthy individual may receive full benefits so long as he or she has retired from active employment. In other words, earned income rather than wealth or investment income is the standard used to establish whether a person has a presumed need for OASDHI benefits.

Benefits Under OASDHI

Eligibility Requirements

Covered Employment. To be eligible for benefits of any type under the OASDHI program, an individual must have an earnings record in covered employment. For purposes of OASDHI coverage, there are four groups of workers: (1) those covered on a compulsory basis, (2) those covered at the election of the employer (or employing unit), (3) those covered only if they meet certain eligibility requirements, and (4) those excluded from coverage.

COMPULSORY COVERAGE. Most employees and self-employed persons are covered on a compulsory basis. Ministers (and some members of religious orders) are automatically covered as self-employed persons, but may request exemption on grounds of conscience or religious principles.

ELECTIVE COVERAGE. State and local government employees are covered only if the governmental unit elects coverage; employees under an existing retirement system also must vote in favor of such action (in some states, coverage is provided for all those under an existing retirement system who elect this and for all new employees). Employees of nonprofit organizations are covered only if the organization consents; those who are employed at the time of election may choose to participate or not and, after that time, coverage is compulsory for all new employees. The elective provisions for nonprofit organizations do not apply to ministers because they have automatic coverage as self-employed workers (unless they request exemption as noted above).

United States citizens employed outside the country by an American firm are compulsorily covered, while those employed by a foreign subsidiary of an American employer are covered if the company enters into an agreement consenting to pay OASDHI taxes for them. If the parent company of the foreign subsidiary elects coverage, all United States citizens employed by the subsidiary are covered on a compulsory basis.

COVERAGE WITH SPECIAL ELIGIBILITY REQUIREMENTS. Farm workers, to be covered, must earn at least $150 a year from one employer or work at least twenty days during the year for cash wages based on time rather than piecework.

Domestic workers are covered if they receive $50 or more in cash wages in a calendar quarter from one employer.

Self-employed persons are covered if they have net annual earnings of at least $400. Farmers have an option of coverage if their gross income is at least $600, even if their net annual earnings are under $400.

EXCLUDED OCCUPATIONS. Persons excluded from coverage fall into four occupational groups: (1) federal employees covered under the Civil Service Retirement System; (2) railroad workers covered under the Railroad Retirement Act; (3) family employees, including children under age twenty-one employed by a parent, the employment of a spouse by the other spouse; and (4) employees in miscellaneous small occupational groups, such as student nurses, students working for schools, and local newspaper carriers under age eighteen.

Insured Status. To be eligible for OASDHI benefits, a person must achieve insured status, defined in terms of quarters of coverage.

The earnings requirements for a quarter of coverage are the same for all workers, namely, in 1978, one quarter of coverage for each $250 of earnings, up to a maximum of four quarters of coverage per year. In future years, the $250 unit will be increased according to changes in wage levels.

For a worker's dependents to qualify for survivorship benefits, a worker must be *fully insured* (or, alternatively, for survivor benefits for children and the surviving parent and for lump-sum death payments, *currently insured*). To be currently insured, a person must have six or more quarters of coverage in the thirteen-quarter period immediately preceding death. A person who has forty quarters of coverage is always fully insured, even if the worker spends no additional time in covered employment. A person with less than forty quarters of coverage can qualify as fully insured by having at least one quarter of coverage for each year elapsing after 1950 (or after the year in which the person reaches age twenty-one, if later) and before the year when age sixty-two is reached or, if earlier, the year of death or disability subject to a minimum of six quarters.

Disability insured status requires that a worker have at least twenty quarters of coverage in the forty-quarter period ending with the quarter in which disability begins. Special, more liberal, eligibility requirements apply if the worker is disabled before age thirty-one or is blind.

Benefit Computation All OASDHI benefits are based on the insured worker's *primary insurance amount* (PIA), which for persons attaining age sixty-two after 1978, or dying or becoming disabled before age sixty-two in 1978, or after, is determined after the insured worker's *average indexed monthly earnings* (AIME) is computed. The AIME is calculated by taking the total indexed earnings credited to the worker's account over the benefit computation years and dividing by the number of months in those years. Earnings are indexed to the second year before attaining age sixty-two or, if earlier, the second year before the year of death or disability, which means that the actual earnings in a year are multiplied by the ratio of the national average wage in such second year to the national average wage in the particular year—which thus expresses all past earnings in terms of the level prevailing in such second year; earnings in and after such second year are used as reported—i.e., are not indexed. ("Earnings" means *both* wages as an employee *and* self-employment income.)

An individual's OASDHI account is credited only with earnings from covered employment, and earnings above the maximum earnings base are not counted. The ceiling on creditable earnings since 1937 is shown in Table 6-5.

Table 6-5

OASDHI Maximum Earnings Base—1937-1977

Period	Wage Base
1937-1950	$ 3,000
1951-1954	3,600
1955-1958	4,200
1959-1965	4,800
1966-1967	6,600
1968-1971	7,800
1972	9,000
1973	10,800
1974	13,200
1975	14,100
1976	15,300
1977†	16,500

† After 1977, the earnings base will be adjusted automatically whenever there is a cost of living increase in benefits.

Benefit Computation Years. The AIME equals the indexed earnings for a selected number of years averaged over the number of months in those years. The number of years is equal to five less than the number of years elapsing after 1950 (or the year in which the person attained age twenty-one, if later) and before the year in which the person attains age sixty-two or dies or becomes disabled before age sixty-two. Once this number of years is determined, a like number of years of highest credited indexed earnings is selected from the worker's social security account. If a person does not have covered earnings in as many years as are required by the benefit computation formula, zero earnings must be averaged in for the missing years.

The law allows a person to omit the five years of lowest earnings after 1950 or, if later, after age twenty-one. However, there are no restrictions on the years that may be selected. Years before the person reached age twenty-two or years after age sixty-two may be included whenever it is to the worker's advantage. Credit for earnings received after age sixty-two does not change the number of years counted in figuring average earnings.

Several special provisions apply to workers who have an established period of disability. First, the average wage for disability benefits is determined as if the person had reached age sixty-two in the year in which disability began. Thus, the years included completely within a period of disability are not counted in computing the average wage. Without this provision, if the person died or returned to work before reaching retirement age, the years of zero earnings during the period of disability could reduce the PIA for old-age and survivors' (OASI) benefits.

To illustrate the computation of the AIME, consider the case of Mr. S who retired upon reaching age sixty-two on January 1, 1979. In every year since Mr. S was twenty-one (1939 and after), he earned more than the maximum amount of creditable earnings. Earnings in twenty-three years must be used in computing the AIME (by taking twenty-eight years after 1950 and before 1979, the year of Mr. S's sixty-second birthday, and subtracting five years). The total indexed earnings for Mr. S for the twenty-three highest years amount to $305,769. This amount is divided by 276, the number of months in 23 years, which results in an AIME of $1,107 (the cents are always dropped).

Primary Insurance Amount. Once the AIME is known, the PIA is obtained from the benefit formula that is applicable to each yearly cohort (i.e., persons attaining age sixty-two in a particular year, or dying or becoming disabled before age sixty-two in that year—see Table 6-6). The formula for the 1979 cohort is:

90% of the first $180 of AIME,
plus 32% of the next $905 of AIME,
plus 15% of AIME in excess of $1,085,
with a minimum benefit of $122.

Accordingly, an AIME of $1,107 yields a PIA of $454.90.

For future cohorts, the AIME dollar bands are adjusted for changes in the national average wage after 1977 but the $122 minimum will not be changed. Persons retiring after age sixty-two receive the same automatic adjustments for increases in the Consumer Price Index (CPI) as are applicable to those who retire at age sixty-two. It should be noted from the foregoing formula that greater weight is given to the lower earnings levels in computing the PIA and hence in determining OASDHI benefit levels.

All benefits (except the $255 lump-sum death benefit) increase automatically whenever there is an increase of 3 percent or more in the CPI since the last previous benefit adjustment. This includes retirement, disability, dependents' benefits, and survivors' benefits. This automatic cost of living escalator, however, is not operative in years in which Congress enacts a general benefit increase.

To illustrate the application of the PIA in determining the benefit amount: Mr. H, a married man, reached age sixty-two in January 1979 and retired then, but waited until age sixty-five to draw benefits. Mr. H

Table 6-6

Table for Determining Primary Insurance Amount and Maximum
Family Benefits (Effective January 1, 1977)†

Average Monthly Wage	Primary Insurance Amount	Maximum Family Benefits
Up to $76	$114.30	$ 171.50
77— 78	116.10	174.20
79— 80	118.80	178.30
81— 81	121.00	181.60
82— 83	123.10	184.70
320— 323	273.20	461.10
324— 328	275.80	468.20
329— 333	278.10	475.30
334— 337	281.00	481.20
338— 342	283.00	488.10
624— 627	433.00	758.50
628— 630	435.10	761.20
631— 634	437.10	764.90
635— 637	439.20	768.50
638— 641	441.40	772.20
936— 940	530.40	928.10
941— 945	531.70	930.50
946— 950	533.00	932.80
951— 955	534.50	935.30
956— 960	535.90	937.60
1,236—1,240	603.80	1,056.70
1,241—1,245	605.00	1,058.60
1,246—1,250	606.10	1,060.60
1,251—1,255	607.20	1,062.50
1,256—1,260	608.30	1,064.60

†Selected numbers for purposes of illustration only.

has always been credited with the maximum taxable earnings for social security purposes. His monthly retirement benefit is equal to his PIA of $454.90 (plus any CPI increases that occurred in 1979-81). His wife, also age sixty-five receives 50 percent of his PIA, or $227.50. The total monthly retirement benefits for Mr. and Mrs. H are $682.40. (Actually, a special transitional benefit calculation method is applicable for retirement cohorts of 1979-83; in this particular case, it yields a larger PIA, $481.60 and would therefore be used.)

Although benefits are generally based upon a percentage of the PIA, there are two other provisions that can affect the normal method of benefit computation. These are the *Special Minimum Benefit* and the *Maximum Family Benefit*.

The special minimum benefit applies to persons who have worked in covered employment for many years but at low earning levels. Beginning in 1979, the benefit is equal to $11.50 for each *year of coverage* under social security in excess of ten years, up to a total maximum of thirty years (thus effectively allowing a maximum of twenty years in computing the special minimum benefit). The special minimum benefit applies only when it is larger than the regular benefit. The effect of the special minimum benefit is to increase the benefit for persons with more than about twenty-two years of coverage. For example, a person with thirty or more years of coverage would be entitled to a special minimum benefit of $230 a month (20 × $11.50). The $11.50 figure will be increased in the future for changes in the CPI.

There is no limit to the number of members of an insured worker's family eligible for benefits, but there is a limit on the total amount of monthly benefits payable to a single family. Whenever the combined benefits payable on one social security account exceed the family maximum, all benefit rates, except that of the worker, are reduced proportionately until the combined benefits are brought within the family ceiling.

The maximum family benefit is determined from a formula involving the PIA. For the 1979 cohort, it is

> 150% of the first $230 of PIA,
> plus 272% of the next $102 of PIA,
> plus 134% of the next $101 of PIA,
> plus 175% of PIA in excess of $433.

In general, the maximum family benefit is between one and one-half and one and three-quarters of the PIA.

To illustrate the application of the maximum, assume that the covered worker was fully insured at the time of death in 1979. The PIA is $500. Each eligible dependent (widow or widower and children) of the deceased is entitled to 75 percent of the PIA, or $375. However, if there are three eligible dependents, the total benefit must not exceed the maximum family benefit of $875. Therefore, the benefit actually payable to each dependent beneficiary is $291.70 (because 3 × $291.70 = $875.10).

Table 6-7

Summary of Insured Status Requirements for OASDHI Benefits

Type of Benefit	Requirement as to Insured Status of Worker
Retirement Benefits	
Retired worker	Fully insured
Spouse of retired worker	Fully insured
Child of retired worker	Fully insured
Survivorship Benefits	
Lump sum death benefit	Fully or currently insured
Widow or widower	Fully insured
Surviving spouse with child(ren)	Fully or currently insured
Child	Fully or currently insured
Parents	Fully insured
Disability Benefits	
Worker and his/her dependents	Fully and disability insured
Disabled survivors	
Child	Fully or currently insured
Widow or widower	Fully insured
Disabled child of a	
Retired worker	Fully insured
Disabled worker	Fully and disability insured

Types of Benefits Benefits under OASDHI may be classified as shown in Table 6-7, together with the insured status that is required for each.

Retirement Benefits. Monthly retirement benefits are similar to a life annuity and are payable to a retired worker, a spouse of a retired worker, and a child of a retired worker.

RETIRED WORKER. A worker who is fully insured and retired at age sixty-five is eligible for the full retirement benefit, equal to 100 percent of the PIA. The worker may elect to retire as early as age sixty-two and receive a permanently reduced benefit. The early retirement reduction is equal to five-ninths of 1 percent of the PIA for each month below age sixty-five. At age sixty-two, for example, the lifetime monthly retirement benefit is equal to 80 percent of the worker's PIA. A person retiring after age sixty-five receives a delayed retirement credit. This credit, for persons attaining age sixty-two after 1978, is a lifetime monthly benefit increase of one-fourth of 1 percent of the PIA for each month after age sixty-five and up to age seventy-two that benefits are deferred (only one-twelfth of 1 percent for those attaining age sixty-two before 1979). The delayed retirement credit results in a maximum increase of 21 percent for a person who works to age seventy-two.

SPOUSE OF A RETIRED WORKER.   At age sixty-two or over, a spouse of a fully insured worker entitled to old-age benefits is also entitled to monthly benefits. The spouse's full monthly benefit, payable when benefits are first received at age sixty-five or after, is equal to 50 percent of the PIA of the retired covered individual. The spouse may elect to take a reduced benefit as early as age sixty-two (with a 25 percent reduction—i.e., a benefit of 37.5 percent of the PIA).

A wife who has in her care a child entitled to a child's benefit (except a child receiving benefits solely because he or she is a student aged eighteen to twenty-one) receives the full benefit amount regardless of his or her age. If the wife is under age sixty-two when the child becomes ineligible for the child's benefit, her benefit temporarily ceases. She again becomes eligible for the full benefit at age sixty-five or for a reduced benefit at age sixty-two. A divorced wife of a retired worker is eligible for benefits at age sixty-two or after, provided the marriage lasted at least ten years.

CHILD OF A RETIRED WORKER.   Each natural child, adopted child, or stepchild of a fully insured worker eligible for retirement benefits may receive a benefit equal to 50 percent of that worker's PIA if the child is under age eighteen (age twenty-two if a full-time student) or is disabled and the disability began before age twenty-two, and is not married.

Survivors' Benefits.   In addition to a small lump-sum death benefit, monthly survivors' benefits are payable to a deceased worker's family. These benefits include a widow's or widower's benefit, mother's benefit, child's benefit, and dependent parent's benefit.

LUMP-SUM DEATH BENEFIT.   A lump-sum death benefit equal to $255 is payable. The payment is made to the surviving spouse if living with the deceased at the time of death; otherwise, it is applied to any unpaid funeral expenses or paid to the person who paid the funeral expenses.

WIDOW'S OR WIDOWER'S BENEFIT.   A widow or widower (including a divorced widow or widower who was married to the deceased for at least ten years) of a fully insured person is eligible for benefits at age sixty. If first received at age sixty-five, a widow's or widower's monthly benefit is equal to the deceased spouse's PIA. An actuarially reduced benefit is payable if benefit payments start between the ages of sixty and sixty-five. The actuarial reduction produces, for example, a benefit rate of 71.5 percent at age sixty and 82.9 percent at age sixty-two. Benefits are not payable if the survivor remarries before age sixty. In the event of remarriage after age sixty, the survivor will continue to receive the full widow's or widower's benefit.

MOTHER'S BENEFIT.   While a widow of a deceased fully or currently insured individual has in her care a child of the deceased who is under age eighteen (or disabled) and eligible for a child's benefit, she receives monthly mother's benefits. The mother's benefit is equal to 75 percent of the deceased worker's PIA. The mother's benefit terminates when the child reaches age eighteen (unless the child is disabled) or when the widow remarries. A widow who has not remarried retains her right to receive her regular widow's benefits at or after age sixty. Thus, a widow may be without benefits from the time her youngest child reaches eighteen until she becomes entitled to reduced widow's benefits at age sixty (or full benefits at age sixty-five). This is often referred to as the "social security blackout period."

CHILD'S BENEFIT.   At the death of a fully or currently insured individual, each child of the deceased is entitled to a monthly benefit equal to 75 percent of the deceased parent's PIA. The benefit is payable if the child is under age eighteen (age twenty-two if a full-time student) and is unmarried. If a child is disabled before age twenty-two, the benefit is payable regardless of age.

PARENT'S BENEFIT.   At the death of a fully insured person, a parent of the deceased who is age sixty-two or older and was receiving at least one-half of his or her support from the deceased at the time of death, and has not married since the worker's death, is entitled to a monthly parent's benefit. If only one parent is entitled to parent's benefits, the benefit is 82.5 percent of the PIA of the deceased worker. When more than one parent is entitled to parent's benefits, the benefit for each parent is 75 percent of the deceased worker's PIA.

Benefit Reduction or Termination.   After a person has established eligibility for benefits, the subsequent occurrence of certain events may cause the benefit either to be reduced or terminated.

BENEFIT REDUCTION.   Benefits are reduced according to the provisions of the *earnings test* (or retirement test) which provides a standard for determining whether a retired worker or other beneficiary is engaged in substantial employment. The concept of the retirement test is consistent with the basic purpose of the OASDHI program—to replace, in part, earnings lost because of retirement in old age, disability, or death. The earnings test allows an individual to earn up to a given amount without affecting the dependents' benefits; but, if earnings exceed that amount, there will be a partial or total loss of benefits. A beneficiary age seventy-two or older (age seventy, beginning in 1982), however, receives full benefits regardless of the amount of earnings.

As of 1977, a beneficiary aged sixty-five or over, but under age seventy-two, receives full benefits if he or she earns $4,000 or less in a year; for younger beneficiaries, this amount is $3,240. For each $2 of covered or noncovered earnings in excess of such amounts, the benefits will be decreased by $1. However, in the initial year of benefit receipt, the benefit will not be withheld for any month in which earnings are less than one-twelfth of such amount and no substantial services in self-employment are rendered. The text does not apply to disabled beneficiaries.

The excess earnings of a retired worker are chargeable not only to the worker's own benefit but also to those of other persons receiving benefits on the workers' social security account. But the excess earnings of a person receiving dependents' or survivors' benefits are charged only against that person's own benefit and do not reduce the benefits payable to other family members. For purposes of the earnings test, income from such nonwork sources as investment income, interest, and annuity, pension, and life insurance proceeds are not counted as earnings. If the test took account of income other than earnings from work, it would no longer be a retirement test, but an income test. If it became an income test, the fundamental idea that OASDHI benefits are intended as a partial replacement of earnings would be diluted or lost.

BENEFIT TERMINATION. Benefits terminate for such causes as death and changes in family or marital status that alter the conditions under which payments are made. For example, a wife's benefit ordinarily is dependent upon her remaining married to the covered worker; a mother's benefit is withheld for any month during which she does not have in her care a child entitled to benefits; and a child's benefit is discontinued at age eighteen (age twenty-two if a full-time student) or upon marriage. In addition, benefits may be lost upon conviction of certain crimes or as the result of deportation from the country.

OASDHI Financing

OASDHI benefits are financed by payroll taxes paid by employers and employees under the Federal Insurance Contributions Act (FICA) and by self-employed persons under the Self-Employment Contributions Act. The funds collected are allocated to three trust funds: The Old-Age and Survivors Insurance Trust Fund, Disability Insurance Trust fund, and Hospital Insurance Trust Fund.

Taxes Two factors determine the annual amount of social

security taxes paid: (1) the social security tax rate, and (2) the earnings subject to taxation (or the so-called wage base).

Tax Rate. The social security tax consists of two separate taxes: the OASDHI tax for old-age, survivors', and disability benefits and the hospital insurance tax for Medicare benefits.

The tax rate is expressed as a percentage of the taxable income up to the maximum earnings base. OASDHI taxes paid by employees are matched by employers; the rate for self-employed persons is approximately one and one-half times the employee rate. The hospital insurance tax rate is the same for employers, employees, and self-employed persons. For 1978, the combined rate for the total OASDHI tax is 6.05 percent each for employers and employees and 8.1 percent for self-employed inividuals.

Taxable Earnings. The social security tax rate is applied to earnings up to the maximum taxable earnings base each year. This base is the same for employers, employees, and the self-employed, and it is increased automatically following each cost-of-living increase in social security benefits. The amount of the increase is determined from the changes in the average of all wages in the country. For 1978 the maximum earnings base is $17,700. In 1979-81 the automatic-adjustment provision will not apply, but rather there will be ad hoc increases to $22,900 for 1979, $25,900 for 1980, and $29,700 for 1981 (which are far more than the automatics would have produced).

The employee is taxed on wages received, and the employer pays the same amount. For social security tax purposes, wages are not limited to the actual money received but include the cash value of all remuneration other than cash, such as room and board. Cash tips count as wages if they equal $20 a month or more. Tips are taxed to the employee, but the employer tax does not apply. The self-employed are taxed on self-employment income, not including interest, dividends, and rent unless these are received in the course of business.

If an employee works for more than one employer during the course of a year, taxes must be paid on earnings up to the maximum ceiling from each employer. If the worker pays taxes over the limit, the overpayment is credited against the federal income tax for that year or may be refunded. A tax overpayment by an employee, however, does not entitle the employers to a refund. Each employer is liable for the taxes on all wages paid to employees during the taxable year up to the maximum earnings base.

THE GROUP INSURANCE TECHNIQUE

Characteristics of Group Insurance

Group insurance provides coverage to a number of individuals under a master contract issued to a sponsoring organization. The insured members are not parties to the contract and do not receive individual policies. Instead, they receive certificates of insurance as evidence of their protection.

Eligible Groups Initially, group insurance was issued only to employer-employee groups, but now group insurance is issued to many types of groups. All states restrict the types of groups that are eligible for group insurance, but there is considerable variation in these restrictions. In general, however, the different types of eligible groups may be classified into four basic categories:

1. Employers. Individual employers represent the largest category covered by group insurance. Employers may be covered as a sole proprietorship, partnership, or corporation. Employee eligibility for coverage is determined by state law and company underwriting standards. Generally employees may be covered if they are directors of a corporation, partners, sole proprietors, retired, employees of a subsidiary or affiliated firm, or independent contractors. Most states permit dependents of employees to be covered in a group life plan.

   The multi-employer arrangement makes it possible to provide group insurance coverage for employees of different organizations generally within the same industry. This includes negotiated trusteeships that arise from collective bargaining (as, for example, when members of the same union work for several employers) and voluntary trade associations (for example, groups made up of employers in the same industry).
2. Unions. A master contract may be issued directly to a union to cover union members.
3. Debtors of a Common Creditor. Organizations that routinely accept consumer debt (such as commercial banks, finance companies, appliance dealers, and credit unions) often provide group insurance as a method of protecting the debt. The master contract is issued to the creditor. In the event of the debtor's death, the proceeds are paid to the creditor and the debt is extinguished. Generally, the amount of group insurance equals the outstanding indebtedness.

4. Miscellaneous Groups. Most states permit many other types of groups to participate in a group insurance arrangement. These include, but are not limited to, members of professional, trade, or veterans associations, alumni groups, religious groups, and even avocational groups.

Size Requirements. The minimum number of lives necessary to qualify for group insurance has declined over the years. State laws, as well as underwriting practices, have been liberalized to the point that small groups may now qualify for group insurance. While some state laws do not specify any minimum number, the usual minimum for single employer groups is ten lives. For other types of groups a larger number is normally required. The Model Group Life Bill requires 100 lives for a multi-employer plan, twenty-five members for a union group, and a creditor-debtor plan must have at least 100 new lives each year (and a minimum of twenty-five lives at any one time).

A primary purpose for requiring a minimum number of lives is to reduce the expense rate by spreading the fixed costs over a larger number of people. Secondly, the larger the group, the smaler the chance that the plan is adopted to provide life insurance for unhealthy persons. Furthermore, with a larger group there is a greater likelihood that the mortality experience will be stable and therefore close to that expected by the insurer.

Eligibility Requirements. Generally group insurance protects all regular, full-time employees (or members) of an organization; however, this is not a statutory requirement. According to state laws (and most insurer underwriting rules) an employer may establish standards to cover only certain classes of employees, but the standards cannot exclude individuals on the basis of age, sex, race, or religion. In general, methods of excluding classes of employees must be based on conditions of employment. For example, a plan may cover salaried workers and exclude those who are compensated on an hourly basis. Part-time and seasonal employees are almost always excluded.

In noncontributory plans (those that are financed solely by employers and without any explicit contributions from employees), coverage automatically becomes effective on the date when employees complete the probationary period, if one exists. The probationary period is a period of time, usually ranging from one to three months after joining a company, when there is no coverage. The purpose of this requirement is to exclude temporary workers and those who are in poor health when they are hired. If a plan is contributory (requires explicit contributions from employees), individual employees are not covered even after completing the probationary period unless they elect coverage and agree to the appropriate payroll deductions.

In addition to the probationary period requirement, most plans also require that employees must be actively at work on the first day after the probationary period expires before coverage commences. This underwriting requirement has the effect of excluding some employees who would otherwise be covered. This rule applies to employees at the inception of a plan, to new employees, and at times when benefits are increased. An employee cannot become eligible for benefits (or an increase in benefits) while absent from work for any reason. This requirement minimizes the insuring of those who are too ill to work.

Benefits.   The amount of group insurance that may be sold on one life is subject to restriction. The law requires the use of some method, usually a formula or schedule, that prevents individual employees from selecting the amount of their coverage. In other words, the benefit amount must be determined automatically to minimize selection against the insurer. Those in poor health are likely to choose large amounts of insurance, which would adversely affect the mortality experience of the insurance company.

Ideally, the benefit formula should recognize (1) the life insurance needs of individual employees, (2) the employees' ability to pay (if the plan is contributory), (3) the overall cost of the plan, and (4) the need for administrative simplicity. Under any type of schedule, the amount of insurance is adjusted as employees move from one employment classification to another.[2]

The most common type of benefit formula is one that uses an employee's earnings to determine the amount of coverage. This approach is illustrated as follows:

Monthly Earnings	Amount of Insurance
Less than $1,000	$10,000
$1,000—$1,500	16,000
$1,500—$2,000	22,000
$2,500—$3,000	28,000
More than $3,000	34,000

Although there are many formulas or schedules for relating the amount of insurance to earnings, a common practice is to provide insurance equal to one, one and a half, or two times an employee's annual earnings, rounded off to the nearest $500 or $1,000.

If a plan is based on earnings, only the regular compensation of an employee usualy is considered; bonuses, overtime pay, and other supplements are excluded in the computation.

Another type of benefit formula relates the amount of insurance to the employee's position. For example:

Position	Amount of Insurance
Officers	$20,000
Department Heads	18,000
Supervisors	15,000
Salespersons	10,000
All Other Employees	7,500

One of the problems with a position schedule is that it is sometimes difficult to classify each employee by position.

A third type of benefit formula which is used infrequently relates the amount of insurance to an employee's length of service. For example, employees with less than six years of service may have $5,000 of insurance; those with more than six but less than twelve years of service may be provided with $10,000 of insurance; and $15,000 of life insurance may be provided to employees who have worked for the company more than twelve years. This method rewards long service, but it tends to give the smallest amounts of insurance to younger employees, who are likely to have greater insurance needs than older employees. Also, it may cause some funding problems because larger amounts of insurance become very expensive on older workers.

Flat amount plans (those that provide the same amount of insurance to all employees) are not common, except in multiple-employer and labor union groups. Generally this method is used where all employees' earnings are fairly uniform.

A fifth type of benefit formula is a combination of two or more of the above approaches. Some plans, for example, provide benefits that are based on earnings and length of service, or position and length of service.

Regardless of the type of benefit formula or schedule, insurance companies stipulate a minimum and maximum amount of insurance that may be issued on any life. Many companies impose a minimum such as $1,000, $5,000, or $7,500 depending on group size to spread expenses over a larger volume of insurance.

The maximum amount of group life insurance that should be issued on one life has been a source of much controversy. Most states no longer limit the amount of group life insurance coverage that may be provided to an individual. While no state uses it, the Group Life Model Bill contains a provision known as the 20/40 rule. With this approach, the limit for one life is $20,000 without regard to income, but amounts up to $40,000 are permitted if the amount is not more than 50 percent greater than the employee's salary. For example, a $20,000 employee could have up to $30,000 of life insurance under this rule. In some other states, a flat maximum amount, such as $20,000 or $25,000 or $100,000 is specified.

Each state may impose its own statutory maximum but the

underwriting practices of insurers may restrict the coverage to an amount below that allowed by law.

The federal government does not impose a limit on the amount of group insurance sold on one life but federal tax law may affect the amount of coverage. According to federal income tax law, an employee must include in gross income the cost of group life insurance in excess of $50,000 if it is paid for by the employer or the excess over a lower state limit. The cost may be calculated from tables prescribed by the Internal Revenue Service, and any amount the employee contributed toward the premium may be deducted from the amount to be included in gross income.

Types of Group Life Coverage

Group life insurance is available as either (1) yearly renewable term insurance, (2) group paid-up insurance, or (3) group ordinary insurance.

Yearly Renewable Term Insurance More than 90 percent of all group life insurance in force is sold on a yearly renewable term basis. This type of insurance is pure protection and does not develop a cash value. If a covered employee dies, a death benefit is payable, but no benefits are payable if an employee lives beyond the period of protection.

The name *yearly renewable term* arises from the fact that the protection expires at the end of each year but is automatically renewed. The premium charged the employer may change annually to reflect the experience of the group being insured.

The popularity of the yearly renewable term plan is due to three factors: (1) the premiums are lower for term insurance than for other plans, (2) it is simple to administer, and (3) there are several income tax advantages. For example, the employer's contributions generally do not represent taxable income to the employee. Section 79 of the Internal Revenue Code allows an employer to provide $50,000 (or the maximum limit imposed by state law if less) of term insurance to an employee without any income tax consequences, providing certain liberal requirements are met. The cost of the protection in excess of the limit is determined by using Table 6-8.

The tax treatment of a group term insurance plan (from an employee's point of view) can be illustrated by a simple example. Assume that an employee is forty-seven years of age and has $100,000 of group term insurance that is financed entirely by the employer. Assume further that the state limit on such benefits is not below $50,000. Therefore:

Table 6-8

Uniform Premiums for $1,000 of
Group-Term Life Insurance Protection

Age	Monthly Cost Per $1,000 of Protection
Under 30	$0.08
30—34	0.10
35—39	0.14
40—44	0.23
45—49	0.40
50—54	0.68
55—59	1.10
60—64	1.63

Excess coverage $=$ ($100,000 $-$ $50,000) $=$ $50,000

Amount to be included in employee's gross income $=$

$$(50 \times \$.40 \times 12) = \$240$$

The employee would be required to pay income tax on $240 at year-end. If the employee is in a 35 percent tax bracket, taxes would be increased by $84 ($240 $\times$ 0.35). If the employee pays part of the cost, the employee's contribution is deducted from the amount to be included in the employee's gross income.

Group Paid-Up Insurance With this approach of providing group life insurance, employer contributions purchase term insurance, and employee contributions are applied to purchase units of fully paid-up whole life insurance which provides protection to age 100.

The amount of fully paid-up insurance that an employee's contribution purchases is determined by the size of the contribution and the employee's attained age. The amount of paid-up insurance builds up as each premium is paid. Employer contributions purchase the amount of term insurance necessary to make up the difference between the total amount of insurance called for by the benefit schedule and the accumulated amount of paid-up insurance. The premium rate for the term insurance increases as the employee gets older, but the cost is kept within manageable bounds because the amount of term insurance purchased each year decreases over time.

Group Ordinary Insurance Prior to 1966, employer contributions toward the cost of permanent insurance were regarded as taxable income to an employee. While this was not a problem for group paid-up plans (because employer contributions are used to finance the term insurance protection), the tax law effectively thwarted the use of other group permanent coverages.

In 1966, Section 79 of the Internal Revenue Code was revised, and group permanent plans became more practical. These plans also are known as group ordinary, group permanent, and Section 79 plans.

A group ordinary plan allows an eligible employee to change all or a portion of his or her group term insurance coverage to permanent insurance. According to present IRS regulations, employer contributions toward the cost of the permanent insurance will not be taxable as income to the employee under certain conditions. Basically, to achieve the desired result, all covered employees must be able to elect the permanent coverage, the group policy must identify the part of the premium that is attributable to term insurance, and the employer's contribution cannot exceed the portion of the premium that is properly allocable to term insurance.

Group Survivor Benefit Insurance Historically, many pension plans provided an ancillary benefit known as a survivors benefit. In recent years this benefit frequently has been provided as a supplement to a group life insurance plan.

One of the distinguishing features of survivor benefit plans is that benefits are payable only to qualified survivors. A surviving spouse (widow or widower) is eligible for benefits, but usually only if living with the deceased spouse at the time of death. Some plans stipulate that the spouse must have been married for a certain period of time, such as one or two years. Dependent children also are eligible for benefits in most plans.

Another feature of these plans is that benefits are paid in monthly installments. The amount often is related to the deceased's income immediately before death. The benefit may range from 10 percent of the employee's income, depending on the plan. The benefit may be determined in a number of other ways. For example, it may be related to the employee's job classification, or it may be based on the employee's projected or accrued pension benefits at the time of the employee's death. Another approach is to simply provide a flat dollar benefit.

The duration of the monthly benefits varies from plan to plan. Some plans provide spouse's benefits for only a short period, such as two or three years, while others provide lifetime benefits. More plans provide spouse's benefits until the spouse reaches age sixty-five or becomes eligible for social security benefits. Almost all plans discontinue benefits immediately if a spouse remarries, but some continue benefits for a period, such as one or two years after remarriage.

Benefits for dependent children are terminated when the child reaches a certain age such as eighteen, twenty-one, or up to age twenty-three as long as the dependent child is a full-time student.

Survivor benefit plans generally provide larger benefits than a typical group life insurance plan and therefore are relatively expensive. Despite this, these plans have grown rapidly in recent years due to the following advantages:

1. Lump-sum death benefits paid in a typical group life insurance plan often are spent by the beneficiaries in a short period of time; with survivor income benefits, the funds are likely to be available over a longer duration.
2. Group life insurance benefits are paid even when there are no closely related survivors who are dependent on the deceased employee's income; this does not occur with survivor benefit plans.
3. Many group life plans provide larger benefits to older employees because their earnings or position calls for higher benefits, but they often have less need for survivor's income than do younger employees.

Characteristics of Group Life Insurance

Low Cost to Employees   Group life insurance almost always costs less than individual insurance. The premium seldom is paid entirely by employees. As indicated previously, a noncontributory plan is paid for entirely by the employer. Even in contributory plans, employees pay only a portion of the cost. In fact, most state laws, as well as the underwriting requirements of most insurance companies, require employers to pay at least a portion of the group life insurance premiums. There are several reasons for this requirement. First, if part of the cost is paid by the employer, the plan will be attractive to employees, and more will participate. Secondly, it allows the employee contribution rate to remain stable with the employer absorbing annual fluctuations. Third, employers will have an incentive to operate the plan efficiently and economically if they pay part of the cost.[3]

Another reason for the low cost of group life insurance is that expenses are relatively low due to reduced agent's commissions and low administrative expenses, since employers normally assume many administrative functions associated with the plan. For example, the collection of premiums in a contributory plan is handled automatically by payroll deduction. Other administrative functions, such as a change in beneficiary and increases in benefit amounts, also are routinely handled by employers.

Since all employees in a contributory plan pay the same rate, regardless of age, the coverage is a greater bargain for older employees than for younger employees. Even though young employees pay more than seems equitable, the cost normally is lower than for individual insurance.

Group Selection An important characteristic of group insurance is that it generally is provided without a medical examination or other evidence of insurability. A person in poor health who is unable to purchase individual life insurance often may obtain group coverage with no difficulty. Obviously, this is advantageous to those in poor health, but is also advantageous to other employees because of low administrative (underwriting) expenses.

Mortality experience is slightly higher in group insurance than it is in the case of individually selected coverage because group selection is not concerned with the specific health, morals, habits, or heredity of individuals within the group. Instead, the characteristics of the group as a whole are underwritten. If the group is acceptable then all members of the group are covered; otherwise, the entire group is rejected regardless of how healthy any given member of the group is.

Insurance Incidental to the Group. An important underwriting requirement is that the group should exist for some purpose other than the desire of its members to obtain low-cost insurance. Otherwise, the group mortality experience is likely to be worse than that anticipated in the insurance rates.

Flow of Persons Through the Group. From an underwriting standpoint, it is desirable to add young, healthy individuals to the group periodically to replace older members who are removed systematically. Otherwise, the average mortality of the group will increase and the cost of insurance may become prohibitive thereby leading to plan termination.

Automatic Determination of Benefits. Individual participants in a group life plan should not be able to influence the amount of coverage on their lives. If individuals select the amount of their insurance, those in poor health will choose larger amounts than those who are healthy. This is rarely a problem in group plans because the amount of the benefits is determined automatically by one of the formulas described previously.

Minimum Proportion of Group. A safeguard used in group underwriting is to require that a large percentage of the eligible group participate, thereby minimizing the chance of insuring an abnormal proportion of unhealthy lives.

Insurers require 100 percent participation of all eligible employees in a noncontributory plan. If the plan is contributory, some employees may not agree to the necessary payroll deduction. Therefore, the minimum acceptable percentage is lower, generally 75 percent.

Other Characteristics One of the attractions of a group life insurance plan is convenience. For example, payroll deduction is an easy method of paying premiums (although premium payments for individual insurance also may be made automatically). Furthermore, there are few decisions involved in enrolling in a group plan. An employee does not have to be concerned with the amount of insurance to purchase because benefits will be determined automatically. An analysis of cost is unnecessary because the cost is lower than that for individual insurance. Finally, an employer's contributions are not taxable income to an employee unless the amount of group life insurance from all sources exceeds $50,000.

Problems or Limitations of Group Life Insurance

Benefit Amounts Depending upon state law, company under-writing practices, and the benefit schedule, an individual may be able to obtain only a small amount of protection such as $10,000 under a group life insurance plan. Often the benefit schedule provides small amounts of coverage to young employees who generally need more protection than do older workers.

Duration of Coverage Normally an employee's group life coverage is not affected by temporary absences from work for reasons such as vacation, strike, accident, sickness, or even a leave of absence. Protection is continued if premium payments are continued. In deciding whether premium payments will be continued for those temporarily unemployed, an employer must use a system that prevents individual selection. For example, a company may have a policy of continuing to pay premiums for employees who are expected to return to work within some specified period, such as three months.

If an employee's service is terminated, the group life coverage will continue automatically for thirty-one days. In many cases this will be adequate since it will be only a short time before starting another job and acquiring new coverage. However, a person might be unemployed for a long period, and even after becoming employed, the new employer may have no group insurance, or the amount of insurance might be substantially less than the previous amount of protection.

An important feature of most group life plans is the conversion provision which allows an employee to obtain an individual policy if employment is terminated or if the master contract is discontinued. The conversion clause permits an employee within thirty-one days after severing employment to obtain an individual policy without providing evidence of insurability. However, this feature may not solve the problem of continuance of coverage since those who are healthy are likely to be unconcerned, and unhealthy employees may not be aware of the conversion right. The mortality experience on converted group insurance is extremely unfavorable. As a result, a charge for the high mortality rate ($55 to $75 per $1,000 of coverage is typical) is levied on employers, (usually through the dividend account) who therefore may not publicize the conversion feature.

One of the serious limitations of most group life insurance plans is the lack of post-retirement coverage. Most group life plans provide term insurance coverage that builds up no cash values which could extend coverage beyond retirement.

Providing insurance protection after retirement is difficult. First, there is no convenient method of collecting premiums from retired employees, and more importantly, the cost of insurance at advanced ages is prohibitively high.

Despite the cost, many group life plans provide limited coverage for retired employees. The benefit amount may be reduced immediately upon retirement to a flat, small amount or to a percentage such as 25 to 33 percent of the amount of insurance in force at retirement. In some plans the benefit amount will be reduced each year until a certain amount (or percentage of prior benefits) is reached. As a general rule, the employer pays the full cost of benefits during retirement in all the plans that provide decreasing benefits. This is administratively simple and does not impose a financial burden on retired employees, but even with reduced benefits, the cost to an employer is substantial.

Another method for providing life insurance during retirement is through the group paid-up arrangement. As explained earlier, employer contributions purchase term insurance, and employee contributions purchase units of paid-up insurance which provide post-retirement insurance protection. The group paid-up approach provides a solution to the problem of continuing coverage, but most group life insurance plans use yearly renewable term insurance.

Lack of Professional Service Group insurance is sold on a mass production basis and employees normally do not receive expert advice. The insurer and the employer must provide a summary plan description that describes the plan benefits and provisions. If an employee needs answers to nonroutine questions, the employer, or the insurance company, may provide some assistance. However, a group life plan cannot be tailored in amount or in design to meet the specific needs of individual employees. Consequently, most individuals will need individual coverage based on the advice of a competent professional in addition to group coverage to round out his or her insurance portfolio.

THE INDIVIDUAL INSURANCE TECHNIQUE

Social and group insurance participants have few, if any, decisions to make. Participation in the OASDHI program is not voluntary, and the type and amount of benefits provided are beyond the control of individual participants. A participant in a group life insurance plan also has little flexibility because the type and amount of benefits are predetermined.

Individual life insurance, however, requires an individual to make several decisions. A life insurance program should be based on a comprehensive plan which recognizes the existence of social and group insurance benefits. The first step in all individual insurance planning is to analyze the life insurance needs of the individual.

Analysis of Life Insurance Needs

A person's life insurance needs may be classified into (1) family needs, and (2) business and estate planning needs. In the remainder of this chapter the analysis will be simplified by concentrating only on personal (family) needs. Business uses of life insurance and estate planning will be treated in later chapters.

The analysis of personal life insurance needs requires answers to two questions: (1) How much income would be needed for specific purposes by the family if a given individual should die immediately? and (2) When would the income be needed? Although it may seem illogical to base the approach on the assumption of immediate death, this is the only method of determining life insurance needs *at the present time*. Because life insurance needs change over time, a life insurance program should be reevaluated periodically.

Estate Settlement Fund The most immediate need for funds upon death is to pay death expenses and to liquidate outstanding financial obligations. This is accomplished by means of a "cleanup fund," which is also called "estate settlement fund," "executor fund," or "probate fund."

The purpose of an estate settlement fund is to pay expenses such as: (1) last-illness costs,[4] (2) burial expenses, (3) outstanding financial obligations, (4) expenses of estate administration, and (5) taxes.

Readjustment Period Income Most families are unable or unwilling to pay insurance premiums sufficient to provide dependents with as much income as they enjoyed while the breadwinner was alive. Consequently, a family's income (from all sources including life insurance) generally decreases after the breadwinner's death.

It is considered advisable that the family's reduction in standard of living not be forced upon the family immediately after the breadwinner dies, but rather the income level should be maintained at the previous level for a period of time. If the reduction is to be slight, a relatively short period (perhaps one year) is considered sufficient for the readjustment period. If, on the other hand, a major decrease is required, the readjustment period should be longer (perhaps two years or more).

Dependency Period Income Most breadwinners feel a responsibility to ensure that children have sufficient resources to live comfortably until they become self-sufficient.

Generally, the amount of the estate clearance fund can be estimated with reasonable accuracy at a given point in time. However, the expenses of last illness depend largely upon the nature and duration of the disability prior to death, and the amount of health insurance available.

Furthermore, the amount estimated for the estate clearance fund may become out of date quickly since the component expenses in this need change from year to year. Finally, the size of the estate clearance fund varies with the size of the estate, which itself may fluctuate.

The amount of income during this period is a matter of personal choice. This period normally is considered to terminate at age eighteen. If the children are college-bound, the dependency period may be extended to the anticipated age at graduation.

For purposes of simplicity, the dependency period is said to extend from the present until the *youngest* child reaches age eighteen. In the actual computation of needs, it is more accurate to compute the amount needed for each child. If, for example, the children are ages eight and sixteen, the dependency period is not ten years. Instead, it is two years for one child and ten years for the other.

Life Income for Widow Historically, husbands have felt a moral obligation to provide a lifetime income for their widows since many devoted their energies to the traditional role of homemaker and did not develop employment skills. This concept is becoming less relevant as women acquire higher education levels and develop better occupational skills.

Mortgage Redemption It may be desirable to pay off any remaining balance on a home mortgage if the breadwinner dies, since the complete and free ownership of a home relieves the survivors of a major financial obligation and simplifies the family's budgetary planning. Furthermore, there is some personal satisfaction in knowing that the family will not be forced to move from the family residence.

Most mortgages will disclose the amount necessary to pay off the mortgage. In assessing the wisdom of liquidation of a mortgage, the size of any pay-off penalty should be considered. Some lenders use mortgage contracts with prepayment penalties but eliminate the penalty if the debt is repaid through life insurance proceeds.

There are circumstances when it is advantageous *not* to redeem the mortgage. For example, if the mortgage interest rate is favorable compared to the current market rate of interest, it may be wise to invest the money in higher interest-bearing investments. Secondly, if the survivors want to sell the property, it may be more marketable with a transferable mortgage. Consequently, paying off the mortgage may work to the detriment of the survivor.

Education Funds Dependency period income provides funds for the education of children through secondary school. If the dependency period is considered to terminate at age eighteen and a college education is planned, additional funds are needed. The time when such funds are necessary is easy to determine, but the amount of funds needed is difficult to estimate.

The costs to acquire a college education have been escalating rapidly and future levels are impossible to predict accurately. If children are not near college age, it is wise to develop an estimate based on current costs and then adjust the estimate by a compound interest factor in order to recognize the higher future costs.

Emergency Fund It is sound practice to establish an emergency fund when the breadwinner dies. Income during the readjustment and dependency periods is likely to be less than desired and, as a result, a financial emergency during this period may disrupt financial plans.

The size of the fund is a matter of judgment. Generally an emergency fund of $5,000 to $10,000 is considered reasonable for a family. If a larger emergency fund is contemplated, it may indicate that other needs have not been funded adequately.

Insurance on Secondary Income Producers Traditionally families have had one breadwinner, but now both spouses in many families are employed. The human life value concept applies equally to both spouses. While the amount of insurance on the primary breadwinner should be greater than the amount on the life of the secondary breadwinner, both lives logically should be insured since the death of either represents a loss to the family.

The death of a nonwage-earning spouse should also be insured because the spouse's death would involve death costs and, in many cases, future expenses. For example, the death of a housewife would create a need for an estate clearance fund, and additional future expenses may be incurred for the services of a housekeeper, child care, and the like.

A common mistake in life insurance planning is to purchase an excessive amount of life insurance on the life of a nonwage-earning spouse. This is not to say that such an individual's insurable value should not be protected by life insurance. As a practical matter, however, many primary breadwinners have an inadequate amount of life insurance. As the amount of insurance on that individual is increased to a reasonable amount, lower priority needs for life insurance for the nonwage-earning spouse should be recognized.

Methods of Planning Individual Insurance Programs

Life insurance purchased to meet a single need without adequate consideration of other needs and resources may result in costly inefficiencies. Life insurance should be purchased as a method of meeting interrelated financial problems, and this calls for a comprehensive plan that considers all important life insurance needs. The two basic methods for planning an individual life insurance program are discussed briefly.

Programming The traditional method of developing an individual life insurance plan is called programming.[5] It involves three determinations:

1. financial objectives;
2. the extent to which the present plan meets the financial objectives; and
3. the additional amount of life insurance (if any) needed to meet the financial objectives.

Determining Financial Objectives. First, the amount of money needed to meet each life insurance need, assuming the individual were to die immediately, must be determined. This assumption is necessary to determine the amount of life insurance needed *at the present time.*

A portion of this need may be determined easily, such as in the case of a mortgage redemption fund. However, most life insurance needs are difficult to estimate because they cannot be estimated objectively. For example, the amount of income needed during the dependency period depends upon the standard of living desired after the breadwinner dies. Despite these problems, programming necessitates the estimation of the amount of money needed to meet each need as well as the time when income must begin and how long it should continue.

As an illustrative example, assume Mr. A is thirty-five years of age,

Table 6-9

Mr. A's Family's Financial Needs Following His Death

Estate clearance	$ 8,000
Mortgage redemption	45,000
Emergency fund	5,000
Total lump sum needs	$58,000

The estimate of the family's income is:

Dependency period	$1,250 per month for ten years
Life income for the widow	$1,000 per month

Figure 6-2

Mr. A's Life Insurance Needs

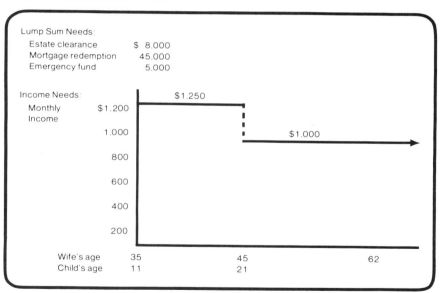

married and has one child, age eleven. Mrs. A is also thirty-five years of age, and has been a housewife since her marriage twelve years ago. Mr. A earns an annual income of $25,000. It is estimated that the amounts shown in Table 6-9 would be needed immediately upon his death. Figure 6-2 illustrates Mr. A's family financial needs.

Evaluating the Present Plan. Secondly, the extent to which Mr. A's needs (illustrated in Figure 6-2) are met must be evaluated. Assume

Figure 6-3

Mr. A's Life Insurance Needs and Present Coverage

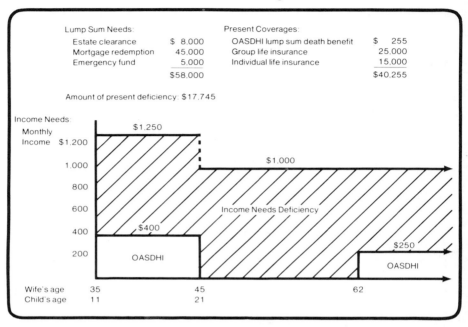

that Mr. A is fully insured in the OASDHI program, has a $25,000 group life insurance policy, and an individual $15,000 policy.

The $255 lump-sum death OASDHI benefit along with the present policies (group and individual) will pay $40,255 of the $58,000 lump-sum needs. OASDHI survivors income benefits are paid to mothers and children while the children are young, and starting at age sixty-two, a widow's benefit is provided. Future increases in benefits normally are ignored in all calculations. Consequently, ignoring possible future increases, OASDHI benefits payable to Mr. A's family are $400 per month during the dependency period and $250 per month starting when Mrs. A reaches sixty-two years of age. The amounts in Figure 6-3 illustrate these facts.

Mr. A's plan clearly fails to meet his objectives. The gap between present income resources and objectives can be divided into three areas: (1) the dependency period spanning ten years after death when the income deficiency is $850 per month, (2) the blackout period when $1,000 per month of additional income is needed, and (3) the widow's life income period when $750 per month is needed. In addition, his lump-sum needs exceed his present resources by $17,745.

Determining the Amount of Additional Insurance Needed. In determining the amount of insurance needed, it is desirable to start with the most distant needs, i.e., the widow's life income after the blackout period. For this period, the unmet need is $750 per month. It takes approximately $1,000 to provide $5.50 of monthly income. Therefore, to provide the needed $750 per month, the amount needed is $750/5.5 × 1,000 = $136,364.

In other words, $136,364 of life insurance will provide Mrs. A with a $750 monthly income for life starting at age sixty-two. This amount ($750) together with the OASDHI benefit ($250) meets the $1,000 per month income objective.

Since Mr. A is assumed to die immediately and the life income will not begin until Mrs. A reaches age sixty-two, the $136,364 may be left on deposit with the insurance company during the blackout period. At 4 percent interest, the interest earnings would be $5,455 per year or about $455 per month. Therefore, the $1,000 monthly deficiency during the blackout period is $545 ($1,000 − $455), which could be satisfied by additional insurance. The amount of insurance needed to provide $545 per month for the seventeen year blackout period when Mrs. A is between the ages forty-five and sixty-two is $77,857 ($545/$7 × $1,000 = $77,857) since $1,000 will provide about $7 per month of monthly income for seventeen years.

The income deficiency during the dependency period is $850 per month. However, interest earnings (assuming 4 percent) on the insurance proceeds of $214,221 ($136,364 + $77,857) held to meet the other needs is about $714 per month, which leaves a deficiency of $136 per month ($850–$714). It takes approximately $13,600 to provide $136 per month for ten years.

The completed programming illustration for Mr. A is shown in Figure 6-4.

The total amount of new life insurance needed is $227,821 ($136,364 + $77,857 + $13,600).

The main advantage of programming is that it provides a reasonably accurate method for matching needs with life insurance policies. Furthermore, the process can be adapted to recognize needs for disability and retirement purposes.

There are several limitations associated with programming. First, accurate estimates require the use of a computer.

Secondly, since the objective is to determine a person's life insurance needs at the present time, it must be assumed that the individual dies immediately, which is unrealistic. Traditional programming, because it assumes immediate death, has been called *static programming.* A much more complex method, called *dynamic program-*

Figure 6-4
Mr. A's Additional Life Insurance Needs

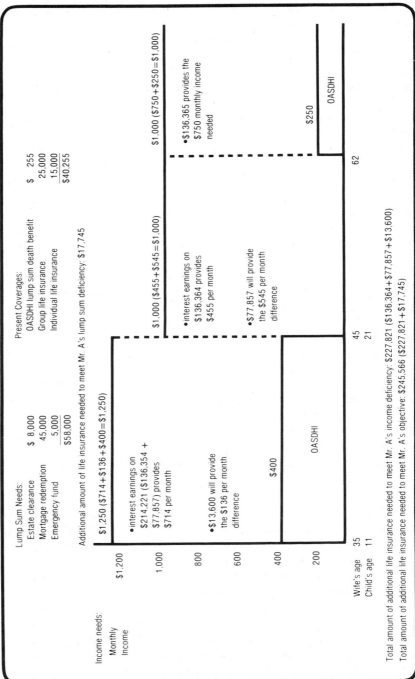

ming, does not assume immediate death, but rather is composed of a series of static programs.

Third, the process assumes that a beneficiary will use one of the *settlement options* described in the next chapter. In reality, however, only a small portion of life insurance proceeds are paid out under the settlement options.

Fourth, it ignores inflation which can result in grossly deficient insurance needs.

The Capital Need Analysis Method of Life Insurance Planning A newer, relatively simple, and increasingly popular approach to life insurance planning is called capital need analysis.

Valuing the Estate. The first step in capital need analysis is to construct a personal balance sheet. The logic of capital need analysis will be developed by means of an extended example. Assume that Mr. B's personal balance sheet is as shown in Table 6-10.

It is not necessary to be completely accurate and consequently, all figures have been rounded to the nearest $500 and minor assets and liabilities have been ignored.

Determining Amount of Income Producing Capital. Secondly, it is necessary to estimate the amount of capital available to meet the income needs of the family.

In Table 6-11, Mr. B's liabilities from his personal balance sheet have been placed in the left column. The amount to be included for "taxes and costs of administration" can be taken from tables that show average amounts for estates of various sizes. The balance on the home mortgage should be included on the next line if the mortgage is to be liquidated.

Assume Mr. B wishes to provide educational funds for his child who is eleven years of age. The $12,000 figure (line 5) is the current cost of four years of college. Since the funds will not be needed for about seven years, the interest earnings on the $12,000 may offset the effects of inflated educational costs.

Assets that do not produce any family income such as equity in the homestead and personal property are included on line 6. This totals $30,000.

The total deductions from Mr. B's assets are shown on line 7. The difference between line 1 and line 7, shown on line 8, indicates the amount of income producing capital available to the family if Mr. B should die.

Income Analysis. The third step in capital need analysis is to examine the income position of the family.

Line 1 of Table 6-12 lists the total, before-tax, annual family income.

Table 6-10

Balance Sheet for Mr. B

Assets	
Net equity in home	
Market value: $80,000 Mortgage: $40,000	$ 40,000
Other real estate	– – –
Personal property	10,000
Death benefits under retirement plans	25,000
Securities	15,500
Stock options	– – –
Life insurance[†]	40,000
Business interest	– – –
Checking and savings accounts	3,500
Other assets	5,000
Total	$139,000

Liabilities	
Current bills	$2,500
Notes	6,500
Other debts	– – –
Total	$9,000

[†] This item should include benefits from employer-provided plans as well as personal (individual) life insurance. Only the basic death benefit should be included, rather than any additional benefits such as the accidental death benefit (described in Chapter 8).

Line 2 shows the proportion of that income needed by the family should Mr. B die. This percentage can be determined by using the figures at the bottom of the table under Income Objective.

The capital available for income (line 3) is taken from line 8 of the capital aanalysis section (discussed previously). The assumed interest rate should be conservative, probably no greater than 5 percent, since it represents the average rate that can be earned on safe investments over a long period of time. Furthermore, the excess earnings resulting from a higher rate will help offset the ravages of inflation. Interest in this example is estimated to be $2,075.

OASDHI and other government sources of income are depicted on line 4. The amount to be inserted can be calculated precisely, but a common practice is to use tables that show maximum benefits. In this example, $9,000 is used.

Table 6-11

Capital Analysis for Mr. B

Line			
1	Total assets		$139,000
2	Liabilities	$ 9,000	
3	Taxes and costs of administration	6,500	
4	Payment of mortgage	40,000	
5	Cost of education	12,000	
6	Nonincome-producing property	30,000	
7	Total deductions		97,500
8	Capital available for income		$ 41,500

Table 6-12

Income Analysis for Mr. B

(1)	Present income	$25,000
(2)	Income objective [60% of (1)]	15,000
	Income presently provided	
(3)	Capital available for income ($41,500 at 5%)	2,075
(4)	Social Security (and other government benefits)	9,000
(5)	Other income	— — —
(6)	Total income provided now	$11,075
(7)	Income shortage	3,925
(8)	Total new capital required	$78,500

Income Objective	
Annual Gross Income	Percentage of Gross Income Required
Less than $20,000	70%
$20,001 — 24,000	65
24,001 — 28,000	60
28,001 — 32,000	55
More than 32,000	50

Table 6-12 shows that $11,075 is available annually from all sources (line 6), which is $3,925 less than desired. This shortfall can be eliminated by purchasing $78,100 of additional insurance. This figure was derived by dividing the income shortage by the assumed interest rate, 5 percent (i.e., $3,925/0.05 = $78,500).

Capital need analysis is simpler and so consequently is easier to understand than the programming concept. Moreover, this approach deals with inflation better than does programming, which simply ignores it. An important assumption of capital need analysis is that the life insurance proceeds will be conserved, and that beneficiaries will use the interest earnings on the proceeds, but will not liquidate the principal. This analysis allows educational funds to accumulate before they are needed, thus providing some protection against increased educational costs. The assumption that capital will be preserved rather than liquidated is an indirect method of offsetting the impact of inflation.

Programming is a more accurate method of calculating life insurance needs when prices are not increasing. However, inflation seems certain to continue over any long period into the future.

Types of Individual Insurance

Traditionally private insurance has been marketed in one of three ways. It has been sold on either an industrial, ordinary, or group basis. This section compares the industrial and ordinary types of life insurance.

Ordinary Life Insurance   Ordinary life is the predominant form of individual life insurance marketed. It is based on the assumption that level premiums will be paid throughout the lifetime of the insured or to age 100. This coverage is normally sold in face amounts such as $5,000, $10,000, $25,000, or $100,000. It is not sold with a face amount of less than $1,000. Normally, an applicant selects the amount of coverage rounded off to the nearest $1,000 desired and then pays the necessary premium directly to the company monthly (automatic check withdrawal is gaining popularity), quarterly, semi-annually, or annually.

The policyholder has a great deal of latitude with respect to this policy. The policy can be assigned by simply notifying the company, and a number of options can be selected at will, e.g., dividend (if the policy is participating), nonforfeiture, or settlement. Other policyholder rights include the right to make the beneficiary designation, selection of a settlement option, the right to borrow the cash value, and the right to add options such as the waiver of premium, disability income, accidental death benefit, or guarantee insurability option. This latitude permits policyholders to tailor ordinary policies to meet their specific needs.

Industrial Life Insurance   Industrial life insurance was developed at the beginning of the twentieth century and was sold primarily to factory workers. Today, "industrial life" is used synonymously with "debit life" and refers to a marketing technique rather than to any particular type of clientele. The distinguishing characteristics of industrial life insurance are as follows.

Face Amount. The average industrial life policy in force has a face amount of $580, and the face amount usually is less than $1,000.[6] However, this is changing since the average size of new policies slightly exceeds $1,000. The NAIC Model Bill for Industrial Life limits any one industrial life policy to $1,000, and the New York insurance law limits the total of all weekly premium industrial life insurance to $1,000 *per person.*

Unit of Sale. Generally, the amount of industrial life sold on the life of an applicant is determined by first asking the applicant to specify the size premium the applicant desires to pay weekly. The policy face is then a function of the premium size selected, the type of policy, and the age and sex of the applicant.

Payment of Premiums. Historically, premiums were collected in person by the agent at the insured's residence or place of employment. Now, most companies reduce the premium rates of policyowners who mail or deliver premiums to a regional or district office.

Types of Life Insurance Policies. The vast majority of industrial life policies are the whole life or endowment type; term insurance is seldom available.

Frequency of Premium Payments. Historically, premiums were collected weekly, but increasing costs have caused companies to move toward bi-weekly and monthly premium collections.

Selection/Underwriting Standards. Generally medical examinations are not required due to the small amounts of insurance involved, but the application does include a relatively simple health questionnaire which must be filled out by the applicant.

Option for Early Surrender. Normally, the policyowner may surrender the policy—usually within two weeks of issue—and receive a full refund of all premiums paid. This cooling-off period permits the insured to change his or her mind without penalty.

Facility of Payment Clause. In the absence of a surviving or locatable beneficiary, this clause permits the insurance company to pay the policy proceeds to anyone equitably entitled to such payment (e.g., the individual who pays for the insured's funeral). This allows the insurance company to discharge its liability without having to contend with a missing beneficiary.

Prohibition of Assignment. Most industrial policies prohibit assignment of the policy to other than banks or trust companies.

Table 6-13

Comparative Life Insurance Costs*

	Industrial	Ordinary	Group
Total in force (in millions)	$39,175	$1,177,672	$1,002,647
Average size policy outstanding	580	8,610	10,010
Average size policy sold in 1976	1,044	6,400	12,600

*Adapted from *Life Insurance Fact Book 1977* (Washington, DC: American Council of Life Insurance, 1977), pp. 7, 13, 15, 22.

Lack of Dividend Options. Each company designates one method for the policyowner to receive divisible surplus. Usually companies prescribe either reduction of premiums or paid-up additions.

Automatic Inclusion of Benefits. Industrial life policies include, without a separate, extra charge, accidental death and dismemberment benefits. Often this added feature continues throughout the entire duration of the policy without regard to the attained age of the life insured.

Lack of Settlement Option. Death benefits are almost always paid in a lump sum since the small amounts involved do not warrant the use of settlement options.

Cost. On a per unit of coverage basis, industrial life insurance costs more than either group or ordinary as a result of the higher expenses and mortality associated with this type of policy. The heavy expense factor results from the collection costs and the need to spread fixed costs per policy over the relatively low face amounts. The extra mortality costs reflect the lack of vigorous selection standards and the higher mortality rates experienced by low income insureds. Due to the low face amounts involved, this type of policy is sold primarily as burial insurance.

At the end of 1976, a comparison of the costs of each type gave the results shown in Table 6-13.

Comparisons of Industrial, Ordinary, and Group Life Insurance Table 6-14 summarizes the major characteristics of each of the insurance techniques for dealing with the premature death exposure.

PRESENT VALUE CALCULATIONS

The underlying assumption of the time value of money concept is that money has a different value depending upon when it is received or paid. Currently held funds are more valuable than funds to be received in the future, since they may be invested at some positive interest rate. In other words, current possession allows the investor to increase the size of his holdings whereas dollars to be received in the future cannot be so invested.

The present value concept is closely associated with the concept of compound interest. By means of a compound interest table, it is possible to calculate what an investment account will accumulate to over specified periods of time at different rates of interest. For example, $100 invested at 5 percent for 5 years will grow to $127.60 (table not provided).

Present Value of $1

The concept of present value has been described as "compound interest in reverse." If we know (or can assume) a future value and can assume a certain interest rate, the appropriate value at present can be determined. For example, assume that $127.60 is payable five years from now, and 5 percent interest can be earned during that time period. How much must be deposited now to accumulate to $127.60? Stated differently, what is the present value of $127.60 five years from now at 5 percent interest?

Present value tables (such as Table 6-15) provide factors for different durations and interest rates and can be used to solve this problem. The amount of $127.60 payable in five years at 5 percent is now worth 0.784 × $127.60, or $100. In other words, the present value of $127.60 payable in five years at 5 percent is $100. A person who has an obligation of $127.60 due in five years could place $100 in a savings account at 5 percent and the $100 would grow to $127.60.

The fundamental unit used in Table 6-15 is $1. The present value of some other amount is determined by multiplying the future amount by the appropriate number found in Table 6-15. To illustrate, the present value of $5,000 payable in ten years at 6 percent interest is 0.558 × $5,000, or $2,790.

Present Value of an Annuity of $1

If there is more than one equal future value, that is, a *series* or *stream* of equal future values, then Table 6-15 is awkward to use. A compound interest table that shows values for compounding deposits made *each period* would be needed. This type of table is not provided in this text because this chapter is not concerned with this type of problem.

Table 6-14

Principal Comparative Characteristics of Industrial, Ordinary, and Group Life Insurance

Characteristic	Industrial	Ordinary	Group
Face amount	Average $500 Historically less than $1,000 but trend is toward face amounts in excess of $1,000	At least $1,000 Average $7,690 No maximum	At least $500 per life Average $8,840 Typically less than $50,000 per life Automatic determination of benefit amount
Frequency of premiums	Weekly, bi-weekly, or monthly	Monthly, quarterly, semi-annually, and annually May be single premium	Usually monthly One premium to insurer on behalf of all participants in the group
Method of premium collection	By debit agent at insured's residence or place of employment	Agent collects first premium only; subsequent premiums paid directly to insurer	Premiums paid directly to insurer

Forms of life insurance	Typically limited-payment life or endowment	All forms available	Typically yearly renewable term
Selection/underwriting standards	Typically simple nonmedical issue	Individual selection—may be with medical examination or nonmedical issue	Select/underwrite the group, not individual participants; Actively-at-work and other requirements
Facility-of-payment clause	Available for entire amount of proceeds	Inapplicable	Available for up to $500 of amount of proceeds
Assignability	Typically prohibited	Assignable	Assignable
Other benefits	Automatic inclusion of accidental death and dismemberment	Available at extra rate (some include waiver of premium automatically)	Available at extra rate
Settlement options	Rarely available	Available	Usually available if policy face large enough to warrant
Dividends (rate credits)	No policyowner option	All options to policyowner	Paid to insured, not certificate holder
Unit insurance cost	Highest (because of collection expense and mortality)	Average	Lowest (because of expense saving)

Table 6-15

Present Value of $1

Period	3%	5%	6%	8%	10%	12%
1	0.971	0.952	0.943	0.926	0.909	0.893
2	0.943	0.907	0.890	0.857	0.826	0.797
3	0.915	0.864	0.840	0.794	0.751	0.712
4	0.889	0.823	0.792	0.735	0.683	0.636
5	0.863	0.784	0.747	0.681	0.621	0.567
6	0.838	0.746	0.705	0.630	0.564	0.507
7	0.813	0.711	0.665	0.583	0.513	0.452
8	0.789	0.677	0.627	0.540	0.467	0.404
9	0.766	0.645	0.592	0.500	0.424	0.361
10	0.744	0.614	0.558	0.463	0.386	0.322
15	0.642	0.481	0.417	0.315	0.239	0.183
20	0.554	0.377	0.312	0.215	0.149	0.104
25	0.478	0.295	0.233	0.146	0.092	0.059
30	0.412	0.231	0.174	0.099	0.057	0.033
35	0.355	0.181	0.130	0.068	0.036	0.019
40	0.307	0.142	0.097	0.046	0.022	0.011

However, it is concerned with finding the present value of a stream of equal future payments. Table 6-2 (referred to earlier in the chapter) can be used for this purpose. It is labeled as the "Present Value of an Annuity of $1," and the word "annuity" denotes a stream or series of equal payments. This table shows present values for a series of equal payments at various interest rates and various durations. For example, the present value of $100 paid (or received) *each year* for ten years at 5 percent is 7.722 × $100, or $772.20. Likewise, the present value of $4,000 each year for twenty years at 6 percent is 11.470 × $4,000, or $45,880. A person could deposit $45,880 in a savings account and if the account earned 6 percent each year, $4,000 could be paid each year for twenty years before all funds would be exhausted.

Chapter Notes

1. A conservative interest rate assumption results in a larger present value *if* in fact the rate is conservative. Such an overstatement of present value is preferable to an understatement, particularly in view of the impact of inflation. Of course if the average annual salary is adjusted for inflation, the interest rate assumption need not be as conservative.
2. Many plans provide that the amount of insurance on an employee will not be adjusted downward.
3. The cost of group credit life insurance is not borne by the sponsoring organization. In fact, dividends on group credit insurance have provided a source of profits for many lending organizations that provide this coverage. Although the rates for group credit life insurance are now subject to strict regulation in most states, the cost for this type of life insurance may be relatively high.
4. Actually, these expenses should be attributed to the disability peril and covered by health insurance. As a practical matter, however, it is often easier to treat them as a death expense.
5. There is no clear distinction between life insurance programming and estate planning, but the latter term usually is used for more complicated, sophisticated cases—for example, when taxes or business interests are major considerations.
6. *Life Insurance Fact Book*, Washington, D.C.: American Council of Life Insurance, 1977, p. 22.

CHAPTER 7

Types of Individual Life Insurance Policies

INTRODUCTION

Despite the apparent complexity in the types of life insurance policies available, there are only three basic types of life insurance plans: (1) term, (2) whole life, and (3) endowment contracts.[1] Two reasons explain why there are so many apparently different policies in the market. First, life insurance companies often use their own names for the policies they issue. A specific policy, for example, might be called an "Executive Accumulator" by one company and something else by another company. Second, many contracts are combinations of more than one of the basic plans, and may on the surface seem to be different policies altogether.

TERM INSURANCE

Basic Characteristics

Term insurance provides financial protection for a limited period of time only. If the insured dies during that period, the face amount of the policy is paid to the insured's beneficiary. If, on the other hand, the insured survives the policy period, the policy expires and the obligations of the insurance company terminate.

This characteristic of term insurance makes it the simplest form of life insurance coverage and the type most comparable to property and liability policies. If a building is insured against loss by fire, for example, and does not suffer any damage during the policy period, the obligation of the insurer ceases, and the premium is fully earned by the insurance company. Although the insured has received no financial indemnity from the insurer, the policyowner received value by having insurance protection during the policy period. The same is true with regard to term life insurance, since the insurance company is liable for the face amount only if the insured dies during the policy period.

Types of Term Insurance Policies

Term insurance policies can be classified according to (1) the length of the policy period, (2) special features in the contract, and (3) whether or not the face amount remains level.

Policy Duration Most term policies provide protection for a specified duration (usually five, ten, fifteen, twenty years, or to some specified age such as sixty-five or seventy).[2] Consequently, term insurance often is referred to as "temporary" protection.

Premiums for term policies are level during the policy period. For example, an individual who purchases a five-year term insurance policy would pay the same premium each year for five years. Annual premiums vary directly with the duration of the contract, since the policies with longer durations provide protection at older ages when mortality rates are higher. For any given age, the premium for term insurance is lower than the premium for any other plan of insurance, since term policies generally do not accumulate a cash value to provide protection at the advanced ages when mortality rates are increasing rapidly.

Special Features

Renewability. A feature commonly found in term insurance policies (especially those of shorter durations) is a provision that gives the insured the option to renew the contract without proof of insurability. Without this option, an unhealthy insured could be without insurance after the policy has expired and would be unable to purchase new coverage. In effect, this provision permits continuation of the coverage at the option of the policyowner, rather than at the option of the company.

Every time a term policy is renewed, the premium increases accordingly, to reflect the current age of the insured. The original contract stipulates this guaranteed scale of renewal rates. Figure 7-1 illustrates how premiums increase for a person who continues to exercise the renewal option.

Increases in the premium are slight at the younger ages, but as a

Figure 7-1

Annual Premiums for a
Five-Year Renewable Term Policy

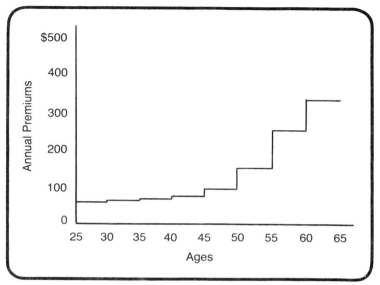

person grows older they become larger to reflect the higher mortality rates at advanced ages.

Obviously, the renewal privilege is a valuable option for those insureds who become uninsurable, but it is also beneficial to insurable policyowners. It is normally more convenient for a policyowner to renew an existing term policy than it is to purchase a new one. Written notice to the company is all that is required to exercise the renewal option. Another advantage of renewal for insurable policyowners is that the suicide and incontestable clauses (described in the following chapter) are not operative in a renewed policy as they are in a newly purchased contract.

Insurance companies, however, face a serious problem with renewable policies. Policyowners who believe they are in good health become increasingly reluctant to pay the higher premiums required upon renewal, and some allow their coverages to expire. At the same time, insureds who believe they are in poor health generally renew their policies, and as a result, the mortality experience of those remaining in the plan becomes increasingly unfavorable. This is known as *adverse mortality selection*, which can be defined as policyowners' decisions that tend to serve their own interests to the detriment of the company. Insurance companies provide extra margins in the premium rates to offset this tendency. Furthermore, insurers place limitations on the policyowner's right to renew the contract. For example, a ten-year renewable term policy issued at age thirty-five might be renewable twice—at ages forty-five and fifty-five—or the contract might stipulate a maximum age beyond which the contract cannot be renewed. This age is usually sixty or sixty-five but may be even higher.

Convertibility. A convertible term policy is one that allows a policyowner to exchange the term policy for another form of insurance (other than term) without providing evidence of insurability. The basic function of the renewal feature and the conversion provision is the same (that is, protecting the insured's insurability), but frequently both features are contained in the policy. The conversion feature is a more effective method of protecting insurability, since it gives the policyowner access to an insurance plan that can be continued for life. In other words, a policyowner can obtain "permanent" insurance through conversion, but with the renewal option, the policyowner can only extend coverage for a specified period.

A policyowner is not required to wait until the end of the policy period to exercise the conversion privilege. In fact, many convertible term policies stipulate that the option can only be exercised a certain amount of time prior to the expiration of the coverage. For example, a five-year policy may be convertible only during the first four policy years, or a fifteen-year plan may be convertible only during the first twelve policy years. Restrictions of this type minimize adverse mortality selection. The effectiveness of these restrictions, however, is questionable, and many companies use conversion provisions that permit conversion at any time during the policy period.

In most term policies a policyowner may use either the *attained age method* or the *original age method* of conversion. The simpler and more common method is to convert on an attained age basis. With this approach, the premium rate and policy form of the new contract are the same as those being used by the company on the conversion date. This is similar to terminating the old policy and purchasing a new one, the important difference being that (1) evidence of insurability is not required, (2) the suicide and incontestable provisions usually do not apply to the new policy, and (3) the policyowner may benefit from a conversion credit. If a conversion credit is available (not all companies follow this practice), it is usually based on the policy reserve and is available to the policyowner only as a credit toward conversion; i.e., it cannot be taken in cash.

Some companies use policy provisions that allow conversion only on the attained age basis. Many of these companies, however, permit original age conversion when it is requested, as a matter of company practice rather than contractual right.

With the original age method of conversion, the new policy premium is the same as would have been paid had the policyowner purchased the new policy initially. The advantage to the policyowner is that future premiums will be lower than they would be with an attained age conversion. Depending upon the terms of the conversion privilege, the policyowner may receive the same policy form as provided by the company at the insured's original age, or the new policy may be exactly the same as those currently being issued (at the insured's attained age).

An original age conversion necessitates an adjustment in order to place the insurance company in the same financial position it would have been had the policyowner initially purchased the new (higher premium) policy. The original term contract stipulates how the lump sum payment must be computed. Usually, it equals the difference in reserves or cash values between the two policies, or the difference in premiums, with interest at 5 or 6 percent.

Original age conversion may be attractive to policyowners because of the lower premium and the belief that the lump sum payment to the insurance company is invested and credited with retroactive interest. Actually, the financial adjustment is designed to place both parties in the financial position that would have resulted if the new policy had been purchased initially. Consequently, there is no substantial financial advantage to the policyowner with original age conversion.

The primary factors to be considered when choosing between an original age and attained age conversion are the insured's health and preference with regard to spreading the insurance cost. A healthy person with the financial resources to pay the required adjustment and who prefers lower future premiums might logically choose an original age conversion. If these conditions are generally not met, the preferable choice would be an attained age conversion. For example, an insurable person with a health impairment which might result ultimately in his or her becoming uninsurable should purchase additional insurance with the funds that otherwise would be used to adjust for the original age conversion. If the person is uninsurable, it makes little sense to make the lump sum payment to the insurance company for original age conversion, because the death benefits would be no greater than they would be by converting with the attained age approach.

Some life insurers issue nonrenewable term policies that are automatically converted at some specified date. The policyowner may choose to convert before the automatic date, but if no such decision is made, the policy automatically converts to a predetermined form. These plans are designed to encourage the purchase of insurance other than term and to minimize the problems of adverse selection. The effectiveness of this approach is questionable because healthy insureds may simply choose to terminate the coverage when the policy automatically converts to a higher premium contract.

Nonlevel Term Insurance The face amount of insurance in a term policy is not necessarily the same throughout the policy period. Many term policies have a level face amount, but decreasing term insurance (either as a rider to a basic policy or as a separate contract) is very common, and increasing term insurance sometimes is issued.

The face amount of a decreasing term policy (or rider) declines yearly or monthly according to a stipulated schedule. The premium usually remains level but in some cases is not payable for the full policy period. For example, a twenty-year decreasing term policy might require premium payments for only the first seventeen years. Premiums are calculated in this manner to avoid paying a relatively large premium for a small amount of protection in the last years of the policy.

Due to the possibility of adverse mortality selection, the conversion feature in a decreasing term policy never allows a policyowner to convert (without evidence of insurability) for the original amount of the decreasing term coverage. Instead, conversion of the amount of insurance that is effective at the time of the conversion is permitted. In some policies the insured may convert only a certain percentage, such as 75 percent, of the amount of insurance in force.

Life insurers seldom issue increasing term policies as a separate contract because of adverse mortality selection. Unhealthy individuals naturally prefer policies such as increasing term insurance that provide the maximum amount of protection for the lowest possible cash outlay. This type of protection is issued as a rider to other types of policies.

Evaluation of Term Insurance

A thorough evaluation of term insurance necessarily involves careful analysis and comparison with other forms of coverage. This type of treatment would be premature at this point, but it may be helpful to examine some of the basic uses and limitations of term insurance.[3]

Uses of Term Insurance Because term insurance generally does not provide protection beyond age sixty-five when mortality rates are high, it has the lowest premium of any form of individual life insurance. The specific uses of term insurance flow from this basic characteristic.

Substantial Insurance Needs and Limited Resources. A person who needs a large amount of life insurance but who can afford only relatively small premiums should consider purchasing term insurance. For example, consider a married couple who are struggling financially in order for the husband to complete his education. In the face of a limited budget a husband who needs a large amount of protection should purchase term insurance so that his insurance protection will most closely approximate the coverage needed.

Secure Outstanding Loans or Investments. Many lenders, where permitted by law, require a term insurance policy as a prerequisite for the loan. If insurance is required, the lender will insist that the proceeds be made payable to him or her. Even in states where life insurance cannot be required to protect a loan, a life insurance policy still may be used for this purpose. The insurance may make the transaction acceptable to the lender, and therefore provide funds to a borrower that otherwise would not be available.

Term insurance is normally appropriate to secure a loan because of its low premium and because the policy period can be made to coincide exactly with the duration of the loan. If the loan is repaid in installments, a decreasing term policy may be appropriate to reflect the decreasing obligation of the borrower.

At times, an individual may use term insurance to protect his or her investments. For example, a person may switch a substantial amount of money from an insured savings account into a new business. If death occurs while the funds are in the savings account, the heirs of the investor probably would have little or no trouble in obtaining the savings. On the other hand, if death occurs after the savings have been placed in a new business, the heirs might easily lose all or a substantial portion of the funds. Term insurance could protect against this possibility until the business becomes well established.

Protect Insurability. The need for guaranteed access to life insurance (discussed in the previous chapter) can be met by purchasing term insurance that is renewable and convertible. Other methods of meeting this need are available, but term insurance involves the lowest premium outlay.[4]

Renewable and convertible term insurance is an excellent method of protecting a child's insurability. The low premium makes term insurance for children especially attractive.

Dependency Period Income. Term insurance on the life of a father is often used to meet this need for income during the limited dependency period. For example, suppose a family has children aged fifteen, twelve, and six. The father or mother might purchase a fifteen-year decreasing term policy (to expire when the youngest child will be twenty-one). Perhaps a preferable approach would be to purchase a twenty- or twenty-five-year decreasing term policy at the birth of each child. Some common "package" life insurance policies (described later in this chapter), recognizing the importance of the need for dependency period income, include decreasing term protection as an integral part of the contract.

Limitations of Term Insurance Life insurance policies can have "advantages" or "disadvantages" only in reference to how well they meet an individual's needs. In other words, it is the *use* of various policies that can be criticized—not the policies themselves. This point may belabor the obvious, but it is well to keep this in mind because: (1) financial advisers have a strong responsibility for the selection of the appropriate type of policy for their clients, and (2) some arguments against term insurance are irrational if they attack the type of policy itself.

Lack of Cash or Loan Values. Term insurance usually contains no cash or loan value. Therefore, it cannot provide funds to the policyowner (except indirectly by enhancing credit) either while the policy is in force or at its expiration. This may lead some to complain that they pay premiums over a long period of time and "receive nothing in return." However, many of the same individuals would not consider their fire insurance premiums or automobile insurance premiums wasted if they failed to collect from their insurance company. Obviously, a policyowner receives value for term insurance premiums through protection obtained. The reason the argument exists is that many people realize that some types of life insurance have a cash value and conclude that all forms of life insurance should do the same.

Every person who purchases a term insurance policy should realize that the contract normally provides no cash value. Therefore, term insurance should be purchased only to provide death protection.

Limited Period of Protection. A person's needs for life insurance change almost constantly. It is sometimes difficult, therefore, to predict exactly what kind of protection will be required for a specific need. As a result, an individual might purchase term insurance, and find his need for life insurance protection extends beyond the duration of the policy. In an effort to prevent this, many advisers recommend renewable and convertible term in all cases when term insurance is used. Even with this approach, or with long-term policies, coverage will normally expire at age sixty-five.

Increasing Premium. One of the main attractions of term insurance is its low premium. The shorter the policy period, the stronger is this attraction. For example, the premium is lower for a ten-year term than for a twenty-year term, and even lower for a five-year policy. However, the premium will increase each time the policy is renewed.

At the younger ages the increase in the premium upon renewal is slight. With each renewal, however, the premium increases, and at the older ages the increase in the premium becomes substantial. Some policyowners, particularly those in good health, are likely to regard the increased premium as prohibitive at some point and let their protection expire. It is important that the insurance adviser inform each policyowner that the premium increases after each term and may become very expensive at the older ages.

WHOLE LIFE INSURANCE

Early Insurance Plans

Life insurance ideas and methods can be traced back many centuries, but a satisfactory technique for providing "permanent" life insurance has been used only in comparatively recent times. The earliest policies were term—usually for short durations and without the renewal privilege. Until reliable mortality data were developed, the premiums for term policies were crude estimates, at best, and policies were issued only at the younger ages. Obviously, these policies did not provide very strong financial security. Even today, with refined mortality statistics and greater longevity, term policies are not used to provide life insurance protection at the advanced ages.

Associations and fraternal societies were among the first to provide life-long insurance protection. Many of these organizations, which were formed as early as the late 1800s, issued policies that were based, at least initially, on the *assessment technique*. The simplest assessment plans charged each member of the group a flat amount, irrespective of age, in order to pay death benefits. The assessment was levied either when a death occurred or periodically, usually once each year. The basic idea was to bring into the membership a continual flow of new, young members; and by keeping the same average age, it was believed that the total death rate would not increase.

In property and liability insurance many small mutual insurers (as well as some other types of companies) issue assessable policies. These plans have advantages and disadvantages, but there is no theoretical reason why they are necessarily unsound. Assessment *life* insurance, however, is inherently unsound, and it is important to understand exactly why this is so.

Maintaining a constant average age in an assessment plan is very difficult for an organization. Consider this simplified example: Suppose the first year the group is composed of 100 members who are each thirty years of age. Clearly, the average age is thirty. If none of the members dies, the group would have to add ten members aged twenty in the second year of operation to maintain an average age of thirty, because the original members would each become thirty-one. If there are no deaths in the third year, the organization would need eleven new members aged twenty in order to keep the average age the same. Each year the organization would need a larger number of new, young members just to keep the average age from increasing. Of course, it is unrealistic to continue to assume that there are no deaths. But even with normal mortality experience, it would still be extremely difficult as a practical matter to maintain a constant average for the group. This phenomenon explains why assessment life insurance organizations could operate reasonably well in the beginning years, but usually had increasing difficulties as the plan matured.

Another deficiency in assessment plans is more important. In property and liability insurance the probability of loss to a building does not necessarily increase each year. In life insurance, however, the death rate (which is a measure of the probability of loss) increases at an increasing rate each year. Thus, the total death rate for a group will increase even if the average age is held stable. For example, the 1958 C.S.O. Mortality Table shows the following death rates:

Age	Death per 1,000
30	2.13
40	3.53
50	8.32

If a group were composed entirely of members forty years of age, the death rate would be 3.53 and the average age forty. Suppose that years later the membership had changed so that one-half of the group was thirty years of age and the other one-half of the group was fifty years of age. The average would be unchanged (it is still forty), but the average death rate would be 2.13 + 8.32/2, or 5.22. Thus, the average death rate would have increased because the mortality rate increases more rapidly from ages forty to fifty than from ages thirty to forty.

When the deficiencies of assessment life insurance plans became evident, modifications of the assessment technique were introduced. Some plans called for increasing assessments for each member based on attained age. In other words, the premium (assessment) would increase each year. From a conceptual standpoint, this approach is reasonable. But as a practical matter, increasing assessments proved to be impractical. Such a plan is workable at the younger ages, but the cost becomes prohibitive as a member ages. To be more precise, the annual cost appeared to be excessive for healthy members, and as they withdrew from the plan, the average mortality rate for the remaining members increased. From the organization's point of view, the adverse mortality selection proved to be unmanageable.

Because of the difficulties described above, assessment life insur-

Table 7-1

Death Rates at Selected Ages

Age	Deaths[†]	Age	Deaths[†]
25	1.93	65	31.75
35	2.51	75	73.37
45	5.35	85	161.14
55	13.00	95	351.24

[†] Per 1,000.

ance plans have virtually disappeared. The plans that operated on the assessment technique have either collapsed or have changed their methods of operation to conform to the level premium technique and other more modern principles.

The Level Premium Technique

Basic Concept Although simple in concept, the *level premium technique* provides a theoretically sound basis for life insurance protection over a long period. A level premium insurance plan is based on the assumption that annual premiums will not increase during the premium-paying period. The premium-paying period may or may not be as long as the protection is provided.

The 1958 C.S.O. Mortality Table shows the death rates at selected ages as in Table 7-1.

Life insurance premiums are based on mortality, interest, and expense assumptions. However, the above figures can be used to compute "pure" premiums that do not reflect interest or expenses. Imagine a company that issues a $1,000, one-year policy to each of 10,000 individuals, all of whom are twenty-five years of age. Disregarding interest (that could be earned by the company if premiums are collected before death claims are paid) and all expenses of operating the company, how many premium dollars would be needed? The insurer could expect 19.3 deaths, and with $1,000 paid in each case, the amount needed would be $19,300. To build a fund of this amount from 10,000 policyholders, the contribution from each would be $1.93, i.e., ($19,300 ÷ 10,000).

Life insurance costs have a natural tendency to increase with age because of the structure of mortality rates. However, with policies that provide protection over a long period, it is possible to restructure the pattern of annual payments so that they do not increase each year. In fact, if the premiums are calculated in such a manner that they are more than adequate in the early policy years, but remain level, the "overcharge" in the beginning can pay for the high mortality rates at the advanced ages. In other words, a level premium (which, in a sense, is a type of "average" premium) can be substituted for a premium that has a strong natural tendency to increase. Figure 7-2 illustrates this concept.

The solid line in Figure 7-2 represents the net annual level premium that is the mathematical equivalent of a series of annually increasing premiums. The net level premium is not simply the average of each of the annual yearly renewable term premiums. Rather, it is a uniform amount calculated to recognize (1) mortality losses (some insureds will not survive to pay all of the premiums—the yearly renewable term (YRT) premium is adjusted upward each year to reflect that fact), and (2) that interest earnings can be realized on the amount accumulated from the excess of the net level premium over the YRT premium during the early years of the "Term to 65" policy. Furthermore, in actual practice, a life insurance company would charge something more than the net level premium in order to cover its operating expenses and to contribute to the surplus of the organization.

Figure 7-2 is actually an illustration of a policy issued at age thirty-five and providing protection for thirty years. This age and policy duration were selected arbitrarily—other figures could have been used to depict the concept. For a policy issued at an earlier or later age, for example, the level premium would still be "excessive" in the early policy years and "inadequate" later. Only the age figures on the horizontal axis would be different.

It should be emphasized that there is absolutely nothing unfair, illegal, or unethical about the "overcharge" in the early policy years. The word "overcharge" is commonly used to explain that the level premium in the early policy years is more than is needed to pay for *current* mortality costs. The same level premium is inadequate to pay for mortality costs that will be incurred later.

In effect, the level premium system is nothing more than a method of keeping the annual premium within reasonable bounds for policyowners when protection is provided over a long period of time.

Significance of the Level Premium Technique The level premium technique has an important effect on the structure of an individual life insurance policy. The "overcharge" in the early policy years must be accounted for in an individual contract by accumulation of values within the policy. Figure 7-3 shows this effect.

The investment element in a policy is a direct result of the level premium technique. Because of the "overcharge," a policy accumulates cash values that may be taken by the policyowner. In other words, the

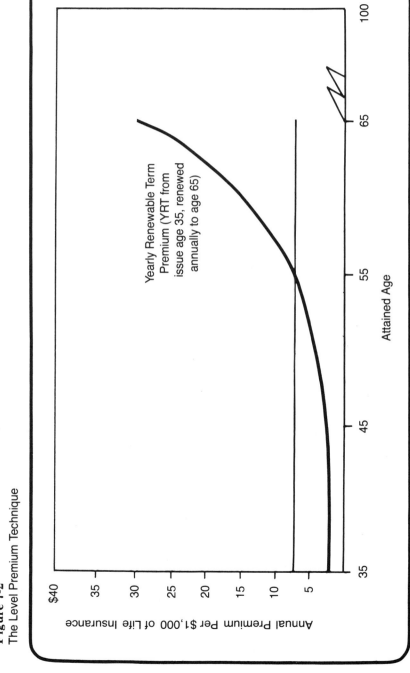

Figure 7-2
The Level Premium Technique

Figure 7-3

Composition of a Whole Life Policy Based
on the Level Premium Technique

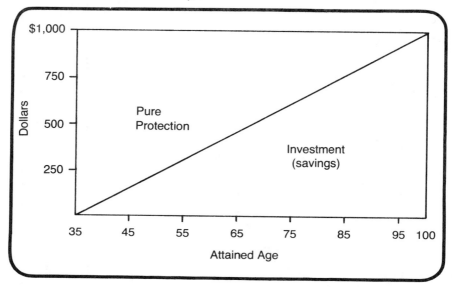

level premium technique causes an "overcharge" which generates an investment element. Policies without completely level premiums may have policy values, as long as premiums in the early years are more than sufficient to pay expected claims. Thus, any policy with a substantial "overcharge" will generate cash values. The level premium is discussed here because it is the most common and simplest method of providing an "overcharge."

Whenever premiums are leveled over a period in which mortality rages are increasing substantially, an "overcharge" necessarily results. Technically, there is an "overcharge" even in term policies of short duration at the younger ages. The amount of the "overcharge," however, in these policies is slight because the policy period is short and the mortality curve is not increasing rapidly. The investment element, therefore, is insignificant; consequently, most term policies have no cash value.

Since the face amount of a policy remains level, and the cash value builds up within a policy using the level premium technique, the amount of pure protection necessarily decreases. Thus, many individuals view a policy as a combination of decreasing amounts of insurance (pure protection) and an increasing investment.

A controversy has developed in recent years about the use of policy values, and about the true nature of level premium life insurance.

Basically, some individuals argue that a policy is not a combination of protection and investment. They argue that the elements are inextricably intertwined and should not be separated. The Institute of Life Insurance, for example, in a recent publication stated:

> [A level premium policy] . . . is a contract of protection—an arrangement by which the insured person, upon regular payment of a level premium, is guaranteed that upon his or her death the beneficiary will receive a stable amount.
> While the central purpose of the contract is insurance protection, the contract also provides auxiliary rights which are available to the policyholder during his or her lifetime if he or she does not wish to continue the original arrangement. These stem from the level-premium plan, the effect of which is to collect from the policyholder more than the cost of the pure risk in the early years to permit accumulation of a reserve against the rising risk of the later years, when the level premium alone would be insufficient.[5]

Whether a life insurance policy is actually composed of protection and savings elements or not is not vitally important for our purposes. It is not inappropriate for an individual policyowner (who has a legal right to a mathematically predetermined and guaranteed value) to regard the policy as consisting of decreasing pure protection and increasing investment as long as the contractual provisions are analyzed correctly. However, individuals in the life insurance industry frequently refer to such policy values as the reserve, the cash value, the nonforfeiture value, or the policy loan value. When these terms are used interchangeably, distortion results.

Policy Reserves. The level premium system assumes that the premiums collected in the early policy years will be more than sufficient to pay claims during this period. This "excessive" amount is invested by the company, accumulated with interest, and later used to pay claims when the premiums being collected are themselves insufficient to pay death claims. This process may generate a tremendous volume of assets and income for the insurance company. Still, without legal safeguards, there is a possibility that the insurance company would not have adequate funds to meet its obligations. The primary purpose of the policy reserve is to assure that adequate funds will be available. A reserve, however, is neither an asset nor a fund and is not used to pay claims. A policy reserve is a *liability* of the insurance company that is established and computed to recognize that the level premium system generates assets for which the company is responsible. The reserve protects the policyowner because the insurance company is required to have assets exceeding the total of all policy reserves. If total assets declined to a point where they barely covered policy reserves, state regulatory authorities might declare the company *insolvent*.[6] In such a case, the assets of the company should be sufficient to meet policy obligations, even without premium payments from a new group of policyowners.

As a practical matter, the level premium technique creates huge reserve liabilities for insurance companies, but it also generates substantial assets and income. When life insurance companies collect premiums from many policyowners years before the funds will be needed to pay death claims, the assets of the company have a strong tendency to grow rapidly. In fact, the level premium technique is the primary reason why the life insurance industry has achieved its present size.

As previously described, the reserve is a liability which must be offset by assets. The amount of the assets, together with future premiums and interest earnings, must be sufficient to meet all future claims. More accurately, the policy reserve can be defined by the following formula:

$$\text{Reserve} = \begin{array}{c}\text{(Present value of}\\ \text{future death claims)}\end{array} - \begin{array}{c}\text{(Present value of}\\ \text{future net premiums)}\end{array}$$

To compute the reserve, certain assumptions regarding mortality and interest are required. The insurance laws of all states spell out minimum requirements for the computation of policy reserves specifying the mortality table and interest rate assumptions that may be used. Companies are allowed to use mortality and interest assumptions that produce higher reserves than the legal standard would indicate, but they cannot report lower reserves in their annual statement.

With the use of a mortality table, one can predict the expected number of deaths that will occur each year. And with a specified rate of interest, the present value of future death claims may be determined. This is an estimate of the amount of money needed, at present, to pay the death claims that will occur in the future. The second element in the reserve formula is an estimate of the amount of future premiums that will be collected, but discounted to their present value. Notice that the assumption is that only *net* premiums will be collected. That is, it is assumed that the loading in the premium will *not* be available to pay death claims. This tends to make the reserve calculation conservative (i.e., makes liabilities higher) because, in practice, after the early policy years the full expense loading in the premium usually is not needed to pay expenses. This is because most expenses associated with a policy are incurred in the early policy years. Reserves are also conservative because the interest and mortality assumptions used are generally not realistic.

The reserve formula should clarify the primary function of the policy reserve. For example, if a company (using legally allowable assumptions for mortality and interest) expects future claims to have a present value of $10 million but the present value of expected net premiums is only $9 million, the company's potential obligations for death claims is greater than the potential net premium income. Therefore, in this situation the company would be required to show a liability (the reserve) for $1 million. By carrying assets (developed from previous net premiums collected), in an amount greater than the reserve, the company indicates that it has the financial strength to meet its long-term obligations.

Confusion about the true nature of life insurance reserves often results from a misunderstanding of the interest assumption. Many states have laws that require insurance companies to specify in the policy the interest rate assumed in the calculation of the reserve. Often the rate specified is 2.5 or 3 percent. This leads unscrupulous or poorly informed life insurance advisers to tell policyowners that they are "earning only 2.5 or 3 percent on their policy reserve." This argument may convince an individual to terminate an existing policy in order to purchase another. First, interest is not earned on the *reserve;* it is impossible for a policyowner to earn any interest on an insurance company's liability. Furthermore, a higher interest assumption in the reserve calculation would produce a *lower* reserve, which provides less security for a policyowner. Perhaps the simplest explanation of this apparent anomaly is that the policy reserve must accumulate to the face amount of the policy at the maturity of the contract. At any time, therefore, the reserve must be larger if it is to accumulate at a lower rate of interest. If a higher rate is assumed, a smaller reserve is established. It is for this reason that state insurance laws specify the *maximum* rate of interest that may be assumed in reserve calculations.

Nonforfeiture Values. When life insurance policies were first issued on a long-term, level-premium basis, policyowners who terminated their coverage did not receive any compensation from the company. Standard nonforfeiture laws are now in effect in all states. In essence, these laws require policies that develop a significant "investment element" to provide some type of value to a policyowner who terminates his or her contract. The word "nonforfeiture" arises from the fact that a terminating policyowner cannot be deprived of the value. If a terminating policyowner fails to select one of the methods of taking the nonforfeiture value, the policy must specify the method that will become effective automatically. As a result, policyowners today always receive a guaranteed value (in one form or another) when they terminate their coverage after paying level premiums over a period of time. Insurers are required to establish nonforfeiture values whenever premiums have been paid for at least three years.

Policy Loan Values. Another policy value that arises from the level premium technique is the policy loan value. The insurance laws of all states require a policy loan provision in any policy that is legally required to generate a nonforfeiture value.

The policy loan provision will be examined in detail in the following chapter, but for immediate purposes it is important to recognize the true nature of a life insurance policy loan.

The loan value of a contract is only indirectly related to the policy reserve, but it is closely tied to the nonforfeiture value. More accurately, the policy loan value is based on the *cash value*, which is the amount of cash that can be obtained if the policy is surrendered. A typical policy loan provision states that a policyowner may require the insurer to advance an amount that, with interest to the next premium due date, does not exceed the guaranteed cash value at that date. Thus, except for the accrual of interest, a policyowner can regard the cash value and loan value as equivalent.

Legally, a policy loan is not a loan at all, but an advance of a portion of the policy proceeds. The primary significance of this distinction is that an insurer must make the value available upon request of the policyowner (subject to the conditions in the contract) but the policyowner is under no obligation to repay the loan. Furthermore, there is no obligation to repay interest on a policy loan. If the loan is not repaid, the amount of the loan plus any interest due will be deducted from the death proceeds.

From a policyowner's view, the loan value of a policy is an asset in every sense of the word because it is available—in a guaranteed amount—at any time it is requested (subject to the "delay clause" which is described in the following chapter). It is erroneous, however, to argue that a policyowner should not pay interest because he or she is "borrowing his or her own money." An insurance company continues to credit interest on policy values even after a policy loan is obtained. Obviously, this cannot be done unless the company charges interest on the loan.

A policy loan is also a genuine insurance company asset. The company can invest its funds in bonds, real estate, or some other asset, or it can provide them to a policyowner by means of a policy loan. As a policy loan, the company has a perfectly secure investment (which will either be repaid by the policyowner or deducted from the death proceeds) and an interest earning asset.

Types of Whole Life Policies

The protection afforded by whole life insurance, unlike that of term and endowment policies, is permanent. That is, it provides protection as long as the individual lives. Stated differently, the premiums and policy values for a whole life contract assume that the policy will be in force for a person's entire life, but the policyowner always has the option to discontinue or modify the protection.

There are two major types of whole life insurance: (1) straight life contracts, and (2) limited payment policies.

Straight Life Policies In the previous chapter the term "ordinary life" was used to separate three major branches of life insurance— ordinary, group, and industrial. Many individuals, in practice, also use the term "ordinary life" interchangeably with "straight life." To avoid this confusion, "ordinary life" is used in this text to refer to a broad category of life insurance policies, including whole' life, and "straight life" is used as one of the basic types of whole life insurance.

Straight life policies provide permanent protection, and the premiums and policy values are based on the assumption that premiums will be paid periodically as long as the insured is alive. Figure 7-4 illustrates a straight life policy issued at age thirty-five.

Notice in Figure 7-4 that the highest attained age shown is age 100. The mortality tables used by most insurance companies for life insurance purposes assume that all insureds die before reaching that age. In the rare cases in which a person lives to celebrate a 100th birthday, the insurance company pays the face amount to the policyowner.

Limited Payment Policies Limited payment life insurance provides permanent protection, but the premiums are paid only for a limited number of years. Terminology again is sometimes confusing because some limited payment policies are described by the number of years premiums will be paid, while others are described by the age to which premiums are payable. For example, at age forty-five, a twenty-payment life policy is identical to a "life paid up at sixty-five."[7]

Limited payment policies may require premiums for other durations, but premium periods of ten, twenty, twenty-five, and thirty years are most common. Of course, the longer the premium period, the more closely the contract resembles the straight life approach.

As illustrated in Figure 7-5, a limited payment policy generates cash values faster than a straight life contract. The reason is simple: both a straight life policy and a limited payment contract provide the same death benefit. Since the limited payment policy requires the same

Figure 7-4
Illustration of a Straight Life Policy

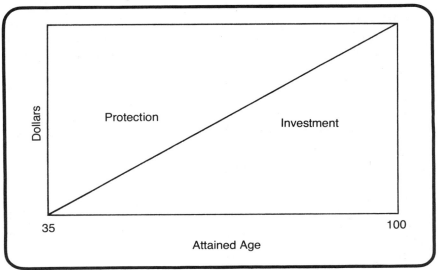

benefit to be purchased by fewer premiums, it follows that each premium must be higher. Higher premiums, of course, imply that the "overcharge" in the level premium system will be greater, and as a result, nonforfeiture values will be greater in the limited payment contract.

A single premium life insurance policy is nothing more than an extreme form of limited payment. Naturally, the premium is relatively large, and an immediate nonforfeiture value is created. Few of these contracts are sold; when they are issued, the primary appeal is for investment purposes.

Evaluation of Whole Life Insurance

Uses of Whole Life Insurance Because whole life insurance provides permanent protection, it can be used to meet life insurance needs that are likely to continue throughout life. The most common example is the need for a last illness and funeral expense fund. Whole life insurance also is used to meet many estate planning needs (which are discussed in a subsequent chapter). On this basis, it can be argued that almost everyone should have some amount of whole life insurance.

Many individuals believe that whole life insurance offers a desirable combination of protection and investment. In a sense, whole life

Figure 7-5
Illustration of a Limited Payment Policy

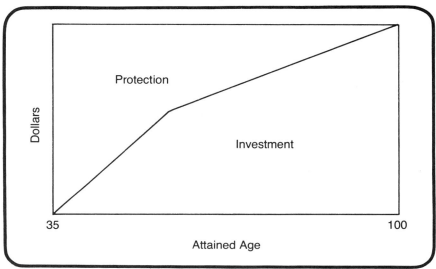

insurance enables a person to guarantee that an estate of a certain size will be created. The insured may allow the protection to continue until death, at which time the face amount is paid to the beneficiary. Or, if he or she lives a long enough time, the nonforfeiture value will accumulate to a sufficiently large amount to be of use in later life.

Whole life insurance offers a greater degree of flexibility than other life insurance policies. Most of the flexibility of whole life insurance is derived from the nonforfeiture options, which will be analyzed in the following chapter. But in addition, the conversion feature of whole life insurance may have advantages for a policyowner. Most companies include a provision in their policies that allows a policyowner to exchange a contract, without evidence of insurability, to any other form of coverage requiring a higher premium. Using this provision, a straight life policy can be converted to any plan other than term insurance.

Limitations of Whole Life Insurance There are very few limitations of whole life insurance for those who want permanent insurance and regard the nonforfeiture values as a reasonable method of accumulating assets. If an individual has insurance needs that are not permanent, however, this form of coverage does not provide as much protection per premium dollar as term insurance.

A common objection to straight life that leads many individuals to choose a limited payment plan is that straight life policies require premium payments for as long as the insured lives. Many people simply prefer to look forward to the date when premium payments can be stopped. Unfortunately, this argument overlooks some important points and can lead to poor insurance planning.

A given premium applied to a limited payment policy will provide a smaller death benefit than it would applied to a straight life policy. For example, suppose a husband who is thirty-five years of age decides he can spend $500 a year for life insurance. Using the figures of one large company, the $500 annually will purchase about $20,000 of straight life insurance, but only about $14,000 of twenty-pay life. If he purchases the straight life policy, he will have $6,000 more life insurance, and his cash value will only be $200 less at age fifty-five. Furthermore, his position is not greatly different if he discontinues premium payments on the straight life policy after twenty years than if he had purchased the twenty-pay policy. The nonforfeiture value of the straight life policy would be large enough to provide $11,100 of paid-up insurance at age fifty-five, only about $3,000 less than the amount of coverage he would have had with the limited payment contract.

The premium-paying period of a limited payment policy usually does not correspond with the maximum earning period of the policyowner. As an illustration, a twenty-pay life policy purchased at age twenty-five will allow the policyowner to discontinue the premium payments at age forty-five, when many employees are just beginning to earn their greatest incomes!

Limited payment policies can also be used in some special situations. Parents, for example, might purchase a limited payment contract and pay all premiums before making a gift of the paid-up policy to the child.

ENDOWMENT INSURANCE

Basic Characteristics

An endowment life insurance policy provides protection for a limited period of time, but the policy pays the full face amount at the end of the specified period if the insured is still living. In other words, the contract pays if the insured dies during the policy period, and it pays if the insured survives to the end of the policy period.

Endowments can be purchased for almost any duration, but the most common contracts are based on ten, fifteen, twenty, twenty-five, or thirty years. Endowments at age sixty or sixty-five are also common. Figure 7-6 illustrates a twenty-year endowment.

The important aspect of Figure 7-6 is that it is identical to a

Figure 7-6
Illustration of a Twenty-Year Endowment

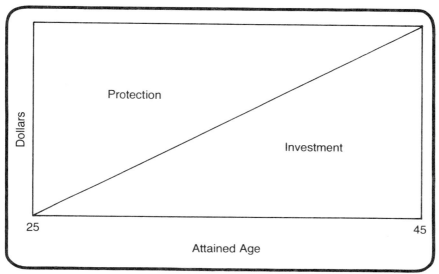

straight life policy illustration except that the illustrated endowment contract matures at age forty-five. In effect, a straight life policy may be regarded as an endowment at age 100.

All life insurance policies are fundamentally the same except that the periods of protection and the premium-paying periods may vary. As a result, it is often helpful to ask, "Over what period of time is protection needed, and over what period should premiums be paid?" rather than, "What kind of policy is best?" If answers to the first question are obtained, the selection of the proper type of policy is automatic. Otherwise, a poor matching of policies and needs may result.

Comparisons of policies may help make unusual policies comprehensible. For example, some life insurance companies issue an "endowment at age ninety." It should be apparent that a policy of this type, for all practical purposes, is a straight life policy—although the premiums are sightly higher and the nonforfeiture values grow a little faster than in a straight life policy. In general, policies of this type are issued to make a contract appear unique.

Premiums for endowment policies usually run the entire length of the policy period. There are, however, some limited payment endowment contracts. For example, a person might purchase a thirty-year endowment with premiums payable for only the first twenty years of the policy.

Evaluation of Endowment Insurance

Uses of Endowment Policies Endowment contracts are often described as "insured savings accounts" because they build nonforfeiture values rapidly. Indeed, endowment policies should be considered only when the primary need is for savings.

Endowments, particularly endowments to age sixty or sixty-five are often used to provide retirement funds. The wisdom of this use for endowments is dependent upon one's views of the investment merits of life insurance contracts. Endowment insurance should be used for retirement purposes only when protection, as well as investment, is needed.

An endowment policy may be issued on the life of a child or a parent to provide an educational fund. The contract is written for the period of time between the child's present age and the age at which he or she will begin college. The use of endowment insurance to provide educational funds guarantees that cash will be available whether the parent lives or dies.

Limitations of Endowment Policies The appeal of endowment insurance, to many people, is that the insured (or the beneficiary) is certain to collect. While this is true, there is a basic flaw in such reasoning. An endowment policy can be viewed as a combination of level term insurance and a *pure* endowment (which pays only if the insured survives to the end of the policy period). A policyowner is certain to "win" on one element of the contract, but obviously he or she is equally certain to "lose" on the other portion. If the insured dies, term insurance would have been a better purchase. If the insured lives, some other noninsurance method of accumulating funds would have been preferred.

It is unwise to use endowment policies to meet permanent insurance needs on the premise that they are similar to permanent policies. However, the duration of the protection in an endowment policy is limited, as in term insurance. If the policy matures while the need for insurance protection still exists, the policyowner may be unable to purchase another policy due to prohibitive premium costs or the lack of insurability. In this case the policyowner would have been in a better position with permanent insurance.

Perhaps the greatest misuse of endowment plans is the inappropriate matching of available premium dollars and insurance needs. Often, policyowners have a need for more insurance than they are willing or able to purchase. Unless an individual clearly has an adequate amount of life insurance, the high premiums required for endowment policies would be taking premium dollars that should be allocated to more pure

Table 7-2

Comparison of Life Insurance Rates

(Age Thirty-Five—Price per $1,000 Face Value)				
Straight Life	Life Paid-Up at 65	20 Payment	Endowment at 65	20 Year Endowment
$21.39	$25.53	$32.29	$35.60	$46.79

insurance protection. Table 7-2 shows the price for a male, aged thirty-five, of $1,000 of life insurance under the various basic plans.

Suppose a thirty-five-year-old husband and his insurance adviser have estimated that $50,000 of life insurance is needed, but the husband is not willing to allocate more than $800 each year. Using the figures in Table 7-2, he can buy more than $37,000 of straight life insurance or about $17,000 of twenty-year endowment insurance. Obviously, his life insurance needs would be more nearly satisfied with the straight life contract. The husband, therefore, would have to weigh the advantages of the endowment (larger cash values) against those of the straight life policy (larger death benefit).

SPECIAL LIFE INSURANCE CONTRACTS

Life insurance policies that do not fit neatly into the basic tripartite of term, whole life, and endowment usually are called "special" policies. They are also called "combination" contracts because many of them are nothing more than combinations of basic plans. Although the term "package policy" is sometimes used, this terminology is not as popular in life insurance as it is in property and liability insurance. In the aggregate, special policies represent a significant portion of all newly issued life insurance policies and can be extremely useful for meeting a complex set of needs.

Family Income Policy

One of the most widely accepted special policies is the family income contract.[8] Its popularity no doubt stems from the fact that it has special attractions for young people with family responsibilities who are unable to afford a large amount of permanent insurance.

In its basic form, the family income policy provides monthly income to the beneficiary beginning upon the death of the insured and continuing to the end of a specified period, when the face amount of the policy becomes payable. The specified period is normally twenty years from the date of issue, but periods of ten, fifteen, or twenty-fiv years are common. Usually, the monthly income is 1 percent of the face amount of the policy, but other percentages are available.

To illustrate this policy, suppose a $10,000 twenty-year family income contract is purchased. If the insured dies four years after issue, the beneficiary receives $100 each month for the next sixteen years, after which time the face amount ($10,000) would be paid. If the insured dies twelve years after the policy is issued, the monthly benefits are paid for eight years. In the event that the insured survives the twenty-year period, only the face amount is payable; payment is made at the time of death.

A family income policy may appear complex, but it is actually a simple contract. Structurally, it is a combination of decreasing term insurance and a basic policy, which is usually whole life. The basic policy provides the funds to pay the face amount at the end of the specified period, whether the insured dies during or after the period. The monthly income payments are made available by the decreasing term proceeds and interest on the proceeds of the basic policy. At 3.5 percent interest, a $10,000 basic policy will provide about $36 each month, leaving a balance of $64 to be met each month by the proceeds of the decreasing term segment of the policy. A decreasing term policy of approximately $22,000 would be necessary. Figure 7-7 illustrates a family income policy, using the numbers in this example.

Many companies have modified the provisions of their family income policy. Probably the most common variation is a provision to make the proceeds of the basic policy payable upon the death of the insured. This provision, of course, necessitates a larger amount of term insurance because interest on the proceeds of the basic policy is not available to supplement the monthly income benefits; this provision, therefore, requires an additional premium.

Another common variation is the payment of a portion (perhaps 25 percent) of the face amount at the insured's death if death occurs within the specified period. The logic of this approach is that the beneficiary is likely to need a sizable lump sum to pay for final expenses such as medical and funeral costs.

When the benefits described above are provided in a single policy, the contract is generally referred to as a family income policy. Essentially the same benefits, however, can be obtained by attaching a decreasing term insurance *rider* to a permanent insurance policy (or to an endowment contract). In fact, some companies issue a decreasing term policy without a basic contract and refer to it as a "family income" policy.

Figure 7-7
Illustration of a Family Income Policy
(Issue Age Thirty-Five—Face Amount $10,000)

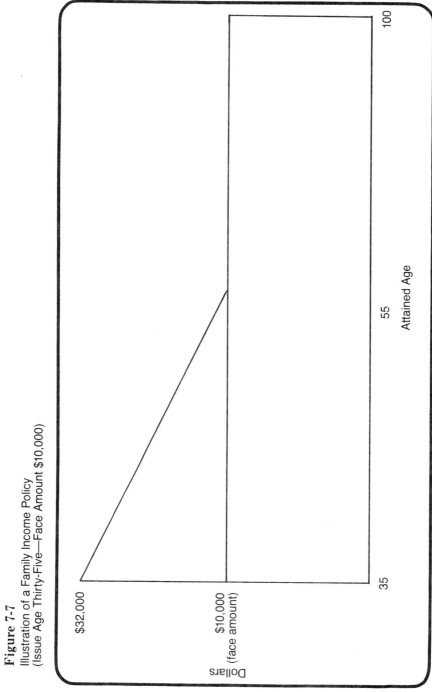

Most life insurance companies will allow a decreasing term rider to be attached to either a new or existing policy. Many of these companies also allow the pattern of benefits to be arranged to duplicate those of a typical family income policy. Naturally, if the term policy is purchased as a rider to attach to an existing policy, the insured must meet the company's insurability standards.

The premium for a family income policy often remains level during the specified period but decreases to the amount required for the basic policy when the decreasing term insurance expires. In many cases, the premium payments for the decreasing term insurance are stopped several years before expiration of the term protection because of the small amounts of protection provided in the last years.

Family Maintenance Policies

The family maintenance policy differs from a family income policy in that it provides a monthly income to the beneficiary—not for the remainder of the family income period, but for a stated period beginning at the time of death.[9] Income benefits are provided in both policies only if the insured dies during the specified period.

A simple example will clarify the family maintenance policy. Suppose an individual, age thirty-five, purchases a $10,000 family maintenance contract with a twenty-year specified period. If the insured dies at any age between thirty-five and fifty-five, monthly income benefits will be paid for twenty years from the time of death. The proceeds from the basic policy would be payable either upon the insured's death or at the end of the twenty-year period, as they are in a family income policy. If the insured survives the twenty-year period, the death benefit is paid at the time of death.

Structurally, a family maintenance policy is composed of a basic policy, usually whole life insurance, and a level term contract for the designated period. Such a policy is illustrated in Figure 7-8.

The term insurance portion of a family maintenance policy is level, not decreasing, because the insurance company agrees to pay monthly income benefits for the full period specified.

The family maintenance policy is appropriate in fewer situations than the family income contract. The family maintenance policy might be desirable for a married couple planning to have additional children over a period of several years. If the couple had purchased a family income policy with a twenty-year designated period and had a child ten years after the policy was purchased, income benefits, if any, would terminate when the child was ten years of age. A family maintenance policy, however, would provide monthly benefits for twenty years after

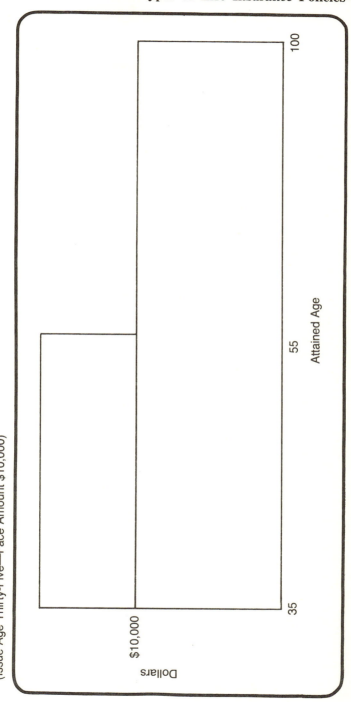

Figure 7-8
Illustration of a Family Maintenance Policy
(Issue Age Thirty-Five—Face Amount $10,000)

the insured died, and benefits would be provided past the child's minority.

Family Policy

One of the most popular special policies is a contract that is most often called a "family policy."[10] This policy provides life insurance protection, in one contract, on all members of the immediate family—husband, wife, and children. Automatic coverage is provided with no increase in premium for children born or legally adopted after the policy becomes effective.

A family policy is usually issued in "units" that provide a stated amount and type of insurance for each family member. For example, one unit of the family policy might consist of $5,000 of straight life insurance on the husband, $2,000 of term insurance on the wife's life to the husband's age sixty-five, and $1,000 of term insurance on each child to age twenty-one. The term insurance on the wife and children is invariably convertible. In many family policies the term insurance on the children is convertible for four, five, or even ten times the original amount of protection.

There are numerous variations in family policies. The amounts of coverage might differ from the 5, 2, and 1 ratio in the above example. The types of insurance on the husband or wife may differ, or children's lives may be insured to some age other than twenty-one (the usual range among companies is age eighteen to age twenty-five). In addition, some companies stipulate that all term coverage becomes fully paid-up if the husband dies before age sixty-five.

The premium for a family policy usually depends entirely on the age of the husband (or wife, if she is the principal source of income). The number of children and their ages have no direct effect on the premium. However, the insurance company makes assumptions with regard to the average number of children and their ages and builds this cost into the premium. This cost is very small because only a small amount of term insurance is involved and mortality rates among children are low, except immediately after birth. The infant mortality problem is handled often by postponing coverage on newly born children until they are fourteen or fifteen days old.

The spouse's age usually has no effect on the premium. If there is a wide difference between the two ages, the premium stays the same, but the amount of insurance on the spouse's life may be adjusted. If the spouse dies before the breadwinner reaches age sixty-five, the premium may be reduced or the amount of the principal insurance policy may be increased.

The family policy is a convenient, usually inexpensive method of providing life insurance for every family member. Family policies are often used to pay last illness and burial expenses.

Another consideration is that the family policy protects the insurability of the children, and possibly the spouse. The conversion feature for children is liberal (usually some multiple of the basic coverage can be converted), and the family policy is one of the few methods of obtaining term insurance for children (many companies will not issue individual term policies below age eighteen or twenty).

One major disadvantage of the family policy is that premium dollars used to purchase insurance on the lives of the spouse and children might be better spent for additional insurance on the principal wage earner. As an example, one company offers five units of the family policy for an annual premium of $431 at age thirty. In the same company, identical insurance for the husband's life can be purchased for $296. The additional family coverage, therefore, costs $135 per year. This amount could be used to purchase almost $40,000 of term insurance on the husband's life. Unless the husband already has adequate life insurance protection, the premium dollars may be poorly distributed by the family policy.

Another possible disadvantage is that the family policy usually requires straight life insurance as the principal policy, which of course carries a higher premium than term insurance.

Juvenile Policies

Life insurance companies are forced to define juvenile policies because these contracts may involve legal problems, and therefore, may require special policy forms and different underwriting rules. Although the definitions vary by company, and in some cases by states, juvenile insurance is usually defined as coverage purchased by an adult on the lives of children under a certain age (often sixteen). A number of states, including New York, have passed laws giving minors over a certain age, usually fourteen, the legal capacity to purchase life insurance on their own lives without the restrictions that apply to juvenile insurance.

A juvenile policy is typically issued when a parent applies for, and becomes the owner of, a life insurance policy on the life of a child under the age of sixteen. Often a special policy provision stipulates that the child automatically becomes the owner when he or she reaches a certain age, usually twenty-one. In certain cases a gift of the policy is made to the child, and a trustee may be designated as the owner.

The plans available for juvenile policies are usually those that build cash values rather quickly. Short-term endowments and limited payment contracts are common. Few policies provide coverage until the child is fourteen, fifteen, or thirty days of age because coverage of infant mortality below these ages would be expensive.

One of the more popular juvenile policies is known as the "jumping juvenile" contract. At age twenty-one, the face amount automatically increases by a multiple of five with no insurability requirement or increase in premium. Again, there are variations among companies in specific policies.

A unique provision included in virtually all juvenile policies is the *payor benefits clause*. This provision states that premiums will be waived until the insured (the child) reaches a certain age, most often age twenty-five, in the event that the person designated as the premium payor (usually the father) dies or becomes totally and permanently disabled. Most juvenile policies, including those with payor benefits, are written without a medical examination. However, evidence of insurability is often required *of the father* if the payor benefits clause is added, and special underwriting rules may be invoked. The premium for the payor benefits provision is determined by the age and underwriting classification of the payor, the age of the insured, and the type of plan. In one major company the annual premium for the benefit is $44.50 (for a $10,000 endowment at age twenty-one when the insured is age six and the payor is age thirty-five).

Juvenile insurance is usually sold (1) to provide funds for last illness and burial expenses, (2) to build a college education fund, (3) to establish a permanent insurance plan at a low annual premium, or (4) to protect a child's insurability. In most cases these needs are poorly met by juvenile insurance.

If the need is to provide a fund for last illness and burial expenses, a health insurance contract and perhaps a family policy would be preferable. Any amount of life insurance on the lives of children other than that needed for funeral expenses seems unwarranted, and a high premium policy is unjustified for this purpose.

Juvenile insurance is an extremely expensive method of building a college education fund. In almost all cases the parent would be well advised to either accumulate the funds through investment or to purchase additional life insurance on his or her own life. To illustrate the latter approach, assume a father, age twenty-five, has an infant son. A $10,000 endowment at age eighteen purchased for the son, age 0 (that is, under six months of age) would require an annual premium of about $450 in one large company. Instead, the father could use the $450 each year to purchase a $40,000 straight life policy on his own life. In the event the father dies before the child reaches age eighteen, $40,000 would be provided, whereas the juvenile policy would have accumulated only a few thousand dollars. Even if the father does not die during the period, the cash value after eighteen years of the straight life policy on the father will amount to about $8,400—only $1,600 less than the amount that would accumulate in the juvenile policy. Furthermore, if the father is alive, he may well have other opportunities for providing financial assistance to his son.

Juvenile insurance that is purchased in order to establish a permanent insurance plan at a low annual premium is particularly interesting. A $20,000 life paid up at age sixty-five will require an annual premium of about $260 if purchased at age fifteen. In the same company, the same type of contract at age thirty-five would cost $495 annually. If the policy is purchased at age fifteen, the total cash outlay (total premiums from age fifteen to age sixty-five) would amount to $13,000, while at age thirty-five the total cash outlay would be $14,850. Thus, both the annual premium and the total cash outlay are lower when the policy is purchased at the earlier age. However, if present values are taken into account, the total premiums are lower for the policy taken at the older age. Specifically, at a 4 percent interest rate, the present value of the premiums for the policy issued at age fifteen is $5,584, but the value for the policy issued at age thirty-five is only $3,905. Therefore, the argument that life insurance should be purchased at the younger ages to obtain a cost advantage is certainly debatable. In general, life insurance purchased at younger ages is more expensive (when adjusted for present values) than insurance purchased later because the policyowner receives more valuable benefits (i.e., protection for a greater number of years). However, deferral of the purchase of insurance raises the possibility that the individual will become uninsurable.

If a family's primary goal is to protect the child's insurability, juvenile insurance might be a legitimate solution. The amount of protection provided by the family policy is limited, and there are few other methods of protecting a child's insurability. A "jumping juvenile" policy is the most appropriate plan for this purpose.

In general, the greatest danger of juvenile insurance is that it uses premium dollars to protect children's lives which would be better used to purchase additional insurance on the breadwinner. Most insurance companies have underwriting rules designed to prevent juvenile insurance when the breadwinner's insurance is obviously inadequate. The effectiveness of these safeguards, however, seems questionable (at least in some companies). The most efficacious control lies in the hands of those who provide life insurance advice.

Life Cycle Policy

A life cycle policy is a hybrid of the term and permanent forms of insurance. A life cycle policy is designated as "permanent-type" and "term-type," depending upon which form of insurance it more closely resembles.

The unique feature of a life cycle policy is the "adaptable provision" that allows a policyowner to switch back and forth from a "permanent-type" plan to a "term-type" plan. Any change that is elected by the policyowner may create a change in premiums, nonforfeiture values, or both. A policy change is accomplished without purchasing a new policy, and in many circumstances, without providing evidence of insurability.

As an illustration, a person who purchases a life cycle policy and later finds that the premiums are an excessive burden may adjust the plan of insurance so that the premiums are lower but the amount of insurance is not decreased. In this case, the nonforfeiture values would increase more slowly; the protection period may also be shortened. If the policyowner later becomes able to pay the original premiums, the policy may be changed back to the original plan, and the policy values will resume their normal growth.

In some situations, a policyowner may wish to maintain the same premium but change the face amount of the contract. If the face amount is decreased, the policy becomes more of a "permanent-type" plan and nonforfeiture values would build more rapidly. The face amount may also be increased (evidence of insurability might be required), with a consequent retardation in growth of nonforfeiture values; this shift would be toward a "term-type" plan.

Although a few policy provisions in life cycle plans are different from the provisions in traditional policies, most of them are essentially the same. Cost comparisons between types of policies are difficult because life cycle plans provide an extra benefit in the form of greater flexibility but apparently the cost of life cycle policies is not a significant problem.

Life cycle policies are too new to permit a reasonable evaluation of these plans. Only a few companies currently issue them, but they are growing in popularity. To date they have been well received, and they may prove to be an important type of life insurance policy.

Mortgage Redemption Policies

The mortgage protection policy is simply a decreasing term

insurance. It can be used for other needs as well as the retirement of a mortgage.

The amount of insurance is sometimes tied rather closely to the mortgage debt. For example, the amount of insurance may be computed to correspond exactly with the amortization of the mortgage, and the death proceeds may be payable directly to the mortgagee. With these plans, the death of the insured automatically absolves the homeowner from the mortgage debt. This feature is usually found in group insurance policies rather than individual contracts. A policy may be referred to as a "mortgage protection policy" even if the amount of insurance and period of protection do not correspond with the mortgage, and the proceeds are not payable to the mortgagee. In this case, the beneficiary has the option of using the proceeds to pay off the mortgage or using the death benefits for some other purpose.

In the process of advising individuals about mortgage redemption policies, it is wise to check the beneficiary arrangement, the relationship between the debt and the policy amount, the duration of both the coverage and the debt, and the terms of a prepayment penalty that may exist in the mortgage agreement. Some policyowners may confuse mortgage life insurance with the mortgage insurance premium that is built into their monthly FHA mortgage payments. The latter is a method of protecting lenders against losses caused by defaults in mortgage payments.

Multiple Protection Policies

A number of life insurance companies provide a policy that promises to pay a multiple of the face amount if the insured dies within a specified period. Only the face amount is payable if the insured dies after the specified period has expired.

The death benefits during the specified period are usually two or three times the face amount, but other multiples are available. The specified period may be a specific number of years, or until the insured reaches a certain age, such as sixty or sixty-five.

Premiums for a multiple protection policy are usually higher during the period of higher death benefits than they are after the multiple coverage expires. In some contracts, however, the premium is level throughout the plan.

Multiple protection policies may appeal to prospective policyowners because the face amount is increased substantially at an apparently low cost. It should be recognized, however, that a multiple protection policy is very similar to a family maintenance policy. For example, a double protection policy to age sixty-five issued at age forty-five is composed of a twenty-year level term policy or rider to age sixty-five and a permanent form of coverage, which is essentially the same structure as a family maintenance contract. In both forms (multiple protection or family maintenance) the term coverage is usually convertible, and the plans are similar in many other respects.

Modified Life Policies

A modified life contract is a straight life contract that carries lower than "normal" premiums in the early policy years. The premium patterns for plans other than straight life can also be modified, however.

In most cases a modified life plan provides lower premiums for three, five, or ten years, but other "lower premium periods" are available. In some plans referred to as "graded premium" or "step rate" plans, the premiums increase annually.

There are many variations in premium patterns for modified life policies. For example, the pattern may vary by the number of premium increases, by size of increase, and by the existence and by length of deferral of each increase. In some cases, the premiums may increase only at the election of the policyowner.

Premium modifications can be accomplished either by utilizing term insurance in the beginning years of the plan or by simply redistributing the premiums for some type of permanent or endowment policy. For example, a plan may include term insurance which automatically converts after a specified period; or it might be composed of decreasing amounts of term insurance and increasing amounts of some other plan.

If the plan does not involve term insurance, the lower premium in the early policy years is accomplished by offsetting the lower premiums with higher premiums later, providing a slower growth in cash values, or both. In a typical plan, both premiums and cash values are lower in the early years; when premiums are increased, cash values tend to grow at a faster rate. At age sixty-five, the cash value of a modified life plan is usually slightly lower than that of an "unmodified" plan.

Modified life plans may be useful in situations where a policyowner expects to improve his or her financial status within a few years. Thus, they may have special appeal to students or recent graduates. Careful consideration must be given to the fact that the premiums will increase and that over the entire policy period there is no financial advantage to be gained from a modified life plan.

"Preferred-Risk" and "Special" Policies

With the increasing price competition of recent years, life insurers have developed a number of techniques designed to make their policies more attractive than those of their competitors. Techniques which can produce a lower cost of insurance for the policyowner include:

1. specification of a minimum acceptable face amount,
2. restriction of issue to those insureds who meet superior underwriting standards,
3. modification of the policy so that policyowners receive lower benefits, or
4. requirement that premiums be paid at less frequent intervals.

Traditionally, the life insurance underwriting process has been primarily concerned with classifying applicants into one of three categories: standard, substandard, and uninsurable.[11] Most insurers, in other words, do not attempt to separate the superior applicants. Some companies, however, offer so-called "preferred-risk" plans to applicants meeting rigorous underwriting rules. According to the rate book of one company such "preferred-risk" policies should be offered only to individuals who are "superior from the viewpoints of build, physical condition, personal history, family history, habits and environment, and who are engaged in healthful, nonhazardous occupations."

From a policyowner's point of view, a "preferred-risk" policy might be advantageous, but it is wise to keep three factors in mind: (1) many companies use the word "preferred" in describing policies which may not be based on superior underwriting characteristics, (2) the cost of a policy is only one of the many factors that should be considered in selecting an insurance plan, and (3) "preferred-risk" policies are available from only a few companies and then usually on a whole life plan.

Minimum amount policies are available from many companies, and they may produce significant savings for a policyowner. The minimum amount specified, for a given type of policy varies from $5,000 to $100,000 or more. Many plans call for a minimum face amount of $20,000, $25,000, or $50,000. The basic purpose of these minimum requirements is to reduce the expense rate per $1,000 of insurance. Some expense items that are built into a premium are virtually independent of the size of the policy. For example, the medical examiner's fee, inspection report, and general overhead costs may be about the same regardless of a policy's size. When these costs are allocated to larger policies, the expense rate per $1,000 of coverage is lower. When these savings are taken into account, the advantage is passed along to buyers who purchase a larger policy.

Some companies recognize lower costs per $1,000 of face amount by separating policies by size into "bands" for which different rates are applied. For example, a company might charge $20 per $1,000 for policies of less than $10,000, $19.25 per $1,000 for policies between $10,000 and $20,000, and $18.50 per $1,000 for policies above $20,000. The same effect is achieved by a quantity discount that is applied for each $1,000 of insurance purchased.

Another common technique is the policy fee system. Although the term "policy fee" appears to connote a disadvantage to the policyowner, the effect is the same as a quantity discount. If, for example, the policy fee is $10, the cost is $2 per $1,000 on a $5,000 policy, but only $.20 per $1,000 on a $50,000 policy.

The word "special" is applied to an endless variety of life insurance policies. In a narrow context, a "special" life insurance policy is one that carries a lower premium rate than one issued on a regular policy form. While the premium reduction may be accomplished in many ways, one or more of the following techniques are common methods:

1. The cash values of the policy may be lower.
2. Policy dividends may be reduced or eliminated.
3. Commissions to agents may be less than normal.
4. The settlement options (discussed in the following chapter) may be less favorable to the policyowner.
5. Premium payments may be allowed only on an annual basis.

"Special" policies are not necessarily advantageous for policyowners and should be purchased only after careful analysis of their particular needs.

Return of Premium Policies

Some companies issue policies that guarantee the beneficiary will receive not only the face amount but also the total of all premiums paid on the policy—if the insured dies within a certain period. To the unsophisticated insurance buyer, this type of contract seems to provide the possibility for "free" insurance.

The return of premium benefit is provided by a term rider with a face amount always equal to the total amount of premiums paid to date. In some plans this benefit is optional for the policyowner, but in others it is provided as an integral part of the policy. If the benefit is not provided as an optional term rider, the contract still must contain an increasing term insurance portion.

The cost of term protection increases rapidly as an insured gets older, and of course *increasing* term insurance accelerates the expense to policyholders. For this reason, the return of premium benefit is best used for a limited period of time at a young age. Rarely is the benefit provided past age sixty.

If an insured lives beyond the period of the term protection, previous premiums cannot be returned when the insured dies. However, the premium for the increasing term rider is discontinued when the benefit expires, and only the premium for the basic policy is payable.

The same concept can be applied to guarantee that the beneficiary will receive an amount equal to the *cash value* of the policy in addition to the face amount, if the insured dies within a stipulated period.

Whether the plan calls for a return of total premiums or the cash value (or both), these benefits are difficult to justify. It appears that a return of premium benefit is a type of "gimmick" to promote policies that otherwise are not competitive. A policy that guarantees the return of cash values is sometimes defended on the grounds that policyowners often believe the cash value is theirs as a matter of right *in addition* to the face amount. It is probably true that some policyowners have this erroneous concept, but the correct solution should lie in policyowner education—not policy modification and further policyowner confusion.

Joint Life Policies

If more than one person is named *as an insured*, the contract is known as a *joint life policy*. These contracts probably are most often used for a married couple, but some policies may jointly insure several business associates.

In a typical joint life policy, the death proceeds are paid upon the death of the first insured; coverage on the surviving insureds terminates. Most joint life policies are either whole life or endowment, but an increasing number of companies are issuing joint life policies on a term basis. Some of those policies allow a surviving insured to convert to a permanent plan at the time the other insured dies.

The premium rate for a joint life policy, of course, is greater than that of an individual policy. However, the premium for a joint life policy is always less than the sum of the premiums for an equivalent amount of insurance on each life. As an example, the rates for one large company show that a husband and wife (both age thirty-five) can purchase a $10,000 joint life policy for an annual premium of $269.20, but a $10,000 policy on each life would require total annual premiums of $418.10.

Joint life policies are appropriate when death of *either* spouse would cause a need for substantial funds. This might be the case, for example, when substantial death taxes would be payable when either the husband or wife died. With a greater number of wives providing income to a family and increasing recognition of the monetary value of nonworking wives, joint life policies may become increasingly popular.

Minimum Deposit Plans

Accurate figures are not available to indicate the amount of minimum deposit life insurance currently in force, but there is no doubt that this type of insurance is enormously popular. In many large agencies, minimum deposit life insurance comprises the bulk of the business.

A minimum deposit plan actually is not a type of insurance. Instead, it is a method of financing the purchase of an insurance policy. The policyowner buys a policy, periodically borrows on the cash value (by means of a policy loan) to pay (all or part of) the premium, and takes income tax deductions for interest paid on the policy loans. An arrangement of this type produces, in effect, decreasing term insurance for the policyowner because the policy loans (which are accumulated with interest) are deducted from the face amount when the insured dies.[12] But even if the amount payable to the beneficiary declines over time, the plan can be attractive because of its low cost. The cost, of course, is made more attractive if the policyowner is able to deduct the interest on the policy loans in the computation of his or her income tax liability. Essentially the same results can be achieved by obtaining loans from a financial institution other than an insurance company; these arrangements are known as "bank loan plans."

The deductibility of the policy loan interest for minimum deposit plans was carefully spelled out in the 1964 amendments to the Internal Revenue Code. Briefly stated, interest on policy loans is deductible if any one of the following conditions is met:

1. No part of four of the first seven annual premiums is paid by policy loans.
2. The total amount of the policy loan interest for the taxable year is less than $100.
3. The indebtedness was incurred because of an unforeseen substantial loss of income or increase in financial obligations.
4. The indebtedness was incurred in connection with the policyowner's trade or business.

In most cases the practical effect of the above rules is that an individual may set up a minimum deposit plan if he or she plans to pay four of the first seven annual premiums from sources other than policy loans.

Table 7-3

Flexible Deposit Ledger Statement—
Preceding Years Dividend Applied to Reduce Current Premium

			Age 30 Male Date Sept. 10, 1975		Amount of Insurance Annual Premium		$100,000.00 $ 1,825.00			
Premium Payment By—										
	(1)	(2)	(3)	(4)	(5)	(6)	(7)	(8)	(9) CSV Less Loan	(10) Total Death Benefit Beneficiary
Year	Net Premium	Cash	Policy Loan	Annual Interest	Gross Outlay	Net Outlay	Guaranteed CSV	Total Loan		
1	1,825	1,825			1,825	1,825				100,000
2	1,636	1,636			1,636	1,636	898		898	100,000
3	1,590		1,590				2,420	1,590	830	98,410
4	1,543		1,543	95	95	67	3,991	3,133	858	96,867
5	1,497		1,497	188	188	120	5,613	4,630	983	95,370
6	1,449	1,449		278	1,727	1,627	7,286	4,630	2,656	95,370
7	1,401	1,401		278	1,679	1,579	9,010	4,630	4,380	95,372
8	1,352		1,352	278	278	178	10,783	5,982	4,801	94,018
9	1,302		1,302	359	359	230	12,605	7,284	5,321	92,7˙6
10	1,251		1,251	437	437	280	14,475	8,535	5,940	91,465
11	1,199		1,199	512	512	328	16,150	9,734	6,416	90,266
12	1,159		1,159	584	584	374	17,862	10,893	6,969	89,107
13	1,118		1,118	654	654	418	19,614	12,011	7,603	87,989
14	1,078		1,078	721	721	461	21,406	13,082	8,317	86,911
15	1,040		1,040	785	785	503	23,237	14,129	9,108	85,871
16	1,002		1,002	848	848	543	25,109	15,131	9,978	84,869
17	962		962	908	908	581	27,020	16,093	10,927	83,907
18	922		922	966	966	618	26,971	17,015	11,956	82,985
19	882		882	1,021	1,021	653	30,960	17,897	13,063	82,103
20	841		841	1,074	1,074	687	32,988	18,738	14,250	81,262
at 60	137		137	1,342	1,342	859	50,368	22,502	27,866	77,498
at 65	86cr			1,356	1,356	868	58,748	22,513	36,235	77,487

Table 7-3 can be very helpful in understanding the mechanics of a minimum deposit plan. Although the figures in the table are actually used by a large company, they should be interpreted as illustrative only and do not necessarily depict the most favorable minimum deposit arrangement.

Column 1 of Table 7-3 shows that the annual premium for the policy is $1,825. The premium decreases over time and is labeled the "net" premium because policy dividends will be used to reduce premiums (policy dividends and dividend options are discussed in the following chapter).

The plan illustrated in Table 7-3 calls for the policyowner to pay the first premium ($1,825) of a $100,000 policy without a policy loan. In the first policy year, the plan does not differ from a traditional policy. In the second policy year, the policyowner pays the premium of only $1,636 because a dividend of $189 is used to reduce the premium. Notice that a cash value of $898 is developed but a policy loan is not obtained. In the third policy year, a cash value of $2,420 is available, and $1,590 of it is borrowed to pay the third annual premium. The total death benefit in the third year, therefore, is $98,410 ($100,000 less $1,590). Again, a policy loan is obtained in the fourth year to pay the premium. But notice that interest on the loan from the preceding year is $95, and this amount would be out-of-pocket expense for the policyowner (column 5). In the 36 percent income tax bracket that is assumed, the net outlay (column 6) is only $61. In other words, the "aftertax" cost to maintain the plan in the fourth year is $61, but since the total policy loan has accumulated to $3,133 (column 8), the death benefit has declined to $96,867 (column 10). The same process is continued in the fifth policy year, but notice that net outlay has increased to $120 (column 6) and the death benefit amounts to $95,370.

In order to meet the IRS rules for deducting the policy loan interest, the plan requires the policyowner to pay the sixth and seventh annual premiums from sources other than a policy loan. In the sixth year, a cash payment of $1,449 for the premium and interest cost of $278 makes the gross outlay (column 5) $1,727. After taxes, this amounts to $1,627 (only the interest and not the premium is deductible). The death benefit does not decrease in the sixth and seventh policy years (it remains at $95,370 as shown in column 10) because policy loans are not used.

After the seventh policy year, the policyowner has met the "four out of seven" tax rule and therefore can use policy loans to pay the premium and deduct interest paid. If policy loans are used in all subsequent years (as illustrated) to pay the premiums, the annual interest will increase and the death benefit will steadily decline.

Although the totals are not shown in Table 7-3 (the figures for ages fifty to sixty-five are not included), the total net payments (payments for premium and interest less the tax advantage) for the plan would amount to $25,943. Since the cash value available at age sixty-five is $36,235, the policyowner could expect an "excess" of $10,292 if the plan is continued to age sixty-five. The death benefit at age sixty-five, although it has declined in most of the years, would still amount to $77,487.[13]

A common variation of the minimum deposit plan is to keep the death benefit level (or almost level). This is frequently accomplished by using dividends to purchase term insurance each year or by using fewer policy loans to pay premiums.

A number of life insurance companies have developed "high early cash value" policies that are particularly well suited for minimum deposit plans. These policies allow the policyowner to have lower out-of-pocket costs for the policy—at least in the beginning of the plan.

Many life insurers are reluctant to encourage minimum deposit plans primarily because they create a large volume of policy loans which are not an advantageous company investment. Also, minimum deposit plans often are terminated because policyowners either fail to understand the plan or are opposed to an increasing cash outlay for interest at the same time that the total death benefit is decreasing.

A policyowner may employ the minimum deposit concept whether or not the insurance company favors it. Furthermore, it may also be used on an existing policy.

Minimum deposit plans are more useful to individuals in higher income tax brackets, but the income tax effect is only one consideration in choosing a life insurance plan. It is much more important to coordinate a person's life insurance needs with the cash that is available for life insurance. In this regard, minimum deposit plans may be appropriate when decreasing term insurance meets the need and large cash outlays in the beginning years are not a problem for the policyowner.

Deposit Term Policies

Perhaps the most interesting life insurance contract to be developed in recent years is the deposit term policy. This contract appeared in the early 1960s and, although still offered by a limited number of companies, seems to be gaining popularity. The policy is highly controversial. It is regarded by some as a genuine breakthrough for consumers; others, however, believe the policy to be deceptive. Deposit term policies are sold freely in many states, issued in other states under stringent regulations, and prohibited in several states.

Deposit term contracts have a number of unique characteristics. Stated in terms in which they are usually presented, the most important of these characteristics are:

1. Policyowners earn 7 to 10 percent interest (compounded annually for ten years) on a deposit that can be continued for a long period of time. Moreover, the interest on the deposit accumulates tax free. At 10 percent, the deposit increases by a factor of approximately 2.6 every ten years. Furthermore, the 10 percent rate of interest is guaranteed, provided the policyowner keeps the contract in force for the entire ten-year period.
2. The plan is renewable without evidence of insurability every ten years and may be renewed to very advanced ages, perhaps as high as age 100.
3. The policy, which is considered term insurance by some companies and permanent insurance by others, may be con-

Table 7-4

Table of Loan and Surrender Values

Issue Age 35	
Policy Year	Cash or Loan Value (per $1,000 of face amount)
1	$ 0
2	0
3	0
4	0
5	0
6	3
7	8
8	12
9	16
10	21

verted without evidence of insurability to whole life insurance or decreasing term insurance to age 100.

Since most companies normally earn less than 10 percent on their investments, they cannot guarantee such a rate on all the funds they have available for investment from deposit term policies. However, they can require an additional premium in the first policy year and calculate cash values in such a manner that the tenth-year cash value equals the additional premium compounded each year for ten years.

The amount of the additional premium or deposit is determined by the policyowner's age and the face amount of the policy. For example, many companies require a deposit of $10 per $1,000 of face amount (at many ages), but other companies require a smaller amount, often $7 or $8 per $1,000 of face amount.

Contracts of many companies include a death benefit (in addition to the face amount of the policy) equal to the deposit, or, in some companies, the deposit plus interest.

Like all permanent and endowment contracts, a deposit term policy contains a table of loan and surrender values. An excerpt of this table from the deposit term policy of one company is shown in Table 7-4.

The first-year premium rate for this policy is $12.72 per $1,000 of face amount. The annual premium rate for each of the subsequent nine years is $4.66. The company is, in effect, charging an additional single premium of $8.06. If the tenth-year cash value is $21, the policyowner has earned 10 percent on his "deposit." There is nothing "magical" about the 10 percent figure. In fact, some companies use interest rates of 7 or 7.2 percent. Occasionally the rate amounts to only 4 or 5 percent. Ten percent, however, is the most common rate in deposit term policies.

It can be argued that the "deposit" is nothing more than an additional premium (that is paid only in the first policy year) and that it is misleading to refer to this extra charge as a "deposit." Some state insurance departments require the deposit term policy to avoid the word "deposit." In these states the extra amount must be described as "premium."

The "taxfree" aspect of the contract should be no mystery at all. According to the Internal Revenue Code, income taxes are payable when a policy is surrendered for cash only if the cash value exceeds the total premiums paid. If a deposit term policy is surrendered in the tenth year, the cash value is less than the total premiums that have been paid, so there is no taxable gain.

The pattern of cash values in a deposit term policy should raise some very substantive questions. Notice that in the cash values shown above there is absolutely no cash value at all until the sixth policy year. Even in the eighth policy year the cash value is only $12 per $1,000 of face amount. Surrender at this point would have produced interest on the "deposit" of only 5.1 percent. Deposit term policies, in other words, contain large forfeitures if the policy is discontinued prior to the tenth year.

Opponents of deposit term policies argue that the forfeitures are unnecessarily large. Few policyowners, they maintain, can be assured that their future will unfold exactly as forecast, and it is unrealistic to plan to surrender (or convert) the policy only on ten-year anniversaries.

Deposit term proponents quickly point out the logic of the slow increase in the cash values in the early years. These proponents, in fact, argue that *other* policies are unfair. All life insurance policies build in costs to cover sales and administrative expenses. Generally, these costs cannot be fully paid by policyowners who terminate their contracts within a few years. These costs, of necessity, must be borne by policyowners who continue their coverage. To be more equitable, the argument continues, cash values should either be low or nonexistent until the sales and administrative expenses are recovered.

A complete evaluation of the forfeiture aspects of deposit term policies in comparison to other types of policies is beyond the scope of this book. However, a point that ought to be transmitted to prospective policyowners is that deposit term policies may involve substantial forfeiture "penalties" if the contract is not carried ten years.

The renewable feature in deposit term policies gives the policyowner the contractual right to continue coverage without evidence of insurability. An important consideration, however, is the fact that the

Table 7-5

Illustration of a Deposit Term Policy

Issue Age Thirty-Five—Face Amount $100,000				
Policy Year	Age	Premium	Cash Value	Total Outlay
1	35	$1,272	0	$1,272
2–10	36–44	466	$2,100	466 each year
11	45	1,962		−138
12–20	46–54	902	2,800	902 each year
21	55	3,464		664
22–30	56–65	1,980		1,980 each year
		Total		$31,930

deposit, as well as the pure protection, is renewed. That is, the second ten-year period operates exactly as the first ten-year period, except that the premium (including the deposit) is on an attained age basis.

A policyowner who purchases a $100,000 deposit term policy at age thirty-five and renews to age sixty-five would have relatively large premiums or deposits to make at age thirty-five, forty-five, and fifty-five, but he or she would be entitled to the tenth-year cash value to help pay these costs at age forty-five and fifty-five. Using the figures from one company, the experience would be as shown in Table 7-5.

The policyowner in the above example would have a total cash outlay over the period of $31,930. In return, he would have had protection of $100,000 plus the amount of the deposit.

The deposit term policies of some companies permit renewal to very advanced ages. Renewal to age seventy, seventy-five, or even eighty is not uncommon. However, renewal premiums at those ages may be prohibitively expensive. Some contracts permit renewal for a larger face amount than the original policy. These larger amounts are based on increases in the Consumer Price Index or some other measure designed to reflect inflation.

Conversion to a level term policy may be elected by a policyowner at the end of every ten-year period, as long as the policyholder has not reached a specified age.

A special conversion option available in most deposit term contracts is the option to convert to a decreasing term policy. In many policies this option is automatic at a stipulated age unless the policyowner chooses otherwise. The unique feature of the decreasing term option is that often the coverage is provided to age 100. This option might very well meet a legitimate consumer need, but the danger is that policyowners are apt to misunderstand the true nature of their coverage. This problem is compounded by agents who refer to their deposit term policies as "permanent" insurance on the basis that the decreasing term option can provide "whole life" protection. Strictly speaking, the "permanent" label is not incorrect; still, it may be misleading.

An arrangement very similar in concept to deposit term is collateral term insurance. The deposit for collateral term is in the form of collateral rather than cash. Mutual fund shares are most often used for collateral, but some companies will accept stock certificates, savings accounts, life insurance cash values, or other assets.

The insurance company has the right in a collateral term plan to convert the pledged asset into cash and charge a termination premium if the policy is surrendered in the early years. The termination premium decreases each year the policy is in force. After several years, the charge is zero and the collateral is returned to the policyowner.

The advantage to policyowners of collateral term over other forms of term coverage is the lower premium. The chief disadvantage, of course, is that the policyowner is, in effect, making a "guarantee" that the policy will be maintained.

Cost of Living Policies

In the inflationary environment of recent years, more and more companies are providing a cost of living rider that automatically increases the death benefit as prices increase. Although most policies of this type are linked to the Consumer Price Index (CPI), other indexes are used.

Most cost of living plans operate by automatically purchasing one-year term insurance whenever the CPI increases a specified amount. If the CPI does not increase (or does not increase enough), no additional term insurance is purchased. Thus, the face amount never decreases below the face amount of the original policy.

One advantage of the cost of living rider is that evidence of insurability is usually not required. Another possible advantage is that the additional term protection may not be fully loaded for expenses (since agents' commissions normally are not paid on the additional insurance). These advantages should not imply that all policyowners should request a cost of living rider. The rider, of course, requires an increasing premium in periods of inflation. Furthermore, an individual's life insurance needs are not necessarily correlated to changes in consumer prices.

Variable Life Insurance

Variable life insurance has received more attention in recent years than any other type of life insurance innovation. A few years ago some authorities were predicting that variable life insurance might account for as much as 40 percent of all new life insurance sales by 1980. Even if these predictions prove to be unduly optimistic, there is a strong possibility that variable life insurance will become a popular form of coverage.

In general, variable life insurance is any form of life insurance providing a death benefit which may change with time. A narrower definition, however, has evolved. According to the NAIC Model Variable Life Insurance Regulation, variable life insurance is a policy in which the death benefit varies with the investment experience of a segregated investment account maintained by the life insurance company. Under this definition, cost of living policies are not considered a form of variable life insurance.

The motivation for a variable life contract arises from a desire for a product based on equity values. The insurance company may view variable life as a product that will be competitive in the marketplace. The individual may see variable life as possible protection against inflation.

Since the values in a variable life contract are dependent upon the performance of an investment account, there is an inflation hedge only to the extent that the underlying investments keep pace (or outperform) the movement in prices. In the past, equity investments have surpassed general price increases in most years, but occasionally equity prices and consumer prices have moved in opposite directions.

According to the NAIC Model Variable Life Insurance Regulation, all variable life policies share three important features. First, although the policy will provide variable death benefits and policy values, the premiums paid by the policyowner will remain level. A second important feature is the requirement that the death benefit be greater than or equal to the original face amount of the policy. A third common characteristic of variable life policies is that coverage must be permanent. There is no variable term or endowment insurance. As a general rule, the annual premiums on the variable life coverage must be payable for a minimum of fifteen or twenty years.

At present, variable life policies may follow several designs. All methods, however, depend upon an "excess investment return" concept. Basically, this approach involves a comparison between the actual net investment rate (ANIR) and the assumed investment rate (AIR). In the determination of the ANIR, all elements of investment performance are considered, including dividends received, realized and unrealized capital gains and losses, taxes, investment expenses, and risk contingencies. Death benefits will remain level if the ANIR is exactly equal to the AIR, but the face amount will change when a difference between the two rates arises.

The NAIC Model Regulation permits four methods of adjusting the death benefit in a variable life insurance contract. One approach is to provide paid-up variable life insurance at the net rate for the attained age of the insured (if the ANIR is greater than the AIR). In other words, with favorable investment experience, dollars are applied, in effect, to purchase a single premium policy in the amount that can be purchased at the insured's attained age. Since the additional insurance is being purchased on a single premium basis, the amount that can be purchased in any one year will be modest, but over time and with favorable investment experience, the total amount of paid-up insurance will accumulate. If the ANIR is less than the AIR, the appropriate amount of paid-up life insurance is deducted from the death benefit, as long as the face amount does not fall below the original amount.

A second method permitted by the NAIC Model Regulation involves purchasing additional insurance that is not paid up. These purchases are made at net rates based on the insured's original age (not his attained age). With favorable investment experience, larger amounts of insurance will be purchased in the early policy years than would be purchased under the paid-up method. However, as time passes, a smaller amount of insurance will be purchased because the funds available from the excess investment performance must first be used to pay the premiums on policy additions that were purchased in previous years; only the remainder, if any, is available to purchase new insurance.

A third method permitted by the NAIC Model Regulation is the purchase of paid-up term insurance. The Regulation does not stipulate the term period, but the term insurance would probably run until the next valuation period. The fourth method permitted is a combination of two of the three other approaches.

Variable life policies may be more expensive than comparable fixed dollar products because of higher administrative expenses and the cost of satisfying additional regulatory requirements. Furthermore, certain benefits may be more liberal in variable life contracts. However, it is too early to make accurate cost comparisons.

The future for variable life insurance is presently clouded by the regulatory environment. The Securities and Exchange Commission (SEC) has ruled that variable life insurance is a security as well as a life insurance policy. As a result, both the SEC and state insurance departments are involved in a complex regulatory pattern that may take years to prove workable. Indeed, a fair assessment of variable life insurance is that much depends upon the regulatory path that will evolve.

SELECTING THE APPROPRIATE TYPE OF POLICY

The first step in addressing the problem of policy selection is to determine the primary life insurance need to be satisfied. If the primary need is for death protection, for example, term insurance might be indicated. A policy that builds a relatively large cash value may be appropriate if the principal aim is to accumulate savings. When both death protection and savings are needed, a straight life policy might be a reasonable choice.

Most people have more than one need for life insurance, and therefore, more than one type of policy may be necessary for the best matching of needs and policies. However, a separate policy may not be necessary for each need because some policies may be used for several purposes. Furthermore, combination (special) policies often may be purchased to meet different types of needs.

In the process of matching needs and policies, the answers to four questions should be developed:

1. Over what period of time will life insurance protection be needed?
2. Over what period of time should premiums be paid?
3. Does the individual regard the cash value element in a policy as an attractive method of saving?
4. Does the person impose a limit on the amount that will be allocated to life insurance premiums, and if so, how much can be spent?

The answers to these questions may be inconsistent. The most obvious conflict arises when a person is unable or unwilling to pay the premiums required to meet his or her needs. Despite these conflicts, it is helpful to analyze each question separately, and then make adjustments to resolve any conflicts that may arise.

The Period of Protection

The nature of the need itself is often indicative of the period of protection that ought to be provided. Some examples follow.

The estate clearance need is lifelong. In fact, the general tendency of this need is to become greater as a person ages. The need for an emergency fund is also permanent. In both cases, therefore, permanent protection, i.e., whole life insurance, is indicated.

An education fund is a temporary need. Even if a person plans to have additional children in the future, the need for educational funds will not exist when the children are past college age. Using only the protection period as a guideline, temporary insurance, either term or endowment, would be implied. The choice between term and endowment requires additional information (considered later).

Needs for readjustment income and income for the dependency period also are temporary. The same is true for a mortgage fund, unless a person plans to maintain a mortgage as long as he or she is alive. In the latter case, a mortgage fund should be regarded as a permanent need. Life income for a spouse generally is regarded as a permanent need because a spouse certainly has a need for income as long as he or she is alive.

Accumulating Savings Through Life Insurance

If a person views life insurance cash values as an attractive method of saving, he or she should consider permanent insurance. Even temporary needs may be met with permanent insurance in these cases. Some people, however, believe life insurance cash values are inadequate savings devices. These individuals, therefore, are inclined toward term insurance. Unfortunately, in many cases a person's attitudes toward life insurance cash values are based on incomplete or inaccurate analysis.

The evaluation of life insurance cash values as a savings vehicle often surfaces as the "buy term and invest the difference" argument. The proponents of this concept argue that a person's financial welfare would be improved if he or she bought term insurance, instead of whole life insurance, and invested the difference in the premiums in some other form of savings or investment. According to this view, a whole life policy is composed of increasing savings (the cash value) and decreasing protection. Essentially the same benefits could be achieved by a decreasing term insurance policy and a separate savings or investment program. The underlying assumption of this approach is that a person can achieve greater investment returns than those implicit in the cash value schedule.

Comparing Rates of Return A comparison of the rate of return obtainable through a life insurance policy with that available from other sources is an exceedingly complex problem.[14] Although generalizations about the rate of return in a cash value life insurance policy are common, they are often misleading.

To estimate the rate of return for a policyowner the major facts or assumptions needed are:

1. the premium that would be required for a cash value policy,
2. the cost of term insurance in an amount equal, each year, to the amount of protection needed,
3. the period of time over which the comparison will be made,
4. the amount of the cash value in the whole life or endowment policy at the end of the given period of time,
5. the amount of life insurance policy dividends that will be paid each year (if any), and
6. the income tax bracket of the individual (each year).

With this information, a person can determine whether "buy term and invest the difference" would be a worthwhile strategem. The objective is to determine the interest rate necessary to make the separate investment fund (accumulated from the difference between the premiums on the term and cash value policies) equal to the cash surrender value of the whole life or endowment policy at the end of a specified period.

This process can be made clear with a simple example. Suppose Mr. A can purchase a cash value policy in the amount of $50,000 for an annual premium of $1,200.[15] This contract has a guaranteed cash surrender value at the end of twenty years of $19,500. Alternately, Mr. A can "buy term and invest the difference." Assume that Mr. A can buy yearly renewable term insurance each year in any amount. If Mr. A bought $48,990 of term insurance at a cost of $190, he would have $1,010 to invest or save. The $1,010 is the "difference" between the premium on the cash value policy ($1,200) and the premium for the term policy ($190). It is not coincidental that $1,010 is also the difference between the cash value policy face amount ($50,000) and the amount of term coverage ($48,990). The amount of term coverage is chosen so that the two differences (between face values and premiums) are equal.

At the start of the second policy year Mr. A would have his separate savings fund, which has increased with interest, plus the "difference" in premium to invest or save. Assume that the cost of $47,940 of term insurance would cost $200 at his higher age. If so, Mr. A's separate investment fund would be $1,010 (from the deposit in the first year), $50 (assumed interest earnings during the first year), and $1,000 (the difference in premiums in the second year). This fund, therefore, would begin the second year worth $2,060. Notice that the total amount of the term insurance and the separate invested fund would be $50,000 each year, the same as it would be if Mr. A purchased the cash value policy.

The plans described above can be summarized as shown in Table 7-6. The calculation would have to be continued for twenty years. Then, the amount in the separate savings fund would be compared to the cash value of the other policy ($19,500 in our example). If the separate savings fund exceeded $19,500, the entire calculation would be made again, using a lower interest rate for the separate fund. Through trial and error, an interest rate could be found that would make the separate

Table 7-6
Summary of Plans

Cash Value Policy				
Face Amount				$50,000
Annual Premium				$1,200
Cash Value (end of 20 years)				$19,500
Buy Term and Invest the Difference				
Policy Year	Cost of Term Insurance	Amount of Term Insurance	Separate Savings Fund	Total Term Insurance and Savings
1	$190	$48,990	$1,010	$50,000
2	$200	$47,940	$2,060	$50,000

savings fund equal to $19,500. This interest rate would be the implicit rate the person would earn on the cash value policy. Obviously this rate can be calculated only with a substantial amount of effort or a computer.

Using techniques similar to these, periodic studies have been made to estimate the returns in cash value policies. The studies most often quoted are those of Albert Linton, a noted actuary. He calculated an annual return of 4.77 percent for straight life policies issued at age thirty-five and terminated at age fifty-five.[16] Other studies have shown substantially different rates of return.

The interpretation of any published rates must be made with caution. The rates of return can vary greatly depending upon (1) the age of issue, (2) the number of years projected, (3) the premiums, dividends, and cash values of the whole life or endowment policy, (4) the term insurance rates assumed, (5) the type of policy, and (6) the tax bracket of the policyowner. For most people, the two dominant considerations are the time period used for the calculation and the tax effect. The time period is important because rates of return in a policy often are negative in the first few years but tend to increase annually. An estimate of the return for a twenty-year period is relevant only for that period. The true return is likely to be greater than the estimated return if the policy is maintained longer than twenty years; conversely, the actual return probably will be less than expected if the policy is terminated in less than twenty years.

The income tax effect provides an advantage that varies directly in importance with the tax bracket. The annual increments in life insurance cash values are not taxable as current income to the policyowner. Interest earnings (or dividends) in most other savings or

Table 7-7

Distribution of Assets of U.S. Life Insurance Companies*

Type of Asset	Amount	Percentage of Total
Government Securities	$11,965	4.5%
Corporate Bonds	96,652	36.7
Stocks	21,920	8.3
Mortgages	86,234	32.8
Real Estate	8,331	3.2
Policy Loans	22,862	8.7
Miscellaneous	15,385	5.8

*Reprinted with permission from *Life Insurance Fact Book* (New York: Institute of Life Insurance, 1975).

investment vehicles are taxed each year. A person in the 30 percent tax bracket earning 4 percent in a life insurance policy would have to earn 5.71 percent (before taxes) in another vehicle to have the same aftertax return.[17]

Other Considerations The expected rate of return is only one consideration in the "buy term and invest the difference" debate; others are presented below.

Safety of Principal. Historically, no type of private financial institution or business organization has equaled the solvency record of the life insurance industry. Three major reasons account for this remarkable safety record. First, the volume of assets in many companies is tremendous, by almost any standard, and therefore life insurers strive to obtain competent investment personnel. Secondly, life insurance companies generally place their funds in rather conservative, safe investments. Table 7-7 shows the volume of assets held by life insurance companies in each of the major types of investments.

Note that the preponderance of life insurance company investments is in bonds and mortgages, with a relatively small portion in more speculative assets. Of course the relative proportions of the investments change over time. At the end of World War II, U.S. government bonds accounted for almost one-half of the assets, but in recent years only a small percentage of assets are in government bonds.

Diversification is another reason for the safety record of the industry. Several methods of diversification are possible and the life insurance industry uses all of them. Life insurance companies place their funds into many types of industries. An adverse experience in one particular industry will have only minor effects upon the entire investment portfolio. Another method of diversification is obtained by spreading investments over a wide geographical territory. This restricts losses that might occur if one region of the country suffered an economic recession. If investments in Canada are excluded, only a small proportion of life insurance company funds are allocated to foreign securities.

Diversification of investments over time is also employed by life insurers. Securities are purchased so that the maturity dates will be spread into the future. If maturities were not spread over time, insurance companies might be forced to obtain a large amount of funds at a time when investment conditions were unfavorable. Diversity by date of maturity increases the regularity of their income. Because of the persistent excess of current income over current disbursements, life insurers are seldom forced to liquidate investments to meet obligations. Even during the depths of the Great Depression, few companies had cash needs that could not be satisfied by current premium and interest income. This regularity enables insurance companies to take full advantage of the most favorable security prices.

A final method of diversification is by size. If a policyowner has $10,000 invested in life insurance and the company has 500 different investments, the policyowner has, in effect $20 invested in each of the investments. Therefore, the sheer number of investments acts to minimize risk.

In purchasing a life insurance policy as an investment, a policyowner obtains a degree of diversification that is impossible for an individual investor to achieve. There are only a limited number of savings vehicles offering the same degree of safety as life insurance.

Liquidity. The ability to quickly convert investments or savings into cash with little or no loss of principal is an important consideration. Life insurance cash values are almost perfectly liquid. Normally, cash can be obtained from a policy in a matter of hours or a few days.

Only one factor detracts from the otherwise perfect liquidity of life insurance savings. As a result of the Great Depression, 1929-33, life insurance companies include a delay clause in the policy. This provision gives the company the right to postpone the payment of the cash value for a period up to six months. In actual practice, however, very few companies have ever exercised the delay provision. To do so would tend to encourage a "run" on cash values, and therefore, companies have a strong incentive to ignore the clause and pay cash values promptly.

Convenience. The time, effort, and ability required to manage an investment or savings program should not be underestimated. A life insurance policyowner has virtually no managerial problems with the investment or savings program. These are turned over to the professional staff of the insurer.

Semicompulsory Nature. Perhaps the most important consideration for a person considering the "buy term and invest the difference" approach is the question of whether the "difference" will actually be invested regularly over a long period of time. Most individuals find it extremely difficult to continue a savings program over a long duration. It is easy for a savings program to be interrupted or discontinued when unusual financial needs arise.

A savings program through life insurance is much easier to continue than most other savings plans because of its "semicompulsory" nature. A policyowner is under no genuine obligation to continue a life insurance policy, but in many cases, he or she is reluctant to let the protection terminate. Consequently, he or she continues to pay the premium and the savings in the form of cash values continue to grow.

Capital Rationing

In selecting the appropriate type of life insurance policy a person often places a constraint on the amount that will be allocated for life insurance premiums. A person, for example, might impose a limit of $500 each year for the purchase of life insurance. This can be labeled "capital rationing."

A person considering capital rationing has a choice. He or she can either limit the amount of cash value insurance to be purchased, or use term insurance to meet all (or a portion) of the life insurance needs. There is no scientific method for making the choice. Much depends upon how the person views the attractiveness of the savings element. Another important consideration is the priority a person places on the death protection.

Capital rationing for life insurance premiums may be a logical, and even necessary stipulation. The discomforting aspect of capital rationing is that there is no generally accepted method of placing a dollar limit on the amount that should be spent for life insurance. Rules of thumb based on what other people spend are of little value to an individual. A budgeting approach seems reasonable, but as a practical matter, budgets often are unreliable. In theory, a person should rank his or her total exposures (property and liability as well as the other exposures) and allocate premium dollars according to the importance of each exposure.

The methods for establishing the appropriate amount to spend for life insurance simply are not reliable or accurate. The practical implication, therefore, is that the dollar limitations imposed by capital rationing are subject to change. While a financial advisor should not extract premium dollars that will be an unreasonable burden, he or she might be able to convince an individual to modify the previously established dollar limits.

Chapter Notes

1. The whole life contract may be properly viewed as a special form of endowment policy, one that matures at age 100. According to this view, there are only two distinct types of life insurance, term and endowment. In keeping with common usage, however, and in recognition of their long-standing and widespread usage, whole life contracts will be treated separately. In an even broader perspective, annuities may be considered a fourth type of policy. Annuities will be discussed in Chapter 11.

2. In some unusual situations, term policies are issued for less than a year.

3. The "buy term and invest the difference" approach is analyzed later in this chapter.

4. The premium for a life insurance policy is normally a poor measure of the cost of the policy. The problem of determining life insurance cost is considered later in this text.

5. *The Nature of the Whole Life Contract*, Institute of Life Insurance, June 1974. See also, Robert I. Mehr, "The Concept of the Level-Premium Whole Life Insurance Policy—Reexamined," *The Journal of Risk and Insurance*, Vol. XLII, No. 3 (Sept., 1975), p. 419.

6. Actually, regulators would stop a company from issuing new policies if the surplus of the company (which is a safety margin equivalent to the excess of assets over liabilities) slipped below regulatory standards.

7. Actually, a twenty-pay life policy issued at age forty-five would be paid up at age sixty-four, rather than age sixty-five.

8. The name "family income policy" is fairly common, but many companies use their own trade name for this contract.

9. The family maintenance policy goes under many different names. It should not be confused with the "family policy" described later in this chapter.

10. Again, these policies are known by many names. Common names are "family plan," "family protector," "family security," and "family insurance."

11. The vast majority of all applicants are classified as standard. For example, of the ordinary life policies underwritten in 1976, 91 percent were standard, 6 percent were substandard, and only 3 percent were declined by the company. Institute of Life Insurance, *Life Insurance Fact Book*, 1977, p. 97.

12. As will be shown later, the decreasing term effect can be avoided in certain plans.

13. Before drawing conclusions about the "profit" on this type of plan, it is necessary to analyze the cost of life insurance. This subject is treated in Chapter 14.

14. It is complex enough to have warranted a substantial amount of academic research in recent years. See articles by Belth, Murray, Scheel, and Schwarzschild in the *Journal of Risk and Insurance*.

15. To simplify the example we will assume that the policy pays no dividends. If

dividends were paid, the estimated dividend for each year should be deducted from the premium to arrive at a "net" premium.

16. For a description and critique of this Linton study see, Joseph Belth, "The Rate of Return on the Savings Element in Cash Value Life Insurance," *Journal of Risk and Insurance*, December, 1968, p. 569.

17. The tax equivalent yield is found by dividing the tax free return by one minus the tax bracket. In our example, 0.04 divided by 1–0.30.

CHAPTER 8

Life Insurance Policy Provisions

COMPARISON OF LIFE
AND PROPERTY-LIABILITY POLICIES

Contract Duration

Most property-liability contracts are written for relatively short periods of time which typically do not exceed three years. Except for term policies, however, life insurance contracts are effective for many years. For example, a policy purchased by a young insured and kept in force until retirement might pay benefits to the insured for many years during retirement and then pay benefits to beneficiaries after the insured's death. In this type of situation, the life insurance contract may be effective for up to 100 years.

The main reason it is possible to issue life insurance contracts for such long durations is that life insurance actuaries can predict, with a high degree of accuracy, how the mortality of a group of lives will change over a long period of time. In property-liability insurance, it is impossible to predict accurately how the claims experience of a group of exposures will change over time. In fact, the insurability of an exposure may change very quickly. Therefore, provisions giving the insurer the right to cancel upon proper notice to the insured are generally found in property-liability contracts. Conversely, life insurance policies do not contain cancellation provisions. This is a valuable safeguard for policyowners since the premium rates are guaranteed for the life of the policy.[1] By contrast, property-liability insurers reserve the right to increase premium rates upon policy renewal or even to refuse to renew the contract.

Control Over Underwriting

Since property-liability insurance is often needed on very short notice, producers possess the underwriting authority to bind the insurer to an exposure without seeking prior company approval. However, insurers normally reserve the right to cancel any coverage that is found to be unacceptable to their underwriting department.

Since life insurers do not have the right to cancel, the underwriting process is centralized within the home or regional office of the company. Life agents do not have the authority to issue unconditionally binding contracts. Instead, they may accept the initial premium and issue conditional receipts, which are very different from property-liability insurance binders.[2]

The long-term nature of the life insurer's commitment and the centralized underwriting process produce the need for a rather detailed insurance application. In addition to identifying information about the insured, the application (and its medical or nonmedical section) elicits information about the applicant's health, occupation, hobbies, and other insurance currently in force. Unlike the situation in most property-liability insurance contracts, this application becomes a part of the policy itself. Statements in a life insurance application are considered representations, not warranties, of the applicant.[3]

Regulation of Rates and Reserves

State regulation of life insurance rates and reserves is very different from that applying to property-liability insurance. In property-liability insurance, emphasis is placed on rate adequacy, reasonableness, and fairness. In general, property-liability insurance rates and reserves (especially the unearned premium reserve) are regulated strictly. The two are related since rate inadequacy will result in reserve inadequacy; similarly, an excessive rate will produce an excessive unearned premium reserve. In other words, the method of calculating the unearned premium reserve (which is a regulatory safeguard intended to provide adequate reserves) assumes that property and liability rates are set at the proper level.[4]

In contrast, life insurance rates are not regulated directly. Basically, a life insurer (with some exceptions) can set its rates at any level desired. There is a regulatory safeguard, however, because the insurance codes stipulate how the reserve must be calculated. Since the laws require minimum reserves and the calculation is independent of the life insurance rate, a life insurance company is virtually forced into charging adequate rates. The general principle is that the insurer must charge a rate sufficient to maintain adequate reserves while meeting all other obligations.[5]

This type of regulation may not adequately protect the life insurance consumer from excessive rates, and there is heavy reliance on competition to force rates down to minimally acceptable levels. Undoubtedly, many life insurance companies do offer competitive rates, but it is extremely difficult for life insurance buyers to evaluate the competitiveness of rates which tend to vary widely in amount. Obviously, some life insurers charge rates that are noncompetitive.

Insurable Interest

In property insurance, the "insurable interest" provision limits the insurer's liability for any loss to the insured's insurable interest at the time of loss. In order to minimize the likelihood of any possible moral hazard, a property insurer may gather information about insurable interests in connection with the underwriting of an insurance contract. Despite the absence of a policy provision requiring an insurable interest in liability insurance, companies are not liable, by law, for losses if an insurable interest is absent at the time of loss.

Life insurance takes a different approach since the insurable interest must exist at the time of policy inception and not at the time of loss. Also, there is no policy provision relating to an insurable interest.

Locations Covered

Most property and liability insurance contracts restrict the extent of their coverage geographically. The 1943 New York Standard Fire Insurance Policy limits coverage to the described location, except for temporary coverage in case of "removal." Most automobile insurance policies limit coverage to the United States, Canada, territories or possessions of the United States, and during transportation between these locations. These territorial restrictions are deemed necessary because of the difference in hazards in other locations.

Life insurance, on the other hand, provides universal coverage. At one time, life insurance companies restricted their coverage geographically, but today policies generally contain no restrictions on travel.

Contract Standardization

Today there are no standard policies in life insurance. However, a substantial degree of policy standardization exists because the Uniform Standard Policy Provisions Law or a variation of it has been enacted in all states.

These laws do not require any standard policy format or prescribe the exact wording of any policy provision. However, they deal with three types of provisions: (1) mandatory, (2) permissible, and (3) prohibited provisions. They permit wording different from that in the law if the change is beneficial to policyowners. If a mandatory provision is omitted from a policy, the courts interpret the policy as though it includes the mandatory provision. Similarly, the courts ignore any prohibited provision that is contained in a policy.

The result is that life insurance policies differ somewhat in general appearance and format, but they are very similar in terms of policy provisions.

Standardization of property-liability insurance contracts varies with the type of insurance, but most are more standardized than life policies. Fire insurance has standard wording mandated by law to the extent that the lines of the standard fire policy are uniformly numbered. Automobile and other liability policies are often standardized through intercompany cooperation in the drafting of a policy or its revision. Marine insurance policies have become standardized through custom, agreement, and tradition.

Additional Comparisons

Valued Policy Life insurance contracts are valued policies since the face amount of the policy is paid in the event of the insured's death. In property insurance, few contracts are valued policies. Generally, valued policies are employed in those instances where it would be difficult or impossible to establish the monetary extent of the loss at the time of loss, such as some coverages for jewelry and fine arts. They are also used in some states where they are dictated by legislation. Even so, valued coverage must be regarded as the exception rather than the general rule in property insurance.

The implications of the valued policy approach are significant. The concept of "insurance to value" is irrelevant in life insurance, so the type of coinsurance clause found in property insurance is not found in life insurance policies. Nor are underwriting techniques designed to deal with underinsurance used in life insurance contracts.

Indemnity The life insurance contract is not a contract of indemnity. Accordingly, there cannot be a legal problem of overindemnity. As a consequence, typical property-liability insurance provisions such as subrogation, appraisal, pro rata distribution, and other insurance clauses are not utilized in life insurance contracts.

Partial Loss Frequent partial losses are a serious problem in property insurance, and are dealt with by means of a deductible. Since there can be no such thing as a "partial death" in life insurance, deductibles are not used in that type of contract, and are not considered in the rate-making process.

Requirements in Case of Loss Property and liability insurance policies specify a number of requirements that the insured must follow in order to collect for a loss. In life insurance, the only policy requirement is to furnish the company with legal proof of the insured's death.

Coverage of Others By means of extensions and liberalizations, many property and liability insurance contracts cover the property and/or activities of persons other than the named insured. For example, a policy may extend coverage to include property of a guest or employee while on the insured's premises. Automobile policies typically insure persons driving the insured's automobile with permission, as well as the insured while driving other vehicles. Conversely, life insurance contracts do not extend coverage to include other people.

Perils and Exclusions Property insurance contracts either cover named perils or provide "all-risks" coverage. Either way, the typical nonlife policy contains many exclusions to limit what is covered within the scope of the insured peril(s). By contrast, a life insurance policy is an "all-risks" contract since it covers the death of the insured by any means. With rare exceptions, there are only three possible exclusions in a life insurance policy: (1) suicide, (2) war, and (3) death resulting from an airplane accident in which the insured was the operator of the plane on a nonscheduled flight. None of the three necessarily apply to any given policy. As described later, the suicide provision has a time limit, and the war and aviation clauses are not uniformly used in all policies.

IMPORTANT POLICY PROVISIONS

Insuring Agreement

The insuring agreement is the heart of an insurance policy since it describes exactly what is being insured by the contract. This provision, typically might read as follows:

> The death benefits under this policy will be paid to the beneficiary immediately upon receipt of due proof of the insured's death. Such proceeds shall include the face amount of the policy together with any other benefit payable under the terms of the policy because of such death.

Notice the requirement for the company to pay upon ". . . receipt of due proof of . . . death." Generally, this is in the form of a certified copy of the death certificate issued by the appropriate official. However, some companies accept a statement by the physician attending the deceased at the time of death. In the unusual circumstances where there is not an attending physician, such as the unexplained absence of the insured for a lengthy duration, a court of competent jurisdiction may, after proper consideration of the evidence, conclude that an individual is dead and enter an order accordingly.

If the insured's absence is unexplained, many states require an absence of seven years before the person will be declared dead. However, if the insured had been exposed to a serious hazard, a court may find that death occurred on the date of the exposure, and a seven-year waiting period will not be required. This circumstance usually arises in combat situations.

The insuring agreement mentions that the death proceeds may be adjusted to reflect additional benefits (described later). Death proceeds may also be adjusted downward to reflect such things as policy loans, unpaid premiums, and the policyowner's exercise of nonforfeiture options.

Entire Contract Provision

At one time it was common practice to declare that the charter and bylaws of an insurance company were to be considered part of the insurance policy. This made it difficult for policyowners to know what their contract contained, and it allowed a company to change the provisions of its policies by modifying the company bylaws. This possible abuse is now prevented by the entire contract clause. The following is an example:

> This policy and the application for it, a copy of which is attached to and made a part of the policy, constitute the entire contract. All statements made in the application will be deemed representations and not warranties. No statement will be used to invalidate the policy nor to defend against a claim under it unless contained in the application.

The contract is made in consideration of such application and the payment of premiums in accordance with the provisions of the policy.

Only the President, Executive Vice President, Vice President, Treasurer or Secretary of the Company at its Home Office can make or modify this contract or waive any of the Company's rights or requirements.

All payments by the Company under this policy are payable at the Company's Home Office in New York City.

While the entire contract clause solves the type of problem described above, the provision cannot be interpreted literally. A policy, even with the application and other amendments, is not considered to be the entire contract. Case law and statutory law modify every insurance policy. For example, even though a fire insurance policy does not define "fire," a clear definition is contained in case law which is used to interpret the policy. As an example of where statutory law modifies insurance contracts, if a company omits a mandatory provision from its policy, the contract will be interpreted as though it contained the required clause.

Since the entire contract provision applies only at policy inception, it does not prevent a company from amending or adding benefits to a policy if the policyowner agrees to the modification.

The statements in the application are deemed to be important to the decision of the insurer to accept and issue the policy. Moreover, the basis for issuance, standard or rated, is based on the information in the attached application which is made a part of the contract.

The statements by the applicant are representations and not warranties. Therefore, if the insurance company contests the contract, it must prove that there was a material misrepresentation (false statement) and that if the company had known the true information, it would have declined to issue the contract, or that it would have charged a higher rate or would have used a more restrictive policy form. For the misrepresentation to be material to the loss, there would have to be a causal link between the information misrepresented and the death of the insured. In some jurisdictions, the insurer would have to prove materiality to the exposure and to the loss. Should there be a concealment (i.e., failure to reveal important information, even though not solicited), the insurer would have to prove willfulness and materiality to both the exposure and the loss.[6]

Effective Date of Policy

In some cases an applicant will request that the policy be effective at a date other than on the issue date of the contract. The usual reason for requesting a back-dated policy is to take advantage of a younger age and therefore a lower premium rate. Many states have laws that prohibit back-dating a policy more than six months. In other cases an applicant may request a post-dated policy in order to make the coverage effective on a future date.

If the policy date differs from the issue date, the contract will contain a clause similar to the following:

> This policy is deemed to have taken effect as of the policy date shown on its first page. Policy years, months, and anniversaries will be determined from the policy date.

This provision establishes a date to measure premium intervals, the effective date of coverage, and the duration of time-related benefits in the contract. However, some provisions, such as the suicide and incontestable clause, are measured from the issue date.

Ownership

In most cases a person applies for insurance on his or her own life and becomes the owner of the policy. This person is the applicant, insured, and owner. However, it is possible for one person to apply for insurance on the life of someone else while another person is the owner. In practice, the most important distinction is between insured and owner.

It may be desirable to designate an owner who is not the insured. For example, if the insured is a child, a parent or guardian may be designated as the owner of the policy. Frequently, the child automatically becomes the owner when he or she reaches a certain age. Also, tax considerations may make it desirable to name someone other than the insured as owner. Finally, life insurance purchased for business purposes is generally owned by someone other than the insured. (Both of these situations are discussed later in the text.)

A change of ownership may be effected at any time during the insured's lifetime by making written notice to the company. A typical policy provision relating to this right is as follows:

> The Owner, by written request to the Company accompanied by the policy for appropriate endorsement, can arrange for a transfer of his entire ownership
> (a) to a new Owner, effective immediately, or
> (b) to an Owner's Designee who, upon the death of the designating Owner before his rights of ownership terminate, will become the new Owner. Any designation of Owner's Designee can be terminated or changed from time to time in a similar manner.

Such new Owner shall succeed to the benefits, rights and privileges of the previous Owner, subject to the terms and conditions of the policy and the interest of any existing assignee. The new Owner is not an "assignee" and the transfer is not an "assignment" within the meaning of those words as used in this policy.

No arrangement for transfer of ownership will take effect unless it is endorsed on the policy, but upon being so endorsed will take effect as of the date such request was signed, subject to any payment made or other action taken by the Company before such endorsement.

Any interest as Owner's Designee shall automatically terminate if a transfer is made under (a) above or if such Owner's Designee does not survive the designating Owner. Transfer of ownership will not act to change the beneficiary nor to transfer the interest of the beneficiary.

Payment of Premiums

A representative provision dealing with the payment of premiums is:

Premiums are payable during the insured's lifetime in accordance with the Premium Schedule, in exchange for a receipt signed by the President or Secretary of the Company and duly countersigned.

Any date in the Premium Schedule which was based on the assumption that the insured would be a specified age on such date shall be corrected, if necessary, to agree with the Insured's true age, nearest birthday.

After payment of the first premium, failure to pay a premium on or before its due date, to the Company at its Home Office or to a duly authorized Office Manager of the Company, will constitute default in payment of premium.

Premiums may be made payable at annual, semi-annual, quarterly or monthly intervals at the Company's applicable premium rate for the mode of payment requested subject to the Company's approval. Payment to and acceptance by the Company of a premium on a new mode of payment shall constitute a change in mode for subsequent premiums.

Generally, premiums are paid on an annual, semi-annual, quarterly, or monthly basis. For example, if the annual premium is $120, typical premium options are as shown in Table 8-1.

As the premium payment frequency is increased, the total annual premium is increased. The extra charge covers the additional clerical and overhead costs in mailing, receiving, and accounting for the additional payments received each year. Second, the time value of money must be considered. With a single annual payment, the insurer has a larger sum to invest for an entire year, whereas with the more

Table 8-1

Typical Premium Options

Premium Mode	Each Premium	Number of Payments Annually	Total Premium Per Year
Annually	$120.00	1	$120.00
Semi-annually	61.20	2	122.40
Quarterly	31.20	4	124.80
Monthly	10.60	12	127.20
Automatic check plan	10.25	12	123.00

frequent premium payments it has a smaller amount of funds available for investment purposes. Third, there is a difference in the "net amount at risk" (i.e., the difference between the face amount and the policy reserve) caused by the different premium intervals. To illustrate, assume that this is the first year of a $5,000 straight life policy, ignore all expenses, and assume that the entire premium is available for investment. With an annual premium of $120, the insurer's "amount at risk" is $4,880 ($5,000 – $120) during the first year, while the "amount at risk" is initially $4,989.40 ($5,000 – $10.60) during the first month of the first year with the monthly mode of premium payment. The initial extra "amount at risk" of $109.40 ($120 – $10.60) must be offset by some additional charge since there is no deduction, upon death, for unpaid premium installments. Fourth, some empirical evidence shows a slight increase in adverse mortality selection and lapse rates associated with policies paid for on an other than annual basis.

Premiums may also be paid by means of a pre-authorized check plan whereby the insurer is authorized to draw the premium payment directly from the owner's checking account. Frequently this is done for monthly premiums, and the insured's cost is less than that associated with a regular monthly premium since collection expenses are lower. Also, there is less likelihood of lapse and adverse mortality selection.

Grace Period

The laws of most states require insurers to include a grace period in their policies. This provision continues a policy in full force for thirty or thirty-one days after the premium due date during which time the policyholder can pay the overdue premium without penalty.

A typical grace period provision states:

A grace period of thirty-one days will be allowed for payment of a premium in default. This policy shall continue in full force during the grace period. If the Insured dies during such period, the premium in default shall be deducted from the proceeds of this policy.

The laws of most states allow an insurer to charge interest on overdue premiums, but few companies follow this practice. They are more concerned with preventing a lapse and the lost interest is relatively insignificant. A more serious problem arises from the possible application of waiver and estoppel (analyzed in CPCU 6) when an insurer accepts premium payments after expiration of the grace period.

Even if the insurer is notified that the policyowner does not intend to pay the premium, the grace period continues for its full duration. Accordingly, the insured may change his or her mind during the grace period, resume premium payments, and keep the policy in full force.

Misstatement of Age and Sex Provision

Most state laws require that all life insurance policies include a misstatement of age clause. A typical provision states:

If the age or sex of the Insured has been misstated, any amount payable under this policy shall be such as the premium paid would have purchased on the basis of the correct age and sex according to the Company's published rate at date of issue.

To illustrate, assume that a company issued a $10,000 ordinary life policy at a time when the company's rates were as follows:

Age	Rate per Thousand
34	$24.25
35	$25.00
36	$26.00

If the insured's true age at the time the policy was issued was thirty-five, but the policy was rated on an incorrect age of thirty-four, the annual premium will be $242.50 when it should have been $250.00. If the mistake is discovered when the insured dies years later, the correct amount of death proceeds would be $9,700; i.e., ($242.50/$250) × $10,000 = $9,700.

If the insured incorrectly gave his age as thirty-six, the amount payable would be $10,400; i.e., ($260/$250) × $10,000. While some companies follow this approach, most companies limit the coverage to the amount applied for initially (e.g., $10,000) and return the excess premium to the insured. This protects the company from the possibility of adverse selection. A misstatement of sex is treated by adjusting the face amount of the policy since different premiums usually apply for males and females. Normally, such a "misstatement" is the result of a clerical error in completing the application or in physically preparing the contract. In essence, the age and sex provision is designed to adjust the benefits (and proceeds) to what they would have been for the premium paid at the insured's correct (true) age and sex.

Policy Exclusions

Most life insurance policies contain only one exclusion—suicide—and even it is not permanently excluded from coverage. The only other important exclusions today are aviation and war. Some companies exclude death from other unusual perils, such as hang gliding, scuba diving, or auto racing.

Once a policy is issued, an insurer cannot deny liability for any benefits based on any changes in health, occupation, avocation, or habits. During the underwriting of a new policy, if the company discovers information or conditions different from their standards they generally handle the problem by using one of the following techniques. First, they may charge a higher then standard premium rate. Second, they may place the policy in a special (lower) dividend class. Third, they may issue a policy on a plan of insurance representing less pure protection to the insurer (e.g., issuing an endowment life policy rather than the term life insurance policy applied for). Fourth, they may decline to issue any policy at all. Lastly, an exclusion may be added to the policy which waives coverage for the condition causing the increase in the expected mortality.

Suicide

If there were no suicide provision in a life insurance policy, the contract would probably be interpreted to cover suicide. This would create a possibility of adverse selection (and moral hazard) for an insurance company. Consequently, all companies include a suicide provision such as the following in their policies:

> Suicide of the Insured, while sane or insane, within two years from the date of issue, is a risk not assumed under this policy; in such event premiums paid for the policy, less any indebtedness, will be refunded.

There are several variations in suicide provisions. For example, some policies exclude suicide for only one year from the effective date of the policy. In Missouri, suicide (at any time) does not relieve an insurance company from paying the full amount of the policy unless the company can prove that the insured contemplated suicide when the policy was purchased.

The basic rationale for the suicide provision is that few individuals contemplate suicide, purchase a policy, and then wait a year or two before taking their life. For those who commit suicide years after the policy is purchased, the company can pay the benefits to innocent beneficiaries without being overly concerned with the moral hazard problem.[7]

The general rule of law is that death is presumed to be unintentional. Therefore, the burden of proving suicide within the suicide exclusion period lies with the insurer.

Aviation Restrictions

The treatment of the aviation hazard has changed over the years, and today there is substantial variation among life insurance policies on how it is handled. Most policies today do not refer to aviation, and they pay even though the insured dies as the result of aviation activity. On the other hand, a policy may exclude coverage for all types of aviation deaths except those of fare-paying passengers on regularly scheduled airlines. Many companies include a question about flying activities in the life insurance application, and ask for additional information if the applicant indicates that he or she anticipates any military or private flying. Private pilots are underwritten carefully, and many are required to pay an extra premium for their coverage. Military aviation may be excluded altogether or covered only at an extra premium.

War Exclusion

Usually, war deaths are not excluded from coverage in a life insurance policy. Therefore, war-related deaths are covered in full as a part of the "all-risks" concept of life insurance.

However, in times of impending hostilities or during war, life insurance companies frequently control adverse selection by placing war exclusion clauses in new policies issued during the period to people exposed to the dangers of war. Some insurers do not use war clauses for modest amounts of life insurance (e.g., $10,000).

The war exclusion clause may be one of two types. The *status* clause limits the proceeds to the return of premiums (possibly with interest) or to the reserve of the policy (often whichever is the larger amount) if death occurs *while the insured is in military service*. The status clause may be liberalized by restricting the exclusion to military service outside some territorial limit, such as outside the United States. The *results* clause limits benefits for death as a direct result of war to the premiums paid (usually with interest) or the reserve of the policy, whichever is the larger. The status clause is the less liberal of the two since it limits the death benefits while in military service, whereas the results clause requires death to be directly attributable to war before benefits are restricted.

Generally life insurers remove war clauses voluntarily from their outstanding contracts at the end of hostilities in order to provide death protection as completely as possible for their policyholders. In fact, after some past wars some insurers have reviewed their loss experience under policies with war clauses and voluntarily paid the balance of the full death benefits for these policies since they determined that the losses were not as serious as had been anticipated.

The Incontestable Clause

One of the most important provisions in a life insurance policy is the incontestable clause. Although there are some differences among companies and among some of the state standard provisions laws, the typical incontestable clause states:

> This policy shall be incontestable after it has been in force during the lifetime of the Insured for a period of two years from the date of issue, except for nonpayment of premiums.

The incontestable clause insures that the validity of the life insurance contract will not be challenged by the insurance company after the contestable period has expired. Without the clause, a policyowner could not be certain that a death claim would be paid because the company might deny the claim by showing that the policy was obtained by fraud, misrepresentation, concealment, or by some other questionable means. For example, without the incontestable clause, a company could claim that the insured had misrepresented a material fact when the policy was purchased. In this case, the company might deny liability for the claim even though the policy was obtained many years earlier and the insured, the one best able to defend against the insurer's allegation, is dead.

For a life insurance company to successfully deny a claim on the grounds of misrepresentation, fraud, or concealment, the company must contest the policy during the contestable period.[8] Consequently, the incontestable clause is valuable not only to policyowners who plan to mislead an insurance company; it also is valuable to innocent policyowners and their beneficiaries as well, since it protects them against the possibility of a legal challenge to the contract.

The incontestable clause does not insure that an insurance company must pay every death claim that occurs after the contestable period. The incontestable clause simply prevents an insurance company from questioning the validity of a life insurance policy after the contestable period. In some cases a company might admit the existence of a valid contract but deny liability for a claim because of the terms of the contract. For example, the company would not be liable for a death caused by an excluded peril such as private aviation.

The adjustment of benefits for misstatement of age and sex is not a contest of the validity of a life insurance policy. Therefore, the incontestable clause is not operative insofar as the age and sex provision is concerned.

The aviation clause does not conflict with the incontestable provision. If a policy contains an aviation exclusion, a company may deny liability for an aviation death even after the contestable period has passed. In this situation, usually there is a return of premiums paid or the policy's reserve, whichever is larger.

Loan Value

Life insurance policies that develop a cash value contain a loan provision similar to the following:

> The Company will advance, on the sole security of the values provided under this policy, an amount up to its loan value at any time after the policy has a loan value, unless it is being continued as Extended Insurance. The loan value on a premium due date, or during the grace period, will be equal to the policy's cash value. The loan value at any other time will be the amount which, with interest, will equal the cash value on the next interest due date or next premium due date if earlier.

> Such advance shall bear interest, at the rate of 5 percent per annum, due on each policy anniversary or on any other date approved by the Company. Interest not paid when due will be added to the principal and will bear interest at the same rate. Any such advance, together with interest as it accrues from day to day, will constitute an indebtedness.

> The advance will be made upon receipt of such evidence of it as the Company may require. Any existing indebtedness will be deducted from such advance. The Company may defer making an advance, other than to pay any premium due the Company, for a period not exceeding six months from the date application for such advance is received by the Company.

Any indebtedness may be repaid, in whole or in part, at any time before this policy matures by the Insured's death or as an endowment, except that, if the policy is being continued under its Non-Forfeiture provisions, any indebtedness which was deducted in determining the non-forfeiture benefit may not be repaid unless the policy is reinstated.

Whenever the indebtedness exceeds the cash value, the policy shall be void thirty-one days after the Company has mailed notice to the last known address of the Owner and of the assignee of record, if any.

This provision provides a valuable benefit to policyowners since the policy's cash value may be borrowed promptly by sending a written request to the company. The company *may* defer the granting of a loan up to six months, but loans are seldom postponed. The deferment clause was put into contracts during the 1930s when bank failures created "runs" on life insurance cash values, but this is not considered to be a problem now.

Unlike commercial loans, a policy loan does not require a credit investigation. Furthermore, the policyowner has maximum flexibility in repaying the loan. It may be repaid at any time since there is no repayment schedule or due date. If a loan has not been repaid at the time of the insured's death, the amount of the loan, plus unpaid interest, is deducted from the death proceeds. If a loan is outstanding when the policy is surrendered for cash, the loan, plus unpaid interest, is deducted from the cash surrender value.

The interest rate payable on policy loans has been the subject of much debate in recent years. In the past, most policies stipulated a rate of 5 or 6 percent, and the rate was embodied in the contractual guarantees of the policy and could not be changed. In many cases this provided a valuable benefit to policyowners because the policy loan interest rate was usually lower than most other interest rates. Consequently, policyowners frequently found that policy loans involved the lowest possible cost for obtaining funds. On occasion, this has caused a problem for the insurer since it obligates the company to provide funds to policyowners at a lower rate than the company could obtain from other investments. This is an example of adverse *financial* selection and has caused many companies to favor changes in policy loan laws. One possible solution would be the establishment of a flexible interest rate system that would allow the policy loan interest rate to vary according to prevailing rates at the time of the loan. Another approach which is being followed in some states is to increase the policy loan rate.[9] The important point for a policyowner is that under any approach the policy loan interest rate (or method of determining the interest rate) must be specified in the policy and cannot be changed during the life of the contract.[10]

In recent years policy loan interest rates have been lower than commercial rates. This market condition has not always been the case, and the situation may be reversed in the future. If so, a policyowner may still obtain a lower rate by using the policy as collateral for a loan from a bank or other lender. Of course, the interest rate is only one factor to consider. It may be more convenient, quicker, more private, and more flexible to obtain a policy loan from the insurance company than to borrow money from a commercial lender.

Policyowners sometimes question the insurer practice of charging interest for policy loans since they are paying interest to borrow their *own* money. The fallacy of this criticism is apparent when the following factors are considered. First, if the insurer did not lend the cash value to the policyowner, it would have been able to keep these funds invested and earning income for the company. Second, in its rate-making and reserve calculations, the insurer assumed that it would earn interest on the reserve. Third, by analogy, if the policyowner had an interest-bearing bank deposit and withdrew part or all of the funds, the depositor would lose interest on the "borrowed" amount. However, the insured continues to accumulate nonforfeiture values on policies on which policy loans are outstanding. Fourth, there are assorted clerical costs involved in making policyowner loans which are properly allocated to those making loans. Fifth, there is an element of adverse financial selection in that those requiring policy loans cause the life insurer to invest substantial amounts in liquid, low-yielding assets. Policyowner equity dictates that those who make policy loans "pay" for this higher liquidity and lower yield.

Many policies contain an automatic premium loan option which acts as a special application of a policy loan provision. Illustrative of such a provision is the following:

> The automatic premium loan option will be in effect if requested in the application for this policy or in a written request received by the Company from the Owner before expiration of the grace period for payment of a premium in default. If this option is in effect, any premium in default will be automatically paid immediately before expiration of the grace period by making an advance as under the Policy Loans provisions and subject to the terms and conditions of such provisions, sufficient to pay such premium unless (a) the resulting indebtedness would exceed the loan value of the policy, or (b) the two consecutive premiums immediately preceding such overdue premium were payable at other than monthly intervals and were paid by automatic premium loans, or (c) the six consecutive premiums immediately preceding such overdue premium were payable at monthly intervals and were paid by automatic premium loans.
>
> Upon receipt by the Company of the Owner's written request for termination of this option, it will cease to be in effect with respect to

any premium then due but unpaid and to subsequent premiums, but may be made effective again by the Owner's subsequent written request.

In most cases a life insurance applicant is asked whether the automatic loan provision is desired. In some policies the provision is always included but a policyowner has the option of deleting it. Today most companies make the provision available.

As a general rule, a policyowner should include the automatic premium loan provision in his or her policy. It provides a convenient method of handling premium payments that are missed inadvertently or premiums that the policyowner is temporarily unable to meet. However, frequent reliance on the automatic loan provision is unwise since the policy will terminate if the remaining cash value is inadequate to pay the premium.[11]

When the premium payments are made automatically by a policy loan, all the benefits, such as dividends and options like waiver of premium, remain in effect just as though the premiums were paid directly by the policyowner. If a policyowner decides to resume premium payments after they have been paid automatically by loans, no evidence of insurability is required.

To protect the policyowner against an unintended serious reduction in the policy proceeds should death occur during the operation of the automatic premium loan option, some companies limit its use to two consecutive missed premiums if the mode of premium payment is other than monthly, or to six consecutive missed premiums if monthly. Further exercise of this option may be arranged by application to the life insurance company at the premium due dates, but such payments are not automatic.

Assignment

The policyowner has the right to transfer ownership of the policy (i.e., assign) to anyone else, even to an individual who lacks an insurable interest in the insured's life and even without receipt of financial consideration. The assignment provision is designed to clarify the conditions under which the insurance company will be responsible for honoring an assignment. An illustrative clause reads:

A duplicate copy of any assignment of this policy, or of any interest in it, must be filed with the Company. Any assignment shall be subject to any payment made or other action taken by the Company before the assignment is received and recorded at the Company's Home Office. The Company assumes no responsibility for the validity of any assignment.

The interest of any beneficiary or Owner's Designee under this policy shall be subordinate to the interest of any assignee and may be assigned by the Owner while the Insured is living.

An assignee cannot change the beneficiary nor exercise the rights set forth in the Arrangements for Transfer of Ownership provisions of this policy.

Notice that this provision is different from the assignment clause found in most property and liability contracts. For example, the standard fire policy states: "Assignment of this policy shall not be valid except with the written consent of this Company." In property insurance an assignment *is not valid* unless the company gives its consent. By contrast, assignment of a life insurance policy may take place without the consent of the insurance company, but the assignment is not binding until written notice is received by the insurer.

Types of Assignments There are two basic types of assignments—absolute and collateral. However, most assignments follow a form developed by the American Banker's Association (ABA) which is a hybrid of these two types.

An absolute assignment transfers to the assignee all of the ownership rights and interests possessed by the assignor. If an assignor is sole owner of a contract (or if all owners join in the assignment), an absolute assignment makes the assignee the new owner of the policy. As the new owner, the assignee may exercise any and all ownership rights.

One of the problems with an absolute assignment is that the parties to the assignment may not intend to effect a complete change of ownership. Although the courts generally will look to the intention of the parties to determine the effect of the transaction, it is preferable to avoid the courts if possible. Because an absolute form is not always reliable (in transferring complete ownership), many insurance companies prefer to transfer ownership through the ownership clause rather than through an absolute assignment.

A collateral assignment transfers ownership only to the extent necessary to provide adequate collateral for a loan. In the event of the borrower's death, the lender would be entitled to receive the amount of the unpaid debt, with interest, and the remaining proceeds would be payable to the borrower's beneficiaries. The lender is protected to the extent of the debt, and the lender's rights to any proceeds are extinguished when the debt is repaid.

A collateral assignment may involve a number of problems. In some cases the rights of the parties are not spelled out clearly, and conflicts may arise between the assignee and assignor. For example, consider the situation where a policyowner assigns his contract to a bank as collateral for a loan and then defaults on both the periodic installments on the debt and the policy premium. Does the bank have the unquestionable right to surrender the policy, and will the insurance company pay the surrender value to the bank without the consent of the debtor? Also, does the bank have the right to pay the premiums on the policy and add the amounts paid to the indebtedness? Questions such as these sometimes arise when a collateral assignment is used.

Because of such problems, the formerly mentioned ABA form was developed for use in assigning life insurance policies as collateral. This form specifies the rights that are transferred as well as those that are not used by most banks, and many insurance companies now use this form.

The ABA assignment form specifies that the assignee has the right to:

1. collect from the insurer the net proceeds of the policy when it becomes a claim by death or maturity;
2. surrender the policy and receive the surrender value;
3. obtain policy loans or advances on the policy, either from the insurer or other persons, and to assign the policy as security for such loans;
4. receive all distributions of surplus (dividends) from the insurer and to exercise all dividend options, provided appropriate notice is given to the company by the assignee; and
5. exercise all nonforfeiture rights.

Unless the contract is surrendered, the assignor does *not* not have the right to:

1. collect from the insurer any cash disability benefit that does not reduce the amount of insurance;
2. designate and change the beneficiary; and
3. select settlement options (but this right must not impair any of the assignee's specified rights).

The ABA form stipulates that the assignee will:

1. pay to the beneficiary any amounts received from the insurer in excess of the existing indebtedness;
2. not surrender or borrow upon the contract except for the purpose of paying premiums (The assignee must give at least twenty days' notice to the assignor.); and
3. send the policy to the insurer without delay if the assignee wants an endorsement to change the beneficiary or elect a settlement option.

In a sense, the ABA form is absolute because it gives the assignee rights that may be exercised without the consent of the assignor. More realistically, though, the form is closer to a collateral assignment because it limits the rights of the assignee to those that are necessary to secure a loan, and all rights revert back to the assignor when the assignee's interest terminates.

Reinstatement

When a policyowner discontinues premium payments (on a policy that is not paid up), one of the following will take place:

1. The premiums will be paid by the automatic premium loan provision.
2. The policy will terminate without value (if premiums are discontinued before a nonforfeiture value has developed).
3. The policy will be surrendered for cash.
4. The policy will be placed on one of the other nonforfeiture options (described below).

It is necessary to distinguish among these four alternatives because there is considerable disagreement about the meaning of the word "lapse." Some experts maintain that a policy lapses only if it terminates without value (alternative 2 above). Others maintain that lapse occurs whether alternative 2, 3, or 4 takes place.

The reinstatement provision allows a policyowner to revive a policy after premium payments have been discontinued. Under alternative 1 above, there is no need to reinstate the policy. A policyowner can simply repay the indebtedness and resume premium payments. The death proceeds then would be the same as they were before the policy loans were used.

Reinstatement generally is not allowed if the policy has been surrendered for its cash value (alternative 3 above). However, some companies allow reinstatement by company practice—not policy provision—if the contract has been surrendered for cash.

The typical reinstatement provision allows reinstatement if a policy has been terminated without value (alternative 2 above) or has been placed on one of the other nonforfeiture options (alternative 4 above). In some companies reinstatement is provided only if the policy has been placed on a nonforfeiture option.

A typical reinstatement provision reads:

Within five years after default in payment of premium, this policy, if it has not been surrendered for its cash value, may be reinstated upon receipt by the Company of (a) evidence of insurability satisfactory to the Company, (b) payment of all overdue premiums with interest at 5 percent per annum from their respective due dates and (c) payment of any indebtedness outstanding at the end of the grace period, with compound interest at 5 percent per annum, plus any outstanding indebtedness incurred thereafter. However, if the Company receives the payments required under (b) and (c) within thirty-one days after expiration of the grace period for payment of the premium in default, the Company will not inquire into, nor require submission of, evidence of insurability but, in such case, reinstatement shall not take effect unless the Insured was living when such payments were received.

Upon the Owner's written request, all or part of the payment required to reinstate the policy can be charged against it as a loan under the Policy Loans provisions if the resulting indebtedness does not exceed the policy's loan value on the date of reinstatement.

In some states a reinstatement provision is mandatory, but as a matter of practice, almost all policies contain the clause. The most common variation among companies is that some allow reinstatement within three years of default, other companies permit reinstatement within five years, and some companies use even longer periods.

An important aspect of reinstatement is that the insurance company has the right to require evidence of insurability. Otherwise, insurers would be subject to mortality selection since individuals in poor health are more likely to request reinstatement than those who believe that they are in good health. This problem is particularly relevant when a long period of time has elapsed after the premium default. In these cases, a company may very well impose underwriting standards that are essentially the same as those used for new policies. For example, a medical examination is required normally.

Short-term lapses occur frequently because the policyowner missed the premium payment unintentionally. Recognizing this, many companies are more liberal when reinstatement is requested shortly after premium default, and may require nothing more than a written statement from the insured indicating he or she is in good health. The type of evidence of insurability required will also depend upon the size of the policy.

Several reasons explain why a policyowner might prefer to reinstate an old policy rather than purchase a new one: (1) a new policy will require a higher premium since the insured is older than when the original policy was purchased; (2) a new policy may not develop a cash value for several years; (3) a new contract may contain more restrictive provisions than those found in the original policy (the policy loan interest rate, for example, may be higher in the new contract); and (4) the suicide and incontestable periods may not operate again in a reinstated policy. In general, reinstatement of a policy does not reopen the suicide period, and the contestable period begins anew on a reinstated policy but only with respect to the statements in the reinstatement process.

Beneficiary Designations

The portion of the policy that deals with the beneficiary designation is very important since it focuses on the basic purpose of owning insurance. A typical one follows:

Beneficiary

Unless otherwise provided in this policy or in a beneficiary designation in effect under the policy, the following provisions shall apply.

Beneficiary Classifications. The beneficiary for any death benefit proceeds under this policy will be classified as a first beneficiary, second beneficiary or third beneficiary. Such classification shall determine the interest of that beneficiary with respect to such death benefit proceeds. Surviving beneficiaries in the same beneficiary classification shall share equally in death benefit proceeds payable to the beneficiaries in that classification.

Payment to Beneficiaries. Death benefit proceeds payable to the beneficiaries under this policy will be paid
to any first beneficiaries for such proceeds surviving at the time of the Insured's death, or if no first beneficiary for such proceeds survives the Insured, to any second beneficiaries for such proceeds surviving at the time of the Insured's death, or
if no first or second beneficiary for such proceeds survives the Insured, to any third beneficiaries for such proceeds surviving at the time of the Insured's death.

Death of Beneficiary. If the last surviving beneficiary for any death benefit proceeds payable under this policy predeceases the Insured, the beneficial interest in such proceeds shall vest in the Owner. If any beneficiary dies simultaneously with the Insured or within fifteen days after the Insured but before due proof of the Insured's death has been received by the Company, the proceeds of the policy will be paid to the same payee or payees and in the same manner as though such beneficiary predeceased the Insured.

Change of Beneficiary

While the Insured is living, the beneficiary designation can be changed from time to time by written notice in form satisfactory to the Company. No such change will take effect unless recorded in the records of the Company at its Home Office. Upon being so recorded, the change will be effective as of the date the notice was signed, whether or not the Insured is living when the change is recorded, subject to any payment made or other action taken by the Company before such recording.

Beneficiary designations should be made very carefully since a significant amount of the litigation surrounding life insurance involves the proper allocation of the life insurance proceeds.

Types of Beneficiaries A policyowner has great latitude in naming beneficiaries, and normally may name anyone regardless of the existence of an insurable interest as beneficiary.[12] The basic problem with beneficiary designations, therefore, is seeing that the most appropriate choice is made and that the wishes of the policyowner are fulfilled.

Primary and Contingent Beneficiaries. A primary beneficiary is entitled to the proceeds of the policy upon the death of the insured, but the beneficiaries are extinguished if he or she predeceases the insured. A contingent ("secondary") beneficiary collects the proceeds if the primary beneficiary predeceases the insured. Also, if the proceeds are being paid to the primary beneficiary over time but he or she dies before the proceeds are fully paid, the beneficiary arrangement can stipulate that the remainder of the proceeds will become payable to the contingent beneficiary. Alternatively, the remaining proceeds can go to the primary beneficiary's estate, rather than to the contingent beneficiary. If the proceeds are payable in a lump sum, upon the insured's death the proceeds vest with the primary beneficiary and any rights of a contingent beneficiary are extinguished.

It is often desirable to establish several levels of contingent beneficiaries. That is, a policyowner may name a primary beneficiary, a first contingent beneficiary, a second contingent beneficiary, and even a third contingent beneficiary.

Specific and Class Beneficiaries. An individual named as a beneficiary is known as a specific (or named) beneficiary.[13] A class beneficiary is not identified by name but, instead, is a member of a group of individuals who are equal beneficiaries.

In setting forth a specific designation, it is usual practice to name the person and indicate his or her relationship to the insured. "Mary Jane Doe, wife of the insured," for example, is a common form of specific designation. It is sound practice to include the full name of the person and to avoid designations such as "wife" or "Mrs. John Doe." If both the name and relationship are provided, the name determines the beneficiary; the relationship is regarded as descriptive only. For example, a designation which reads "Mary Jane Doe, wife of the insured" would make the proceeds payable to Mary Jane Doe even if she is not the wife of the insured at the time of his death.

Class designations are appropriate when the life insurance proceeds are to be divided equally among the members of a specific group such as the "children of the insured."

Class designations should be specified with care since it may be difficult to identify clearly those who are members of the group. For example, if the designation makes the proceeds payable to children, some questions similar to the following may arise:

1. Are after-born or adopted children included?
2. What about children from a former marriage of a spouse?
3. Should the insurance company pay the proceeds to a minor beneficiary?

Because of the legal problems that may be involved, insurers generally will not pay life insurance proceeds to a minor.[14] In most cases the company will insist upon paying the proceeds to a guardian who is legally competent to provide a valid receipt. The appointment of a guardian, however, normally involves problems since it takes time and involves expense to establish a guardian, and even then the laws are not always clear about the decisions a guardian may make. For example, does a guardian have the right to select or change a settlement option? One solution (discussed later in the chapter) is to make the proceeds payable to a trustee who will administer the funds for the benefit of the children.

Revocable and Irrevocable Beneficiaries. The usual beneficiary clause states that the policyowner reserves the right to change the beneficiary. This type of designation establishes a revocable beneficiary, and a revocable beneficiary has only a "mere expectation" of benefits. The policyowner may exercise any of the policy rights without the consent of a revocable beneficiary.

The legal status of an irrevocable beneficiary is unclear. At one extreme, an irrevocable beneficiary is regarded as a "co-owner" of the policy, and as such, the consent of the beneficiary is needed to exercise any policy rights. At the other extreme of legal opinion, an irrevocable beneficiary's consent is not needed to exercise any policy right—except the right to change the beneficiary. Some companies use policy language that clarifies the status of an irrevocable beneficiary. With this approach, the policyowner does not have the right to change the beneficiary (without the beneficiary's consent), but the policyowner may exercise other policy rights (such as selection of options) without the approval of the beneficiary. This creates a curious situation because the beneficiary's rights may be destroyed by the policyowner by surrendering the policy or exercising other rights.

Normally, it is preferable to use a revocable beneficiary clause that permits the policyowner to change the beneficiary. If an irrevocable beneficiary clause is necessary, it is usually preferable to use an absolute assignment or an appropriately worded ownership clause, because of the unsettled legal status of an irrevocable designation.

Common Designations and Potential Problems While it is impossible to analyze all of the legal problems that may arise with beneficiary designations, it is helpful to be aware of the major problems that may arise.

Insured's Estate. Insureds frequently designate their estate as a contingent beneficiary. In most cases the wording "insured's estate" would be acceptable, but it is more common to stipulate "the executors or administrators of the insured." Most companies will not accept wording such as "heirs" or "family" because of the problems involved in defining these classes.

Many experts feel that generally it is poor practice to designate the insured's estate as beneficiary because the proceeds are likely to be delayed in reaching other beneficiaries and because the proceeds may be reduced by probate expenses, state inheritance taxes, and the claims of creditors. At times, the insured's estate is named as a third or fourth level contingent beneficiary simply to provide an ultimate recipient. This does not solve the problems mentioned above and may cause additional problems if proceeds are not paid in one lump sum and the insured's estate must be reopened at a later date. An alternative would be to name a charity, educational institution, or religious organization as the ultimate contingent beneficiary.

Succession in Interest of Beneficiaries. If there is more than one beneficiary in a classification (for example, three individuals who are first contingent beneficiaries), it is not always clear exactly how the proceeds will be divided. For example, suppose the insured, A, owns a $100,000 life insurance policy and his children, B, C, and D, are equal beneficiaries. Assume B and C have no children but D has two children, E and F. Assume further that D dies before A. The question is, "How will the proceeds be divided?"

If the life insurance policy itself (or the beneficiary designation if it is separate from the policy) does not deal with this possibility, the proceeds will be divided equally—$50,000 each to B and C. However, this allocation may not be consistent with the policyowner's wishes. If the insured, A in this case, wants his grandchildren, E and F, to participate, the policy must so state. This may be achieved on either a *per stirpes* or *per capita* basis. A per stirpes distribution means "by the branches" or "by the trunk," and could be worded "in equal shares to the surviving children of the marriage of John and Mary Doe, otherwise to the surviving children of any deceased children of the marriage, per stirpes." With this approach, B and C each would receive one-third, and E and F each would receive one-sixth. A less popular approach of including the grandchildren is the "per capita" method, which means "by the heads." This approach would pay equal shares (one-fourth each in this example) to B, C, E, and F.

A clause in a policy which deals with the succession in interest problem usually applies at every beneficiary level. That is, it applies to cases in which a primary or contingent beneficiary predeceases the insured, but it also applies to cases in which a contingent beneficiary dies before a primary beneficiary.

Trusts. In recent years it has become increasingly popular to designate a trustee either as a primary or contingent beneficiary under a life insurance policy. A trust is an arrangement under which a person (the donor or settlor) transfers property to another individual or corporation (the trustee) for the benefit of a third party (the trust beneficiary). A trust is extremely flexible. For example, one may be established as a living (*inter vivos*) trust while the donor is alive, or one may be established at the donor's death (a testamentary trust); it may be revocable, irrevocable, or irrevocable for a period and later become revocable; almost any type of property (including a life insurance policy) may be placed in a trust or it may contain no property; it may provide income tax advantages, estate tax advantages, or no tax advantages at all; and a trustee may be given little or a wide range of discretionary powers.

In using a trust as a beneficiary, it is important to identify clearly the trustee as a beneficiary and refer to the trust agreement. For example, the proceeds may be payable to "the ABC Company, as trustee, in trust under trust agreement dated. . . ." If there is no trust agreement at the insured's death, the plans for the trust will fail because the trustee has no instructions for managing the property.

There are a number of reasons why it may be advisable to designate a trust as beneficiary instead of naming a beneficiary under one of the settlement options (discussed below). First, unlike an insurer, a trust facilitates the adjustment of the level of payments as the needs and circumstances of the beneficiary change. Second, a trust permits extreme flexibility in the management of funds which life insurance companies cannot do. Third, a trustee can be given the power to invest in equity securities, thereby protecting the beneficiary from the ravages of inflation. Life insurers, on the other hand, become debtors to the beneficiary upon the death of the insured and pay "fixed dollar" benefits. Life insurance company investments are mostly of the "fixed dollar" variety (in keeping with their obligation to pay fixed dollar benefits), and provide little protection against inflation. Fourth, the use of a trust arrangement allows the consolidation of all of the insured's assets in one trustee. This could include the proceeds of many small policies, each with benefits inadequate for realistic use of settlement options and noninsurance assets such as securities, real estate, etc.[15] The advantages of consolidation include savings on estate administrative expense(s) (since the percentage cost of these expenses is inversely related to the size of the estate) and the opportunity for the trustee to diversify the investments. With life insurance settlement options there is little if any opportunity for unification of assets.[16] Fifth, a trustee may also serve as a personal counselor to the beneficiary and, in the case of a minor, act as the minor's guardian.[17] Sixth, the trustee may, unless the life insurance policy specifically forbids it, select life insurance settlement options. Seventh, a trustee may be given enough discretion to resolve any survivorship problem. Eighth, a trust may be used as a "portable trust," i.e., the trustor or guarantor may choose the state of domicile. This allows the trustor or guarantor to select the trustee independent of the statutory requirements for a trustee to serve in any domiciliary state. Although it is not an advantage of a trust over settlement options, if the trust is properly arranged, there is no loss of inheritance and estate tax advantages or of creditor protection.[18]

There are several limitations to the use of a trust for life insurance death proceeds. First, there is a loss of the special $1,000 annual interest income tax exclusion given to a surviving spouse receiving a settlement option that combines interest and principal. Second, the investments of a trust are nondiversified segregated funds which must "stand on their own," unless the trust is in a state that permits "common trust funds." In contrast, the investment result of insurance company assets is stable since they are extensively diversified. Third, the trusts lack the safety and stability that are inherent in a life insurance company's guarantee as to the safety of both principal and interest. Fourth, there is an explicit charge for the management of trust assets, whereas life insurers make no additional charge for the use of settlement options.[19]

Protection Against Creditors

Some life insurance companies include a provision which protects beneficiaries from their creditors as well as the creditors of the insured. A typical clause reads:

> To the extent allowed by law and subject to the terms and conditions of this policy, all benefits and money available or paid to any person and relating in any manner to this policy will be exempt and free from such person's debts, contracts and engagements, and from judicial process to levy upon or attach the same.

Note that the clause quoted above begins with the words "To the extent allowed by law . . . ." This is an important phrase because most states have laws that exempt life insurance values from the claims of creditors. These laws recognize the social and humane purposes of life insurance, and therefore, they increase the chances that life insurance values will be used for the purposes intended.

There is considerable variation in the state exemption statutes. However, there are four general types of laws.

1. Insured's Creditors and Proceeds. Most state laws protect life insurance death proceeds from the insured's creditors. In some states the proceeds are fully exempt; in other states the proceeds are exempt up to a certain amount. Often the degree of protection depends upon the beneficiary, with the insured's spouse and children receiving greater insulation from creditors.
2. Insured's Creditors and Cash Values. In many states creditors of the insured cannot attach or seize life insurance cash values.
3. Beneficiary's Creditors and Proceeds. Only a few states protect the proceeds from the beneficiary's creditors. However, protection of this type can be achieved in the majority of the states that specifically permit a "spendthrift trust" clause in life insurance policies. This clause states that a beneficiary who is receiving benefits in periodic payments cannot assign, transfer, commute, encumber, withdraw, or anticipate the proceeds. While the proceeds are being held by the insurance company, they cannot be taken by the beneficiary's creditors.
4. Beneficiary's Creditors and Cash Values. There is little, if any, need to protect cash values from the claims of the beneficiary's creditors. A revocable beneficiary does not have a vested right to cash values. Even an irrevocable beneficiary generally cannot obtain a policy's cash values without the consent of the policyowner.

The result of these statutes is that life insurance values are afforded substantial protection against creditors. An important exception, however, is that the federal government can seize cash values to satisfy delinquent taxes. The government can force the surrender of a policy to satisfy tax claims, and if a lien has been placed on the policy before the insured's death, the government can collect from the death proceeds. The government's rights to collect taxes in this manner supersede state exemption statutes.

Change of Plan Privilege

In an effort to provide maximum flexibility for its policyowners, life insurance companies normally allow policyowners to exchange their policy for coverage under a different plan of insurance.[20] Generally companies include a specific provision to this effect, although such exchange can usually be negotiated for a policy without this provision. For example:

> The following changes can be made in this policy:
>
> (a) *Changes to Higher Premium Plans.* If no premium is in default, the plan of insurance will be changed to an endowment or limited payment life insurance plan for the same level face amount, but with a higher premium rate and a premium paying period which extends for at least five full years beyond the effective date of the change, without evidence of insurability and without any change in the classification of the risk, upon receipt by the Company at its Home Office of the Owner's written request for such change accompanied by the policy and a payment of
>
> (i) the difference in previously due premiums for the basic life or endowment insurance benefits under the two plans, where the change is to take effect on or before the second anniversary of this policy, or
>
> (ii) 103% of the difference in the then current cash values for the two plans, where the change is to take effect after the second anniversary of this policy.
>
> The new plan must be one which was available on the policy date of this policy. Subject to the same condition and such additional payment, if any, as may be required, provision for an Accidental Death Benefit may be included in the new plan if a corresponding provision is included in this policy. However, the inclusion in the new plan of a provision for any benefit other than such Accidental Death Benefit and the basic life or endowment insurance benefit on the life of the Insured shall be subject to the Company's approval and requirements.
>
> (b) *Other Changes.* Any other change in this policy, including changes to a lesser amount of insurance or to a plan of insurance with a lower premium rate, shall be subject to the Company's approval and requirements.

Exchange to any higher premium rate plan (such as whole life to endowment) does not require evidence of insurability because the pure protection provided by the life insurance company is being reduced. On the other hand, change to a lower premium rate plan (such as limited payment life to straight life) requires evidence of insurability satisfactory to the company since it increases the amount of pure protection effective for this insured.

Definitions

Many life insurance companies define some of the terms used in the policy. Without these definitions, these technical terms would be interpreted, if there is a dispute as to meaning, by a court of law. Since courts are guided by the principle that an insurance policy is a contract of adhesion, any ambiguities would be interpreted against the maker of the contract. Illustrative of such a provision is:

> Every reference in this policy to: "dividend credits" means outstanding dividends and dividend deposits and the reserve on outstanding dividend additions;
>
> "indebtedness" means indebtedness to the Company against the policy;
>
> "tabular cash value" means the cash value determined in accordance with the Table of Cash, Loan and Non-Forfeiture Values shown in the policy;
>
> "age" means age nearest birthday. Any reference to a specified age in the Table of Cash, Loan and Non-Forfeiture Values or the Premium Schedule in the policy shall mean the policy anniversary on which the Insured's age, nearest birthday, is the specified age.

Additional definitions appear within the context of other provisions of the policy contract.

Indebtedness

A provision describing how the company treats any policy loan or unpaid premium upon policy maturity or surrender is included. This is covered in a separate provision to emphasize that loans, with interest, will be deducted from the policy proceeds. An example of such a provision is:

> Any indebtedness will be deducted in determining the amount of proceeds payable in any settlement under this policy.

Settlement on Maturity or Surrender

A provision that describes how the policy face is affected by the existence of either advance or delinquent premiums at policy maturity is generally placed in a life contract. Typical of this provision is the following:

> This policy will be settled in accordance with its terms upon receipt of due proof of the Insured's death or upon its maturity as an endowment or its surrender for cash value. Surrender of the policy will be required when such settlement is made.

Death Benefit Premium Adjustment. Death benefit proceeds under this policy will be subject to adjustment, as follows

(a) Such proceeds will be increased, if a premium was paid for the premium interval current at the time of the Insured's death, by such pro rata part of that premium as is applicable to the period, if any, between the end of the policy month in which death occurs and the end of such premium interval.

(b) Such proceeds will be decreased, if the insured dies during a grace period, by such pro rata part of any overdue premium as would be applicable to the period ending with the last day of the policy month in which death occurs.

Surrender of the policy contract is required for payment of the proceeds. If the policy cannot be found, the policyowner or beneficiary is required to complete an appropriate form attesting to this fact. This prevents the insurer from being called upon to pay twice if the original policy should be presented later.

The second aspect of this policy clause deals with advance premiums. The usual company practice is to treat the date of death as being on the same date as the premium due date. Assume, for example, that a semi-annual premium of $61.20 was paid on March 16 (the premium due date), and the insured died on May 12 of the same year. In this illustration, the premium was paid four months beyond the date of death. Accordingly, four-sixths of the advance premium, or $40.80 ($\frac{4}{6}$ × $61.20 = $40.80) would be added to the proceeds of the policy. Although many life insurance companies follow this liberal procedure, some companies treat advance premiums as "earned when received."

Normally, if the insured dies during the grace period and before the payment of the due premium, the pro rata part of the overdue, unpaid premium for that policy month will be deducted (without interest) from the policy proceeds. For example, assume that a quarterly premium of $31.20 is due on January 12 and the insured dies on February 2 of the same year, i.e., during the grace period. The deduction for the unpaid premium will be one-third of the quarterly premium, or $10.40 ($\frac{1}{3}$ × $31.20 = $10.40).

Another clause sometimes added to the settlement or surrender provision relates to interest earned on the death benefit if payable in a single sum. For example:

Interest on Single Sum Death Benefit. Interest at the rate (not less than 3% per annum) declared by the Company will be included in death benefit proceeds which are paid in a single sum. Such interest will be for the period from the date of the insured's death to the date the proceeds are paid, but not for a period of more than two years.

This provision is not particularly important since life insurance claims generally are paid promptly.

POLICYOWNER DECISIONS

Many life insurance provisions are included automatically in a policy, and an applicant or policyowner has no choice about their inclusion or wording. There may be variation in contract language among companies or policies, but the policyowner cannot modify the contractual language. The policyowner normally must accept most of the provisions described previously in this chapter or decline the entire policy. Nevertheless, there are some important decisions that must be made by life insurance applicants or policyowners.

Supplementary Benefits

Waiver of Premium   The waiver of premium benefit is the most common option added to a life insurance policy. Frequently, the benefit is included automatically in the contract. The premium required for this benefit is usually no more than 1 to 3 percent of the premium. Representative of the waiver of premium benefit is:

Provision for Premium Waiver in Event of Total Disability

This Provision is made a part of the contract to which it is attached and all provisions of the basic contract not inconsistent with this Provision are made applicable hereto.

Consideration—This Provision is issued in consideration of the application for it and of the additional premium stated in the SCHEDULE OF BENEFITS; both this Provision and the application are made a part of the contract to which they are attached.

The additional premium for this Provision is payable under the same conditions as the premium for the basic contract. The additional premium for this Provision shall not be payable following its termination.

Total Disability—Except that total disability will not exist under this Provision while the Insured is engaged in any occuption or employment for remuneration or profit, total disability is defined to mean:
1. If on the commencement date of the Insured's total disability, the Insured was engaged in any occuption or employment for remuneration or profit—the Insured's incapacity, caused by disease or bodily injury, to perform, during the first 24 consecutive months of such incapacity, any and every duty pertaining to the Insured's occupation or employment, thereafter, the Insured's incapacity to engage in any occupation or employment for remuneration or profit for which the Insured is or can become reasonably fitted by education, training or experience; or

2. If on the commencement date of the Insured's total disability, the Insured was not engaged in any occupation or employment for remuneration or profit—except as provided in 3 below, the Insured's incapacity, caused by disease or bodily injury, to engage in any occupation or employment for remuneration or profit, for which the Insured is or can become reasonably fitted by education, training or experience; or
3. If on the commencement date of the Insured's total disability the sole occupation of the Insured is that of student or housewife—the Insured's incapacity, caused by disease or bodily injury, to engage in that occupation; or
4. The entire and irrecoverable loss of sight of both eyes, or of the use of both hands or both feet, or one hand and one foot.

Notice of Claim—Written notice of claim under this Provision must be given to the Company during the lifetime of the Insured and during the period of total disability. However, failure to give such notice of claim shall not invalidate or diminish any claim if it shall be shown that such notice was given as soon as was reasonably possible.

Proof of Total Disability—Upon receipt of due proof that the Insured has, after payment of the initial premium under the basic contract and under this Provision, during their continuance and on or after the anniversary of the Contract Date on which the Insured's age was 5, become totally disabled and has been so disabled for a period of not less than six consecutive months, the benefits described below will be granted.

Benefits—The Company will waive the payment of any premium which may fall due under this contract during such disability and will refund any premium previously paid during such disability, but no premium will be waived or refunded which became due more than one year prior to notice of claim, except that failure to give such notice shall not invalidate or diminish any claim if it shall be shown that such notice was given as soon as was reasonably possible. The provisions, values and benefits of this contract shall be the same as if such premium payments were made to the Company. Premiums shall be waived in accordance with the mode of payment in effect at the commencement of such disability. Any premium so waived will not be deducted in any settlement under this contract.

Premium in Default—If, after payment of the initial premium under the basic contract and under this Provision, any subsequent premium shall be in default when written notice of claim under this Provision is received, disability benefits as described above shall be allowed if total disability shall have existed continuously from a date prior to expiration of the grace period of the first premium in default when such notice is received. If the inception of such disability shall have occurred during such grace period, the premium then due shall not be waived by the Company.

Proof of Continuance of Disability—Commencing one year after receipt of initial proof of disability, the Company may require proof of continuance of such disability from year to year. If due proof is not furnished, or when total disability has terminated, no further premium will be waived on account of such disability.

Resumption of Premium Payments—The benefits for disability as defined above shall be discontinued if and when the Insured shall cease to be totally disabled, and the premiums falling due thereafter shall be payable to the Company.

Incontestability—As applied to this Provision, the period of time stated in the Incontestability provision of the basic contract shall be measured from the Date of Issue of this Provision.

Date of Issue—The Date of Issue for this Provision is the same as that for the basic contract unless otherwise stated in the SCHEDULE OF BENEFITS.

Termination—Except as provided in the paragraph entitled "Premium in Default," this Provision will terminate upon the earliest of:

1. Failure to pay any premium due under this Provision or the basic contract on or before the expiration of the grace period; or
2. The Expiry Date or Maturity Date, if any, of the basic contract; or
3. The operative date of any paid-up insurance option or any non-forfeiture benefit of the basic contract; or
4. The anniversary of the Contract Date on which the Insured's age is 60; or
5. The owner's written request for cancellation, accompanied by this Provision.

The insured peril is total disability so the benefit is a form of health insurance protection. Because disability is more difficult to determine than death, all life insurance policies with this benefit contain a careful definition of total disability.

Typically, total disability requires the inability of the insured to engage in any occupation for remuneration or profit for a period of six months. This definition requires an insured to be unable to perform the duties of *any* occupation, which excludes all cases except the most extreme forms of disability. Therefore, the definition is interpreted generally to mean the inability to perform the duties of any occupation for which the insured is reasonably suited in terms of his or her education, training, and experience.

A more liberal definition of disability is used by many companies. These companies waive premiums during an initial period of time (usually two to five years) so long as the insured cannot perform the major obligations of *his or her own* occupation. After the stipulated period, the definition becomes more strict, requiring that the insured be unable to perform the duties of *any* occupation. This usually is interpreted to mean any occuption for which the insured is fitted by reason of education, training, and experience.

Most companies use a six-month waiting period, but many

companies require a shorter period such as four months. The waiting period is actually a method of defining the insured peril. Originally, life insurers intended to insure only against total and *permanent* disability. With a waiting period, the effect is nearly the same as insuring only permanent disability because relatively few individuals who are totally disabled for more than six months ever recover. The wording of most provisions is such that a disability that persists longer than the waiting period qualifies for the benefit even if it is obvious that disability will not continue. On the other hand, some disabilities are obviously permanent, yet benefits are not payable until the disability extends beyond the waiting period. The waiver of premium benefit is retroactive; i.e., premium payments that become due during the waiting period must be paid by the policyowner, but the insurer will reimburse the policyowner for them if the disability continues past the waiting period.

The waiver of premium benefit covers disabilities resulting from both accident and sickness. Virtually all provisions exclude self-inflicted injuries and disabilities resulting from war. Some companies also add other exclusions such as injuries or diseases resulting from private air travel or travel in foreign countries.

To be eligible for the benefit, a disability must occur prior to a stipulated age. Most contracts stipulate age seventy or lower. The premium for the benefit is discontinued after the insured reaches the stipulated age (except for those policies that include this feature as an indivisible part of their coverage).

The age cutoff specifies the age before which the disability must occur if the premiums are to be waived. It does not operate to terminate benefits. If a disability occurs before the stipulated age, all premiums, including those due after that age, are waived. Many whole life policies provide that the premiums will be waived until the insured reaches age sixty-five and at that time, the policyowner will be granted a paid-up policy. Other whole life contracts provide that the policy will mature as an endowment at age sixty-five. In the case of nonrenewable term, limited payment, ordinary life, or endowment policies, the waiver of premium benefit simply continues until the end of the premium payment period. Most renewable term contracts are renewed automatically (and thus continued) if premiums are being waived. Convertible term policies are handled in one of several ways. An uncommon method that is least favorable to a policyowner is to continue the contract as a term policy. The most liberal method is to convert the term policy automatically and to continue to waive the premiums. Premium waiver is not a universal practice after the conversion.

Disability Income Rider   In many respects the disability income feature is similar to the waiver of premium benefit. If both provisions are contained in a policy, the benefits are likely to share much of the contractual language. Typically, the provisions that apply to both are: (1) definition of total disability, (2) waiting period, (3) limiting age, and (4) exclusions.

This similarity should not be surprising since the waiver of premium feature is a form of disability income used for a designated purpose, namely, for the payment of the premium. The basic difference between the two riders is that one is paid in cash to the policyowner, and the benefit amount is independent of the premium for the basic life policy.

Generally, income provided by a disability income rider is related to the policy face amount. The most common practice is to pay $10 per month for each $1,000 of face amount, but the amount may range from $5 to $20. Most companies employ underwriting practices that limit the maximum amount of disability income that may be provided by all policies owned by the insured.

In some policies the maximum benefit period may be limited to only two or five years. As riders to life policies, it is common to pay benefits until age sixty or sixty-five, but some policies pay benefits for life. Lifetime benefits normally are reduced (often to $5 per month for each $1,000 of coverage) after age sixty-five. Many policies mature as an endowment if the insured is totally disabled at age sixty or sixty-five.

Another difference between the two riders is that the disability income benefit normally is not paid retroactively. Payments begin at the end of the waiting period, and the company has no liability for benefits during the waiting period.

Few policies contain a disability income provision due to its relatively high cost while many include the waiver of premium benefit. For example, a male thirty-five years of age paying about $500 a year for a $20,000 whole life policy can expect to pay about $110 annually for a $200 per month disability income rider while the waiver of premium feature would add only $6 per year to the premium.

Accidental Death Benefits   This rider, popularly known as *double indemnity,* is added to many life insurance policies. A few companies include the benefit automatically in the policy and do not make a separate charge for the rider. A typical benefit provision states:

Accidental Death Benefit

These provisions are included in and made a part of the policy to which they are attached by the Company in consideration of the application for such provisions and payment of the amount that is included in the premium for such policy on account of the Accidental Death Benefit.

The amount of the Accidental Death Benefit and the amount included in the premium for the policy on account of such benefit are shown on the first page of this policy, and these Accidental Death Benefit provisions will be deemed to have taken effect as of the policy date of the policy except where such provisions have been added to a policy which was already in force in which case such amounts and such effective date shall be as specified in the provisions for Addition of Supplementary Benefits which make these Accidental Death Benefit provisions a part of this policy.

Subject to the terms and conditions of the policy and these Accidental Death Benefit provisions, the Company will pay the Accidental Death Benefit, as part of the policy's death benefit proceeds, upon receipt of due proof that the Insured's death resulted directly, and independently of all other causes, from accidental bodily injury and that such death occurred within 90 days after such injury and before the earliest of the following

(1) expiration of the grace period following the due date of a premium in default;

(2) maturity of this policy as an endowment or its surrender for cash value;

(3) any other termination of coverage under these Accidental Death Benefit provisions.

However, the Accidental Death Benefit will not be payble if death occurs before the Insured's fifth birthday or results from (a) suicide, whether sane or insane, or (b) war (including any armed aggression resisted by the armed forces of any country or combination of countries), whether such war is declared or undeclared, or any act incident to any such war, or (c) travel or flight in any kind of aircraft (including falling or otherwise descending from or with such aircraft in flight) while the Insured is participating in aviation training in such aircraft, or is a pilot, officer or other member of the crew of such aircraft or has any duties aboard the aircraft while it is in flight if such duties relate in any way to the aircraft, its operation or equipment, or to any purpose of the flight; nor will such benefit be payable if death is caused or contributed to by infirmity of mind or body, or any illness or disease other than a bacterial infection occurring in consequence of an accidental injury on the exterior of the body.

The Company shall have the right and opportunity to examine the body and unless prohibited by law, to make an autopsy.

These Accidental Death Benefit provisions will not affect tabular cash values under this policy.

Notwithstanding anything in this policy to the contrary, its Incontestability provision will not apply to these Accidental Death Benefit provisions where the Accidental Death Benefit provisions were added to the policy when it was already in force. Instead, in such case, these Accidental Death Benefit provisions shall be incontestable, except for nonpayment of premium, after the policy has been in force during the lifetime of the Insured for two years from the date of issue specified for these Accidental Death Benefit provisions in the applicable provisions for Addition of Supplementary Benefits.

Upon receipt by the Company within thirty one days of any premium due date of the Owner's written request accompanied by this policy for appropriate indorsement, coverage under these Accidental Death Benefit provisions will terminate as of such premium due date. If not previously terminated, such coverage will terminate automatically on the policy anniversary when the Insured's age is 65.

Any premium due under this policy on or after termination of coverage under these Accidental Death Benefit provisions will be reduced by any amount included in such premium for the Accidental Death Benefit.

In most cases the amount of the accidental death benefit is equal to the face amount of the basic policy—hence the name "double indemnity."[21] A $25,000 policy, for example, would pay $50,000 to the beneficiary if the death of the insured meets the requirements of the clause. In some policies the amount of the accidental death benefit is some other multiple of the face amount, such as twice the face amount of the policy (which might be called "triple indemnity").

In the wording quoted above, death must result from "accidental bodily injury." This is a much more liberal approach than that followed by many companies which requires that death result from "violent, external, and accidental means." The significance of the phrase "accidental means" is examined carefully in Chapter 9. Basically, it requires that the cause and the result be accidental. This would exclude a death caused by an insured's intentional act even though death resulted accidentally.

The typical accidental death benefit (ADB) provision stipulates that the death of the insured must occur within ninety days of the injury. This minimizes the problem of establishing whether or not the accidental injury was the proximate cause of death. The 90-day requirement is becoming a problem as medical technology is better able to prolong life. Therefore an increasing number of companies is specifying a longer period, such as 120 or 180 days.

The accidental death benefit generally terminates on the policy anniversary just after the insured reaches some specified age (i.e., sixty, sixty-five, or seventy), but some policies provide lifetime AD benefits. The extra premium for the benefit terminates with the coverage. This rider has no effect on cash values.

There is considerable variation in the exclusions that apply to the accidental death benefit. Some policies contain many exclusions; others contain few exclusions. The most common exclusions are the following:

1. suicide and self-inflicted injuries
2. inhalation of gas or fumes
3. injuries occurring during commission of a felony
4. aviation (except as a fare-paying passenger)

Table 8-2

Death Rates (Deaths Per 1,000 Individuals)

Age	Accidental Deaths [1]	Deaths from All Causes [2]
25	0.490	1.93
35	0.386	2.51
45	0.431	5.35
55	0.514	13.00
65	0.809	31.75

1. Taken from the 1959 Accidental Death Benefits Table.
2. Taken from the 1958 C.S.O. Mortality Table.

5. war
6. illness or disease

The ADB is added to many policies probably because the cost is low, and many individuals have the view that their death is unlikely while they are young unless they die accidentally. The cost varies, but at age thirty-five it costs approximately $.60 per $1,000 of coverge. At this rate, an individual can add the rider to a $25,000 policy for only $15 per year. To evaluate the chances of accidental death, Table 8-2 is helpful.

Table 8-2 shows that accidental deaths, even at the younger ages, are only a small portion of total deaths. Furthermore, because of medical expenses, the economic loss is often greater when death results from illness than it is in cases of accidental death. Consequently, the desirability of the accidental death benefit is questionable. Critics point out that the rider is detrimental if the benefit absorbs premium dollars that should be used to buy a larger policy. Furthermore, this coverage gives many policyowners an inaccurate perception of the amount of life insurance protection they have. For example, it is not uncommon for a person who owns a $25,000 policy with an accidental death benefit to believe that he or she has a "$50,000 policy."

Despite these weaknesses, the ADB does provide a form of limited protection. Because of its low cost, it is unlikely that it diverts substantial premium dollars from the purchase of more life insurance. However, due to its uncertain occurrence, the ADB should not be included for life insurance planning purposes.

Guaranteed Purchase Option This option has a variety of names but is often called the guaranteed purchase option (GPO), guaranteed insurability option (GIO), or option to purchase additional insurance. It may be added to many policies, particularly to those issued at the younger ages. Since it provides a means of purchasing life insurance at specified times in the future without evidence of insurability, the option normally must be purchased prior to a certain age, often age forty. The amount of insurance that may be purchased under this option is limited, usually to the face amount of the original policy or some specified maximum portion of the face. Often a minimum amount applies to the exercise of each option. The option dates usually are set at uniform intervals based on the insured's attained age. A common approach is to allow purchases every three or five years, but some companies use other time intervals. In some cases the rider permits acceleration of option dates upon the occurrence of certain events such as marriage, or the birth or adoption of a child. A policyowner usually has thirty or sixty days before or after the option date to exercise the purchase privilege. An unexercised option cannot be used after the purchase period expires, but future options are unaffected by failure to exercise an option.

The guaranteed purchase option usually allows the purchase of any whole life or endowment plan and rarely permits a policyowner to purchase additional term insurance. One guaranteed purchase option reads:

RIGHT TO PURCHASE ADDITIONAL INSURANCE POLICIES

(Additional Purchase Benefit)

1. THE BENEFIT

The Company agrees to issue an additional policy of insurance on the life of the Insured, without evidence of insurability, as of each Purchase Date.

2. PURCHASE DATES

The Purchase Dates shall be each policy anniversary on which the Insured's age nearest birthday is 25, 28, 31, 34, 37, and 40. The right to purchase an additional policy as of any Purchase Date will expire on the 30th day after that date.

3. ADVANCE PURCHASE PRIVILEGE

If the Insured is a male, upon his marriage or upon the birth of his child, the right to purchase an additional policy as of the next available Purchase Date may be exercised immediately. The additional policy shall be in lieu of the policy which otherwise might be purchased as of such date. Each such privilege shall expire on the 90th day after it becomes exercisable.

4. AUTOMATIC TERM INSURANCE

The Company will automatically provide term insurance on the life of the Insured beginning on the date of a marriage or of a birth which gives the right to purchase a policy under the Advance Purchase Privilege and ending on the day preceding the expiry of such Privilege. However, if an additional policy is purchased under the Advance Purchase Privilege, any proceeds of the term insurance will be payable only if the additional policy is surrendered to the Company without any payment thereunder other than a refund of the premiums paid.

The amount of the term insurance shall be the maximum amount which could be purchased as an additional policy. The term insurance shall be subject to the beneficiary designation and the other terms and conditions of this policy.

5. ADDITIONAL POLICY

(a) **Face Amount.** The face amount of each additional policy may not be less than $5,000. It may not be more than $10,000 or the face amount of this policy, whichever is the smaller.

However, in the event of a multiple birth the face amount which may be purchased under the Advance Purchase Privilege will be the amount available from a single birth multiplied by the number of children of such multiple birth.

(b) **Plan.** Each additional policy shall be on any level annual premium life or endowment plan being issued by the Company on the date of purchase of such additional policy.

(c) **Waiver of Premium Benefit on Disability.** If the Waiver of Premium Benefit is a part of this policy at the time an additional policy is issued:

(1) An additional policy on the Whole Life or 65 Life plan may contain the Waiver of Premium Benefit even though premiums are then being waived under this policy. If premiums are being waived under this policy when such additional policy is purchased, premiums will also be waived under the additional policy.

(2) An additional policy on other than the Whole Life or 65 Life plan may contain the Waiver of Premium Benefit only if premiums are not then being waived under this policy. The Waiver of Premium Benefit of such additional policy will apply only if total disability resulted from bodily injury or disease originating after the effective date of such policy.

(d) **Accidental Death Benefit.** Each additional policy may contain the Accidental Death Benefit in an amount equal to its face amount if such benefit is a part of this policy when the additional policy is issued.

(e) **Provisions.** Each additional policy, and any Waiver of Premium Benefit on Disability and Accidental Death Benefit which are a part of it, shall include all such provisions as are regularly included in new policies at the time of purchase of such additional policy including any war and aviation restrictions. The incontestability provision in each additional policy shall be effective from the date of issue of this policy. The suicide provision in each additional policy shall be effective from the date of issue of such additional policy.

(f) Premiums. The premium for each additional policy shall be at the standard premium rates of the Company on the date of issue of such policy for the plan and amount of insurance requested at the Insured's then attained age.

6. APPLICATION AND EFFECTIVE DATE

Written application and the first premium for an additional policy must be received by the Company during the lifetime of the Insured and not more than sixty days before nor more than thirty days after a Purchase date. If so received, the additional policy will be dated and effective upon receipt of the application or the first premium, whichever is the later.

Under the Advance Purchase Privilege, written application including proof of marriage or birth, and the first premium must be received by the Company during the lifetime of the Insured and not later than ninety days following the date of such marriage or birth. If so received, the additional policy will be dated and effective upon receipt of the application or the first premium, whichever is the later.

7. TERMINATION

This benefit shall be in effect while this policy is in force other than under the Extended Term Insurance or Paid-up Insurance Provisions but shall terminate on the policy anniversary on which the Insured's age nearest birthday is 40 or upon previous exercise of all available purchase privileges. It may be terminated upon receipt at the Home Office, within thirty-one days of a premium due date, of the Owner's written request accompanied by this policy for endorsement.

8. GENERAL

An additional policy shall not be issued unless the Owner has an insurable interest in the life of the Insured. This benefit shall not participate in the surplus of the Company.

One difference among GPOs deals with what happens to the policyowner's rights for additional purchases when premiums on the base policy are being waived because of disability. One approach allows the policyowner to purchase new insurance at each option date and the premiums for the newly acquired policies are waived as well as those for the original contract. The policyowner is permitted no choice in selecting the type of policy that may be purchased in order to minimize adverse selection. Obviously, insureds would prefer to purchase a short-term endowment at no cost rather than a whole life policy. A second approach permits the disabled insured to exercise this GPO but the new premiums are not waived.

The guaranteed purchase option is a wise purchase, since it provides a reasonable method of protecting the future insurability of the insured. Its cost varies from about $.50 per thousand to approximately $2 per thousand, depending upon age.

Nonforfeiture Options

To protect the financial interest of policyowners who terminate their policies, all states have enacted nonforfeiture laws. These statutes generally follow the model legislation known as the Standard Nonforfeiture Law. Basically, the law sets forth the assumptions and method of calculating *minimum* nonforfeiture values. A life insurer may use any method to compute nonforfeiture values and, in general, may set the values at any level above that required by the law. Furthermore, the actuarial assumptions do not necessarily have to be the same as those used in computing premiums and reserves.

Generally, a minimum nonforfeiture value is required in the second or third policy year. However, in some plans a value will be required in the first policy year, while in others a nonforfeiture value may not be necessary until the fourth, fifth, or subsequent years. The formula embodied in the Standard Nonforfeiture Law creates a minimum surrender value in some term policies, especially level term policies of long duration purchased at a young age.

Since the nonforfeiture laws are concerned with minimum values, insurance companies have a wide latitude in setting surrender values. Some companies adopt the philosophy that in order to be fair to persisting policyowners, relatively low benefits should be paid to those who terminate their policies prematurely. These companies set their surrender values near the minimum required by law. At the other extreme, some companies offer liberal surrender values to increase the competitiveness of their policies.[22]

A policyowner who voluntarily terminates a life insurance policy may choose one of three methods of taking the nonforfeiture value: (1) cash, (2) paid-up insurance, or (3) extended term insurance.[23] The typical nonforfeiture benefit provision states:

Cash and Non-Forfeiture Benefits

1. Cash Value

This policy can be surrendered for its cash value at any time after it first has such a value.

If no premium is in default, the cash value of this policy will be its tabular cash value plus any dividend credits. If the policy has become fully paid-up its cash value will be the reserve on the paid-up insurance plus any dividend credits.

Within three months after the due date of a premium in default, the cash value of this policy will be the same as on that due date, reduced by any subsequent withdrawal of dividend credits.

After such three months the cash value will be the reserve on any insurance provided under the policy's Non-Forfeiture provisions plus any dividend credits, however, if the policy is surrendered within thirty-one days after a policy anniversary, the reserve on such insurance will be taken as not less than on that anniversary.

The Company may defer payment of any cash value for a period not exceeding six months from the date of surrender. If payment is deferred for thirty days or more, such cash value, less any indebtedness, will bear interest at the rate of 3% per annum for the period of deferment.

2. Non-Forfeiture

The following non-forfeiture benefits will apply if this policy has a cash value and a premium in default remains unpaid:

(a) *Extended Insurance.* Upon expiration of the grace period, this policy will be automatically continued as non-participating term insurance commencing as from the due date of the premium in default. The amount of such insurance will be equal to the face amount of the policy plus any outstanding dividends, dividend deposits and dividend additions and less any indebtedness. The term period will be such as the cash value, less any indebtedness, would provide if applied as a net single premium at the Insured's attained age on the due date of the premium in default.

The election of Paid-up Insurance or the surrender of the policy for cash value within three months after the due date of such premium will revoke any Extended Insurance from such due date.

(b) *Paid-up Insurance.* Within three months after the due date of the premium in default, this policy will, upon written request, be continued as participating paid-up life insurance for such amount as the policy's cash value, less any indebtedness would provide if applied as a net single premium at the Insured's attained age on such due date.

(c) *Cash Value.* The policy can be surrendered in accordance with the Cash Value provisions.

3. Basis of Computation

Tabular cash values and the corresponding non-forfeiture values are based on the assumptions that (a) this policy has been in force and all premiums due have been paid to the end of the number of policy years stated, (b) there are no dividend credits and (c) there is no indebtedness. Any value not shown in the table will be furnished by the Company upon request.

Tabular cash values are computed by the Standard Non-Forfeiture Value Method, using the applicable non-forfeiture factors set forth in the Table of Cash, Loan and Non-Forfeiture Values. Such values at any time during a policy year will be determined by the Company with due allowance for the time elapsed in that year and the date to which premiums that have become due have been paid. Tabular cash values are equal to the full net premium reserve from the policy anniversary specified in the table.

A detailed statement of the method of computation of cash and nonforfeiture values has been filed with the insurance supervisory official of the jurisdiction in which this policy is delivered. All values for this policy are equal to or greater than those required by statute in such jurisdiction.

Reserves, net single premiums, and cash and nonforteiture values referred to in the Cash and Non-Forfeiture Benefits provisions, and reserves on, and net single premiums for, outstanding dividend additions wherever referred to in this policy are based on the Commissioners 1958 Standard Ordinary Table of Mortality where the Insured is a male, or the Commissioners 1968 Standard Ordinary Female Table of Mortality where the Insured is a female, with continuous functions and interest at the rate of 3% compounded annually.

Cash The nonforfeiture value of a life insurance contract is referred to frequently as the "cash surrender value" because a policyowner may discontinue a policy and receive the value in cash. The delay clause gives companies the legal right to postpone the payment of the cash surrender value for a period up to six months, but this is rarely done.

When a life insurance policy is surrendered for cash, a check is sent to the policyowner, and all future obligations of the insurer are terminated. The value of any policy indebtedness (policy loans plus accumulated interest) will be deducted from the cash surrender. The cash option should not be exercised unless the policyowner's need for funds exceeds the need for life insurance protection. If this is not the case, one of the other surrender options should be used.[24] For example, a straight life policy issued to a male, age twenty-five, will have a twentieth-year cash surrender value of approximately $255 for each $1,000 of face amount. Figure 8-1 illustrates the status of the contract.

Paid-Up Insurance If this option is selected, the net surrender value (the cash value, plus the cash value of any dividend additions or accumulations, less any policy indebtedness) is applied as a net single premium to purchase fully paid-up insurance.[25] The amount of the paid-up insurance is determined by the net surrender value, the insured's attained age, and the mortality and interest factors specified in the original contract. Since the amount of paid-up insurance is always less than the original face amount, this option is often called the "reduced paid-up option."

The type of paid-up policy is the same as the original contract. A straight life policy, for example, would be converted to a reduced amount of paid-up, whole life insurance. An endowment policy would continue as an endowment, but with the face amount reduced and no

Figure 8-1

Impact of the Cash Surrender of a Straight Life Policy in the Twentieth Year—
Issue Age Twenty-Five*

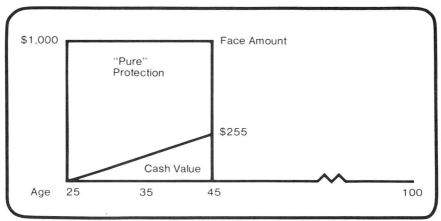

*The figure shows nothing after age forty-five, indicating that cash surrender terminates all benefits of the contract.

future premiums required. Few, if any, life insurance companies make the reduced paid-up option available in term policies.

Normally, when a policy is converted to paid-up status, all supplementary contract benefits are eliminated including term riders, disability and accidental death riders, and so on. Participating policies continue to pay dividends.

This option is appropriate if the policyowner needs life insurance but cannot make the premium payments. This option provides greater flexibility than the other nonforfeiture options since the reduced, paid-up policy contains a cash value. As a result, the paid-up policy may still serve as a source of funds in the event of a financial emergency.

Figure 8-2, which shows the amount of paid-up insurance available for a straight life policy issued at age twenty-five, indicates that the reduction in the amount of insurance as a result of exercising this option may be substantial. Note, however, that the cash value is not reduced upon selection of the paid-up option. As a matter of fact, the cash value of a policy under this option will continue to increase but at a slower rate than it would have under the original policy.

Figure 8-2 illustrates the status of a straight life policy issued to a male, age twenty-five, placed under the reduced paid-up nonforfeiture option in its twentieth year. This option is desirable when the policyowner is in good health but would like to stop paying premiums such as at the time of retirement.

Figure 8-2

Impact of the Reduced Paid-Up Nonforfeiture Option of a Straight Life Policy
—Issue Age Twenty-Five

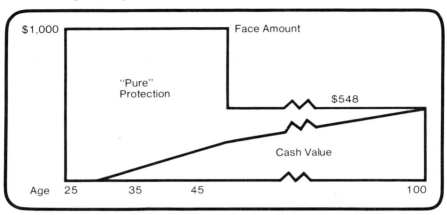

Extended Term Insurance Under this nonforfeiture option, the net cash value of the policy is applied as a net single premium to purchase term insurance for as long a period as possible.[26] The face amount of the term coverage is the same as the face amount of the original policy. If there is an outstanding policy loan, the face amount of the term coverage will be reduced by that amount rather than shortening the period of coverage in order to protect the company from adverse selection. For example, assume that an unhealthy person owns a $25,000 policy with a $10,000 policy loan value. If the face amount were not reduced, the policyowner could obtain $10,000 as a policy loan, and the beneficiary could receive $25,000 as a death benefit for a total of $35,000.

In many endowment policies the cash value is larger than the amount needed to purchase term insurance to the end of the endowment period. Since the original endowment policy was purchased for a specific period of time, it would seem unreasonable to extend term insurance protection past the original period of protection. This is handled by continuing term insurance for the full amount of protection to the endowment date and applying the excess value to purchase a *pure* endowment that will mature at the end of the original policy period. A pure endowment is payable only if the insured lives to the maturity date.[27]

As was the case with the reduced, paid-up option, supplementary benefits are eliminated when this option is exercised. Furthermore, dividends are paid infrequently under this option since they are too small to justify the administrative expense of paying them.

Figure 8-3

Extended Term Insurance for a Straight Life Policy in the Twentieth Year—
Issue Age Twenty-Five

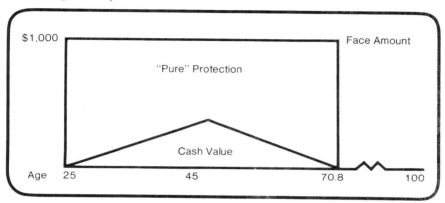

The nonforfeiture value table located in the policy shows how long the extended term period is, depending on the length of time the contract has been in force. For example, after twenty years, one straight life policy, issued to a male age twenty-five, has an extended term of twenty-five years plus 303 days. Figure 8-3 illustrates this policy assuming this option is selected when the insured is age forty-five. A nonforfeiture table is included in all policies. As an example, see Table 8-3.[28]

Insurance companies must designate one nonforfeiture option that becomes operative *automatically* upon premium default if the policyholder does not elect another one within a period of time which is usually sixty days.[29] Most companies designate the extended term option since it does not involve a reduction of benefits (which sometimes leads to misunderstandings), and it has a definite expiration date.

When a policy is placed under the reduced, paid-up option, the amount of coverage is often small and, particularly if a long time elapses, beneficiaries may not file a death claim which results ultimately in the company incurring the expense of attempting to locate the beneficiary.

The selection of the cash surrender option results in the discontinuance of the insurance protection. If a policyowner wants to continue some protection, the choice is between the reduced, paid-up option and the extended term option. The health of the insured is normally the major consideration in the decision process. If the insured is in good health, the reduced, paid-up option is often the best choice while the extended term option is normally more appropriate if the insured is in poor health.

Table 8-3

Table of Cash, Loan, and Non-Forfeiture Values for Whole Life Insurance—Issue Age Twenty-Five (Per $1,000 of Face Amount)

End of Policy Year	Tabular Cash or Loan Value	Participating Paid-Up Insurance	Non-Participating Extended Insurance	
			Years	Days
1	...	...	...	...
2	$ 9	$ 31	4	244
3	23	76	11	162
4	38	122	16	175
5	53	166	19	318
6	64	195	21	155
7	76	226	22	274
8	88	255	23	266
9	100	282	24	160
10	113	311	25	28
11	126	338	25	189
12	139	364	25	297
13	153	390	26	32
14	167	415	26	88
15	181	439	26	110
16	195	462	26	101
17	210	485	26	96
18	225	507	26	64
19	240	528	26	11
20	255	548	25	303
Age 60	500	780	20	334
Age 65	582	832	18	288

A second consideration is the ease and availability of reinstatement. If the policy is surrendered for cash, this contractual privilege may be permanently lost. However, reinstatement privileges are retained by the policyholder if either of the other two options is utilized.

The automatic premium loan, technically speaking, is not a nonforfeiture option, but it does serve a similar purpose in that a policyowner may discontinue premium payments, and the policy will remain in force for a specified period of time. Subsequent automatic premium loans and accumulating interest eventually will exhaust the policy's cash value. Figure 8-4 illustrates the status of a policy using the automatic premium loan feature.

This type of loan is most appropriate when the policyowner intends to resume the premium payments or when it is important to keep the

Figure 8-4

Impact of the Automatic Premium Loan (Straight Life Policy, Issue Age Twenty-Five, Beginning at the Twentieth Policy Year)

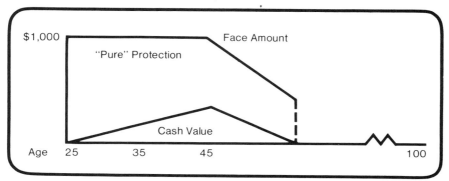

supplementary benefits in force. If premiums are not resumed under the automatic premium loan feature, the amount of the death benefit will be less than it would have been under extended term insurance since the accumulated indebtedness must be deducted from the proceeds. Furthermore, coverage will last longer if the extended term insurance is used—the term insurance is purchased at net rates, while the automatic premium loan pays gross premiums.

Life Insurance Dividends

After prospective policyowners have decided to purchase insurance, they must then decide whether to purchase a participating or nonparticipating policy. The term "participating" stems from the fact that policyowners participate in the actual mortality, investment, and expense experience of the company. To the extent that the experience is more favorable than expected, dividends will increase and vice versa. A *par* policy pays dividends to policyowners while a *nonpar* policy does not. Assuming the decision is to purchase a participating policy, the policyowner must then decide which dividend option should be selected.

Par Versus Nonpar Policies   All policies issued by mutual life insurers are par, while stock companies generally issue both par and nonpar contracts.

Stockholders' dividends (in life insurance companies as well as other companies) represent a distribution of profits and as such, are subject to federal income taxation. Policyowners' dividends represent the return of part of the insurance premium and are not subject to federal income taxation.

Life insurance premiums are a function of three major factors: mortality, interest, and expenses. Life insurers estimate their mortality experience, administrative expenses, and interest earnings. The premiums for nonpar policies are based on realistic assumptions and contain relatively small margins for variation between expected (or assumed) and actual experience. The premiums for par policies, however, are based on more conservative assumptions (i.e., higher mortality and expenses and lower interest earning) than the company expects to realize that probably will be higher than those actually experienced. Conservative assumptions are used purposely to provide a margin of safety for the company.

As experience proves more favorable than the assumptions used in the rate-making process, the surplus of the company is increased which the directors of the company may distribute as dividends. The directors attempt to adhere to the dividend scale that has been projected for each series of policies, but occasionally changes will be made in the dividend scale for some contracts.[30] In recent years, favorable investment experience has resulted in many companies increasing their dividend scales.

Typically, annual dividends are small in the early policy years and increase over time.[31] However, there is substantial variation among companies in their basic dividend philosophy. Some companies pay relatively small dividends that do not increase rapidly. Other companies favor small dividends but use a steeply increasing dividend scale. Other companies plan for relatively large dividends, with or without rapid increases.

Nonpar policy premiums are lower than would be the case if they were adjusted to provide for dividends. Since dividends are not paid on nonpar policies, policyowners can determine the actual premium outlay in advance. In participating policies, the amount of the net premiums (premiums less dividends) cannot be known in advance since dividends cannot be guaranteed.

Participating insurance provides a slight margin of safety not available to nonpar policyholders. If a company that issues par policies runs into adverse mortality, interest, or expense experience, it may reduce dividends and thereby minimize financial problems. Favorable experience should result in dividends larger than those initially projected. Participating insurance provides greater flexibility than a nonpar plan since results may be obtained through the five dividend options (discussed below) which cannot be achieved if there are no dividends.

The debate over which of the two types of insurance is superior is meaningless. Which is better for a particular policyholder is dependent on his or her own needs. Other factors (i.e., cost, service, terms, whole life, and so on) are of greater importance to policyowners.

Dividend Options If an individual purchases a par policy, he or she may select one of several methods of receiving dividends. In most cases the choice is made when the application is completed, but generally may be changed later. If no option is selected, one method will automatically be effective. The automatic option differs among companies, and some states specify the choice. A typical provision reads:

> This is a participating contract and its share of divisible surplus will be determined annually by the Company. On each anniversary of this policy, any share of divisible surplus apportioned to it will be payable as a dividend if this policy is then in force and all premiums due have been paid to such anniversary. The dividend, when payable, will be applied under one of the following options, as elected:
> (a) *Cash*—Paid in cash.
> (b) *Premium*—Applied toward payment of a premium due if the balance of such premium is paid.
> (c) *Dividend Addition*—Applied at net single premium rates to provide a participating paid-up addition to the sum insured.
> (d) *Dividend Deposit*—Left with the Company at interest, subject to withdrawal. On each succeeding policy anniversary, interest will be credited on outstanding dividend deposits at such rate (not less than 3% per annum) as the Company may declare.
>
> If no option is elected, option (c) will apply.
>
> It is not expected that a dividend will be payable on this policy before its second anniversary.
>
> Any outstanding dividend addition can be surrendered at any time for an amount equal to the reserve on such addition as of the latest policy anniversary. Dividend additions and dividend deposits outstanding at the maturity of the policy by death will be payable as part of the policy proceeds.
>
> *Post-Mortem Dividend.* If this policy matures by the death of the Insured, any post-mortem dividend apportioned to it will be paid as part of death benefit proceeds.
>
> *Fully Paid-up Policy Privilege.* This policy will be made fully paid up by application of dividend credits as of any premium due date on which its tabular cash value plus such dividend credits equals or exceeds the net single premium (calculated on the same basis as the premium for this policy) for such fully paid-up participating policy at the Insured's attained age, upon written request within thirty-one days of such premium due date.
>
> *Endowment Privilege.* This policy will be matured as an endowment by application of dividend credits upon written request when its tabular cash value plus such dividend credits equals or exceeds the face amount of the policy.

Cash. Generally, policyowners have the opportunity to receive cash dividends; however, other options generally offer advantages over this option. This option may be a reasonable choice when the policy is paid up, or when the policyowner has an urgent need for cash—such as when he or she is totally disabled.

Reduce Premiums. If this option is selected, a policyowner remits only the net premium (premium less the dividend). The premium notice will show the gross premium, the current dividend, and the difference that is payable. Some companies stipulate in their policies that the company has no obligation to apply the dividend to the premium due unless the balance of the amount due is paid. The similarity between this option and the cash option is obvious.

Accumulate at Interest. Under this option, dividends are accumulated by the company with interest compounded annually. The interest rate credited to the accumulated dividends usually is determined annually by the company, but most policies specify a guaranteed minimum rate of interest.[32]

Most companies allow a policyowner to withdraw the accumulated dividends at any time.[33] In most cases the accumulated dividends are distributed when the policy is surrendered, when the insured dies, or upon retirement of the insured. This has the effect of increasing the amount available to the policyholder or beneficiaries by supplementing the guaranteed cash value at those times.

Interest earnings on accumulated dividends are taxable income in the year credited. This may make this option undesirable for some policyholders.

Paid-Up Additions. If this option is selected, dividends are used each year to purchase amounts of single-premium, paid-up insurance. The amount of insurance is the amount that the dividend will purchase at net rates at the insured's attained age. These additions mature at the same time as does the basic policy. Generally, this option is not available on term policies.

To illustrate, assume a twenty-year-old individual purchases an endowment at age sixty-five with a face amount of $40,000. Assume that the dividend at the end of the first year is $.50 per $1,000 and $1 of dividends will purchase $2.50 of paid-up endowment at age sixty-five. The company will apply the dividend of $20 (i.e., $.50 × 40) to purchase $50 (i.e., $2.50 × $20) of paid-up insurance. In the following year $1 of dividends will purchase less paid-up endowment insurance (i.e., $2.45), but the dividend should increase, perhaps to $.60 per $1,000 of insurance. The dividend would be $24 (i.e., $.60 × 40) and this would purchase a paid-up addition in the amount of $58.80 (i.e., $2.45 × $24). The policyowner would then have a total of $108.80 of paid-up additional insurance. Over time, the single premium for the paid-up endowment additions increases (tending to decrease the amount of insurance that can be purchased), but this is offset by the fact that dividends increase. Moreover, the paid-up additional insurance itself pays dividends which operate to build up the amount of insurance. Frequently, paid-up additions grow to equal 40 or 50 percent of the face of the policy, especialy if the contract is purchased at a young age and maintained for a long time.

The paid-up additions increase the basic death benefit and add to the cash value of the basic policy. A policyowner may surrender the paid-up insurance for its cash value without disturbing the basic policy.

One advantage of this option is that the additions are relatively inexpensive since they are purchased at *net* rates (i.e., some or all of the loading for expenses is not included in the premium).[34] Moreover, they are purchased without evidence of insurability. Unlike the accumulation at interest option, this option does not create a current income tax liability, and the cash values of the paid-up additions may not be substantially less than the cash that could be provided through dividend accumulations. Evidence of insurability may be required if a policyowner wants to change to this option after the policy is issued.

Purchase Term Insurance. Some companies will apply the current dividend to purchase as much term insurance as possible. A more popular form of this option, usually called the "fifth dividend option," does not necessarily purchase the maximum amount of term insurance. Instead, the dividend is used first to purchase one-year term insurance in the amount of the cash value of the policy, and any remaining dividend value is accumulated at interest.[35] Later, when the premium for the term insurance is higher than the amount of the dividend, the accumulated dividends are used to increase the amount of term insurance to the cash value. With this approach a policyowner purchases one-year term insurance equal to the cash value for a long period of time. The option terminates when the dividends are inadequate to purchase term insurance equal to the cash value. From then on the dividends are applied under one of the other options. Illustrative of this type of provision is the following.

Provisions for Application of Dividend Deposits to Provide One Year Term Insurance

The Dividends provisions of this policy are hereby modified by the addition of these Provisions for Application of Dividend Deposits to Provide One Year Term Insurance.

These provisions will be deemed to have taken effect as of the date of the policy, except where they have been added to a policy which was already in force, in which case the effective date of these provisions shall be as specified in the provisions for Addition of Supplementary Benefits which make these Provisions for Application of Dividend Deposits to Provide One Year Term Insurance a part of this policy.

Provision for One Year Term Insurance

The Company, on each policy anniversary while these provisions are in effect, will withdraw from outstanding dividend deposits an amount sufficient to provide non-participating term insurance on the life of the Insured for a period of one year beginning on that policy anniversary. Such term insurance will be for an amount equal to this policy's tabular cash value on the next policy anniversary if outstanding dividend deposits are sufficient to provide that amount of term insurance. Otherwise, the amount of such term insurance will be the amount that can be provided by such application of all outstanding dividend deposits.

Outstanding dividend deposits will be applied to provide one year term insurance under these provisions at the Company's then current premium rate for such one year term insurance. The Company's premium rate for such one year term insurance on standard risks will not exceed the net single premium therefor determined in accordance with the Commissioners 1958 Standard Ordinary Table of Mortality where the Insured is a male, or the Commissioners 1958 Standard Ordinary Female Table of Mortality where the Insured is a female, with continuous functions and interest at the rate of 3% compounded annually.

Conversion Privilege

While $2,000 or more of one year term insurance is in effect under these Provisions for Application of Dividend Deposits to Provide One Year Term Insurance, these provisions can be surrendered in exchange for a new policy on the life of the Insured as of any date before the policy anniversary on which the Insured's age is 60, if the Insured is living and is not totally disabled as defined in any Waiver of Premium Benefit of this policy and, where this policy provides endowment insurance, if at least five full years remain until the endowment date. Such exchange will be made upon receipt by the Company at its Home Office of a written request for it, accompanied by this policy for appropriate indorsement and by the first premium for the new policy, subject to the following condition:
(a) The effective date of the new policy will be the date as of which the exchange is made;
(b) The amount of insurance under the new policy may not be greater than the amount of term insurance then in effect under these provisions nor less than $2,000;
(c) Subject to (d) below, the new policy may be on any life or endowment plan elected in the written request;
(d) The new policy shall be one which would be available on its effective date under the Company's rules as to amount, plan of insurance and age of the Insured. However, the inclusion in the new policy of any benefit other than the basic life or endowment insurance benefit shall be subject to the Company's approval and

requirements, including evidence of insurability satisfactory to the Company.

The new policy will be of the same edition, with the same provisions and conditions, as policies being issued by the Company on the effective date of the new policy, and the premium for it will be based on the Company's then current rate for such policy at the Insured's attained age.

No change will be made in the classification of the risk and no evidence of insurability will be required in connection with any exchange effected under this Conversion Privilege except as may be required under (d) above.

The period of time specified in any provisions relating to Incontestability and Suicide in any new policy effected under this Conversion Privilege will run, not from the date of issue of the new policy, but from the date of issue of these Provisions for Application of Dividend Deposits to Provide One Year Term Insurance, except with respect to any benefit which required the Company's approval for inclusion in the new policy.

Incontestability and Suicide

Notwithstanding anything in this policy to the contrary, its Suicide and Incontestability provisions will not apply to these provisions where these Provisions for Application of Dividend Deposits to Provide One Year Term Insurance were added to this policy when it was already in force. Instead, in such case:

(a) suicide of the Insured, while sane or insane, within two years from the date of issue of these provisions is a risk not assumed under these provisions and, in event of the Insured's suicide within that year, any amount withdrawn from outstanding dividend deposits to provide term insurance under these provisions will be refunded by crediting it to the policy as a dividend deposit; and

(b) these Provisions for Application of Dividend Deposits to Provide One Year Term Insurance shall be incontestable, after the policy has been in force during the lifetime of the Insured for two years from the date of issue of these provisions;

and the date of issue of these Provisions for Application of Dividend deposits to Provide One Year Term Insurance shall be as specified in the applicable provisions for Addition of Supplementary Benefits.

Termination of Insurance

Any one year term insurance under these provisions will terminate on the date these provisions terminate. These provisions will automatically terminate:

(i) immediately before the policy anniversary next following receipt by the Company at its Home Office of the Owner's written request to terminate these provisions;

(ii) immediately before the policy anniversary on which a dividend option other than the Dividend Deposit option becomes effective;

(iii) upon termination of this policy by maturity, surrender or otherwise, or upon any non-forfeiture benefit becoming applicable;

(iv) upon exchange of this policy for a policy on another plan of insurance or a policy of lesser amount;

(v) upon exchange of these provisions for a new policy under the Conversion Privilege of these provisions;

(vi) upon issuance by the Company of a policy providing term insurance on the life of the Insured in accordance with the provisions for Term Insurance for Policy Loan under the Policy Loan Provisions of this policy;

(vii) immediately before any policy anniversary on which any indebtedness under this policy exceeds its loan value less the amount which would be withdrawn from outstanding dividend deposits on that anniversary to provide term insurance under these Provisions for Application of Dividend Deposits to Provide One Year Term Insurance.

If any one year term insurance provided under these provisions is terminated between policy anniversaries, its termination value will be equal to the pro rata part of the amount applied to provide such one year term insurance corresponding to the number of full policy months between the date such insurance is terminated and and the end of the one year term period. Any such termination value will be credited to the policy as a dividend deposit.

The fifth dividend option is useful when the cash value is borrowed regularly as in, for example, a minimum deposit plan. In this case a policyowner may borrow the cash value and maintain the amount of death protection by purchasing term insurance equal to the policy loan.

Many companies require evidence of insurability if the fifth dividend option is selected after the policy has been in force for a while.

Other Dividend Options.   If a policyowner elects either the paid-up additions or accumulate at interest option, the dividends can be used to mature the contract as an endowment or convert to a paid-up policy, when the cash value plus accumulated dividends or cash value of dividend additions equal the net single premium (required at the insured's attained age for the same type of policy in the same amount). No additional premiums are required after the policy is paid up and the policy face will be paid whenever the insured dies. However, subsequent dividends on the fully paid-up policy will increase the death benefit unless the dividends are taken in the form of cash.

The endowment option is somewhat similar. When the cash value of the policy plus the cash value of the accumulated dividends (or cash value of the paid-up additions) equals the face amount of the contract, the policyowner may mature the policy as an endowment. This is comparable to "cashing in" both the policy and the accumulated dividends.

Settlement Options

Life insurance proceeds are payable in a single sum or in the form of periodic income by using one of the "settlement options." The options are: (1) interest only, (2) fixed-period installments, (3) fixed-amount installments, and (4) payments as a lifetime income.

A distinction should be made between settlement options and nonforfeiture options. Basically, settlement options are alternative methods of receiving death proceeds, while nonforfeiture options are exercised by living policyowners. Many companies, however, allow living policyowners to liquidate their cash values under one or more of the settlement options. Thus, the policy may specifically state that cash values may be taken under the settlement options. Even if the contract does not grant this right, many companies will, upon request, pay cash values in this manner.

Prior to the death of the insured, the policyowner may select one of the settlement options, and may change the selection at any time. Generally, the beneficiary has no rights before the insured's death. The policyowner may give the beneficiary no discretion, or conversely, the right to make a wide range of decisions in the use of settlement options. Which method is more appropriate depends on the ability of the policyowner to foresee accurately the needs of the beneficiary as well as the ability of the beneficiary to make intelligent decisions in a period of stress. Obviously, neither approach is always best but depends on the circumstances and individuals involved.

The use of settlement options may be specified in the policy itself in connection with the beneficiary designation, or in a separate settlement agreement by endorsement to the contract. Once the periodic income payments of the settlement option begin, the life insurance policy itself is surrendered, and the company issues a new contract (usually called a supplementary contract or supplementary agreement) which sets forth the provisions of the optional mode(s) of settlement. An illustrative policy provision for the optional methods of settlement follows.

Optional Methods of Settlement

The death benefit, matured endowment or cash value proceeds of this policy, in whole or in part, can be settled under one of the following options instead of being paid in a single sum if every payee under the option is a natural person taking in his own right, subject to the terms and conditions of these Optional Methods of Settlement provisions.

Option 1. Withdrawable Deposit. Left on deposit, subject to withdrawal in sums of not less than $100. Interest will be credited annually at the rate (not less than 3%) declared by the Company each year under this option on the amount remaining with the Company on the interest credit date.

Option 2. Income for Specified Period. Equal monthly payments for the number of years elected, in accordance with the Option 2 Table.

Option 3. Annuity for Life:

With Certain Period. Equal monthly payments for five, ten, fifteen or twenty years (the certain period), as elected, and thereafter for the remaining lifetime of the payee; or

With Installment Refund. Equal monthly payments until the sum of such payments equals the proceeds settled under this option (at which time the instalment refund period ends) and thereafter for the remaining lifetime of the payee.

The amount of each monthly payment will be in accordance with the Option 3 Table.

Option 4. Interest Payments. Left with the Company with interest payable at the rate declared by the Company each year under this option, until the death of the payee. The Company guarantees that such interest, per $1,000 remaining with the Company under this option on the interest due date, will not be less than the following, according to the frequency of payment elected:

Annual	*Semi-annual*	*Quarterly*	*Monthly*
$30.00	$14.89	$7.42	$2.47

Option 5. Income of Specified Amount. Equal monthly, quarterly, semiannual or annual payments of specified amount, as elected, if the total amount payable each year is at least five percent of the proceeds settled under this option. Payments will be made until such proceeds, together with accrued interest at the rate (not less than 3%) declared by the by the Company each year under this option, have been paid.

Option 6. Annuity for Life—Two Persons. Equal monthly payments, in accordance with the Option 6 Table, for the joint lifetime of two payees and continuing for the remaining lifetime of the survivor. Such payments will be payable for ten years certain if both payees die sooner.

If one of the payees named in an election of Option 6 dies before becoming entitled to the first payment, settlement will be made instead under Option 3 (Ten Years Certain) with the surviving payee.

Deferred Settlement Option. Left with the Company at interest, as under Option 4, for not more than two years, subject to withdrawal in sums of not less than $100. At any time during such two year period the payee designated in the original election of this option may direct that any unpaid sum remaining with the Company, together with accrued interest thereon, be applied under any other optional method of settlement available under this policy. Any unpaid sum which has not been so applied at the end of such two year period will then be paid in a single sum.

Additional Interest Under Options 2, 3 and 6. The tables for Options 2, 3 and 6 are based on an interest rate of 3% per annum. The payment due on each anniversary of the due date of the first payment will be increased during the specified period of Option 2, or the certain period or instalment refund period of Option 3 or 6, by any additional interest as determined by the Company at the rate declared each year under the option, on the commuted value of the remaining payments for the applicable period.

Election of Options. Election of an optional method of settlement must be made by written notice in form satisfactory to the Company. While the policy is in force during the insured's lifetime, a previous election can similarly be revoked or changed. Such election, revocation or change will, upon being recorded by the Company at its Home Office, take effect as of the date it was signed, whether or not the Insured is living when it is recorded, subject to any payment made or other action taken by the Company before such recording. An assignee cannot elect an optional method of settlement for unmatured death benefit proceeds nor revoke or change an election previously made.

An election for settlement of death benefit proceeds under these Optional Methods of Settlement provisions can be made by the person entitled to such proceeds if no previous election was in effect at the time of the Insured's death. Such election must be made before payment of the death benefit proceeds and within six months after the Insured's death. An election for settlement of matured endowment proceeds must be made within sixty days of maturity of this policy and an election for settlement of cash value proceeds must be made upon surrender of this policy.

Payee Not a Natural Person Taking in Own Right. Notwithstanding anything in these Optional Methods of Settlement provisions to the contrary, anyone, whether a natural person or not, who has the right to elect an optional method of settlement and who is acting for the benefit of the Insured, or the spouse, child or parent of the Insured, can elect to have death benefit, matured endowment or cash value proceeds settled under Option 2 or 5 or under Option 3 with amount and duration of payments based on the life of the person for whose benefit the election was made. In such case, either the person making the election or the person for whose benefit the election was made may be the payee, as elected.

In addition, any person, other than a natural person, who has the right to elect an optional method of settlement and who is taking in its own right, can elect to have death benefit, matured endowment or cash value proceeds settled under Option 2 or 5 or can elect to have matured endowment or cash value proceeds settled under Option 3 with amount and duration of payments based on the Insured's life. In any of these cases, either the person making such election or the Insured may be the payee, as elected.

Policy Assigned as Collateral. Any amount payable under this policy to a collateral assignee will be paid in a single sum but any remainder of the policy proceeds can be settled in accordance with these Optional Methods of Settlement provisions.

Purchase of Single Premium Life Annuity at Reduced Premium Rate. As a supplement to any settlement under these Optional Methods of Settlement provisions, the payee under the option, if a natural person taking in his own right, may purchase, on his own life, any single premium life annuity being issued by the Company on the date of such settlement by making appropriate written application to the Company within thirty-one days of such date accompanied by payment of the single premium for such annuity. The premium rate for such annuity will be 2% less than the Company's then published premium rate, and the amount of the single premium which can be paid for such annuity may not exceed the proceeds of this policy before deduction of any outstanding indebtedness.

Payments Other Than Monthly. In the election of an optional method of settlement, quarterly, semiannual or annual payments may be requested. The amount of each such payment under Option 2, 3 or 6 will be determined by multiplying the amount of the monthly payment by the appropriate factor in the following table:

	Frequency of Payment Elected		
Option Elected	*Quarterly*	*Semi-annual*	*Annual*
Option 2	2.99	5.96	11.84
Option 3 or 6	2.99	5.94	11.74

Minimum Payment. If any monthly payment under an optional method of settlement would be less than $10, the frequency of payment will be automatically changed to quarterly. If any quarterly, semi-annual or annual payment would be less than $10, the Company may discharge its entire remaining obligation by payment of a single sum to the person who would be entitled to any amount then due.

Settlement Certificate. A settlement certificate setting forth the rights and benefits of the payee under any optional method of settlement elected will be issued when the proceeds of this policy become due. If the policy matures by the death of the insured, the effective date of the settlement certificate will be the date of death, if the policy matures as an endowment or is surrendered for cash value, the effective date of the settlement certificate will be the date of maturity or surrender. The first payment under Option 2, 3, 5 or 6 will be payable as of the effective date of the settlement certificate except where such option is elected by the payee under a settlement certificate issued for a Deferred Settlement Option. Payments under Option 4 will be made at the end of each interest period according to the frequency of payment elected.

Miscellaneous Provisions. Any person making an election of an optional method of settlement can, at the time of such election, designate one or more contingent payees to receive any benefits which may be payable, after the death of the primary payee (the death of the survivor of the two primary payees under Option 6), under the provisions of a written settlement agreement. If no duly designated contingent payee is living at the time of such primary payee's death, such benefits, if any, will be settled by payment of a single sum to the executors or administrators of the deceased primary payee. The amount of any such single sum payment will be equal to:

Under Option 1, 4 or 5, any unpaid sum remaining with the Company together with any accrued interest to the date of death;

Under Option 2, 3 or 6, the commuted value as of the date of such death, on the basis of interest at the rate of 3% compounded annually, of any remaining payments (a) for the specified period of Option 2, (b) for the period certain of Option 6 or Option 3 (With Certain Period), or (c) as may be necessary to complete the payments which would equal in total the proceeds settled under Option 3 (With Installment Refund).

If an optional method of settlement is elected by a person other than the payee and such person does not otherwise direct in writing, the benefits under such optional method of settlement will not be transferable nor subject to commutation, anticipation or encumbrance during the lifetime of the payee.

Evidence satisfactory to the Company may be required as to the age and continuing survival of any person on whose life Option 3 or 6 is based.

Special Agreements. Provision may be made for settlement of the proceeds of this policy in any other manner that may be agreed to by the Company.

Table 8-4 shows the monthly payments under the optional methods of settlement.

Interest Option   Under the interest option, the company retains the proceeds of the policy and pays only interest to the beneficiary at periodic intervals. Usually the company guarantees a minimum rate of interest, such as 3 percent, but the insurer actually pays a higher rate that is a function of the rate the company is currently earning. These interest payments to the beneficiary may be monthly, quarterly, semi-annual, or annual.

Treatment of interest in excess of the guaranteed minimum rate varies among companies. Some pay the guaranteed rate at the interval selected and any excess amount once each year. Other companies include any excess interest earnings with each payment. With one exception (noted below), companies will not accumulate interest under this option.

This option is an interim method of handling the proceeds and must be followed either by a lump sum payment or one of the other settlement options. It may seem to have limited appeal, but it provides great flexibility and is useful in a number of situations. For example:

1. When the proceeds are not needed until some time after the insured's death. For instance, funds needed for estate clearance purposes normally are not required for several months after the

Table 8-4

Tables of Monthly Payments Under Optional Methods of Settlement
Per $1,000 of Proceeds Settled Under Option

Option 2. Income for Specified Period

Years	1	2	3	4	5	6	7	8	9	10	11	12	13	14	15
Payment	$84.47	$42.86	$28.99	$22.06	$17.91	$15.14	$13.16	$11.68	$10.53	$9.61	$8.86	$8.24	$7.71	$7.26	$6.87

Years	16	17	18	19	20	21	22	23	24	25	26	27	28	29	30
Payment	$6.53	$6.23	$5.96	$5.73	$5.51	$5.32	$5.15	$4.99	$4.84	$4.71	$4.59	$4.47	$4.37	$4.27	$4.18

Option 3. Annuity for Life
(based on payee's age on due date of first payment)

Men

Age	5 Years	Certain Period 10 Years	15 Years	20 Years	Installment Refund
15*	$2.93	$2.92	$2.91	$2.90	$2.89
16	2.95	2.94	2.93	2.92	2.91
17	2.97	2.96	2.95	2.94	2.93
18	2.98	2.97	2.96	2.95	2.94
19	3.00	2.99	2.98	2.97	2.96
20	3.02	3.01	3.00	2.99	2.98
21	3.04	3.03	3.02	3.01	3.00
22	3.06	3.05	3.04	3.03	3.02
23	3.08	3.07	3.06	3.05	3.04
24	3.11	3.10	3.09	3.08	3.07

Women

Age	5 Years	Certain Period 10 Years	15 Years	20 Years	Installment Refund
15*	$2.86	$2.85	$2.84	$2.83	$2.82
16	2.88	2.87	2.86	2.85	2.84
17	2.89	2.88	2.87	2.86	2.85
18	2.90	2.89	2.88	2.87	2.86
19	2.92	2.91	2.90	2.89	2.88
20	2.94	2.93	2.92	2.91	2.90
21	2.95	2.94	2.93	2.92	2.91
22	2.97	2.96	2.95	2.94	2.93
23	2.99	2.98	2.97	2.96	2.95
24	3.00	2.99	2.98	2.97	2.96

Men

Age	5 Years	Certain Period 10 Years	15 Years	20 Years	Installment Refund
50	$4.39	$4.35	$4.27	$4.17	$4.18
51	4.48	4.43	4.35	4.24	4.25
52	4.58	4.52	4.43	4.30	4.32
53	4.68	4.62	4.51	4.37	4.40
54	4.79	4.72	4.60	4.44	4.49
55	4.90	4.82	4.69	4.51	4.58
56	5.02	4.93	4.78	4.58	4.67
57	5.15	5.04	4.87	4.64	4.77
58	5.28	5.16	4.97	4.71	4.87
59	5.42	5.29	5.07	4.78	4.97

Women

Age	5 Years	Certain Period 10 Years	15 Years	20 Years	Installment Refund
50	$3.97	$3.96	$3.93	$3.89	$3.87
51	4.04	4.02	3.99	3.95	3.94
52	4.12	4.10	4.06	4.01	4.00
53	4.20	4.18	4.14	4.08	4.07
54	4.28	4.26	4.21	4.15	4.14
55	4.37	4.34	4.29	4.21	4.22
56	4.47	4.44	4.38	4.28	4.29
57	4.57	4.53	4.46	4.35	4.38
58	4.68	4.64	4.55	4.43	4.47
59	4.80	4.75	4.65	4.50	4.56

Age										
25	2.98	2.99	3.00	3.01	3.02	3.09	3.10	3.11	3.12	3.13
26	3.00	3.01	3.02	3.03	3.04	3.12	3.13	3.14	3.15	3.16
27	3.02	3.03	3.04	3.05	3.06	3.14	3.15	3.16	3.17	3.18
28	3.05	3.06	3.07	3.08	3.09	3.17	3.18	3.19	3.20	3.21
29	3.07	3.08	3.09	3.10	3.11	3.20	3.21	3.22	3.23	3.24
30	3.09	3.10	3.11	3.12	3.13	3.22	3.24	3.25	3.26	3.27
31	3.12	3.13	3.14	3.15	3.16	3.26	3.27	3.28	3.29	3.30
32	3.14	3.15	3.16	3.17	3.18	3.29	3.30	3.31	3.32	3.33
33	3.17	3.18	3.19	3.20	3.21	3.32	3.34	3.35	3.36	3.37
34	3.20	3.21	3.22	3.23	3.24	3.35	3.37	3.39	3.40	3.41
35	3.23	3.24	3.25	3.26	3.27	3.39	3.41	3.43	3.44	3.45
36	3.26	3.27	3.28	3.29	3.30	3.43	3.45	3.47	3.48	3.49
37	3.29	3.30	3.31	3.32	3.33	3.47	3.49	3.51	3.52	3.53
38	3.32	3.34	3.35	3.36	3.37	3.51	3.53	3.56	3.57	3.58
39	3.36	3.37	3.38	3.39	3.40	3.55	3.58	3.60	3.62	3.63
40	3.40	3.41	3.42	3.43	3.44	3.60	3.62	3.65	3.67	3.68
41	3.43	3.45	3.46	3.47	3.48	3.64	3.67	3.70	3.73	3.74
42	3.47	3.49	3.50	3.51	3.52	3.69	3.72	3.76	3.78	3.80
43	3.52	3.53	3.55	3.56	3.57	3.74	3.77	3.81	3.84	3.86
44	3.56	3.58	3.60	3.61	3.62	3.80	3.82	3.87	3.90	3.92
45	3.61	3.62	3.64	3.66	3.67	3.85	3.88	3.93	3.97	3.99
46	3.65	3.67	3.70	3.71	3.72	3.91	3.93	4.00	4.04	4.06
47	3.71	3.72	3.75	3.77	3.78	3.97	3.99	4.06	4.11	4.14
48	3.76	3.78	3.81	3.83	3.84	4.04	4.05	4.13	4.19	4.22
49	3.81	3.83	3.87	3.89	3.90	4.10	4.11	4.20	4.26	4.30

*and under †and over

Age										
60	4.66	4.58	4.75	4.86	4.92	5.09	4.85	5.17	5.42	5.57
61	4.76	4.65	4.85	4.98	5.05	5.21	4.91	5.27	5.55	5.73
62	4.87	4.73	4.96	5.11	5.20	5.33	4.98	5.38	5.70	5.90
63	4.98	4.80	5.07	5.25	5.35	5.46	5.04	5.48	5.85	6.08
64	5.11	4.87	5.18	5.39	5.51	5.60	5.09	5.59	6.00	6.28
65	5.23	4.94	5.29	5.54	5.68	5.75	5.15	5.70	6.17	6.48
66	5.37	5.01	5.41	5.70	5.87	5.90	5.20	5.80	6.34	6.70
67	5.51	5.07	5.52	5.86	6.06	6.06	5.24	5.90	6.51	6.93
68	5.66	5.13	5.64	6.04	6.28	6.23	5.28	6.00	6.69	7.18
69	5.82	5.19	5.75	6.22	6.50	6.41	5.32	6.09	6.87	7.44
70	5.99	5.24	5.86	6.40	6.74	6.60	5.35	6.18	7.05	7.72
71	6.17	5.29	5.97	6.59	7.00	6.80	5.38	6.27	7.23	8.01
72	6.36	5.33	6.07	6.78	7.27	7.01	5.41	6.35	7.42	8.32
73	6.56	5.37	6.17	6.98	7.57	7.23	5.43	6.42	7.60	8.64
74	6.77	5.40	6.27	7.18	7.87	7.46	5.45	6.49	7.78	8.98
75	6.99	5.42	6.36	7.38	8.20	7.71	5.46	6.55	7.95	9.33
76	7.23	5.45	6.44	7.58	8.54	7.96	5.48	6.60	8.12	9.70
77	7.48	5.46	6.51	7.77	8.90	8.24	5.49	6.65	8.28	10.07
78	7.74	5.48	6.58	7.97	9.28	8.52	5.49	6.69	8.44	10.45
79	8.02	5.49	6.63	8.15	9.67	8.82	5.50	6.73	8.58	10.84
80	8.32	5.50	6.68	8.33	10.07	9.14	5.50	6.76	8.72	11.24
81	8.63	5.50	6.73	8.50	10.49	9.46	5.50	6.79	8.84	11.64
82	8.97	5.50	6.76	8.65	10.92	9.81	5.50	6.81	8.96	12.04
83	9.33	5.50	6.79	8.80	11.36	10.18	5.50	6.82	9.06	12.45
84	9.70	5.50	6.81	8.94	11.81	10.57	5.50	6.84	9.15	12.86
85†	10.11	5.50	6.83	9.06	12.28	10.97	5.50	6.85	9.24	13.27

Continued on next page

Option 6. Annuity for Life—Ten Years Certain—Two Lives
(based on payees' ages on due date of first payment)

Payees of Equal Age	One Man and One Woman	Two Men	Two Women
25	$2.86	$2.88	$2.82
26	2.87	2.90	2.84
27	2.89	2.92	2.85
28	2.91	2.94	2.87
29	2.93	2.96	2.89
30	2.95	2.97	2.90
31	2.97	3.00	2.92
32	2.99	3.02	2.94
33	3.01	3.05	2.96
34	3.03	3.07	2.98
35	3.05	3.10	3.00
36	3.08	3.13	3.03
37	3.11	3.16	3.05
38	3.14	3.19	3.08
39	3.17	3.22	3.10
40	$3.19	$3.25	$3.13
41	3.23	3.29	3.16
42	3.27	3.33	3.19
43	3.30	3.37	3.22
44	3.34	3.41	3.26
45	3.37	3.45	3.29
46	3.42	3.51	3.33
47	3.47	3.56	3.37
48	3.51	3.61	3.42
49	3.56	3.67	3.46
50	3.61	3.72	3.50
51	3.67	3.79	3.56
52	3.73	3.86	3.61
53	3.79	3.93	3.67
54	3.85	4.00	3.72
55	$3.91	$4.07	$3.78
56	4.00	4.17	3.86
57	4.08	4.26	3.93
58	4.17	4.36	4.01
59	4.25	4.45	4.09
60	4.33	4.54	4.16
61	4.45	4.67	4.27
62	4.56	4.80	4.38
63	4.68	4.93	4.48
64	4.79	5.06	4.59
65	4.91	5.19	4.60
66	5.07	5.35	4.84
67	5.22	5.52	4.99
68	5.38	5.69	5.14
69	5.54	5.86	5.28
70	$5.69	$6.03	$5.43
71	5.89	6.23	5.63
72	6.09	6.44	5.82
73	6.29	6.64	6.01
74	6.49	6.84	6.21
75	6.69	7.05	6.40
76	6.91	7.25	6.63
77	7.13	7.46	6.86
78	7.35	7.66	7.08
79	7.57	7.87	7.31
80	7.79	8.08	7.54
81	7.98	8.25	7.75
82	8.18	8.41	7.97
83	8.37	8.58	8.18
84	8.57	8.75	8.40
85 & over	8.76	8.92	8.61

The amount of the payment for any other combination of ages will be furnished on request.

insured dies. There is no reason why interest should not be earned until the funds are needed.

2. When interest on the proceeds is large enough to provide an adequate income to the primary beneficiary. It is not uncommon to provide for interest income to a spouse (as primary beneficiary) and later pay the remaining proceeds to children (as contingent beneficiaries). The primary beneficiary often is granted liberal (or total) rights of withdrawal.

3. When the proceeds are payable to a minor beneficiary. Many companies will accumulate the proceeds and interest until the minor reaches the age of legal capacity.

4. When there is a need to supplement a spouse's income during the "social security gap period" and preserve the policy proceeds to the end of that period. Recall that the "gap" period is the time when social security benefits are not payable to a surviving spouse (i.e., between the time when the youngest child reaches age eighteen or twenty-two, and when the surviving spouse reaches sixty-two years of age). The dependent spouse may need an income supplement during the years when he or she is capable of working but he or she may have a greater need for funds when no longer able to work.

Assuming a 3 percent guaranteed minimum interest rate for this option, $25,000 of proceeds would provide: an annual income of $750, a semi-annual income of $372.25, a quarterly income of $185.50, or a monthly income of $61.75. Excess interest earnings could significantly increase this periodic income. For example, one company (at the time of this writing) is paying 6.25 percent with the excess paid annually regardless of the method of regular payments. This excess interest raises the annual income from the guaranteed minimum of $750 to $1,562.50.

Fixed Period Option   The fixed period option is also known as the *installment certain, installment time,* or *period certain* option.

With this option, the proceeds are liquidated over a specified period of time. The periodic payment is a function of the amount of proceeds, the rate of interest, the frequency of benefit payments, and the time period selected. The installment benefits are not contingent upon the death or survival of any person. A primary beneficiary may outlive the benefits, or if the primary beneficiary dies before the benefits are exhausted, they will be paid to a secondary beneficiary or will be paid to the primary beneficiary's estate.

The typical policy provision specifies the monthly payment for each $1,000 of proceeds for different durations. For example, the policy provision above shows that if the period selected is ten years, the

Table 8-5

Amounts of Principal Required for Guaranteed Monthly Benefits Under the Fixed Period Option (3 Percent Interest Assumption)

Years of Income	Monthly Income			
	$10	$50	$100	$500
1	$ 118	$ 592	$ 1,184	$ 5,920
5	558	2,792	5,583	27,915
10	1,041	5,203	10,406	52,030
15	1,456	7,278	14,556	72,780
20	1,815	9,075	18,149	90,745
25	2,123	10,616	21,231	106,155
30	2,392	11,962	23,923	119,615

monthly income would be $9.61 for each $1,000 of proceeds. Suppose, however, that one wishes to arrange for a guaranteed minimum monthly income of $100 for ten years. Dividing $100 by $9.61 shows that the proceeds of the policy would have to be $10,406 (rounded to the nearest thousand). Table 8-5 is derived by using this approach.

This option is convenient when it is possible to ascertain how long income will be needed. For example, if the insured's youngest child is eight years of age and income is desired until the child reaches age eighteen, benefits are needed for ten years. However, one disadvantage of this option is that it requires periodic evaluation and changes before death to adapt the period to changing needs. Moreover, partial withdrawals during the liquidation period normally are not permitted.

Fixed Amount Option The *installment amount, installments of a fixed amount,* or *amount certain* options usually are called simply the *fixed amount* option. This option pays periodic payments of a predetermined amount to the beneficiary. The individual determines the amount of income needed which determines the duration of the benefits. Suppose, for example, that a policyowner wants to provide $500 a month to the beneficiary. Given proceeds of $25,000 and 3 percent interest, $500 a month can be provided for four years and five months. Because the amount of each installment is "fixed" under this option, excess interest extends the benefit period.

The primary difference between the fixed amount and fixed period options is that a number of factors can influence the amount of the proceeds, and changes in the amount of proceeds are treated differently under the options. Consider the effect of policy loans, accumulated dividends, paid-up additions purchased with dividends, accidental death benefits, and excess interest earnings. If the fixed period option has been selected and any of the above change the death proceeds, the *amount* of each installment benefit will be altered, but the duration of benefits will not change. Conversely, if the fixed amount option has been selected and any of the above change the amount of the proceeds, the *duration*, and not the amount, of benefits will change. This difference between the two options makes it necessary for the policyowner to decide which is more important—a fixed benefit period or a fixed benefit amount.

There are other differences between these two options which generally favor the fixed amount option. If the fixed amount option is selected, the beneficiary may:

1. Obtain a limited or unlimited right of withdrawal. Withdrawals decrease the benefit period, but it is unnecessary to recompute the benefit amount.
2. Change the benefit amount. For example, a beneficiary may decide to take $500 a month rather than $400 a month originally intended by the policyowner. It is even possible to vary the monthly benefits, i.e., to take various amounts as needed. In some cases a beneficiary may decline benefits during selected months.[36]
3. Place any unpaid proceeds under another option.

The amount of flexibility given to a beneficiary under the fixed amount option is subject to the policyowner's discretion.

Life Income Options   Several forms of life income options which are similar to individual annuities are available as settlement options. The treatment of annuities and settlement options is located in Chapter 11.

The annuity "rates" quoted in life insurance contracts are *net* rates in that they do not include a charge for selling costs. Therefore, a given annuity income will "cost" less than would an annuity purchased outright. Furthermore, these annuity option rates are guaranteed when the contract is issued. Assuming continued improvement in longevity, these contractually guaranteed rates could easily be more favorable than those available at the time when the policy matures.

EVALUATION OF SETTLEMENT OPTIONS

Policyowner Decisions

Policyowners have complete discretion in the amount of latitude they give beneficiaries to select one of the settlement options, withdraw part or all of the proceeds, or select a contingent beneficiary. The policyowner may permit the beneficiary to change from one settlement option to another or to request a lump-sum payment. This right may be limited to a specified period of time.

The policyowner also can specify whether or not the beneficiary has the right to withdraw any or all of the proceeds held by the company. Some insurers limit the number of such withdrawals in one year. Moreover, most companies permit the withdrawal privilege under the fixed amount option, but restrict withdrawals under the fixed period and life income options. Some companies do not permit withdrawals of less than a specified amount such as $100.

Advantages and Limitations of Settlement Options

The policyowner has control over the degree of flexibility that the beneficiary has to select a settlement option. For example, it is possible to apply different settlement options to different portions of the proceeds. The beneficiary may be given no flexibility for a portion of the proceeds but may be given considerable flexibility in determining how the remainder will be used.

Settlement options represent valuable rights to beneficiaries for several reasons. Funds so invested are not subject to market loss and earn interest that cannot fall below some minimum rate. Also, no financial institutions other than life insurance companies are able to offer a guaranteed, lifetime income. Further, $1,000 annual *interest exclusion* from federal income taxation of interest is paid to the spouse of a deceased insured. This exclusion applies to the fixed amount, fixed period, and life annuity options only. It does not apply to the interest only option.

There are certain disadvantages associated with using the settlement options. The interest rate applied to funds invested with insurance companies may not be attractive when compared to current yields on alternative investments. Secondly, settlement options do not offer a hedge against inflation. Of course, this argument applies equally well to other fixed-dollar investments. Thirdly, settlement options may be inflexible if the beneficiary is given little freedom to invade the principal. However, this type of inflexibility may be good in that it insures that the funds are used as the policyholder had desired rather than be dissipated by the beneficiary.

Trusts offer a higher degree of flexibility than do settlement options. They are particularly suitable if discretionary decisions for beneficiaries are needed (i.e., the beneficiary cannot handle his or her own affairs). Generally, a trustee arrangement is better suited for managing larger estates due to the complications involved.

Chapter Notes

1. Group life insurance rates may be increased in certain situations. On individual policies, premiums may be increased in modified life insurance plans (as described in the previous chapter), but the premium increases are guaranteed in the contract.
2. Conditional receipts of life insurance applications are described in detail in CPCU 6.
3. Representations and warranties are described in CPCU 1 and CPCU 6.
4. Regulation of rates and reserves for property and liability insurance is covered in CPCU 5 and CPCU 8. In addition, CPCU 10 treats some current issues concerned with these areas.
5. In those instances in which the rate charged for life insurance is less than that needed to produce the legally required minimum reserve, the life insurer must maintain deficiency reserves. See Davis W. Gregg and Vane B. Lucas, *Life and Health Insurance Handbook,* 3rd ed. (Homewood, IL: Richard D. Irwin, 1973), pp. 169-170.
6. This subject is covered in detail in CPCU 6.
7. It is assumed that love of one's own life is far stronger than the desire to provide insurance benefits to beneficiaries, in effect reducing moral hazard. It is also assumed today that suicide is rarely committed exclusively to enable beneficiaries to receive life insurance proceeds.
8. There are at least three situations that have been adjudicated that hold that if the policy never legally existed, it could never become incontestable. These are cases in which the applicant purchased the policy with the intent to murder the insured (no valid contract as it is against public policy); cases in which a healthy person impersonated the person to be insured to the medical examiner (the "person to be insured" was not the *life* insured, hence no contract on that life); and cases where the applicant was other than the insured and lacked an insurable interest at the formation of the contract.
9. The rate usually contemplated is 8 percent.
10. There have been rare cases in which the policy loan interest rate was decreased.
11. As with all policy loans or other indebtedness, should death occur before the loan is repaid, the amount of the loan plus any unpaid interest is deducted from the proceeds at death. The automatic premium loan option reduces these proceeds rather dramatically if allowed to operate for several years. See the discussion on nonforfeiture options.
12. As a practical matter, the underwriting practices of life insurers may raise questions about the beneficiary's insurable interest. However, these are not legal restrictions.
13. Actually, a named beneficiary need not be identified by name; but if not, he or she must be identified in some manner as an individual.
14. Many states have statutes that permit a life insurer to pay life insurance

proceeds to a minor without any legal problems. Almost all of these laws, however, limit the amount that may be paid safely, usually to a rather nominal amount (such as $3,000).

15. Life insurance companies usually require that there be a minimum principal amount or a minimum periodic income.

16. Only in unusual circumstances will a life insurer accept other assets upon the death of the insured for administration under the settlement option provision of a policy. One such circumstance is the "pour-over" provision of a Keogh Act retirement plan where the life insurer will accept and administer funds that had accumulated in a savings account or a mutual fund pursuant to a deed of trust established during the lifetime of the insured. See Chapter 11 of this text.

17. With a trust arrangement rather than a guardianship, there may be, in some jurisdictions, less frequent (and therefore less expensive) periodic accounting to the court.

18. If the trust is a "living trust" it qualifies as a "named beneficiary" for state inheritance and estate tax exemption and is also qualified for employee death benefits for the purposes of Section 2039(c) of the Internal Revenue Code.

19. Life insurers, in preparing their settlement option payment scales, assume certain overhead expenses which are implicit charges in their policy guarantees.

20. Such flexibility may be required because of a change in the insured's circumstances. For example, when the family is no longer financially dependent upon the insured's income, consideration should be given to a change from the need for maximum protection to the need for maximum accumulation for retirement purposes.

21. Of course, since the life insurance policy is not regarded as a contract of indemnity, the expression "double indemnity" is technically inaccurate.

22. From the point of view of a potential policyowner, it is not easy to determine which approach, high or low surrender values, is preferable. Obviously, high values are better for policyowners who terminate their policies voluntarily, but low surrender values may be advantageous for those who continue their contracts.

23. In many cases, a living policyowner may use one of the settlement options as a method of receiving the nonforfeiture value.

24. It is often preferable to borrow the loan value rather than to surrender the policy for its cash value. The loan value is often identical with the cash surrender value, the only possible difference in some companies being the deduction of an interest charge in advance. However, if the contract is surrendered for its cash value, many life insurance companies, by contract provision, will not permit reinstatement. If the loan value is borrowed, restoration of the full benefits of the contract is automatic upon repayment of the loan (and applicable interest) *without* the necessity for a reinstatement application and evidence of insurability. Moreover, if surrendered for cash, there would not be any death benefit; while if a loan is made, the death benefit woud be the face of the policy less the indebtedness.

25. In a few companies, policy indebtedness is not deducted (in order to purchase

a larger amount of paid-up insurance), but the policy loans are continued under the new policy.

26. Under the Standard Nonforfeiture Laws, life insurers are permitted to use an increased mortality assumption in calculating the net single premium for extended term insurance. The reason for this is the adverse mortality selection associated with this option. Other things equal, this option is more likely to be selected by those in poor health.

27. For example, a typical $1,000 twenty-year endowment issued to a person age thirty would show a fifteenth-year extended term nonforfeiture option of five years and $775. This means that the face amount will be continued until the original maturity date without further premium payments, and will mature as an endowment at that time for the reduced amount of $775.

28. The cash surrender value is often referred to as the "tabular" cash value since it appears in this table. Values for years not shown in the table may be obtained by writing to the life insurance company.

29. Many life insurance companies delete the extended term insurance nonforfeiture option from policies issued to substandard insureds.

30. In the past twenty or thirty years, most changes in dividend scales have been upward because of favorable investment earnings and improvements in longevity. Most recently, these upward dividend adjustments have been moderated by increases in expenses because of inflation. During the Great Depression of the 1930s, some companies had to reduce their dividend scales as a result of lower investment earnings.

31. A dividend scale that establishes an annual increase is fully justifiable on actuarial and business grounds. In addition, it may serve as a marketing tool to minimize policy lapse.

32. Interest in excess of the guaranteed minimum rate is often declared on the dividend deposit. If left to accumulate at interest, this deposit is almost identical with a time deposit with a bank or savings and loan association. A significant difference between a time deposit and the dividend deposit is that under the latter, the only means of entry into the "account" is from a declared dividend or interest. Once withdrawn by the policyowner, the amount withdrawn may not be redeposited.

33. In some companies accumulated dividends may be withdrawn only on the policy anniversary.

34. For this reason, the dividends on the paid-up additions do not benefit from savings in expenses.

35. In some policies the excess dividend is applied to one of the other basic dividend options.

36. For example, many life insurance companies make available, upon policy-owner request, an educational settlement option. This could, for example, provide $100 monthly for four years plus an additional $1,000 payable during each September and January of those years.

Index

463

Property in control of insured, *97*
Property interests, other, *18*
Property loss exposures, *15*
Property owned by an insured, *94*
Property ownership, forms of, *16*
Proposals, *59*
Protect insurability, *337*
Protection, additional personal property, *263*
  limited period of, *388*
Protection against creditors, *416*
Protection against premature death, source of, *27*
Protection period, *380*
Protection policies, multiple, *365*
Protective devices, *248*
Provision, misstatement of age and sex, *399*
Provision for retirement income, *33*
Provisions, contract, *394*
  life insurance policy, *389*
  policy, *393*
Purchase option, guaranteed, *428*
Purchase term insurance, *443*
Purpose, *215*

Q

Questionnaire, exposure identification, *4*

R

Rate, tax, *299*
Rates, commission, for agents and brokers, *249*
Rates and reserves, regulation of, *390*
Rating a flood policy, *259*
Rationing, capital, *386*
Readability, policy, *190*
Readjustment period income, *312*
Record, driving, *202*
Redemption, mortgage, *312*
Reduce premiums, *442*

Reduction, benefit, *297*
Reductions in coverage (internal limits), *214*
Regulation of rates and reserves, *390*
Reinstatement, *409*
Reinsurance and joint underwriting facilities for residual markets, *228*
Reinsurance operation, *239*
Removal, *247*
  automatic, *143*
  debris, *144*
Renewability, *332*
Renewable term insurance, yearly, *304*
Rental value, *108*
Replacement cost, *260*
Reproducing equipment, sound, *230*
Requirements, eligibility, *288, 301*
  size, *301*
Reserves, policy, *345*
Reserves and rates, regulation of, *390*
Residence, construction of new, *98*
Residential coverages, other, *143*
Residual automobile markets, *215*
Residual markets, reinsurance and joint underwriting facilities for, *228*
Responsibility, industry, *56*
Responsibility laws, financial, *166*
Restrictions, aviation, *401*
Restrictions, territorial, *189*
Restrictions and exclusions, *119, 245*
Retired worker, *295*
  child of a, *296*
  spouse of a, *296*
Retirement benefits, *295*
Retirement income, provision for, *33*
Retirement needs, *37*
Return, comparing rates of, *381*
Return of premium policies, *368*
Revocable and irrevocable beneficiaries, *413*
Rider, disability income, *424*
Risk management in a changing society, *45*